American Library History

American Library History
A Bibliography

Michael H. Harris & Donald G. Davis, Jr.

Foreword by Edward G. Holley

University of Texas Press, Austin & London

Library of Congress Cataloging in Publication Data

Harris, Michael H
 American library history.

 Includes indexes.
 1. Libraries—United States—History—
Bibliography. 2. Library science—United States—
History—Bibliography. I. Davis, Donald G.,
joint author. II. Title.
Z731.H28 021'.00973 77-25499
ISBN 0-292-70332-5

Copyright © 1978 by University of Texas Press

All rights reserved

Printed in the United States of America

Contents

Foreword vii

Preface ix

Abbreviations of Journal Titles xi

I. Historiography and Sources 3

II. General Studies of American Library History 10

III. Private Libraries, Reading Tastes, and the Book Trade from the Colonial Period to the Present 19

    A. Private Libraries 22
    B. Reading Tastes and the Book Trade 29

IV. Predecessors of the Public Library 41

    A. Thomas Bray and American Libraries 43
    B. Social Libraries 45
    C. Circulating, Sunday School, School District, and YMCA Libraries 55

V. Public Libraries 58

    A. General Studies 60
    B. Special Studies Arranged by State 68

VI. Academic Libraries 99

    A. General Studies 101
    B. Special Studies Arranged by State 105

VII. School Libraries 126

VIII. State Libraries 132

IX. Special Libraries 136
- A. General Studies 138
- B. Private Research Libraries 139
- C. Historical Society, Museum, and Institute Libraries 142
- D. Business and Industrial Libraries 144
- E. Law Libraries 145
- F. Medical Libraries 147
- G. Government Libraries 151

X. Education for Librarianship 158

XI. Library Associations 164

XII. Special Aspects of American Librarianship 174
- A. International Relations 176
- B. Cataloging and Classification 178
- C. Reference Work 182

XIII. Biographies of Librarians and Library Benefactors 184

Author Index 219

Subject Index 242

Foreword

Those of us who have worked in the field of American library history have long been frustrated by the lack of a good, standard bibliography. We have our own bibliographical notes, which we have developed over the years, and we can depend upon some of the older works like Cannon's *Bibliography of Library Economy* (1927) with the Jordans' author index (1976), Burton and Vosburgh's *A Bibliography of Librarianship* (1934) and *Library Literature*, as well as Michael H. Harris' *Guide to Research in American Library History* (1974) for much useful material, but our searches have been a laborious process. There has been no single source where we could go for an immediate check and say, "Ah, there is the item for which I was looking!" This particular gap in the bibliographical tools became especially noticeable for those of us working on centennial essays for the American Library Association's celebration in 1976. For that reason I welcome the appearance of *American Library History: A Bibliography* and expect to be one of its frequent users. Any source which allows the historian to devote himself or herself to the examination of evidence as opposed to searching for the documents can only be greeted with applause.

Both the compilers, Michael H. Harris and Donald G. Davis, Jr., are well known to American library historians. Davis' *The Association of American Library Schools, 1915–1968: An Analytical History* (1974) is likely to stand as the definitive history of that association, while Michael H. Harris' *A Guide to Research in American Library History*, in both editions (1968, 1974), has been a tool of general usefulness for those needing quick information on the numerous master's theses and doctoral dissertations which have been completed on library history topics. Harris' work on the social foundations of the public library movement has brought him an accumulation of large numbers of titles both in library history and in areas peripheral to it. The joint effort of these two historians on this project has resulted in a significant and original contribution to the American library history field.

Any steady user of this bibliography will discover, as is true of bibliographies in general, that there have been errors and omissions. There is an old saying in librarianship that, if you are troubled by a pride of accuracy and would have it taken completely out of you, compile a bibliography. Nonetheless, this writer is impressed with the remarkable amount of material which has been included. The bibliography is as comprehensive as such a work can be. Supplements to it will doubtless include additional materials which users bring to the compilers' attention. While Harris and

Davis are in a better position than anyone else to have received copies of the many articles which the ALA centennial spawned, even they are unlikely to have discovered everything.

Users will also disagree occasionally with the compilers' judgment about a work. "Definitive," "standard," and "landmark" are designations about which conscientious and able historians can and do disagree. Yet it is still better to have them so that the user will understand the compilers' judgment. It is also a good thing for them to have included the seemingly less useful material. For example, I am delighted that they have included the autobiographies, not because they are major contributions (most are not), but because they are valuable as resource materials. Autobiographies partially compensate for the lack of manuscript material of librarians which frustrates so many potential biographers.

While one might quarrel with some of the entries as not fitting the compilers' definition of items "written consciously as library history," I am also pleased that these have been included. In general the historian is better served by the principle of inclusion than of exclusion. Also Harris and Davis have generally done a good job of identifying those major items which will unquestionably be of value to the American library historian. As they have pointed out in their comments on historiography, there is really nothing comparable to this bibliography.

Fortunately *American Library History: A Bibliography* will make its appearance at roughly the same time as another much-needed and long-awaited reference tool: the *Dictionary of American Library Biography*. Both will be indispensable tools for the library historian and this writer predicts that they will have a long and useful life. Any future historian of the American library scene will find it imperative to begin with Harris and Davis. If their work had appeared earlier, it would have saved many a master's and doctoral student a great amount of time-consuming research.

I congratulate the compilers on their achievement and expect their bibliography to make a substantial contribution to the improvement of research and publication in American library history.

Edward G. Holley, Dean
The School of Library Science
University of North Carolina
Chapel Hill, North Carolina

Preface

1976 marked the one hundredth anniversary of the founding of the American Library Association, and that year can be legitimately considered a major landmark in American library history. It is also symbolic of the librarian's growing concern with questions of philosophy and service to the nation's library users—real and potential. As librarians search increasingly for answers to the basic questions underlying a philosophy of service, they turn repeatedly to the history of the profession as one means of understanding the library's rise and current state in America.

In the light of this frequent return to history, and in the light of the occasion of the celebration of the centennial of the American Library Association, it seemed both appropriate and necessary to compile this bibliography of writings on American library history. We hope that it will provide librarians with some guidance in their examination of the history of American librarianship, while at the same time pointing the way for those scholars in other disciplines who would like to investigate one aspect or another of the history of library development in this country as part of broader studies of American social or intellectual history.

This guide should prove of special interest to scholars interested in the social, intellectual, and literary history of the country. In the past this group generally overlooked library and book history in their studies, viewing ideas as merely camouflage for deeper motives, and they thus tended to ignore ideas in order to focus on social and, especially, economic forces in American history. More recently, however, scholars have become convinced that the connection between ideas and behavior is indeed significant, and we have witnessed the rise of a very extensive interest in the impact of ideas. This new emphasis on the nature and dissemination of ideas in various eras of American history—especially the colonial and early national periods—has encouraged scholars to pay close attention to the printed word, whether transmitted by means of books, newspapers, or magazines, and to the repository of the printed word, the library. As a result, the study of the origins, contents, and evolution of private and public libraries now plays an important part in the writing of American intellectual history.

This bibliography represents the work of over a decade and is felt to reflect a comprehensive picture of what has been written about American libraries and related areas. Every effort has been made to make the list as complete as possible, but it should be noted that this is not a definitive list of materials *about* American libraries. Such a list would run to many volumes and would include the tens of thousands of descriptive or analytic items written over the years. Our purpose has been to include primarily those items written *consciously* as library history. As the user will note, this body of literature alone constitutes some three thousand items and represents, in our view, the most important literature relating to the historical development of American libraries published through 1976.

Every attempt has been made to avoid unnecessary duplication of entries in the various sections of the bibliography, although in certain cases some duplication was deemed essential. In the introductory essays to each part of the bibliography we have attempted to direct the reader to other parts of the list which may produce items of interest. However, users of this bibliography should consult the subject index for guidance to materials related to subjects that may cut across the topical divisions used here. For instance, studies of American library architecture will be found listed under the various types of libraries, in the biography section, and in the section on general studies.

The compilers of a bibliography such as this owe an obvious debt to all those scholars who have carried out original research on aspects of the history of libraries and, more importantly, to the many librarians and historians who have prepared bibliographies of special aspects of the subject covered here. Section I of the following bibliography will demonstrate the extent of our debt to the latter group. More specifically, we must acknowledge the aid of the editors of the *Journal of Library History*, who for over a decade have been publishing the compilers' essays on "the year's work in American library history." Further, a number of scholars have critically examined the list and have made many useful suggestions as to its improvement. Edward Holley of the University of North Carolina, Arthur Young of the University of Alabama, and Wayne Wiegand of the University of Kentucky were especially helpful. Patricia Boyle of the University of Kentucky prepared a careful typescript of the manuscript and contributed significant editorial suggestions during the compilation. All these individuals and many others cooperated in making this a truly cooperative endeavor, and they deserve much of the credit for the bibliography's strengths, while we, of course, must take all the responsibility for its shortcomings.

I. Historiography and Sources

Generally speaking, library historians have chosen to pattern their research after that being undertaken by the historical profession at large. As a result, few works devoted to American library historiography have been written. Several provocative articles on the "value of library history" have appeared over the years, and the scholar interested in this aspect of library history should begin by seeing Jesse Shera's essay (1973, **72**) on this topic, as well as the work of John Colson (1969, **14**; 1976, **15**) and Raymond Irwin (1958, **50**).

Several book-length studies are of particular value to the beginner in American library history. Michael H. Harris's *Guide to Research in American Library History* (1974, **38**) contains chapters on method, sources, and the state-of-the-art but is devoted primarily to an annotated list of master's theses and doctoral dissertations on the subject. James Ollé's *Library History* (1971, **66**) focuses heavily on the British scene but does give some attention to American development.

A number of skilled library historians have written on the mechanics of the study of library history. Especially important are the papers prepared by Haynes McMullen and Edward G. Holley for the Conference on Historical and Bibliographical Methods in Library Research held at the University of Illinois in 1971; McMullen (**58**) deals with primary source materials in library research, while Holley (**49**) treats textual criticism in library history. Other works of value to the scholar seeking insights into specific methodological and thematic problems in library history are Michael H. Harris's essays (1975, **36**; 1976, **42**) on interpretive frameworks, Sidney Ditzion's paper (1973, **22**) on the writing of public library history, and Felix Reichmann's classic essay, "Historical Research and Library Science" (1964, **68**).

The quickening of interest in American library history over the past decade has stimulated the production of a series of very useful guides to primary source materials. Illustrative of this type of tool are the papers delivered at the Third Library History Seminar by Bill M. Woods on library association archives (1966, **89**) and Robert V. Williams on document sources for the history of federal government libraries (1966, **86**). Portions of the Fourth Library History Seminar (1972) were also devoted to papers on "sources," and important essays were presented by Jack Goodwin (**31**) on primary materials in the Washington D.C., area; Nancy V. Menan (**63**) on similar resources in New York City; and Howard Winger and Francis Miksa (**87**) on the American Library Association Archives. Notice should also be made of guides to significant manuscript collections, such as Maynard

Brichford's essay on the material available at the University of Illinois (1970, **8**); Loraine Correll's study of sources of information on American theater libraries (1972, **17**); and Barbara Yate's analysis of the Joseph Wheeler papers (1973, **90**).

The published literature on American library history has always been the subject of considerable attention, and the bibliographic control of this literature is now quite good. The most impressive critical essay on this literature remains Jesse Shera's assessment (1973, **72**). For the past decade the *Journal of Library History* has been publishing Michael Harris's (**44, 45, 46**) and (since 1974) Donald Davis's (**20, 21**) periodic reviews of the "Year's Work," and that feature is to continue. The *Journal of Library History* has also sponsored a series of state library history bibliographies, some dozen of which have been published to date, and publishes numerous essays on sources and methods. Finally, a number of bibliographic essays are available on various aspects of American library history. Examples of some of the most useful would be Harry Bach's essay on scholarly libraries in the United States (1959, **3**), Nathaniel Stewart's study of the sources for the history of the American college library (1943, **82**), and Donald Oehlerts's review of the literature on the history of American library architecture (1976, **65**).

Historiography and Sources

1. Agriesti, P. A. "A Bibliography of Ohio Library History." *JLH* 7 (1972): 157–88.
2. Andrews, F. E. "A Handguide to Writing Your Library's History–The Time Is Now." *WLB* 48 (1973): 324–28.
3. Bach, H. *Bibliographical Essay on the History of Scholarly Libraries in the United States, 1800 to the Present.* Urbana: University of Illinois Graduate School of Library Science, Occasional Paper no. 54, 1959.
4. Bartlett, R. A. "The State of the Library History Art." In *Approaches to Library History*, edited by J. D. Marshall, pp. 13–23. Tallahassee: *JLH*, 1966.
5. Beck, E. R. "Critique of Representative Library Histories." In *In Pursuit of Library History*, edited by J. D. Marshall, pp. 8–18. Tallahasse: Florida State University Library School, 1961.
6. Bergquist, C. C. "A Bibliography of Florida Library History." *JLH* 5 (1970): 48–65.
7. Blazek, R. "The State of Historical Research; or Please Save the Bloody Beast." *JLH* 8 (1973): 50–51.
8. Brichford, M. "Original Source Materials for the History of Librarianship." *JLH* 5 (1970): 177–81.
9. Bronson, B. *Bibliographical Guides to the History of American Li-*

braries. Urbana: University of Illinois Graduate School of Library Science, Occasional Paper no. 32, 1953.
10. Butler, P. "The Intellectual Content of Librarianship." *LQ* 15 (1945): 349–50.
11. Carpenter, R.; Bruce, B.; and Oliver, M. "A Bibliography of North Carolina Library History." *JLH* 6 (1971): 212–64.
12. Coleman, G. P. "Documenting Librarianship via Oral History." In *Proceedings of the Fourth Library History Seminar*, edited by H. Goldstein and J. Goudeau, pp. 30–32. Tallahassee: Florida State University School of Library Science, 1972.
13. ———. "Making Library History." *JLH* 7 (1972): 130–40.
14. Colson, J. C. "Speculations on the Uses of Library History." *JLH* 4 (1969): 65–71.
15. ———. "The Writing of American Library History, 1876–1976." *LibT* 25 (1976): 7–22.
16. Conmy, P. T. "CLA's Library History Chapter: Why History?" *CalL* 33 (1972): 205–09.
17. Correll, L. "American Theatre Libraries: Sources of Information." *JLH* 7 (1972): 197–207.
18. Cummings, C. S., comp. *A Biographical-Bibliographical Directory of Women Librarians*. Madison: University of Wisconsin Library School Woman's Group, 1976.
19. Cutliffe, M. R. "The Value of Library History." *LibR* 21 (1967): 193–96.
20. Davis, D. G., and Harris, M. H. "Three Years' Work in American Library History, 1971–1973." *JLH* 9 (1974): 296–317.
21. ———. "Two Years' Work in American Library History: 1974–1975." *JLH* 11 (1976): 276–96.
22. Ditzion, S. "The Research and Writing of American Library History." In *Toward a Theory of Librarianship: Papers in Honor of Jesse Hauk Shera*, edited by C. Rawski, pp. 55–69. Metuchen, N.J.: Scarecrow Press, 1973.
23. Dixon, E. I. "The Implications of Oral History in Library History." *JLH* 1 (1966): 59–62.
24. ———. *Writing Your Library History*. Menlo Park, Calif.: Ritchie Press, 1967.
25. Downs, R. B. "Resources for Research in Librarianship." *LibT* 13 (1964): 6–14.
26. Drazan, J. "Alaskan Libraries in Print, 1905–1971." *JLH* 7 (1972): 50–60.
27. Ellsworth, D. J., and Stevens, N. D. *Landmarks of Library Literature, 1876–1976*. Metuchen, N.J.: Scarecrow Press, 1976.
28. Fain, E. "Manners and Morals in the Public Library: A Glance at Some New History." *JLH* 10 (1975): 99–105.
29. Gillespie, D., and Harris, M. H. "A Bibliography of Virginia Library History." *JLH* 6 (1971): 72–90.

30. Goldhor, H. *An Introduction to Scientific Research in Librarianship.* Urbana: University of Illinois Graduate School of Library Science, 1972.
31. Goodwin, J. "A Preliminary Survey of Materials Available for the Study of American Library History in Washington, D.C." In *Proceedings of the Fourth Library History Seminar,* edited by H. Goldstein and J. Goudeau, pp. 23–29. Tallahassee: Florida State University School of Library Science, 1972.
32. Gormley, D. M. "A Bibliographic Essay on Western Library Architecture to the Mid-Twentieth Century." *JLH* 9 (1974): 4–24.
33. Hagler, R. "Needed Research in Library History." In *Research Methods in Librarianship: Historical and Bibliographical Methods in Library Research,* edited by R. E. Stevens, pp. 128–38. Urbana: University of Illinois Graduate School of Library Science, 1971.
34. Halsell, W. D. "A Bibliography of Mississippi Library History." Published in a supplemental issue of the *JLH,* fall 1973, pp. 27–50.
35. Harris, M. H. "American Librarians as Authors: A Bibliography of Bibliographies." *BB* 30 (1973): 143–46.
36. ———. "Externalist or Internalist Frameworks for the Interpretation of American Library History–The Continuing Debate." *JLH* 10 (1975): 106–10.
37. ———. *Fugitive Literature in Library Science: American Library History as a Test Case.* Albany: State University of New York, School of Library Science, 1968.
38. ———. *A Guide to Research in American Library History.* 2nd ed. Metuchen, N.J.: Scarecrow Press, 1974.
39. ———. "Historians Assess the Impact of Print on the Course of American History: The Revolution as a Test Case." *LibT* 22 (1973): 127–47.
40. ———. "Library History: A Critical Essay on the In-print Literature." *JLH* 2 (1967): 117–25.
41. ———. "Pennsylvania Library History: A Bibliography." *PLAB* 25 (1970): 19–28.
42. ———. "'The Priest Who Slew the Slayer and Shall Himself be Slain': Revisionism in American Library History." *JEL* 16 (1976): 229–31.
43. ———. "Probate Records as a Source of American Library History." In *Proceedings of the Fourth Library History Seminar,* edited by H. Goldstein and J. Goudeau, pp. 140–49. Tallahassee: Florida State University School of Library Science, 1972.
44. ———. "The Year's Work in American Library History, 1967." *JLH* 3 (1968): 342–52.
45. ———. "The Year's Work in American Library History, 1968." *JLH* 5 (1970): 133–45.
46. ———. "Two Years' Work in American Library History, 1969–70." *JLH* 7 (1972): 33–49.

47. Hart, M. L. "A Bibliography of Connecticut Library History." *JLH* 7 (1972): 251–74.
48. Heaney, H. J. "Bibliographical Scholarship in the United States, 1949–1974: A Review." *CRL* 36 (1975): 493–510.
49. Holley, E. G. "Textual Criticism in Library History." In *Research Methods in Librarianship: Historical and Bibliographical Methods in Library Research*, edited by R. E. Stevens, pp. 95–105. Urbana: University of Illinois Graduate School of Library Science, 1971.
50. Irwin, R. "Does Library History Matter?" *LibR* 128 (1958): 510–13.
51. Jackson, S. L. "Materials for Teaching Library History in the U.S.A." *JEL* 12 (1972): 178–92.
52. Keller, J. D. "A Bibliography of Minnesota Library History." Published in a supplemental issue of the *JLH*, fall 1973, pp. 51–85.
53. Kittelson, D. "A Bibliography of Hawaii Library History." *JLH* 5 (1970): 341–55.
54. Kunkle, H. J. *Bibliography of the History of Libraries in California*. Tallahassee: *JLH*, 1976.
55. Ladd, J. "Cornerstones and Landmarks in Ohio Library History." *OLAB* 46 (1976): 19–32.
56. Lopez, M. D. "Bibliography of the History of Libraries in New York State." Published in a supplemental issue of the *JLH*, fall 1971, 140 pp.
57. McMullen, H. "How Should We Tell Librarians of the Future About Libraries of the Past?" *JEL* 6 (1965): 65–68.
58. ———. "Primary Sources in Library Research." In *Research Methods in Librarianship: Historical and Bibliographical Methods in Library Research*, edited by R. E. Stevens, pp. 23–41. Urbana: University of Illinois Graduate School of Library Science, 1971.
59. ———. "Research in Backgrounds of Librarianship." *LibT* 6 (1956): 110–19.
60. ———. "Through History with Punch and Needle: Edge Notched Cards for Data on Early American Libraries." In *Approaches to Library History*, edited by J. D. Marshall, pp. 81–90. Tallahassee: *JLH*, 1966.
61. ———. "Why Read and Write Library History." *WLB* 26 (1952): 385–86.
62. Mead, C. D. "Popular Education and Cultural Agencies." In *Research Opportunities in American Cultural History*, edited by J. F. McDermott, pp. 155–67. Lexington: University of Kentucky Press, 1961.
63. Menan, N. V. "Library History Resources in New York City." In *Proceedings of the Fourth Library History Seminar*, edited by H. Goldstein and J. Goudeau, pp. 12–22. Tallahassee: Florida State University School of Library Science, 1972.
64. Mishoff, W. O. "Academic and School Library History." In *In Pursuit of Library History*, edited by J. D. Marshall, pp. 23–32. Tallahassee: Florida State University Library School, 1961.

8 Historiography & Sources

65. Oehlerts, D. E. "Sources for the Study of American Library Architecture." *JLH* 11 (1976): 68–78.
66. Ollé, J. *Library History: An Examination Guidebook*. 2d ed. London: Bingley, 1971.
67. Pearlove, S. *A Guide to Manuscript Materials Relating to the History of the Library of Congress*. Washington, D.C.: Government Printing Office, 1949.
68. Reichmann, F. "Historical Research and Library Science." *LibT* 13 (1964): 31–41.
69. Schlachter, G. A., and Thomison, D. *Library Science Dissertations, 1925–1972*. Littleton, Colo.: Libraries Unlimited, 1974.
70. Schwarz, P. J. "A Bibliography of Wisconsin Library History." *JLH* 11 (1976): 87–166.
71. Sessa, F. "Public Library History." In *In Pursuit of Library History*, edited by J. D. Marshall, pp. 19–22. Tallahassee: Florida State University Library School, 1961.
72. Shera, J. H. "The Literature of American Library History." In his *Knowing Books and Men, Knowing Computers Too*, pp. 124–61. Littleton, Colo.: Libraries Unlimited, 1973.
73. ———. "A Renaissance in Library History." *WLB* 40 (1965): 281.
74. ———. "On the Value of Library History." *LQ* 22 (1952): 240–51.
75. Shores, L. "The Importance of Library History." In *American Library History Reader*, edited by J. D. Marshall, pp. 3–7. Hamden, Conn.: Shoestring Press, 1961.
76. ———. "The Library and Society." *JLH* 8 (1973): 143–49.
77. ———. "Place of Library History in Library Schools." *JLH* 3 (1968): 291–95.
78. ———. "The School Librarian as Historian." *SchL* 18 (1969): 9–15.
79. Sills, R. M. "The 'Trumbull Manuscript Collections' and Early Connecticut Libraries." In *Papers in Honor of Andrew Keogh, Librarian of Yale University*, edited by M. C. Withington, pp. 325–42. New Haven: Privately printed, 1938.
80. Smith, J. M. *A Chronology of Librarianship*. Metuchen, N.J.: Scarecrow Press, 1968.
81. Stevens, N. D. "A Plea for the Librarian as Collector." *JLH* 4 (1969): 173–75.
82. Stewart, N. "Sources for the Study of American College Library History, 1800–1876." *LQ* 13 (1943): 227–31.
83. Thompson, D. E. "A History of Library Architecture: A Bibliographic Essay." *JLH* 4 (1969): 133–41.
84. Vleeschauwer, H. J. "Library History in Library Science." *Mousaion*, no. 29–30, 1958.
85. Wilkins, B. "A Bibliography of South Carolina Library History." Published in a supplemental issue of the *JLH*, fall 1973, 1–25.
86. Williams, R. V. "Document Sources for the History of Federal Gov-

ernment Libraries." In *Approaches to Library History*, edited by J. D. Marshall, pp. 61–80. Tallahassee: *JLH*, 1966.
87. Winger, H., and Miksa, F. "Historical Records of the American Library Association." In *Proceedings of the Fourth Library History Seminar*, edited by H. Goldstein and J. Goudeau, pp. 1–11. Tallahassee: Florida State University School of Library Science, 1972.
88. Woodford, F. "Second Thoughts on Writing Library History." *JLH* 1 (1966): 34–42.
89. Woods, B. M. "Library Association Archives and Library History." In *Approaches to Library History*, edited by J. D. Marshall, pp. 49–60. Tallahassee: *JLH*, 1966.
90. Yates, B. "The Joseph L. Wheeler Papers." *JLH* 8 (1973): 96–98.
91. Zachert, M. J. K. "Oral History Interviews." *JLH* 5 (1970): 80–87.
92. ———. "Personal Records as Historical Sources." *JLH* 9 (1969): 337–40.
93. ———. "Sources: A 'Modern' Letter, by Sally Huckaby." *JLH* 7 (1972): 189–91.

II. General Studies of American Library History

Few book-length surveys of the history of American libraries have been written. However, a number of short overviews have appeared which treat the history of American libraries as part of the history of libraries in the West, and taken together they provide the student with an overview of American library history. Most useful of these works are Elmer Johnson and Michael H. Harris, *History of Libraries in the Western World* (1976, **156**); Sidney Jackson, *Libraries and Librarianship in the West: A Brief History* (1974, **150**); and Albert Predeek, *A History of Libraries in Great Britain and North America* (1947, **194**).

Also of use to the student attempting to get a quick grasp of the history of American libraries are two chronologies now available: Josephine M. Smith, *A Chronology of Librarianship* (1968, **212**), and Elizabet W. Stone, *American Library Development, 1600–1899* (1977, **215**). The latter work is a revision and augmentation of the first segment of an earlier effort published in 1967. A sequel volume, continuing the chronology to the present, awaits completion. While systematic surveys of American library history are scarce, there are several collections of articles that attempt to provide an overview of the development of American libraries. Three of the most useful are Thelma Eaton, *Contributions to American Library History* (1961, **123**); Michael H. Harris, *Reader in American Library History* (1971, **144**); and John David Marshall, *An American Library History Reader* (1961, **171**). More recently, two very ambitious collaborative volumes have appeared. Both volumes were designed as up-to-date surveys of American library history since 1876, and together they constitute basic readings on recent American library history. They are Sidney Jackson et al., *A Century of Service: Librarianship in the United States and Canada* (1976, **149**), and Howard Winger, *American Library History, 1876–1976*, which was published as the July 1976 issue of *Library Trends* (**228**) and then as a separate book.

Readers will also find a number of entries in this section of the bibliography treating subjects viewed as too general for inclusion in other sections of the list. Among this group are major statistical compilations relating to the history of American libraries, such as Charles Coffin Jewett's *Notices of Public Libraries in the United States of America* (1851, **153**). These older statistical compilations have been reviewed and extended by a number of recent studies, such as Haynes McMullen, "The Prevalence of Libraries in the United States Before 1876: Some Regional Differences" (1972, **174**);

Kenneth Peterson, "Library Statistics and Libraries of the Southeast Before 1876" (1972, **192**); Elmer Johnson, "Southern Public Libraries in the 1850's: Correcting an Error" (1969, **155**); and Frank Schick's "Library Statistics: A Century Plus" (1971, **202**). We have also listed in this section a number of foreign travelers' observations on American librarianship. Especially revealing in this category is Wilhelm Munthe, *American Librarianship from a European Angle* (1939, **182**).

Finally, a number of other "general aspects" of American librarianship are covered here, such as the "philosophy of library service" in impressive works by David Berninghausen (1975, **103**) and Judith Krug (1972, **162**); "the government and American librarianship" in works by Richard Burns (1968, **114**), Clark Elliot (1968, **126**), and Robert Havlik (1968, **145**) and Kathleen Molz's award-winning book (1976, **179**); the "literature of librarianship" as covered in important studies by J. Periam Danton (1976, **121**), Donald Krummel (1966, **163**), Donald Lehnus (1971, **167**), Guy Lyle (1967, **169**), and Francis Miksa (1973, **178**); or "women in librarianship" as represented by the recent and controversial work by M. A. Corwin (1973, **120**), Dee Garrison (1976, **134**), Margaret Myers and M. Scarborough (1975, **183**), and Jody Newmyer (1976, **185**).

General Studies of American Library History

94. Allanson, V. L. *Profile of a Library Magazine: Fifty Years of the Wilson Library Bulletin.* Kent, Ohio: Kent State University School of Library Science, 1970.
95. Allen, W. C. "Library Buildings." *LibT* 25 (1976): 89–112.
96. Altick, R. D. *Librarianship and the Pursuit of Truth.* Second Annual Richard L. Shoemaker Lecture. New Brunswick, N.J.: Rutgers University Graduate School of Library Service, 1974.
97. Barker, T. D. *Libraries of the South: A Report on Developments, 1930–1935.* Chicago: American Library Association, 1936.
98. ———. "Libraries in the Southeastern States, 1942–1946." In *Twelfth Biennial Conference, Papers and Proceedings*, pp. 13–29. Asheville, N.C.: Southeastern Library Association, 1946.
99. ———. "Library Progress in the South, 1936–1942." *LQ* 12 (1942): 353–62.
100. Beagle, A. M. "Typewriters in Libraries: A Short History of Mechanization." *LJ* 96 (1971): 46–47.
101. Beasley, K. E. "Librarians' Continued Efforts to Understand and Adapt to Community Politics." *LibT* 24 (1976): 259–81.
102. Beddie, J. S. "Libraries in the Twentieth Century." Doctoral dissertation, Harvard University, 1928.
103. Berninghausen, D. K. *The Flight from Reason: Essays on Intellectual Freedom in the Academy, the Press, and the Library.* Chicago: American Library Association, 1975.

12　General Studies of American Library History

104. ———. "The Librarian's Commitment to the Library Bill of Rights." *LibT* 19 (1970): 19–38.
105. Blackshear, E. C. "Wisconsin Library Bulletin Fifty Years Ago." *WisLB* 51 (1955): 3–6.
106. Blough, N. L. "Histories of Some Major Library Periodicals." Master's thesis, Western Reserve University, 1955.
107. Boll, J. J. "Library Architecture, 1800–1875." Doctoral dissertation, University of Illinois, 1961.
108. Bolton, C. K. *American Library History.* Chicago: American Library Association, 1911.
109. Borden, A. K. "Sociological Beginnings of the Library Movement." *LQ* 1 (1931): 278–82.
110. Born, L. K. "History of Microform Activity." *LibT* 8 (1960): 348–58.
111. Bowker, R. R. "Women in the Library Profession." *LJ* 55 (1920): 545–49, 587–92, 635–40.
112. Boyer, P. S. *Purity in Print: The Vice Society Movement and Book Censorship in America.* New York: Charles Scribner's Sons, 1968.
113. Burgh, A. E., and Beede, B. R. "American Librarianship." *Signs: Journal of Women in Culture and Society* 1 (1976): 943–55.
114. Burns, R. K. "The White House National Advisory Commission on Libraries: A Background Report." *DCL* 39 (1968): 28–36.
115. Casey, G. M., ed. "Federal Aid to Libraries: Its History, Impact, Future." *LibT* 24 (1975): whole issue.
116. Chang, H. C. "Library Goals as Responses to Structural and Milieu Requirements: A Comparative Study." Doctoral dissertation, University of Minnesota, 1974.
117. Clopine, J. "A History of Library Unions in the United States." Master's thesis, Catholic University of America, 1951. Published: Association of College and Research Libraries Microcard, Number 43.
118. Coil, N. *American Librarianship, 1876–1976: An Attempt at Identifying Some Bench Marks Useful in Measuring Achievement, and a Selective Bibliography.* Muncie, Ind.: The Third in the 1975–76 Ball State University Faculty Lecture Series, 1976.
119. Conduitte, G. G. "The Changing Character of Southern Libraries." *LJ* 81 (1956): 1112–18.
120. Corwin, M. A. "An Investigation of Female Leadership in State Library Organizations and Local Library Associations, 1876–1923." Master's thesis, University of Chicago, 1973.
121. Danton, J. P. "The Library Press." *LibT* 25 (1976): 153–76.
122. Ducsay, W. J. "A Translation of the 'History of Libraries in the United States of America' from the Milkau Collection." Master's thesis, Western Reserve University, 1959.
123. Eaton, T., ed. *Contributions to American Library History.* Champaign: Illini Union Bookstore, 1964.
124. ———. *Contributions to Mid-west Library History.* Champaign: Illini Union Bookstore, 1964.

General Studies of American Library History   13

125. Edgar, N. L. "Image of Librarianship in the Media." In *A Century of Service: Librarianship in the United States and Canada*, edited by S. L. Jackson, et al., pp. 303–20. Chicago: American Library Association, 1976.
126. Elliot, C. A. "The U.S. Bureau of Education: Its Role in Library History, 1876." In *Library History Seminar Number 3*, edited by M. J. Zachert, pp. 98–111. Tallahassee: *JLH*, 1968.
127. Esterquest, R. T. "War Literature and Libraries: The Role of the American Library in Promoting Interest and Support of the European War, 1914–1918." Master's thesis, University of Illinois, 1940.
128. Evans, C. "A History of Community Analysis in American Librarianship." *LibT* 24 (1976): 441–58.
129. Fiske, M. *Book Selection and Censorship: A Study of School and Public Libraries in California*. Berkeley: University of California Press, 1959.
130. Fleming, E. M. "The Publishers Weekly and the Library Movement, 1882–1900." In *R. R. Bowker, Militant Liberal*, pp. 175–95. Norman: University of Oklahoma, 1952.
131. Fletcher, W. I. "The Great Libraries of the United States." *BookB* 11 (1894): 343–46.
132. Fry, J. W. "LSA and LSCA, 1956–1973: A Legislative History." *LibT* 24 (1975): 7–26.
133. Fulcino, S. A. "'The Right to Know' and the Library: A Case History in the Popularization of a Slogan." Master's thesis, University of Chicago, 1974.
134. Garrison, D. "Women in Librarianship." In *A Century of Service: Librarianship in the United States and Canada*, edited by S. L. Jackson et al., pp. 146–68. Chicago: American Library Association, 1976.
135. Gecas, J. G. "The Depository Library Act of 1962: A Legislative History and Survey of Implementation." Master's thesis, University of Chicago Graduate Library School, 1975.
136. Geller, E. "Intellectual Freedom: Eternal Principle or Unanticipated Consequence." *LJ* 99 (1974): 1364–67.
137. ———. "The Librarian as Censor." *LJ* 101 (1976): 1255–58.
138. Godet, M. *Bibliothèques Américaines: Impressions et Réflexions*. Berne, 1935.
139. Graham, C. A. "Trends in Library Cooperation, 1921–1955: An Analysis Based on Library Literature." Master's thesis, University of Texas, 1961.
140. Green, C. S. "Library Service to the Blind in the United States: Origins and Development to 1931." Master's thesis, University of Chicago, 1967.
141. Hankins, F. D. "The Treatment of Basic Problems in the *Library Journal*, 1900–1930." Master's thesis, University of Texas, 1951.

142. Harris, H. J. "A History of Joseph Ruzicka, Inc., Library Bookbinders." Master's thesis, University of North Carolina, 1966.
143. Harris, M. H. "Portrait in Paradox: Commitment and Ambivalence in American Librarianship, 1876–1976." *Libri* 26 (1976): 311–31.
144. ———, comp. *Reader in American Library History*. Washington, D.C.: NCR Microcards Editions, 1971.
145. Havlik, R. J. "The Library Services Branch of the U.S. Office of Education: Its Creation, Growth, and Transformation." In *Library History Seminar Number 3*, edited by M. J. Zachert, pp. 112–23. Tallahassee: *JLH*, 1968.
146. Hesseltine, W. B., and Gara, L. "Sherman Burns the Libraries." *SCHM* 55 (1954): 137–42.
147. Hoffman, C. *Libraries in the United States, 1940–1947*. Chicago: American Library Association, 1948.
148. Holley, E. G. "Librarians, 1876–1976." *LibT* 25 (1976): 177–208.
149. Jackson, S., ed. *A Century of Service: Librarianship in the United States and Canada*. Chicago: American Library Association, 1976.
150. ———. *Libraries and Librarianship in the West: A Brief History*. New York: McGraw-Hill, 1974.
151. ———. "Research." In *A Century of Service: Librarianship in the United States and Canada*, edited by S. L. Jackson et al., pp. 341–54. Chicago: American Library Association, 1976.
152. Jackson, W. V. "Funding Library Endowments in the United States." *ELIS* 9:138–86.
153. Jewett, C. C. *Notices of Public Libraries in the United States of America*. Washington, D.C.: Printed for the House of Representatives, 1851.
154. Johnson, E. D. *Communication: An Introduction to the History of Writing, Printing, Books and Libraries*. 4th ed. Metuchen, N.J.: Scarecrow Press, 1973.
155. ———. "Southern Public Libraries in the 1850's: Correcting an Error." *JLH* 4 (1969): 268–70.
156. ———, and Harris, M. H. *History of Libraries in the Western World*. 3d ed. Metuchen, N.J.: Scarecrow Press, 1976.
157. Kanner, E. E. "The Impact of Gerontological Concepts on Principles of Librarianship." Doctoral dissertation, University of Wisconsin, 1972.
158. Kaplan, L. "Library Cooperation in the United States." *IntR* 5 (1973): 139–45.
159. Kaser, D., and Jackson, R. "A Century of Personnel Concerns in Libraries." In *A Century of Service: Librarianship in the United States and Canada*, edited by S. L. Jackson et al., pp. 129–45. Chicago: American Library Association, 1976.
160. Kilgour, F. G. "History of Library Computerization." *JLA* 3 (1970): 218–29.

161. Kraus, J. W. "Prologue to Library Cooperation." *LibT* 24 (1975): 169–82.
162. Krug, J. "History of the Library Bill of Rights." *ALib* 3 (1972): 80–82, 183–84.
163. Krummel, D. W. "The Library World of *Norton's Literary Gazette.*" In *Books in America's Past: Essays Honoring Rudolph H. Gjelsness*, edited by D. Kaser, pp. 238–65. Charlottesville: University of Virginia Press, 1966.
164. Lacy, D. M. "War Measures: Past and Present." *LQ* 23 (1935): 283–51.
165. Landram, C. O. "A Study of the Changing Concept of American Librarians as Reflected in the Novels of the Twentieth Century." Master's thesis, Texas State College, 1951.
166. Leary, W. M. "Books, Soldiers and Censorship During the Second World War." *AQ* 20 (1968): 237–45.
167. Lehnus, D. J. "*JEL*, 1969–1970: An Analytical Study." *JEL* 12 (1972): 71–83.
168. Lemke, A. B. "Access, Barriers, Change: The ABC's of Women in Libraries." *SchLJ* 22 (1976): 17–19.
169. Lyle, G. R. "An Exploration into the Origins and Evolution of the Library Survey." In *Library Surveys*, edited by M. F. Tauber and I. R. Stephens, pp. 3–22. New York: Columbia University Press, 1967.
170. Manley, M. C. "Personalities Behind the Development of PAIS." *CRL* 15 (1954): 263–70, 276.
171. Marshall, J. D., comp. *An American Library History Reader: Contributions to Library Literature*. Hamden, Conn.: Shoestring Press, 1961.
172. McMullen, H. "The Distribution of Libraries Throughout the United States." *LibT* 25 (1976): 23–54.
173. ———. "More Statistics of Libraries in the Southeast Before 1876." *SEL* 24 (1974): 18–29.
174. ———. "The Prevalence of Libraries in the United States Before 1876: Some Regional Differences." In *Library History Seminar Number 4*, edited by H. Goldstein and J. Goudeau, pp. 115–39. Tallahassee: Florida State University School of Library Science, 1972.
175. Melrose, L. H. "St. Elizabeth Parish Library: A History and Survey." Master's thesis, Western Reserve University, 1951.
176. Metcalfe, J. *Information Retrieval: British and American, 1876–1976*. Metuchen, N.J.: Scarecrow Press, 1976.
177. Meyer, A. B. *Amerikanische Bibliotheken und Ihre Bestrebungen*. Berlin: R. Friedlander & Sohn, 1906.
178. Miksa, F. "The Making of the 1876 Special Report on Public Libraries." *JLH* 8 (1973): 30–40.
179. Molz, R. K. *Federal Policy and Library Support*. Cambridge, Mass.: M.I.T. Press, 1976.

180. Moore, E. T. "The Intellectual Freedom Saga in California: The Experience of Four Decades." CalL 35 (1974): 48–57.
181. Munn, R. "Library Objectives." BALA 30 (1963): 583–86.
182. Munthe, W. *American Librarianship from a European Angle: An Attempt at an Evaluation of Policies and Activities.* Chicago: American Library Association, 1939.
183. Myers, M., and Scarborough, M., eds. *Women in Librarianship: Melvil's Rib Symposium.* New Brunswick, N.J.: Rutgers University Graduate School of Library Service, 1975.
184. Newell, M. M. "The Development of Library Services to the Blind in the United States." Master's thesis, Southern Connecticut State College, 1966.
185. Newmyer, J. "The Image Problem of the Librarian: Femininity and Social Control." *JLH* 11 (1976): 44–67.
186. Nitecki, J. Z. "The Concept of Public Interest in the Philosophy of Librarianship: The Implications of a Multiple Approach." Master's thesis, University of Chicago, 1963.
187. Oboler, E. M. *The Fear of the Word: Censorship and Sex.* Metuchen, N.J.: Scarecrow Press, 1974.
188. "Outline of the Modern Library Movement in America with Most Important Foreign Events." *LJ* (1901): 73–75.
189. Pafford, J. H. *American and Canadian Libraries: Some Notes on a Visit in the Summer of 1947.* London: Library Association, 1949.
190. [Pearson, E. L.] *The Old Librarian's Almanac . . .* Woodstock, Vt.: The Elm Tree Press, 1909.
191. Peirce, P. "A Study of the Philosophy of Librarianship: A Review of the Relevent Literature, 1930–1950." Master's thesis, Drexel Institute of Technology, 1951.
192. Peterson, K. G. "Library Statistics and Libraries of the Southeast Before 1876." *SEL* 22 (1972): 67–73.
193. Powell, L. C. *Bibliographers of the Golden State.* Berkeley: University of California School of Librarianship, 1967.
194. Predeek, A. *A History of Libraries in Great Britain and North America.* Translated by L. Thompson. Chicago: American Library Association, 1947.
195. Radtke, L. S. "Librarians Turn Publishers: A Study of the Shoe String Press." Master's thesis, Florida State University, 1962.
196. Rairigh, W. N. "Judicial Opinion Concerning Censorship of Library Materials, 1926–1950." Master's thesis, Drexel Institute of Technology, 1950.
197. Ranganathan, S. R. *Library Tour 1948, Europe and America: Impressions and Reflections.* Delhi: Indian Library Association, 1950.
198. Rayward, W. B. "Librarianship in the New World and the Old: Some Points of Contrast." *LibT* 25 (1976): 209–26.
199. Rehfus, R. O., and Skearns, E. I. *"The Library Quarterly,* 1931–1966:

An Index with Commentary." Master's thesis, Kent State University, 1967.
200. Rhees, W. J. *Manual of Public Libraries, Institutions, and Societies in the United States and British Provinces of North America.* Philadelphia: J. B. Lippincott, 1859.
201. Rogers, A. R. "Library Buildings." In *A Century of Service: Librarianship in the United States and Canada*, edited by S. L. Jackson et al., pp. 221–42. Chicago: American Library Association, 1976.
202. Schick, F. L. "Library Statistics: A Century Plus." *ALib* 2 (1971): 727–31.
203. ———. "Statistical Reporting of American Library Developments." *LibT* 25 (1976): 81–88.
204. Schiller, A. R. "Women in Librarianship." In *Advances in Librarianship Volume 4*, edited by M. Voigt, pp. 103–47. New York: Academic Press, 1974.
205. Schmidt, V. L. "The Development of Personnel Selection Procedures and Placement Services in the Professional Staffing of the Library, 1935–1959." Master's thesis, University of North Carolina, 1960. Published: Association of College and Research Libraries Microcard, Number 128.
206. Serebnick, J. "The Relationship Between Book Reviewing and the Inclusion of Controversial Books in Public Libraries." Doctoral dissertation, Rutgers University, 1976.
207. Sharp, H. A. *Libraries and Librarianship in America: A British Commentary and Comparison.* London: Grafton & Co., 1936.
208. Sharp, K. "Illinois Libraries." [University of Illinois] *UnivS* 2 (1906): whole issue.
209. Shera, J. H. "Failure and Success: Assessing a Century." *LJ* 101 (1976): 281–87.
210. Shores, L. "Library Cooperation in the Southwest [1939–52]." *LQ* 22 (1952): 335–41.
211. Smith, G. W. "Northern Libraries and the Confederacy, 1861–1865." *VL* 3 (1956): 7–8.
212. Smith, J. M. *A Chronology of Librarianship.* Metuchen, N.J.: Scarecrow Press, 1968.
213. Smith, P. C. "The Tennessee Valley Authority and Its Influence in the Development of Regional Libraries in the South." Master's thesis, University of North Carolina, 1954.
214. Stanford, E. B. "Library Extension Under the WPA: An Appraisal of an Early Experiment in Federal Aid." Doctoral dissertation, University of Chicago, 1942.
215. Stone, E. W. *American Library Development, 1600–1899.* New York: H. W. Wilson, 1977.
216. Stuart-Stubbs, B. "An Historical Look at Resource Sharing." *LibT* 23 (1975): 649–64.

217. Sumner, J. S. "Theological Libraries in the United States." In U.S. Bureau of Education, *Public Libraries in the United States of America* ... , pp. 127–60. Washington, D.C.: Government Printing Office, 1876.
218. Swarthout, A. W. "The Church Library Movement in Historical Perspective." *DLQ* 6 (1970): 115–18.
219. U.S. Bureau of Education. *Public Libraries in the United States of America: Their History, Condition and Management; Special Report, Part I*. Washington, D.C.: Government Printing Office, 1876.
220. Veaner, A. B. "Microfilm and the Library: A Retrospective." *DLQ* 11 (1975): 3–16.
221. Wallace, A. "The Library Movement in the South Since 1899." *LJ* 32 (1907): 253–58.
222. Wasserman, P. "Development of Administration in Library Service." *CRL* 9 (1958): 283–94.
223. Wells, S. B. "The Feminization of the American Library Profession." Master's thesis, University of Chicago, 1967.
224. White, J. L. "Church Libraries." *ELIS* 9:662–73.
225. Wright, W. E. "A Regimental Library in the Confederate Army." *JLH* 4 (1969): 347–52.
226. Williams, Sister M. L. "History and Description of the Baltimore Archdiocesan Library Council." Master's thesis, Catholic University of America, 1950.
227. Wilson, L. R. "The Role of the Library in the Southeast in Peace and War." *JSF* 21 (1943): 463–68.
228. Winger, H., ed. "American Library History, 1876–1976." *LibT* 25 (1976): whole issue.
229. *Women in the Library Profession: Leadership Roles and Contributions*. Ann Arbor: University of Michigan School of Library Science, 1971.

III. Private Libraries, Reading Tastes, and the Book Trade from the Colonial Period to the Present

This part of the bibliography is divided into two sections: (A) Private Libraries and (B) Reading Tastes and the Book Trade. Selectivity has been necessary in preparing this list, especially in Part B. The objective has been to include items that reflect on the development of reading tastes and the book trade as a means of providing a larger context within which questions of library development might be considered. Readers wanting a definitive list of materials on publishing and the book trade are referred to G. Thomas Tanselle's monumental *Guide to the Study of United States Imprints* (1971, **583**).

A. Private Libraries

There is a strange tendency among historians to consider the nature of private book ownership a significant aspect of American intellectual history prior to the Civil War, while ignoring this subject when it comes to exploring the social or intellectual history of the late nineteenth and twentieth centuries. An excellent example of this situation is Daniel Boorstin's award-winning trilogy entitled *The Americans*, the first volume of which (1958, **244**) devotes one of four sections to the history of reading tastes, private libraries, and the book trade, while the second volume contains only scattered references to the subject, and the final volume overlooks this aspect of American intellectual history.

Due to this emphasis, the majority of the work on private libraries focuses on the colonial and early national periods in American history. However, as can be readily seen from the following bibliography, studies of this time span abound. Among the classic surveys of private libraries in colonial America are Louis B. Wright's study of libraries and reading tastes in his *Cultural Life of the American Colonies, 1607–1763* (1957, **381**) and his more focused study, *The First Gentlemen of Virginia* (1940, **382**). New England is treated in Samuel Eliot Morrison's *Intellectual Life of Colonial New England* (1965, **320**) and Thomas G. Wright's *Literary Culture in Early New England, 1620–1730* (1920, **385**). One old but excellent survey of book col-

20 Private Libraries, Reading Tastes, & the Book Trade

lecting is Carl L. Cannon's *American Book Collectors and Collecting from Colonial Times to the Present* (1941, **255**).

A significant number of studies have been written relating to private libraries in various states or cities during the early period as well. Examples of the more substantial studies include Walter Edgar's work on colonial South Carolina (1969, **265**; 1971, **266**), John Goudeau's studies of Louisiana (1965, **275**), William Houlette's work on plantation libraries in the Old South (1933, **289**), E. V. Lamberton's study of libraries in early Pennsylvania (1918, **307**), John McDermott's book *Private Libraries in Creole St. Louis* (1938, **317**), George Smart's analysis of libraries in colonial Virginia (1938, **347**), and Joseph T. Wheeler's studies of private libraries in colonial Maryland (1940, **364**). Readers should also examine Section B of this part of the bibliography, since the material listed dealing with reading tastes frequently reflects on private collecting interests.

A final major category of studies dealing with private libraries consists of those devoted to the collection interests of individuals. Many such studies have been completed, and they range from full-length books analyzing the development of a major collection to catalogues of individual libraries to short articles on such collections. Impressive in this category are Walter Harding, *Emerson's Library* (1967, **282**), Gordon W. Jones, *The Library of James Monroe* (1967, **292**), Margaret Korty, "Franklin's World of Books" (1967, **305**), Daniel Meador, *Mr. Justice Black and His Books* (1974, **318**), William Peden, "Thomas Jefferson: Book Collector" (1942, **329**), Millicent Sowerby, *Catalogue of the Library of Thomas Jefferson* (1952–1959, **348**), and Edwin Wolf, *The Library of James Logan of Philadelphia* (1975, **375**) and "Reconstruction of Benjamin Franklin's Library" (1962, **379**). Frequently the libraries of private individuals formed the nucleus of public or research libraries, and the histories of these libraries often contain useful information on the private libraries involved. For example, the John Carter Brown Library at Brown University, Jefferson's books at the University of Virginia and the Library of Congress, and the Bancroft Library at the University of California.

B. Reading Tastes and the Book Trade

This section treats materials relating to the development of reading tastes and those aspects of the book trade that reflect on reading tastes. Studies of reading tastes have tended to focus on eighteenth- and nineteenth-century America, as is evidenced by the book-length studies by Morison, Louis B. Wright, and Thomas Goddard Wright cited in Section A. However, several excellent surveys of reading tastes in the country do give a general overview of the subject: James D. Hart, *The Popular Book: A History of America's Literary Taste* (1950, **473**), Frank Luther Mott, *Golden Multitudes: The Story of Best Sellers in the United States* (1947, **524**), and Frank Schick, *The Paperbound Book in America* (1958, **536**).

A large number of studies based on the analysis of private libraries, book trade statistics, and advertisements attempt to assess the nature of reading tastes in various parts of the country, or in different time periods in American history. Examples of these are Hugh Baker's work on California (1951, **395**), Glenn E. Barker on New York (1950, **398**), Theodore C. Blegen on Minnesota (1947, **407**), Clyde H. Cantrell on the antebellum South (1960, **417**), H. Trevor Colbourn on the reading interests of colonial leaders (1965, **428**), Richard B. Davis's *Intellectual Life in Jefferson's Virginia* (1964, **438**), Harold H. Dugger on reading tastes in Missouri (1951, **444**), M. P. Fletcher on reading in Arkansas (1949, **455**), Richard M. Gummere on the influence of the classics on colonial America (1963, **463**), Michael H. Harris on reading in Indiana (1971, **468**), Lundberg and May on the "enlightened reader in America" (1976, **504**), Doyce Nunis on reading in early California (1964, **532**), Howard Peckham on books and reading in the Ohio Valley (1958, **540**), Donald A. Sears on reading in Maine (1973, **559**), Don D. Walker on the reading habits of the cowboy (1960, **593**), and Joseph T. Wheeler on reading interests in colonial Maryland (1941, **601**).

Another approach has been to study the vogue of individual authors in America. Classic studies of this nature include Mary Barr on Voltaire (1941, **401**), Esther C. Dunn on Shakespeare (1939, **445**), Chester N. Greenough on Defoe (1935, **462**), Leon Howard on Milton (1935, **479**), Frederic M. Litto on Addison (1966, **503**), Charles F. Mullett on Coke (1932, **527**), G. H. Orians on Scott (1929, **534**), Martin Roth on Sterne (1970, **555**), George F. Sensabaugh on Milton (1964, **561**), Agnes M. Sibley on Pope (1949, **568**), Paul M. Spurlin on Montesquieu (1940, **573**) and Rousseau (1948, **575**), and John M. Werner on Hume (1972, **597**).

Book publishing and the book trade in America have been the subject of substantial surveys, all of which deal in some detail with the question of reading tastes and libraries. Three of the most important are Hellmut Lehmann-Haupt, *The Book in America: A History of the Making and Selling of Books in the United States* (2d ed., 1952, **498**), Charles C. Madison, *Book Publishing in America* (1966, **505**), and John Tebbel, *A History of Book Publishing in the United States* (1972–, **586**; 2 vols. to date). An old, but still useful, history of the book trade is Henry W. Boynton, *Annals of American Bookselling, 1638–1850* (1932, **413**).

A number of more specialized studies deal with individual book sellers or the trade in an area or city. Examples of work in this area are Hugh S. Baker on the California book trade (1951, **394**), Wallace J. Bonk on the Detroit Bookstore, 1817–1828 (1957, **409**), Worthington C. Ford on Henry Knox and his London book store in revolutionary Boston (1927–28, **457**), John Goudeau on booksellers in New Orleans (1970, **460**), Robert Harlan on William Strahan's bookstore (1961, **467**), Michael Harris on the trade in Illinois (1971, **469**) and Indiana (1973, **471**, **472**), John F. McDermott on St. Louis (1939, **513**), Walter Sutton on Cincinnati (1961, **582**), Theodore Vonnegut on Indianapolis (1926, **591**), and Calhoun Winton on colonial South Carolina (1973, **606**).

There are hundreds of histories of individual publishing houses and a selected number are included here since they deal in a substantial way with the development of reading tastes and the book trade. Among the best are Ellen B. Ballou, *The Building of the House: Houghton Mifflin's Formative Years* (1970, **397**), Eugene Exman, *The House of Harper: One Hundred and Fifty Years of Publishing* (1967, **452**), David Kaser, *Messrs. Carey & Lea of Philadelphia: A Study in the History of the Booktrade* (1957, **489**), James P. Pilkington, *The Methodist Publishing House: A History* (1968, **542**), and W. S. Tryon, *Parnassus Corner: A Life of James T. Fields, Publisher to the Victorians* (1963, **589**).

Finally, a number of excellent works on the book trade during certain periods, or the publication and reading of certain types of books, need to be mentioned. Examples of the first type are William Charvat's works on the nineteenth-century book trade (1959, **422**; 1968, **423**), Donald Sheehan's *This Was Publishing: A Chronicle of the Book Trade in the Gilded Age* (1952, **564**), and Madeleine B. Stern's *Imprints on History: Book Publishers and American Frontiers* (1956, **578**). Quality studies of the latter type are Arthur M. Schlesinger, *Learning How to Behave: A Historical Study of American Etiquette Books* (1946, **557**); Mary Noel, *Villains Galore: The Heyday of the Popular Story Weekly* (1954, **531**); or the works of Hillel Black (1967, **405**), Charles Carpenter (1963, **419**), Ruth Elson (1964, **448**), J. Merton England (1963, **449**), Sister M. L. Fell (1941, **453**), Norton Garfinkle (1954, **458**), Clifford Johnson (1904, **485**), John Nietz (1961, **530**), and Erwin C. Shoemaker (1936, **566**) on American text books; and, finally, Jacob Blanck (1938, **406**), John C. Crandall (1969, **432**), and Monica Keifer (1948, **490**) on children's literature.

Private Libraries, Reading Tastes, and the Book Trade from the Colonial Period to the Present

A. Private Libraries

230. Abrahams, A. J. "Chemical Library of Thomas Jefferson." *JCE* 37 (1960): 357–60.
231. Adams, E. B. "Two Colonial New Mexico Libraries, 1704, 1776." *NMHR* 19 (1944): 135–67.
232. ———, and Algier, K. W. "A Frontier Book List–1800." *NMHR* 43 (1968): 49–59.
233. ———, and Scholes, F. V. "Books in New Mexico, 1598–1680." *NMHR* 17 (1942): 1–45.
234. Adams, H. D. "A Note on Jefferson's Knowledge of Economics." *VMHB* 75 (1967): 69–74.
235. Ames, S. M. *Reading, Writing and Arithmetic in Virginia, 1607–1699*. Williamsburg: Virginia 350th Anniversary Celebration Corporation, 1957.

236. Andrews, C. "The Historical Russian Library of Alaska." *PNQ* 3 (1938): 201–04.
237. Baker, C. M. "Books in a Pioneer Household." *JISHS* 32 (1939): 261–87.
238. Bay, J. C. "Private Book Collectors of the Chicago Area: A Brief Review." *LQ* 12 (1942): 363–74.
239. Baym, M. E. "The 1858 Catalogue of Henry Adams' Library." *Colophon* 3 (1938): 483–89.
240. Beck, L. N. "The Library of Susan B. Anthony." *QJLC* 32 (1975): 325–35.
241. Bestor, A. "Thomas Jefferson and the Freedom of Books." In *Three Presidents and Their Books*, pp. 1–44. Urbana: University of Illinois Press, 1963.
242. Blake, M. "Books Taken from Dr. Franklin's Library by Major Andre." *PMHB* 8 (1884): 430.
243. Bondurant, A. M. "Libraries and Books." In *Poe's Richmond . . .*, pp. 91–121. Richmond: Garrett & Massie, 1942.
244. Boorstin, D. *The Americans: The Colonial Experience.* New York: Random House, 1958.
245. Borden, A. K. "Seventeenth-Century American Libraries." *LQ* 2 (1932): 138–47.
246. Boyd, J. P. *The Scheide Library: A Summary View of Its History and Its Outstanding Books Together with an Account of Its Two Founders: William Taylor Scheide and John Hinsdale Scheide.* N.p.: Privately printed, 1947.
247. Bradley, R. "Books in the California Missions." Master's thesis, Columbia University, 1950.
248. Brayton, S. S. "The Library of an Eighteenth-Century Gentleman of Rhode Island." *NEQ* 8 (1935): 277–83.
249. Briggs, R. T. "Books of the Pilgrims as Recorded in Their Inventories and Preserved in Pilgram Hall." *OTNE* 61 (1970–71): 41–46.
250. Browne, C. A. "John Winthrop's Library." *Isis* 11 (1928): 328–41.
251. Bruce, P. A. *Institutional History of Virginia in the Seventeenth Century.* New York: G. P. Putnam's Sons, 1910.
252. Cadbury, H. J. "Anthony Benezet's Library." *BFHA* 23 (1934): 63–75.
253. ———. "John Harvard's Library." *PCSM* 34 (1943): 353–77.
254. ———. "More of Benezet's Library." *BFHA* 25 (1936): 83–85.
255. Cannon, C. L. *American Book Collectors and Collecting from Colonial Times to the Present.* New York: H. W. Wilson, 1941.
256. ———. "William Byrd II of Westover." *Colophon* (1938): 291–302.
257. "A Catalogue of the Books in the Library at Westover . . ." In *The Writings of Colonel William Byrd*, edited by J. S. Bassett, pp. 413–33. New York: Doubleday, Page & Co., 1901.
258. Clemons, H. *Home Library of the Garnetts of "Elmwood."* Charlottesville: University of Virginia, 1957.

259. Clower, G. W. "An Early Nineteenth Century Library: Books of Rev. William Quillin." *GHQ* 49 (1965): 193–99.
260. Commager, H. S. "Jefferson and the Book Burners." *AH* 9 (1958): 65–68.
261. Davis, R. B. "Jefferson as Collector of Virginiana." *SB* 19 (1961): 117–44.
262. Dexter, F. B. "Early Private Libraries in New England." *PAAS* 28 (1907): 135–47.
263. Dumbauld, E. "A Manuscript from Monticello: Jefferson's Library in Legal History." *ABAJ* 38 (1952): 389–92, 446–47.
264. Eddy, G. S. "Dr. Benjamin Franklin's Library." *PAAS* 34 (1924): 206–26.
265. Edgar, W. B. "The Libraries of Colonial South Carolina." Doctoral dissertation, University of South Carolina, 1969.
266. ———. "Notable Libraries of Colonial South Carolina." *SCHM* 72 (1971): 105–10.
267. Evans, E. G., ed. *Inventory of the Library of William Nelson, Jr., of Yorktown, Virginia*. Williamsburg: Botetourt Bibliographical Society, College of William and Mary, 1972.
268. Evans, W. A. "The Library at Beauvoir." *JMH* 6 (1944): 51–54, 119–21, 174–76.
269. Fields, J. E. "A Signer and His Signatures; or the Library of Thomas Lynch, Jr." *HLB* 14 (1960): 210–52.
270. Flanagan, J. T. "The Destruction of an Early Illinois Library." *JISHS* 40 (1959): 387–93.
271. Goff, F. R. "Jefferson the Book Collector." *QJLC* 29 (1972): 32–47.
272. ———. "T.R.'s Big Game Library." *QJLC* 21 (1964): 167–71.
273. Gordon, D. "The Book-Collecting Ishams of Northamptonshire and Their Bookish Virginia Cousins." *VMHB* 77 (1969): 174–79.
274. ———. "The Book-Collecting Ishams of Northamptonshire and Their Bookloving Virginia and Massachusetts Cousins." *HLB* 18 (1970): 282–97.
275. Goudeau, J. M. "Early Libraries in Louisiana: A Study of Creole Influence." Doctoral dissertation, Western Reserve University, 1965. 2 vols.
276. ———, and Goudeau, L. "The Canonage Library." *JLH* 7 (1972): 64–79.
277. ———, and Goudeau, L. "A Nineteenth Century Louisiana Library: The LaRue Library." *JLH* 10 (1975): 162–68.
278. Greenberg, H. "The Authenticity of the Library of John Winthrop the Younger." *AL* 8 (1937): 448–52.
279. Haffner, G. O., ed. "The Medical Inventory of a Pioneer Doctor." *IMH* 56 (1960): 37–63.
280. Hall, H. J. "Two Book-lists: 1668 and 1728." *PCSM* 24 (1920): 64–71.
281. Hamill, R. F. "A Plain Farmer's Library of 1814." *ABC* 5 (1934): 223–25.

282. Harding, W., comp. *Emerson's Library.* Charlottesville: The University Press of Virginia for the Bibliographical Society of the University of Virginia, 1967.
283. Harris, M. H. "Books on the Frontier: The Extent and Nature of Bookownership in Southern Indiana, 1800–1850." *LQ* 42 (1972): 416–30.
284. ———. "The Lawyer's Library on the Frontier: Southern Indiana, 1800–1850, as a Test Case." *AJLH* 16 (1972): 239–51.
285. ———. "A Methodist Minister's Working Library in Mid-Nineteenth Century Illinois." *WQR* 4 (1967): 210–19.
286. Houlette, W. D. "Books of the Virginia Dynasty." *LQ* 24 (1954): 226–39.
287. ———. "Plantation and Parish Libraries in the Old South." Doctoral dissertation, State University of Iowa, 1933. 2 vols.
288. Irrman, R. H. "The Library of an Early Ohio Farmer." *POSAHS* 42 (1948): 185–93.
289. Jackson, W. A. "Henry Stevens and Washington's Library." *PBSA* 53 (1959): 79–80.
290. Johnson, R. D. "Books in the Life of John Quincy Adams." Master's thesis, University of Chicago, 1957.
291. Jones, G. W. "The Library of Doctor John Mitchell of Urbana." *VMHB* 76 (1968): 441–43.
292. ———, comp. *The Library of James Monroe (1758–1831), 5th President (1816–1824) of the United States.* Charlottesville: Bibliographical Society of the University of Virginia, 1967.
293. ———. "A Virginia-Owned Shelf of Early Medical Imprints." *PBSA* 58 (1964): 281–90.
294. Joyce, D. F. "Arthur Alonzo Schomburg: A Pioneering Black Bibliophile." *JLH* 10 (1975): 169–77.
295. Kaplan, L. "Peter Force, Collector." *LQ* 14 (1944): 234–38.
296. Ketcham, J. "The Bibliomania of the Reverend William Bentley, D.D." *HCEI* 108 (1972): 275–303.
297. Keys, T. E. "The Colonial Library and the Development of Sectional Differences in American Colonies." *LQ* 8 (1938): 373–90.
298. ———. "The Development of Private Medical Libraries." In his *Applied Medical Library Practice*, pp. 148–89. Springfield, Ill.: Charles C. Thomas, 1958.
299. ———. "Libraries of Some Twentieth-Century American Bibliophilic Physicians." *LQ* 24 (1954): 21–34.
300. ———. "The Medical Books of Dr. Charles N. Hewitt." *MinnH* 21 (1940): 357–71.
301. ———. "The Medical Books of William Worral Mayo, Pioneer Surgeon of the American Northwest." *MLAB* 31 (1943): 119–27.
302. ———. "Popular Authors in the Colonial Library." *WLB* 14 (1940): 726–27.

303. ———. "Private and Semi-Private Libraries of the American Colonies." Master's thesis, University of Chicago, 1934.
304. Korey, M. E. *The Books of Isaac Norris (1701–1766) at Dickinson College*. Carlisle, Pa.: Dickinson College, 1976.
305. Korty, M. B. "Franklin's World of Books." *JLH* 2 (1967): 271–328.
306. Kraus, J. W. "Private Libraries in Colonial America." *JLH* 9 (1974): 31–53.
307. Lamberton, E. V. "Colonial Libraries of Pennsylvania." *PMHB* 17 (1918): 193–234.
308. Leonard, I. A. "A Frontier Library, 1799." *HAHR* 23 (1943): 21–51.
309. *Library of an Early Virginia Scientist: Dr. John Mitchell, F.R.S. (1711–1763)*. Occasional Papers Number 4. Fredericksburg, Va.: Lee Trinkle Library, Mary Washington College of the University of Virginia, 1971.
310. Maurer, M. "The Library of a Colonial Musician, 1755 [Cuthbert Ogle]." *WMQ* 7 (1950): 39–52.
311. McCorison, M. A. "Donald McKay–A Collector of Western Americana." *WestHQ* 3 (1972): 67–76.
312. McDermott, J. F. "A Frontier Library: The Books of Isaac McCoy." *PBSA* 52 (1958): 140–43.
313. ———. "The Library of Barthelemi Tardiveau." *JISHS* 29 (1936): 89–91.
314. ———. "The Library of Father Gibault." *MA* 27 (1935): 273–75.
315. ———. "The Library of Henry Shaw." *MBGB* 28 (1940): 49–53.
316. ———. "The Library of John Hay of Cahokia and Belleville." *MHSB* 9 (1953): 183–86.
317. ———. *Private Libraries in Creole St. Louis*. Baltimore: Johns Hopkins Press, 1938.
318. Meador, D. J. *Mr. Justice Black and His Books*. Charlottesville: University Press of Virginia, 1974.
319. Metcalf, J. C. "Virginia Libraries in Retrospect." *MadQ* 6 (1946): 154–62.
320. Morison, S. E. *The Intellectual Life of Colonial New England*. New York: New York University Press, 1965.
321. Morris, W. J. "John Quincy Adams's German Library with a Catalog of his German Books." *PAPS* 118 (1974): 321–33.
322. Morrison, H. A. "Alaskana: Description of the Library of Judge Wickersham, Delegate in Congress from Alaska." *SL* 4 (1913): 183–84.
323. Oliphant, J. O. "The Library of Archibald McKinley, Oregon Fur Trader." *WHQ* 25 (1934): 23–36.
324. O'Neal, W. B. *Jefferson's Fine Arts Library: His Selections for the University of Virginia Together with His Own Architectural Books*. Charlottesville: University Press of Virginia, 1976.
325. Parks, E. W. "Jefferson as a Man of Letters." *GaR* 6 (1952): 450–59.
326. Patrick, W. R. "Literature in the Louisiana Plantation Home Prior to

1861: A Study in Literary Culture." Doctoral dissertation, Louisiana State University, 1937.
327. ———. "A Louisiana French Plantation Library." *FAR* 1 (1948): 47–67.
328. Peden, W. H. "Some Notes Concerning Thomas Jefferson's Libraries." *WMQ* 1 (1944): 265–72.
329. ———. "Thomas Jefferson: Book Collector." Doctoral dissertation, University of Virginia, 1942.
330. Pene du Bois, H. *Four Private Libraries of New York: A Contribution of the History of Bibliophilism in America*. First Series. Preface by O. Uzanne. New York: Duprat & Co., 1892.
331. Potter, A. C. "Catalogue of John Harvard's Library." *PCSM* 21 (1920): 190–230.
332. Quinn, D. B. "A List of Books Purchased for the Virginia Company." *VMHB* 77 (1969): 347–60.
333. Read, K. T. "The Library of Robert Carter of Nomini Hall." Master's thesis, College of William and Mary, 1970.
334. Reese, G. H. "Books in the Palace: The Libraries of Three Virginia Governors [Fauquier, Berkeley, Murray]." *VC* (1968): 20–31.
335. Robinson, C. F., and Robinson R. "Three Early Massachusetts Libraries." *PCSM* 28 (1935): 107–75.
336. Rodgers, H. *Private Libraries of Providence*. Providence: Sidney S. Rider, 1878.
337. Rogers, A. E. "Swante Palm: With Notes on the Library of a Nineteenth Century Texas Book Collector." Master's thesis, University of Texas, 1966.
338. Rosenbach, A. S. W. "The Libraries of the Presidents of the United States." *PAAS* 44 (1934): 337–64.
339. Savin, M. B., and Abrahams, J. J. "The Botanical Library of Thomas Jefferson." *JEMSS* 75 (1959): 44–52.
340. Schullian, D. M. "Unfolded Out of the Folds." *MLAB* 40 (1952): 135–43.
341. Seeber, E. D. "The Brute Library in Vincennes." *IQB* 4 (1948): 81–86.
342. Shaffer, E. "Portrait of a Philadelphia Collector: William McIntire Elkins [1882–1947]." *PBSA* 50 (1956): 115–29.
343. Shipley, J. B. "Franklin Attends a Book Auction." *PMHB* 80 (1956): 37–45.
344. Simpson, W. S. "A Comparison of the Libraries of Seven Colonial Virginians, 1754–1789." *JLH* 9 (1947): 54–65.
345. Sioussat, St. George L. "The Philosophical Transactions of the Royal Society in Libraries of William Byrd of Westover, Benjamin Franklin, and the American Philosophical Society." *PAPS* 93 (1949): 99–107.
346. Skallerup, H. R. "For His Excellency, Thomas Jefferson, Esq.: The Tale of a Wandering Book." *QJLC* 31 (1974): 116–21.

347. Smart, G. K. "Private Libraries in Colonial Virginia." *AL* 10 (1938): 24–52.
348. Sowerby, M., comp. *Catalogue of the Library of Thomas Jefferson*. 5 vols. Washington, D.C.: Library of Congress, 1952–1959.
349. ———. "Thomas Jefferson and His Library." *PBSA* 50 (1956): 213–28.
350. Spruill, J. C. "The Southern Lady's Library, 1700–1776." *SAQ* 34 (1935): 23–41.
351. Stern, M. B. "Anton Roman: Argonaut of Books." *CHSQ* 28 (1949): 1–18.
352. Street, T. W. "Thomas Smyth: Presbyterian Bookman." *JPH* 37 (1959): 1–14.
353. Talbert, N. J. "Books and Libraries of the Carolina Charter Colonists, 1663–1763." *NCL* 21 (1963): 68–69.
354. "The Ticknor Library." *MoreB* 3 (1921): 301–16.
355. Tolles, F. B. "John Woolman's List of 'Books Lent.'" *BFHA* 31 (1942): 72–83.
356. Tuttle, J. H. "[Catalogue of Increase Mathers' Library.]" *PAAS* 20 (1910): 280–90.
357. ———. "Early Libraries in New England." *PCSM* 13 (1911): 288–92.
358. ———. "The Libraries of the Mathers." *PAAS* 20 (1910): 312–50.
359. ———. "The Library of Dr. William Ames." *PCSM* 14 (1913): 63–66.
360. Upshur, A. F., and Whitelaw, R. T. "Library of the Rev. Thomas Teackle [1696]." *WMQ* 23 (1943): 298–308.
361. Waterman, J. S. "Thomas Jefferson and Blackstone's Commentaries." In *Essays in the History of Early American Law*, edited by D. H. Flaherty, pp. 451–88. Chapel Hill: University of North Carolina Press, 1969.
362. Watson, H. R. "The Books They Left: Some 'Liberies' in Edgecombe County, 1733–1783." *NCHR* 48 (1971): 245–57.
363. Weeks, S. B. "Libraries and Literature in North Carolina in the Eighteenth Century." Amer. Hist. Ass., *Annual Report for the Year 1895*, pp. 169–77. Washington, D.C.: Government Printing Office, 1896.
364. Wheeler, J. T. "Books Owned by Marylanders, 1700–1776." *NHM* 35 (1940): 337–53.
365. Williams, J. R., contr. "A Catalogue of Books in the Library of Councillor Robert Carter." *WMQ* 10 (1902): 232–41.
366. Wilson, J. E. "An Early Baltimore Physician and His Medical Library." *AMH* 4 (1942): 63–80.
367. Winne, J. *Private Libraries of New York*. New York: E. French, 1860.
368. Wolf, E., 2d. "B. Franklin, Bookman." *BALA* 50 (1956): 13–16.
369. ———. "The Dispersal of the Library of William Byrd of Westover." *PAAS* 68 (1958): 19–106.
370. ———. "Great American Book Collectors to 1800." *GGC* n.s., no. 16 (1971): 1–25.

371. ———. *James Logan, 1674–1751, Bookman Extraordinary.* Philadelphia: Library Company of Philadelphia, 1971.
372. ———. "James Logan's Correspondence with William Reading, Librarian of Sion College." In *Homage to a Bookman: Essays . . . Written for Hans P. Kraus . . .* , edited by H. Lehmann-Haupt, pp. 209–20. Berlin: Gebr. Mann Verlag, 1967.
373. ———. "A Key to Identification of Franklin's Books." *Manuscripts* 8 (1956): 211–14.
374. ———. "The Library of Edward Lloyd IV of Wye House." *WintP* 5 (1969): 87–121.
375. ———. *The Library of James Logan of Philadelphia.* Philadelphia: Library Company of Philadelphia, 1975.
376. ———. "The Library of a Philadelphia Judge [John Guest], 1708." *PMHB* 83 (1939): 180–91.
377. ———. "The Library of Ralph Ashton: The Book Background of a Colonial Philadelphia Lawyer." *PBSA* 58 (1964): 345–79.
378. ———. "A Parcel of Books for the Province in 1700." *PMHB* 89 (1965): 428–46.
379. ———. "The Reconstruction of Benjamin Franklin's Library: An Unorthodox Jigsaw Puzzle." *PBSA* 46 (1962): 1–16.
380. ———. "The Romance of James Logan's Books." *WMQ* 13 (1956): 342–53.
381. Wright, L. B. "Books, Libraries and Learning." In his *The Cultural Life of the American Colonies, 1607–1763 . . .* , pp. 126–53. New York: Harper, 1957.
382. ———. *The First Gentlemen of Virginia: Intellectual Qualities of the Early Colonial Ruling Class.* San Moreno: Huntington Library, 1940.
383. ———. "The Gentleman's Library in Early Virginia: The Literary Interests of the First Carters." *HLQ* 1 (1937): 3–61.
384. ———. "Jefferson and the Classics." *PAPS* 87 (1943): 223–33.
385. Wright, T. G. *Literary Culture in Early New England, 1620–1730.* New Haven: Yale University Press, 1920.
386. Yost, G. "The Reconstruction of the Library of Norborne Berkeley, Baron de Botetourt, Governor of Virginia, 1768–1770." *PBSA* 36 (1942): 97–123.
387. Zachert, M. J. K. "The Peter Early Estate: Inventory and Appraisement." *JLH* 3 (1968): 266–70.

B. Reading Tastes and the Book Trade

388. Agard, W. "Classics on the Midwest Frontier." In *The Frontier in Perspective*, edited by W. D. Wyman and C. B. Kroeber, pp. 165–83. Madison: University of Wisconsin Press, 1957.

389. Bader, A. L. "Frederick Saunders and the Early History of International Copyright Movement in America." *LQ* 8 (1938): 25–39.
390. Baer, E. "Books, Newspapers and Libraries in Pioneer St. Louis, 1808–1842." *MHR* 56 (1962): 347–60.
391. Bailyn, B. *The Ideological Origins of the American Revolution.* Cambridge, Mass.: Harvard University Press, 1967.
392. ———. "Political Experience and Enlightenment Ideas in Eighteenth-century America." *AHR* 67 (1962): 339–51.
393. Baker, H. S. "Gold Rush Miners and Their Books." *QN* 10 (1955): 51–60.
394. ———. "History of the Book Trade in California, 1849–1859." *CHSQ* 30 (1951): 97–115, 249–67, 353–67.
395. ———. "Reading Tastes in California, 1849–1859." Doctoral dissertation, Stanford University, 1951.
396. Baldwin, S. "Book-Learning and Learning Books." *CRL* 1 (1940): 257–61.
397. Ballou, E. B. *The Building of the House: Houghton Mifflin's Formative Years.* Boston: Houghton Mifflin, 1970.
398. Barker, G. E. "What Crown Pointers Were Reading One Hundred Years Ago." *NYH* 31 (1950): 31–40.
399. Barnes, J. C. "A Bibliography of Wordsworth in American Periodicals Through 1825." *PBSA* 52 (1958): 205–19.
400. Barnes, J. J. *Authors, Publishers, and Politicians: The Quest for an Anglo-American Copyright Agreement, 1815–1854.* Columbus: Ohio State University Press, 1974.
401. Barr, M. M. *Voltaire in America, 1744–1800.* Baltimore: Johns Hopkins Press, 1941.
402. Bethke, R. D. "Chapbook 'Gallows Literature' in Nineteenth-Century Pennsylvania." *PF* 20 (1970): 2–15.
403. Bickford, C. P. "Literary Piracy in New Haven: Sidney Babcock and the Publication of Children's Books." *ConnHSB* 40 (1975): 65–74.
404. Bishop, W. P. "The Struggle for International Copyright in the United States." Doctoral dissertation, Boston University, 1959.
405. Black, H. *The American Schoolbook.* New York: Morrow, 1967.
406. Blanck, J. *Peter Parley to Penrod: A Bibliographical Description of the Best-Loved American Juvenile Books.* New York: R. R. Bowker, 1938.
407. Blegen, T. C. "Frontier Bookshelves." In *Grassroots History*, pp. 175–86. Minneapolis: University of Minnesota, 1947.
408. Bode, C. *The Anatomy of American Popular Culture, 1840–1861.* Berkeley: University of California Press, 1959.
409. Bonk, W. J. *Michigan's First Bookstore: A Study of the Books Sold in the Detroit Bookstore, 1817–1828.* Ann Arbor: University of Michigan Department of Library Science, 1957.
410. Boquer, H. F. "Sir Walter Scott in New Orleans, 1818–1832." *LHQ* 21 (1938): 420–517.

Private Libraries, Reading Tastes, & the Book Trade 31

411. Bowes, F. P. *The Culture of Early Charleston.* Chapel Hill: University of North Carolina Press, 1942.
412. Bowker, R. R. *Copyright: Its History and Its Law.* Boston: Houghton Mifflin, 1912.
413. Boynton, H. W. *Annals of American Bookselling, 1638–1850.* New York: Wiley, 1932.
414. Bridenbaugh, C. "The Press and the Book in Eighteenth Century Philadelphia." *PMHB* 65 (1941): 1–30.
415. Bugbee, B. W. "The Early American Law of Intellectual Property: The Historical Foundations of the United States Patent and Copyright Systems." Doctoral dissertation, University of Michigan, 1960.
416. Cambell, K. "Poe's Reading." *UTSE* 5 (1925): 166–96; 7 (1927): 175–80.
417. Cantrell, C. H. "The Reading Habits of Ante-Bellum Southerners." Doctoral dissertation, University of Illinois, 1960.
418. Capps, J. L. *Emily Dickinson's Reading, 1836–1886.* Cambridge: Harvard University Press, 1966.
419. Carpenter, C. *History of American Schoolbooks.* Philadelphia: University of Pennsylvania Press, 1963.
420. Cazden, R. E. "The German Book Trade in Ohio Before 1848." *OH* 84 (1975): 57–77.
421. ———. "The Provision of German Books in America During the Eighteenth Century." *Libri* 6 (1973): 81–108.
422. Charvat, W. *Literary Publishing in America, 1790–1850.* Philadelphia: University of Pennsylvania Press, 1959.
423. ———. *The Profession of Authorship in America, 1800–1870.* Columbus: Ohio State University Press, 1968.
424. Chinard, G., ed. *The Literary Bible of Thomas Jefferson: His Commonplace Book of Philosophers and Poets.* Baltimore: Johns Hopkins Press, 1928.
425. Clark, A. J. *The Movement for International Copyright in Nineteenth Century America.* Washington, D.C.: Catholic University of America Press, 1960.
426. Clive, J., and Bailyn, B. "England's Cultural Provinces: Scotland and America." *WMQ* 11 (1954): 200–13.
427. Cohen, H., ed. *Landmarks of American Writing.* New York: Basic Books, 1969.
428. Colbourn, H. T. *The Lamp of Experience: Whig History and the Intellectual Origins of the American Revolution.* Chapel Hill: University of North Carolina Press, 1965.
429. ———. "The Reading of Joseph Carrington Cabell: A List of Books on Various Subjects Recommended to a Young Man . . ." *SB* 3 (1960): 179–88.
430. ———. "Thomas Jefferson's Use of the Past." *WMQ* 15 (1958): 56–70.

431. Commager, H. S. "The American Enlightenment and the Ancient World: A Study of Paradox." *PMHS* 83 (1971): 3–15.
432. Crandall, J. C. "Patriotism and Humanitarian Reform in Children's Literature, 1825–1860." *AQ* 21 (1969): 3–22.
433. Cross, W. O. "Ralph Waldo Emerson's Reading in the Boston Athenaeum." Master's thesis, Columbia University, 1930.
434. Dale, E. E. "Culture on the American Frontier." *NH* 26 (1945): 75–90.
435. ———. "The Frontier Society." *NH* 31 (1950): 167–82.
436. Davis, C. C. *An Early Novelist Goes to the Library: William Caruthers and His Readings, 1823–29.* New York: New Public Library, 1948.
437. Davis, R. B. *Francis Walker Gilmer; Life and Learning in Jefferson's Virginia. A Study in Virginia Literary Culture in the First Quarter of the Nineteenth Century.* Richmond: Dietz Press, 1939.
438. ———. *Intellectual Life in Jefferson's Virginia, 1790–1830.* Chapel Hill: University of North Carolina Press, 1964.
439. ———. "Literary Tastes in Virginia Before Poe." *WMQ* 10 (1939): 55–68.
440. Dedmond, F. B. "Emerson and the Concord Libraries." *MoreB* 3 (1951): 318–19.
441. Derby, J. C. *Fifty Years Among Authors, Books and Publishers.* New York: Carleton, 1884.
442. Downs, R. B. *Books That Changed America.* New York: Macmillan, 1970.
443. ———. *Famous American Books.* New York: McGraw-Hill, 1971.
444. Dugger, H. H. "Reading Interests and the Book Trade in Frontier Missouri." Doctoral dissertation, University of Missouri, 1951.
445. Dunn, E. C. *Shakespeare in America.* New York: Macmillan Co., 1939.
446. Eaton, A. J. "The American Movement for International Copyright: 1837–1860." *LQ* 15 (1945): 95–122.
447. Edgar, W. B. "Some Popular Books in Colonial South Carolina." *SCHM* 72 (1971): 174–78.
448. Elson, R. M. *Guardians of Tradition: American School Books of the Nineteenth Century.* Lincoln: University of Nebraska, 1964.
449. England, J. M. "The Democratic Faith in American Schoolbooks, 1783–1860." *AQ* 15 (1963): 191–99.
450. Ensor, A. *Mark Twain and the Bible.* Lexington: University of Kentucky Press, 1969.
451. Esarey, L. "Elements of Culture in the Old Northwest." *IMH* 53 (1957): 257–64.
452. Exman, E. *The House of Harper: One Hundred and Fifty Years of Publishing.* New York: Harper & Row, 1967.
453. Fell, Sister M. L. *The Foundations of Nativism in American Textbooks, 1783–1860.* Washington, D.C., 1941.

454. Fiering, N. S. "Solomon Stoddard's Library at Harvard in 1664." *HLB* 20 (1972): 255–69.
455. Fletcher, M. P. "Arkansas Pioneers: What They Were Reading a Century Ago." *AHQ* 8 (1949): 211–14.
456. Ford, P. L. *The New England Primer: A History of Its Origin and the Development with a Reprint of the Unique Copy of the Earliest Known Edition and Many Fac-Simile Illustrations and Reproductions.* New York: Dodd, Mead and Company, 1897.
457. Ford, W. C. "Henry Knox and the London Book-Store in Boston, 1771–1774." *PMHS* 61 (1927–28): 225–303.
458. Garfinkle, N. "Conservatism in American Textbooks, 1800–1860." *NYH* 35 (1954): 49–63.
459. Geary, S. "The Domestic Novel as a Commercial Commodity: Making a Best Seller in the 1850s." *PBSA* 70 (1976): 365–93.
460. Goudeau, J. M. "Booksellers and Printers in New Orleans, 1764–1884." *JLH* 5 (1970): 5–19.
461. Grade, A. E. "A Chronicle of Robert Frost's Early Reading, 1874–1899." *BNYPL* 72 (1968): 611–28.
462. Greenough, C. N. "Defoe in Boston." *PCSM* 28 (1935): 461–93.
463. Gummere, R. M. *The American Colonial Mind and the Classical Tradition.* Cambridge: Harvard University Press, 1963.
464. Hackett, A. P. *Fifty Years of Best Sellers, 1895–1945.* New York: R. R. Bowker, 1945.
465. Haraszti, Z. *John Adams and the Prophets of Progress.* Cambridge, Mass.: Harvard University Press, 1952.
466. Harlan, R. D. "Colonial Printer as Bookseller in Eighteenth-Century Philadelphia: The Case of David Hall." *Studies Eighteenth-Century Culture* 5 (1976): 355–69.
467. ———. "William Strahan's American Book Trade, 1774–76." *LQ* 31 (1961): 235–44.
468. Harris, M. H. "The Availability of Books and the Nature of Book Ownership on the Southern Indiana Frontier, 1800–1850." Doctoral dissertation, Indiana University, 1971.
469. ———. "Books for Sale on the Illinois Frontier." *ABC* 21 (1971): 15–17.
470. ———. "Books Stocked by Six Indiana General Stores." *JLH* 9 (1974): 66–72.
471. ———. "Bookstores on the Southern Indiana Frontier, 1833–1850." *ABC* 23 (1973): 30–32.
472. ———. "The General Store as an Outlet for Books on the Southern [Indiana] Frontier, 1800–1850." *JLH* 8 (1973): 124–32.
473. Hart, J. D. *The Popular Book: A History of America's Literary Taste.* New York: Oxford University Press, 1950.
474. Hedrick, U. P. "What Farmers Read in Western New York, 1800–1850." *NYH* 17 (1936): 281–89.

475. Hemphill, W. Edwin, ed. "The Constitution of the Charlottesville Lyceum, 1837–1840." *PACHS* 8 (1946–47): 47–64.
476. Herrick, C. A. "The Early New-Englanders: What Did They Read?" *The Library* 9 (1918): 1–17.
477. Houlette, W. D. "Books of the Virginia Dynasty." *LQ* 24 (1954): 226–39.
478. ———. "Sources of Books for the Old South." *LQ* 28 (1958): 194–201.
479. Howard, L. "Early American Copies of Milton." *HuntLB* 7 (1935): 169–79.
480. Howe, D. W. "Browsing Among Old Books." *IMH* 11 (1915): 187–210.
481. Hubbell, J. B. *Who Are the Major American Writers? A Study of Changing Literary Canon*. Durham: Duke University Press, 1972.
482. Hurley, G. "Reading in the Gold Rush." *BCCQNL* 15 (1950): 85–91.
483. Ingraham, C. A. "Mason Locke Weems: A Great American Author and Distributor of Books." *Americana* 25 (1931): 469–85.
484. Jantz, H. S. "German Thought and Literature in New England, 1620–1820." *JEGP* 41 (1942): 1–45.
485. Johnson, C. *Old Time Schools and School Books*. New York: Macmillan, 1904.
486. Johnson, T. H. "Jonathan Edwards' Background of Reading." *PCSM* 28 (1930–33): 193–222.
487. Jones, H. M. "The Importation of French Books in Philadelphia, 1750–1800." *MP* 32 (1934): 157–77.
488. Joyaux, G. J. "French Fiction in American Magazines, 1800–1848." *ArizQ* 21 (1965): 29–40.
489. Kaser, D. *Messrs. Carey & Lea of Philadelphia: A Study in the History of the Booktrade*. Philadelphia: University of Pennsylvania Press, 1957.
490. Keifer, M. *American Children Through Their Books, 1700–1835*. Philadelphia: University of Pennsylvania Press, 1949.
491. Kesselring, M. L. *Hawthorne's Reading, 1828–1850*. New York: New York Public Library, 1949.
492. Kimball, L. E. "An Account of Hocquet Caritat, 18th Century New York Circulating Librarian, Bookseller, and Publisher . . ." *Colophon* 5 (1934): whole issue.
493. Kittredge, G. L. "A Harvard Salutatory Oration of 1662." *PCSM* 28 (1935): 1–24.
494. Lancaster, E. R. "Books Read in Early Nineteenth Century Virginia, 1806–1822." *VMHB* 42 (1938): 56–59.
495. Landrum, G. W. "Notes on the Reading of the Old South." *AL* 3 (1931): 60–71.
496. Laurus, J. "The Origin and Development of the 1891 International Copyright Law of the United States." Doctoral dissertation, Columbia University, 1960.

497. Leary, W. M. "Books, Soldiers and Censorship During the Second World War." *AQ* 20 (1968): 237–45.
498. Lehmann-Haupt, H. *The Book in America: A History of the Making and Selling of Books in the United States.* 2d ed. New York: Bowker, 1952.
499. Liebman, S. W. "The Origins of Emerson's Early Poetics: His Reading in the Scottish Common Sense Critics." *AL* 45 (1973): 23–33.
500. Lillard, R. D. "A Literate Woman in the Mines: The Diary of Rachel Haskell." *MVHR* 31 (1944): 81–98.
501. Little, E. N. "The Early Reading of Oliver Wendell Holmes." *HLB* 8 (1954): 163–203.
502. Littlefield, G. E. *Early Schools and School-Books of New England.* Boston: The Club of Odd Volumes, 1904.
503. Litto, F. M. "Addison's *Cato* in the Colonies." *WMQ* 23 (1966): 431–49.
504. Lundberg, D., and May, H. F. "The Enlightened Reader in America." *AQ* 28 (1976): 262–[93].
505. Madison, C. A. *Book Publishing in America.* New York: McGraw-Hill, 1966.
506. Manning, J. W. "Literacy on the Oregon Trail: Books Across the Plains." *OHQ* 61 (1940): 189–94.
507. Matthews, A. "Knowledge of Milton in Early New England." *Nation* 87 (1908): 624–25, 650.
508. McCutcheon, R. P. "Books and Booksellers in New Orleans, 1730–1830." *LHQ* 20 (1937): 606–18.
509. McDermott, J. F. "Best Sellers in Early Saint Louis." *S&S* 47 (1938): 673–75.
510. ———. "Books on Natural History in Early Saint Louis." *MBGB* 23 (1935): 55–62.
511. ———. "Culture and the Missouri Frontier." *MHR* 50 (1956): 355–70.
512. ———. "Everybody Sold Books in Early Saint Louis." *PW* 132 (1937): 248–50.
513. ———. "The First Bookstore in Saint Louis." *MA* 21 (1939): 206–08.
514. ———. "Scientific Books in the Early West." *S&S* 40 (1934): 812–13.
515. ———. "Voltaire and the Freethinkers in Early Saint Louis." *RDLC* 16 (1936): 720–31.
516. McKay, G. L. *American Book Auction Catalogues, 1713–1934: A Union List . . .* New York: New York Public Library, 1937.
517. McMullen, H. "Ralph Waldo Emerson and Libraries." *LQ* 25 (1955): 152–62.
518. ———. "The Use of Books in the Ohio Valley Before 1850." *JLH* 1 (1966): 43–56, 73.
519. Miles, E. A. "The Old South and the Classical World." *NCHR* 48 (1971): 258–75.
520. Mills, R. V. "Books in Oregon: The First Decade." *BCCQNL* 15 (1950): 51–57.

521. Minnich, H. C. *William Homes McGuffey and His Readers*. New York, 1936.
522. Minnick, N. F. "A Cultural History of Central City, Colorado, from 1859 to 1880, in Terms of Books and Libraries." Master's thesis, University of Chicago, 1946.
523. Mosier, R. D. *Making the American Mind: Social and Moral Ideas in the McGuffey Readers*. New York, 1947.
524. Mott, F. L. *Golden Multitudes: The Story of Best Sellers in the United States*. New York: Macmillan, 1947.
525. ———. *A History of American Magazines*. 5 vols. Cambridge, Mass.: Harvard University Press, 1938–68.
526. Mullett, C. F. "Classical Influences on the American Revolution." *CJ* 35 (1939): 92–104.
527. ———. "Coke and the American Revolution." *Economica* 12 (1932): 457–71.
528. Napier, J. "Some Book Sales in Dumfries, Virginia, 1794–1796." *WMQ* 10 (1953): 441–45.
529. Nichols, C. H. "Who Read the Slave Narratives?" *Phylon* 20 (1959): 149–62.
530. Nietz, J. *Old Textbooks . . . from Colonial Days to 1900*. Pittsburgh: University of Pittsburgh Press, 1961.
531. Noel, M. *Villains Galore: The Heyday of the Popular Story Weekly*. New York: Macmillan, 1954.
532. Nunis, D. B. *Books in Their Sea Chests: Reading Along the Early California Coast*. N.p.: California Library Association, 1964.
533. Orians, G. H. "Censure of Fiction in American Romances and Magazines, 1789–1810." *PMLA* 52 (1937): 195–224.
534. ———. *The Influence of Walter Scott on America and American Literature Before 1860*. Urbana: University of Illinois, 1929.
535. Parker, W. W. *Henry Stevens of Vermont, American Rare Book Dealer in London, 1845–1886*. Amsterdam: N. Israel, 1963.
536. ———. "Henry Stevens Sweeps the States." *PBSA* 52 (1958): 249–61.
537. ———. "Henry Stevens: The Making of a Bookseller." *PBSA* 48 (1954): 149–69.
538. Parks, E. W. "Jefferson's Attitude Toward History." *GHQ* (1952): 336–52.
539. Patrick, W. R. "Reading Tastes in Louisiana, 1830–60." In *Studies for William A. Read . . .*, ed. by N. M. Coffee and T. A. Kirby, pp. 288–300. Baton Rouge: Louisiana State University Press, 1940.
540. Peckham, H. "Books and Reading on the Ohio Valley Frontier." *MVHR* 44 (1958): 649–63.
541. Peden, W. H. "A Book Peddler [Samuel Whitcomb, Jr.] Invades Monticello [1972]." *WMQ* 6 (1949): 631–36.
542. Pilkington, J. P. *The Methodist Publishing House: A History*. Nashville: Abingdon Press, 1968.

543. Powell, J. H. *The Books of a New Nation: United States Government Publications, 1774–1814.* Philadelphia: University of Pennsylvania Press, 1957.
544. Powell, W. S. "Books in the Virginia Colony Before 1624." *WMQ* 5 (1948): 177–84.
545. Power, F. M. "American Private Book Clubs." Master's thesis, Columbia University, 1946.
546. Purcell, J. A. "A Book Pedlar's Progress in North Carolina." *NCHR* 29 (1952): 8–23.
547. Quenzel, C. H. "Books for the Boys in Blue [Civil War]." *JISHS* 44 (1951): 218–30.
548. Quinn, D. B. "A List of Books Purchased for the Virginia Company." *VMHB* 77 (1969): 347–60.
549. Rayward, W. B. "Manufacture and Copyright: Past History Remaking." *JLH* 3 (1968): 7–31.
550. Reitzel, W. "The Purchasing of English Books in Philadelphia, 1790–1800." *MP* 35 (1937): 159–71.
551. Ribbens, D. N. "The Reading Interests of Thoreau, Hawthorne, and Lanier." Doctoral dissertation, University of Wisconsin, 1969.
552. Richardson, L. N. *A History of Early American Magazines, 1741–1789.* New York: Nelson, 1931.
553. Robathan, D. M. "John Adams and the Classics." *NEQ* 19 (1946): 91–98.
554. Robbins, C. *The Eighteenth Century Commonwealthman: Studies in the Transmission, Development, and Circumstances of English Liberal Thought from the Restoration of Charles II Until the War with the Thirteen Colonies.* Cambridge, Mass.: Harvard University Press, 1959.
555. Roth, M. "Lawrence Sterne in America." *BNYPL* 74 (1970): 428–36.
556. Schick, F. L. *The Paperbound Book in America: The History of Paperbacks and Their European Backgrounds.* New York: R. R. Bowker Co., 1958.
557. Schlesinger, A. M. *Learning How to Behave: A Historical Study of American Etiquette Books.* New York: Macmillan, 1946.
558. Sealts, M. M. *Melville's Reading: A Checklist of Books Owned and Borrowed.* Madison: University of Wisconsin Press, 1966.
559. Sears, D. A. "Libraries and Reading Habits in Early Portland (1763–1836)." *MaineHSNL* 12 (Spring 1973): 151–65.
560. Seigel, J. P. "Puritan Light Reading." *NEQ* 37 (1964): 185–99.
561. Sensabaugh, G. F. *Milton in Early America.* Princeton: Princeton University Press, 1964.
562. Shaffer, E. "The Children's Books of the American Sunday-School Union." *ABC* 17 (1966): 21–28.
563. Shaw, R. R. *Literary Property in the United States.* Washington, D.C.: Scarecrow Press, 1950.

564. Sheehan, D. *This Was Publishing: A Chronicle of the Book Trade in the Gilded Age*. Bloomington: Indiana University Press, 1952.
565. Shipley, J. B. "Franklin Attends a Book Auction." *PMHB* 53 (1956): 37–45.
566. Shoemaker, E. C. *Noah Webster*. New York: Columbia University Press, 1936.
567. Shove, R. H. *Cheap Book Production in the United States, 1870–1891*. Urbana: University of Illinois Library, 1931.
568. Sibley, A. M. *Alexander Pope's Prestige in America, 1725–1835*. New York: Columbia University Press, 1949.
569. Silver, R. G. "The Baltimore Book Trade, 1800–1825." *BNYPL* 57 (1953): 114–25, 182–201, 248–51, 297–305, 349–57.
570. Simon, H. W. *The Reading of Shakespeare in American Schools and Colleges: An Historical Survey*. New York: Simon and Schuster, 1932.
571. Skeel, E. E. F., ed. *Mason Locke Weems: His Work and Ways*. 3 vols. New York: Plimpton Press, 1929.
572. Skelley, G. T. "The Library World and the Book Trade." In *A Century of Service: Librarianship in the United States and Canada*, edited by S. L. Jackson et al., pp. 281–302. Chicago: American Library Association, 1976.
573. Spurlin, P. M. *Montesquieu in America, 1760–1801*. Baton Rouge: Louisiana State University Press, 1940.
574. ———. "Readership in the American Enlightenment." In *Literature and History in the Age of Ideas*, edited by C. G. S. Williams, pp. 359–74. Columbus: Ohio State University Press, 1975.
575. ———. "Rousseau in America, 1760–1809." *FAR* 1 (1948): 8–16.
576. Stafford, M. "Subscription Book Publishing in the United States, 1865–1930." Master's thesis, University of Illinois, 1943.
577. Starke, A. "Books in the Wilderness." *JISHS* 28 (1935): 258–70.
578. Stern, M. B. *Imprints on History: Book Publishers and American Frontiers*. Bloomington: Indiana University Press, 1956.
579. Stiverson, G. A. "Books Both Useful and Entertaining: Reading Habits in Mid-Eighteenth Century Virginia." *SEL* 24 (1975): 52–58.
580. Stobridge, W. "Book Smuggling in Mexican California." *AN* 32 (1972): 117–22.
581. Stovall, F. "Notes on Whitman's Reading." *AL* 26 (1954): 337–62.
582. Sutton, W. *The Western Book Trade: Cincinnati as a Nineteenth-Century Publishing and Book-Trade Center*. Columbus: Ohio State University Press, 1961.
583. Tanselle, T. G. *Guide to the Study of the United States Imprints*. Cambridge, Mass.: Harvard University Press, 1971.
584. ———. "Indianapolis in the World of Books: The Hoosier House." In *Indianapolis and the World of Books*, pp. 30–49. Indianapolis: Indianapolis-Marion County Public Library, 1974.

585. Tapley, H. S. *Salem Imprints, 1768–1825: A History of the First Fifty Years of Printing in Salem, Massachusetts, with Some Account of the Bookshops, Booksellers, Bookbinders, and the Private Libraries*. Salem: Essex Institute, 1927.
586. Tebbel, J. *A History of Book Publishing in the United States*. 2 vols. to date. New York: R. R. Bowker, 1972–.
587. Tope, M. *A Biography of William Holmes McGuffey*. Bowerston, Ohio, 1929.
588. Tourtellot, A. B. "The Early Reading of Benjamin Franklin." *HLB* 23 (1975): 5–41.
589. Tryon, W. S. *Parnassus Corner: A Life of James T. Fields, Publisher to the Victorians*. Boston: Houghton Mifflin, 1963.
590. Van Orman, R. A. "The Bard in the West." *WHQ* 5 (1974): 29–38.
591. Vonnegut, T. F. *Indianapolis Booksellers and Their Literary Background, 1822–1860*. Greenfield, Ind.: Wm. Mitchell Printing Co., 1926.
592. Wade, R. C. *The Urban Frontier: Pioneer Life in Early Pittsburgh, Cincinnati, Lexington, Louisville, and St. Louis*. Chicago: University of Chicago Press, 1964.
593. Walker, D. D. "Reading on the Range: The Literary Habits of the American Cowboys." *ArizW* 11 (1960): 307–18.
594. Waples, D. *People and Print: Social Aspects of Reading in the Depression*. Chicago: University of Chicago Press, 1938.
595. Warfel, H. R. *Noah Webster: Schoolmaster to America*. New York: Macmillan, 1936.
596. Warren, A. "Hawthorne's Reading." *NEQ* 8 (1935): 480–97.
597. Werner, J. M. "David Hume and America." *JHI* 33 (1972): 439–56.
598. Weyant, R. G. "Helvetius and Jefferson: Studies of Human Nature and Government in the Eighteenth Century." *JHBS* 9 (1973): 29–41.
599. Wheeler, J. T. "Booksellers and Circulating Libraries in Colonial Maryland." *MHM* 34 (1939): 111–37.
600. ———. "Literary Culture and Eighteenth Century Maryland: Summary of Findings." *MHM* 38 (1943): 273–76.
601. ———. "Reading Interests of the Professional Classes in Colonial Maryland, 1700–1776." *MHM* 36 (1941): 184–201, 281–301.
602. Willoughby, E. E. "The Reading of Shakespeare in Colonial America." *PBSA* 31 (1937): 45–56.
603. Wilson, J. S. "Best Sellers in Jefferson's Day." *VQR* 36 (1960): 222–37.
604. Winans, R. B. "The Growth of a Novel-Reading Public in Late Eighteenth Century America." *EAL* 9 (1975): 267–75.
605. Winterich, J. T. "What a New Englander Was Likely to Read in 1711." *PW* 159 (1951): 759–61.
606. Winton, C. "The Colonial South Carolina Book Trade." *Proof* 2 (1973): 71–87.

607. Woolf, H. "Science for the People: Copernicanism and Newtonianism in the Almanacs of Early America." In *The Reception of Copernicus' Heliocentric Theory* . . . , edited by J. Dobrzycki, pp. 293–309. Boston: D. Reidel Publishing Co., 1972.
608. Wright, C. C. "Reading Interests in Texas From the 1830's to the Civil War." *SHQ* 54 (1951): 301–15.
609. Wright, L. B. "Classical Tradition in Colonial Virginia." *PBSA* 33 (1939): 85–97.
610. ———. *Culture on the Moving Frontier*. Bloomington: Indiana University Press, 1955.
611. ———. "Pious Reading in Colonial America." *JSH* 6 (1940): 383–93.
612. ———. "The Purposeful Reading of Our Colonial Ancestors." *JELH* 4 (1937): 85–111.
613. Wright, N. "Horatio Greenough's Borrowings from the Harvard College Library." *HLB* 9 (1955): 406–10.
614. Wroth, L. C. *An American Bookshelf, 1755*. Philadelphia: University of Pennsylvania Press, 1934.

IV. Predecessors of the Public Library

This chapter of the bibliography is divided into three main sections: (A) Thomas Bray and American Libraries; (B) Social Libraries; and (C) Circulating, Sunday School, School District, and YMCA Libraries.

A. Thomas Bray and American Libraries

Thomas Bray was an Anglican clergyman who served for a brief span of time as commissary to Maryland. A number of studies treat his efforts to establish libraries in the colonies at the end of the seventeenth century. The most definitive is Charles T. Laugher's *Thomas Bray's Grand Design* (1973, **625**), which is based on the author's dissertation. However, a number of other works treat various aspects of Bray's short-lived efforts to establish libraries in the colonies and they, too, should be examined by the serious student. Among the most important are William D. Houlette's study of the parish libraries (1934, **622**), Herbert Searcy's essay on the parochial libraries (1963, **635**), Steiner's old but still useful essay (1896, **638**), and Joseph Wheeler's studies of Bray's efforts in Maryland (1939, **642**; 1940, **641**).

B. Social Libraries

The definition of the term *social library* has bothered historians for several decades. In the nineteenth century, librarians frequently labeled all libraries open in any substantial way to the public as "public libraries." However, with the rise of the public library, supported with tax funds, open to all on an equal basis, and administered as a public trust, a new label was required for those institutions which were established on the joint-stock formula and which required a more or less substantial fee for use. These libraries, in all their forms, have come to be known as social libraries. As a group they have been the subject of a considerable body of research.

The standard treatment of the rise of social libraries in the United States is Jesse Shera's *Foundations of the Public Library: The Origins of the Public Library Movement in New England, 1629–1855* (1949, **816**). However, since the publication of Shera's work a number of careful studies of social library development in various states or cities have appeared. All these are listed in the bibliography, but a number deserve to be singled out for special

42 Predecessors of the Public Library

mention. Haynes McMullen has probably done more work in this area than anyone else and has authored substantial essays on Pennsylvania (1965, **767**), Kentucky (1960, **769**), and Ohio, Illinois, and Indiana (1958, **768**). Other important work has been done by Jane Flener on developments in Tennessee (1963, **696**), Ray Held on social libraries in California (1963, **724**), John Francis McDermott on Missouri (1944, **766**), Ruth W. Robinson on social libraries in four Pennsylvania communities (1952, **803**), Harry R. Skallerup on libraries and reading among the seamen of early America (1974, **818**), and Frances L. Spain (1944, **822**; 1947, **821**) and Elizabeth Welborn (1956, **841**; 1959, **842**) on South Carolina.

In addition to these more general studies, a multitude of individual social libraries have been afforded historical attention. The most important of these are as follows: America's first and perhaps most important social library—the Library Company of Philadelphia—has been explored in detail by George Abbot (1913, **645**), Austin Gray (1937, **708**), Dorothy F. Grimm (1955, **712**), Margaret Korty (1965, **741**), and Edwin Wolf (1954, **855**; 1955, **854**; 1956, **856**; 1960, **858**). Other famous social libraries have also been the subject of serious research, and they include Russell Bidlack's history of the City Library of Detroit (1955, **658**); Robert Constantine's study of the Vincennes Library Company (1965–1967, **679**); Sarah Cutler (1917, **682**) and J. B. Nicholson (1955, **777**) on the "Coonskin Library"; Charles W. David on the Longwood Library (1957, **684**); Anne Gregorie (1935, **710**) and Edgar Reinke (1967, **799**) on the Charleston Library Society; Philip A. Kalisch on the Omaha Library Association (1971, **730**); Austin B. Keep (1908, **732**) and Marion King (1954, **738**) on the New York Society Library; Harry M. Lydenberg on the Berkshire Republican Library (1940, **752**); Sister M. V. O'Connor (1956, **781**), Arthur S. Roberts (1948, **801**), and Marcus McCorison (1965, **764**) on the Redwood Library Company; and William Van Beynum on the Book Company of Durham (1968, **833**).

Several other special types of social libraries deserve brief mention here. The athenaeum, an aristocratic offshoot of the social library form, is also covered in this section of the bibliography. Several of the more important studies of this type of library are Charles K. Bolton (1909, **662**; 1927, **660**), William I. Fletcher (1914, **698**), Mary Regan (1927, **797**), Ronald Story (1975, **824**), and Walter Whitehill (1973, **843**) on the Boston Athenaeum; Joseph L. Harrison (1911, **719**) and Grace Leonard and Chesley Worthington (1940, **743**) on the Providence Athenaeum; and Cynthia B. Wiggin on the Salem Athenaeum (1966, **846**; 1968, **847**).

One futher type of social library has been given extensive attention, the mechanics and mercantile library. The standard survey of the subject was Sidney Ditzion's (1940, **687**), but W. D. Boyd's dissertation (1975, **665**) must now be considered the definitive treatment. A number of individual libraries have also been studied, including the San Francisco Mercantile Library by Joyce Backus (1931, **652**), the Young Men's Mercantile Library Association of Cincinnati by Merle Carter (1951, **671**), the Mercantile Library Association of Boston by Gordon Gaskill (1949, **701**), and the Apprentices' Library of Philadelphia by John F. Lewis (1924, **744**).

C. Circulating, Sunday School, School District, and YMCA Libraries

A third group of predecessors of the public library remains to be mentioned here. Circulating libraries have been generally overlooked, but several important works do cover the subject. Jesse Shera's *Foundations of the Public Library* (1949, **816**) remains the most significant overview, but a specialized study of circulating libraries in the Southeast by Mary V. Moore (1958, **880**) is also of considerable value.

Sunday School libraries have garnered a good deal of attention, but much remains to be done. Of particular interest are the general studies by F. A. Briggs (1961, **865**), Alice B. Cushman (1957, **867**), Maxine B. Fedder (1951, **871**), M. E. Hand (1950, **874**), Ellen Shaffer (1966, **887**), and Frank K. Walter (1942, **889**).

School district libraries are covered in classic fashion by Sidney Ditzion (1940, **868**), but a number of more specialized studies are Alice C. Dodge (1944, **869**) on school district libraries in New York State, Ray Held on these libraries in California (1959, **875**), and Helen M. Wilcox (1953, **891**) on their early development.

The YMCA libraries have not received detailed attention. However, a number of useful essays on the subject have been prepared and they include those by Doris Fletcher (1957, **872**) and Joe E. Kraus (1975, **878**).

Finally, the statistical studies of library development in eighteenth- and nineteenth-century America discussed in Chapter II of this bibliography should be consulted for information on that aspect of the history of these libraries.

Predecessors of the Public Library

A. Thomas Bray and American Libraries

615. *America's First Public Library: The Provincial Library in Charlestown in Carolina, 1698*. Columbia: South Carolina State Library, 1970.
616. Bray, T. *An Essay Towards Promoting All Necessary and Useful Knowledge, Both Divine and Human*. Boston: G. K. Hall, 1967.
617. Bultmann, W. A., and Bultmann, P. W. "The Roots of American Humanitarianism: A Study of the SPCK and the APG, 1699–1720." *HMPEC* 33 (1964): 3–48.
618. Fletcher, C. "The Reverend Thomas Bray, M. Alexandre Vattemare, and Library Science." *LQ* 27 (1957): 95–99.

619. Foote, H. "Remarks on King's Chapel Library, Boston, Mass." *PMHS* 1st ser., 18 (1881): 423–30.
620. Gordon, N. S. "Thomas Bray: A Study in Early Eighteenth-Century Librarianship." Master's thesis, Catholic University of America, 1961.
621. Hirsch, C. B. "The Experiences of the SPG in Eighteenth-Century North Carolina." Doctoral dissertation, Indiana University, 1953.
622. Houlette, W. D. "Parish Libraries and the Work of the Rev. Thomas Bray." *LQ* 4 (1934): 588–609.
623. ———. "Plantation and Parish Libraries in the Old South." Doctoral dissertation, University of Iowa, 1933.
624. Hurst, J. F. "Parochial Libraries [of Maryland] of the Colonial Period." *PASCH* 2 (1890): 46–49.
625. Laugher, C. T. *Thomas Bray's Grand Design*. Chicago: American Library Association, 1973.
626. Lydekker, J. W. "Thomas Bray (1658–1730): Founder of Missionary Enterprise." *HMPEC* 12 (1943): 186–224.
627. McCulloch, S. C. "Dr. Thomas Bray's Commissary Work in London." *WMQ* 2 (1945): 333–48.
628. ———. "The Importance of Dr. Thomas Bray's Bibliotheca Parochialis." *HMPEC* 15 (1946): 50–59.
629. Merritt, E. P. *The Parochial Library of the Eighteenth Century in Christ Church, Boston*. Boston: Merrymount Press, 1917.
630. Molz, J. B. "The Reverend Thomas Bray, Planner of Libraries: A Study of an Early Benefactor of Maryland Libraries." Master's thesis, Drexel Institute of Technology, 1950.
631. Nelso, J. K. "Anglican Missions in America, 1701–1725: A Study of the Society for the Propagation of the Gospel in Foreign Parts." Doctoral dissertation, Northwestern University, 1962.
632. Pennington, E. L. *The Reverend Thomas Bray*. Philadelphia: Church Historical Society, 1934.
633. ———. "Thomas Bray's Associates and Their Work Among the Negroes." *PAAS* 48 (1939): 311–403.
634. ———. "The Work of the Bray Associates in Pennsylvania." *PMHB* 58 (1934): 1–25.
635. Searcy, H. L. "Parochial Libraries in the American Colonies." Doctoral dissertation, University of Illinois, 1963.
636. Shali, M. S. "Thomas Bray and the Founding of Libraries in Maryland." Master's thesis, Western Reserve University, 1952.
637. Smith, G. "Dr. Thomas Bray." *LAR* 12 (1910): 242–60.
638. Steiner, B. C. "Reverend Thomas Bray and His American Libraries." *AHR* 2 (October 1896): 59–75.
639. ———. *Rev. Thomas Bray: His Life and Selected Works Relating to Maryland*. Baltimore: Maryland Historical Society, 1901.
640. Thompson, H. P. *Into All Lands: The History of the Society for the*

Propagation of the Gospel in Foreign Parts, 1701–1950. London: Society for Promoting Christian Knowledge, 1951.
641. Wheeler, J. T. "The Layman's Libraries and the Provincial Library." *MHM* 35 (1940): 60–73.
642. ———. "Thomas Bray and the Maryland Parochial Libraries." *MHM* 34 (1939): 246–65.
643. Whitehill, W. M. "The King's Chapel Library." *PCSM* 38 (1949): 274–89.
644. Wroth, L. C. "Dr. Bray's 'Proposals for the Encouragement of Religion and Learning in the Foreign Plantations': A Bibliographical Note." *PMHS* 65 (1936): 518–34.

B. Social Libraries

645. Abbot, G. M. *A Short History of the Library Company of Philadelphia; Compiled from the Minutes, Together with Some Personal Reminiscences.* Philadelphia: Published by order of the Board of Directors, 1913.
646. Albrecht, T. "The Music Libraries of the German Singing Societies in Texas, 1850–1855." *MLAN* 31 (1975): 517–29.
647. Anderson, K. E. *Historical Sketch of the Library Association of Portland, 1864–1964.* Portland, Ore., [1964].
648. Anderson, M. T. "History of Colonial American Libraries, 1607–1776." Master's thesis, University of Missouri, 1966.
649. Ashton, J. N. *The Salem Athenaeum, 1810–1910.* Salem, Mass.: Berkeley Press, 1917.
650. *The Athenaeum Centenary: The Influence and History of the Boston Athenaeum.* Boston: The Athenaeum, 1907.
651. Athens Co., Ohio. Pioneer Association. *Memorial and History of the Western Library Association of Ames Township, Athens County, Ohio.* Published by the Pioneer Association of Athens County, Ohio, 1882.
652. Backus, J. "A History of the San Francisco Mercantile Library Association." Master's thesis, University of California, 1931.
653. Baker, H. S. "'Rational Amusement in Our Midst,' Public Libraries in California, 1849–1859." *CHSQ* 38 (1959): 295–320.
654. Bald, F. C. "Beginnings of Libraries in Michigan." *MichL* 20 (1956): 3–5.
655. Ballard, H. H. "The History, Methods, and Purposes of the Berkshire Athenaeum." *BHSSC* 1 (1891): 293–306.
656. Baroco, J. V. "The Library Association of Pensacola, 1885–1933." Master's thesis, Florida State University, 1953.
657. Berkshire Athenaeum and Museum. *1872–1947: 75 Years of Library Service.* Pittsfield, Mass.: 1947.

658. Bidlack, R. E. *The City Library of Detroit, 1817–1837: Michigan's First Public Library.* Ann Arbor: University of Michigan, Department of Library Science. 1955.
659. Blait, M. G. "Some Early Libraries of Oregon." *WHQ* 17 (1926): 259–70.
660. Bolton, C. K. *The Boston Athenaeum, 1807–1927: A Sketch.* Boston: The Athenaeum, 1927.
661. ———. "Proprietary and Subscription Libraries." In *Manual of Library Economy.* Chicago: ALA Publishing Board, 1912.
662. ———. "Social Libraries in Boston." *PCSM* 12 (1909): 332–38.
663. Bowker, R. R. *The Stockbridge Library (1904–1928), Address by R. R. Bowker, President of the (Stockbridge Library) Association at the Annual Meeting, September 29, 1928.* Pittsfield, Mass.: Sun Printing Co., 1928.
664. Bowman, J. N. "Libraries in Provincial California." *HSSCQ* 43 (1961): 426–39.
665. Boyd, W. D. "Books for Young Businessmen: Mercantile Libraries in the United States, 1820–1865." Doctoral dissertation, Indiana University, 1975.
666. Bradsher, E. L. "A Model American Library in 1793 [Thaddeus Harris' Selected Catalogue of Some of the Most Esteemed Publications in the English Language Proper to Form a Social Library 272 Titles]." *SR* 24 (1961): 458–75.
667. Burbank, M. "Story of the Honolulu Library and Reading Room Association." *ARHHS* 36 (1927): 14–27.
668. Burke, B. L. "The Development of Libraries in Guilford, Connecticut." Master's thesis, Southern Connecticut State College, 1959.
669. Cadbury, H. J. "The Passing of Friends' Library." *The Friend* 103 (1930): 459–61.
670. Canavan, M. J. "The Old Boston Public Library, 1656–1747." *PCSM* 12 (1908): 116–33.
671. Carter, M. "The Young Men's Mercantile Library Association of Cincinnati." Master's thesis, Western Reserve University, 1951.
672. Castagnetti, N. R. "The History of Russell Library Company, Middletown, Connecticut." Master's thesis, Southern Connecticut State College, 1966.
673. Chadbourne, E. H. "Early Social Libraries in Maine." *MLB* 31 (1970): 3–12.
674. Chase, V. "Village Library." *DE* 5 (March 1958): 28, 53–56.
675. Cincinnati Young Men's Mercantile Library Association. *History of the Young Men's Mercantile Library Association of Cincinnati, 1835–1935.* Cincinnati: Ebbert and Richards Co., 1935.
676. Clark, T. D. "Building Libraries in the Early Ohio Valley." *JLH* 6 (1971): 101–19.
677. Cole, G. W. *Early Library Development in New York State (1800–1900).* New York: New York Public Library, 1927.

678. Conmy, P. T. *Oakland Library Association, 1868–1878.* Oakland, Calif.: Oakland Public Library, 1968.
679. Constantine, R. "The Vincennes Library Company: A Cultural Institution in Pioneer Indiana." *IMH* 61 (1965): 305–89; 62 (1966): 121–54, 305–44; 63 (1967): 125–54.
680. Crawford, M. C. "The Boston Athenaeum." *NatM* 20 (1904): 272–77.
681. Crook, M. R. "Collections of Books and the Beginnings of Libraries in the Oregon Territory from the Great Migration to the End of the Frontier Period." Master's thesis, University of Washington, 1960.
682. Cutler, S. B. "The Coonskin Library." *POSAHS* 26 (1917): 58–77.
683. Dalphin, M. "Library Beginnings in Westchester County." *WCHSB* 15 (1939): 73–80.
684. David, C. W. "The Longwood Library." *PBSA* 51 (1957): 183–202.
685. Davis, E. G. "John Bradford's Contributions to Printing and Libraries in Lexington, Kentucky, 1787–1800." Master's thesis, University of Kentucky, 1951.
686. Day, N. J. "History and Administration of the Social Library of Bedford, New Hampshire." Master's thesis, University of Michigan, 1943.
687. Ditzion, S. "Mechanics' and Mercantile Libraries." *LQ* 10 (1940): 192–219.
688. Donze, S. L. "A History of the Dr. Sloan Library." Master's thesis, Western Reserve University, 1958.
689. "Early Documents of the Library Company of Philadelphia, 1733–1734." *PMHB* 39 (1915): 450–53.
690. Edmunds, A. J. "The First Books Imported by America's First Great Library [Library Company of Philadelphia]: 1732." *PMHB* 30 (1906): 300–08.
691. Edwards, A. "The Boston Athenaeum." *MM* 9 (1916): 115–26.
692. Ellis, H. "The First Library in Indiana." *PL* 10 (1905): 509–12.
693. Engebretson, B. L. "Books for Pioneers: The Minneapolis Athenaeum." *MinnH* 35 (1956–57): 222–32.
694. Fitch, A. W. "Ashtabula Social Library." *ONGQ* 12 (1909): 146–47.
695. Flanders, F. V. "History of the Ouachita Parish Library [1951–53]." *LLAB* 16 (1953): 137–40.
696. Flener, J. G. "A History of Libraries in Tennessee Before the Civil War." Doctoral dissertation, Indiana University, 1963.
697. Fletcher, W. I. "Proprietary Library in Relation to the Public Library Movement." *LJ* 31 (1906): 268–72.
698. ———. "Some Recollections of the Boston Athenaeum, 1861–1866." *LJ* 39 (1914): 579–83.
699. Fowler, S. P. "The New Mills Social Library." *DanHC* 1 (1913): 95–96.
700. Freeman, J. "Early Libraries in North Carolina." *NCL* 16 (1958): 125–27.

701. Gaskill, G. A. "The Cultural Significance of the Mercantile Library Association of Boston." Master's thesis, Brown University, 1949.
702. Gay, J. *An Historical Address Delivered at the Annual Meeting of the Village Library Company of Farmington, Connecticut.* Hartford: Hartford Press, 1903.
703. Geiger, M. J. "The Story of California's First Libraries." *SCQ* 46 (1964): 109–24.
704. Goodfellow, D. M. "Centenary of a Pittsburgh Library." *WPHM* 31 (1948): 21–25.
705. Goodwin, D. "Some Early Rhode Island Libraries." *MH* 14 (1911): 182–95.
706. Goulder, G. "Some Early Ohio Libraries." *Serif* 3 (March 1966): 3–8.
707. Gower, C. W. "Lectures, Lyceums and Libraries in Early Kansas, 1854–1864." *KHQ* 36 (1970): 175–82.
708. Gray, A. K. *Benjamin Franklin's Library: A Short Account of the Library Company of Philadelphia, 1731–1931.* Foreword by Owen Wister. New York: Macmillan, 1937.
709. Gray, V. G. "The Friends' Free Library, 1848–1948: Some Notes in Retrospect." *The Friend* 122 (1948): 6–9.
710. Gregorie, A. K. "The First Decade of the Charleston Library Society." *PSCHA* (1935): 3–10.
711. Grimm, D. F. "Franklin's Scientific Institution." *PennH* 23 (1956): 437–62.
712. ———. "A History of the Library Company of Philadelphia, 1731–1835." Doctoral dissertation, University of Pennsylvania, 1955.
713. Gross, S. C. "Tumblin' Creek's Cabin Library." *SS* 87 (Suppl. 1965): 17–19.
714. Haddonfield, N.J., Library Company. *Papers Read at the Hundredth Anniversary of the Founding of the Haddonfield Library Company.* Haddonfield, N.J.: The Library, 1903.
715. Hallenbeck, C. T., ed. "A Colonial Reading List: From the Union Library of Hatboro, Pennsylvania (1762–1787)." *PMHB* 56 (1932): 289–340.
716. Harrell, L. "The Development of the Lyceum Movement in Mississippi." *JMH* 31 (1969): 187–201.
717. Harris, D. G. "History of the Friends' Meeting Libraries." *BFHA* 31 (1942): 42–62.
718. Harris, W. S. "What Our Grandparents Read—A Sketch of the Windham Social Library." *GranM* 38 (March 1906): 85–89.
719. Harrison, J. L. *The Providence Athenaeum, 1753–1911.* [Providence], 1911.
720. Hatch, O. W. *Lyceum to Library: A Chapter in the Cultural History of Houston.* Houston: Texas Gulf Coast Historical Association, 1965.
721. Haverstick, D. C. "History of the Mechanics' Library." *PLHS* 9 (1905): 334–51.

722. Held, R. "Libraries in California Before the Deluge." CalL 28 (1967): 83–93.
723. ———. "The Odd Fellows' Library Associations of California." LQ 32 (1962): 148–63.
724. ———. *Public Libraries in California, 1849–1878*. Berkeley: University of California Press, 1963.
725. Hooker, M. W. "Book Lovers of 1738–One of the First Libraries in America." JAH 1 (1907): 177–85.
726. Ingram, E. F. *The Lucius Beebe Memorial Library: An Historical Sketch*. Wakefield, Mass.: Item Press, 1925.
727. Jackson, S. "Seldom, Snug, and Gave No Scandal; or, the Junto and After." SHBN 24 (1970): 133–36; 25 (1970): 1–3.
728. Johnston, W. D. "Early History of the Washington Library Company and Other Local Libraries." RCHS 7 (1904): 20–38.
729. Jones, L. R. "The Howard Library Association." WMH 23 (1939–40): 304–08.
730. Kalisch, P. A. "High Culture on the Frontier: The Omaha Library Association." NH 52 (1971): 411–17.
731. Kaser, D. "Tom Brown's Library at Rugby." In *Library History Seminar Number 3*, edited by M. J. Zachert, pp. 124–36. Tallahassee: JLH, 1968.
732. Keep, A. B. *History of the New York Society Library, with an Introductory Chapter on Libraries in Colonial New York*. New York: Devinne Press, 1908.
733. Kellogg, A. W. "The Boston Athenaeum." NEM 25 (1903): 167–85.
734. Kelly, E. D. "Berkshire Athenaeum." BA 1 (1971): 15–20.
735. Kelso, J. G. "The Lyceum and the Mechanics' Institutes: Pre-Civil War Ventures in Adult Education." Doctoral dissertation, Harvard University, 1953.
736. Kennedy, A. M. "The Athenaeum: Some Account of Its History from 1814–1850." TAPS 43 (1953): 260–65.
737. Kieffer, E. C. "Libraries in Lancaster." PLSH 48 (1944): 71–80.
738. King, M. *Books and People: Five Decades of New York's Oldest Library*. New York: Macmillan, 1954.
739. Kirkpatrick, L. H. "Gathering Books for the Saints: A History of Libraries in Territorial Utah." MLAB 42 (1954): 1–2.
740. Kitchell, J. "The Old Vincennes Library." IMH 28 (1932): 240–46.
741. Korty, M. B. "Benjamin Franklin and Eighteenth Century American Libraries." TAPS 55 (1965): 1–83.
742. Larned, J. N. "An Historical Sketch of the Buffalo Library, Prior to the Free Library Movement." PBHS 3 (1902): 361–84.
743. Leonard, G. and Worthington, C. *The Providence Athenaeum: A History, 1753–1939*. Providence: The Athenaeum, 1940.
744. Lewis, J. F. *History of the Apprentices' Library of Philadelphia 1820–1920, the Oldest Free Circulating Library in America*. Philadelphia, 1924.

745. "The Library Association of Portland (Oregon, 1864–1950)." *PNLAQ* 14 (July 1950): 126–28.
746. "The Library Company of Baltimore [1795–]." *MHM* 12 (1917): 297–310.
747. Livingood, J. W. "A History of Libraries in Pennsylvania Before 1832." *PLN* 13 (1932): 152–55.
748. Lonn, E. "The History of an Unusual Library." *IMH* 19 (1923): 209–25.
749. Lovett, R. W. "From Social Library to Public Library: A Century of Library Development in Beverly, Massachusetts [1802–1902]." *HCEI* 88 (1952): 219–53.
750. Low, J. F. "A History of the Cuyahoga Falls Library Association and the Taylor Memorial Association." Master's thesis, Western Reserve University, 1955.
751. Lowrey, S. G. R. "A History of Libraries in Madison [East Guilford], Connecticut." Master's thesis, Southern Connecticut State College, 1963.
752. Lydenberg, H. M. "The Berkshire Republican Library at Stockbridge, 1794–1818." *PAAS* 50 (1940): 4–38.
753. Maestri, H. L. "A History of the New Orleans Commercial Library Society, 1831–1842." Master's thesis, Tulane University, 1943.
754. ———. "New Orleans Public Library in the Nineteenth Century." *LLAB* 15 (1952): 35–43.
755. Manning, J. W. "Books in Early Oregon: 1821–1888." Master's thesis, University of Oregon, 1940.
756. Markwell, D. "Liberty and Intelligence Hand in Hand." *Settler* 1 (1952): 4–9.
757. Marta, O. V. "The Truth About Cincinnati's First Library." *OAHQ* 53 (1944): 193–208.
758. Martin, D. V. "A History of the Library Movement in Ohio to 1850 with a Special Study of Cincinnati's Library Development." Master's thesis, Ohio State University, 1935.
759. Mason, A. P. "The Fitchburg Athenaeum (1852–1859)." *FitchHSP* 1 (1892–94): 202–19.
760. Mason, G. C. *Annals of the Redwood Library and Athenaeum.* Newport, R.I.: Redwood Library, 1891.
761. Mayer, V. J. "The Coonskin Library." *WLB* 26 (1952): 43–49.
762. McCauley, E. B. "The Manufacturers' and Village Library in Somersworth, New Hampshire." *HNH* 27 (1972): 89–107.
763. ———. "The New England Mill Girls: Feminine Influence in the Development of Public Libraries in New England." Doctoral dissertation, Columbia University, 1971.
764. McCorison, M. A., ed. *The 1764 Catalogue of the Redwood Library Company at Newport, Rhode Island.* New Haven, Conn.: Yale University Press, 1965.

765. McCutcheon, R. P. "Libraries in New Orleans, 1771–1833." *LHQ* 20 (1937): 152–58.
766. McDermott, J. F. "Public Libraries in St. Louis, 1811–39." *LQ* 14 (1944): 9–27.
767. McMullen, H. "The Founding of Social Libraries in Pennsylvania, 1731–1876." *PennH* 32 (1965): 130–52.
768. ———. *The Founding of Social and Public Libraries in Ohio, Indiana, and Illinois Through 1850*. Urbana: University of Illinois Graduate School of Library Science, Occasional Paper no. 51, 1958.
769. ———. "Social Libraries in Antebellum Kentucky." *RKSHS* 58 (1960): 97–128.
770. Mead, C. D. *Yankee Eloquence in the Middle West: The Ohio Lyceum. 1850–1870*. East Lansing: Michigan State College Press, 1951.
771. Mershon, G. L. "The Kingston, New Jersey, Library of 1812." *PNJHS* 65 (1947): 100–03.
772. Miller, C. E. "St. Louis Mercantile Library: An Old Library and Its Civic Background." *MLAQ* 8 (1947): 23–31.
773. Mills, R. V. "Books in Oregon: The First Decade." *BCCQNL* 15 (1950): 51–57.
774. Morrison, T. *Chautauqua: A Center for Education, Religion and the Arts in America*. Chicago: University of Chicago Press, 1974.
775. Mumford, R. L., and Mumford, R. F. "The New Castle Library Company: The Founding and Early History of a Subscription Library, 1811 to 1850." *DH* 11 (1965): 282–300.
776. Neyman, M. "By the Light of Pine Knots . . . The First Library in Ohio." *OLAB* 46 (1976): 4–7.
777. Nicholson, J. B. *"Coonskin Library": A Legend of Books in the Wilderness*. Aspects of Librarianship, no. 9. Kent, Ohio: Kent State University Library Science Department, 1955.
778. "North Carolina Library Rules: 1817." *NCL* 17 (1959): 118.
779. Norton, W. T. "Early Libraries in Illinois." *JISHS* 6 (1913): 246–51.
780. Nunmeker, F. G. "The Unique Ohioana Library." *WWO* 31 (January 1967): 13–15.
781. O'Conner, Sister M. V. "History of the Redwood Library and Athenaeum of Newport, Rhode Island." Master's thesis, Catholic University of America, 1956.
782. Oldham, E. M. "A Much-Traveled Book Returns to Boston." *BPLQ* 11 (1959): 149–50.
783. "Original Rules and Members of the Charleston Library Society [1750]." *SCHM* 23 (1922): 163–70.
784. Packard, F. R. *Charter Members of the Library Company . . .* Philadelphia: The Library Company of Philadelphia, 1942.
785. Palmer, H. R. "The Libraries of Rhode Island." *NEM* 22 (1900): 478–500.

786. Palmer-Poroner, B. J. "The Library Movement in Reading, 1820–1860." *HRBC* 7 (1942): 70–74.
787. Paltsits, V. H. "Petitioners for Founding the Albany Library in 1792." *BNYPL* 30 (1926): 649–50.
788. Parker, W. W. "The Jarvis Library." *Serif* 1 (July 1964): 5–18.
789. Pennington, E. L. "The Beginnings of the Library in Charles Town, South Carolina." *PAAS* 44 (1934): 159–87.
790. Perkins, F. B. "Young Men's Mercantile Libraries." In U.S. Bureau of Education, *Public Libraries in the United States of America . . .* , pp. 378–85. Washington, D.C.: Government Printing Office, 1876.
791. Peterson, C. E. "The Library Hall: Home of the Library Company of Philadelphia, 1790–1880." *PAPS* 95 (1951): 266–85.
792. Philadelphia Library Company. *A Catalogue of Books Belonging to the Library Company of Philadelphia: A Facsimile of the Edition of 1741 Printed by Benjamin Franklin, with an Introduction by Edwin Wolf,* 2nd. Philadelphia: Library Company of Philadelphia, 1956.
793. Philadelphia. Mercantile Library Company. *Essay on the History and Growth of the Mercantile Company of Philadelphia and Its Capabilities for Future Usefulness.* Philadelphia: Jas. B. Rogers, 1867.
794. "Proposals for a Public Library at Albany in 1758." *BNYPL* 12 (1908): 575–76.
795. Pugh, J. F. "The History of the Library of North Carolina." *UNCM* 31 (1931): 207–13.
796. Quincy, J. *History of the Boston Athenaeum, with Biographical Notices of Its Deceased Founders.* Cambridge, Mass.: Metcalf & Co., 1851.
797. Regan, M. J. *Echoes from the Past: Reminiscences of the Boston Athenaeum.* Boston: The Athenaeum, 1927.
798. Reilly, P. G. "Some Nineteenth-Century Predecessors of the Free Library of Philadelphia." Master's thesis, Drexel Institute of Technology, 1951.
799. Reinke, E. C. "A Classical Debate of the Charleston, South Carolina, Library Society." *PBSA* 61 (1967): 83–99.
800. Ridpath, J. W. *History of Abington Library Society of Jenkintown, Pennsylvania, Prepared and Read by J. W. Ridpath at the One Hundredth Anniversary June 12, 1903.* Jenkintown: Times-Chronicle Print, 1903.
801. Roberts, A. S. *The Redwood Library and Athenaeum, Newport, Rhode Island (1747–1948).* Providence, 1948.
802. Robinson, O. "A Frontier Library–1806." *Americana* 32 (1935): 461–69.
803. Robinson, R. W. "Four Community Subscription Libraries in Colonial Pennsylvania: Darby, Hatboro, Lancaster, and Newtown, 1743–1790." Doctoral dissertation, University of Pennsylvania, 1952.

Predecessors of the Public Library 53

804. Rogers, T. W. "Libraries in the Ante-Bellum South." *AlaHQ* 30 (1968): 15–26.
805. Romberg, A. "A Texas Literary Society of Pioneer Days." *SHQ* 52 (1948): 60–65.
806. Ross, R. R. *Union Library Company of Hatborough: An Account of the First Two Hundred Years Done Out of the Original Records.* Hatboro, Pa.: Union Library Company, 1955.
807. Rowell, J. C. "The First Public Library in California: Monterey Library Association, 1850." *NNCL* 13 (1918): 39–40.
808. Rugheimer, V. C. "Charleston Library Society." *SEL* 5 (1955): 137–40, 154.
809. ———, and Cardwell, G. A. "The Charleston Library Society: Source Materials for the Study of Southern Literary Culture, III." *SAB* 8 (1942): 4–5.
810. Sabine, J. E. "Antecedents of the Newark Public Library." Doctoral dissertation, University of Chicago, 1946.
811. ———. "Books and Libraries in Newark (from 1765) to 1847." *PNJHS* 71 (1953): 254–78.
812. Sanborn, F. B. "Two New Hampshire Libraries in Hampton Falls, 1785." *PMHS* 43 (1910): 33–45.
813. Sears, D. A. "Libraries and Reading Habits in Early Portland (1763–1836)." *MaineHSNL* 12 (1973): 151–65.
814. Serrill, K. W. "A Sketch of the Darby Library Company." *PLN* 6 (1913): 63–65.
815. Shaw, S. S. *The Boston Library Society: Historical Sketch.* Boston: G. H. Ellis, 1895.
816. Shera, J. H. *Foundations of the Public Library: The Origins of the Public Library Movement in New England, 1629–1855.* Chicago: University of Chicago Press, 1949.
817. Sherman, S. C. "The Library Company of Baltimore, 1795–1854." *MHM* 39 (March 1944): 6–24.
818. Skallerup, H. R. *Books Afloat and Ashore: A History of Books, Libraries, and Reading Among Seamen During the Age of Sail.* Hamden, Conn.: Archon Books, 1974.
819. Smith, C. W. "Early Library Development in Washington." *WHQ* 17 (1926): 246–58.
820. Spain, F. L. "Early Libraries in Pendleton." *SCHM* 59 (1949): 115–26.
821. ———. "Libraries of South Carolina: Their Origins and Early History, 1700–1830." *LQ* 17 (1947): 28–42.
822. ———. "Libraries of South Carolina: Their Origins and Early History, 1700–1830." Doctoral dissertation, University of Chicago, 1944.
823. Stiffler, S. A. "The Antecedents of the Public Library in the Western Reserve, 1800–1860." Master's thesis, Western Reserve University, 1957.

824. Story, R. "Class and Culture in Boston: The Athenaeum, 1807–1860." *AQ* 27 (1975): 178–99.
825. Swan, M. M. *The Athenaeum Gallery, 1827–1873: The Boston Athenaeum as an Early Patron of Art* . . . [Boston]: Boston Athenaeum, 1940.
826. Teeter, L. W. "A Brief History of the Growth and Development of the Youngstown Library Association, Youngstown, Ohio." Master's thesis, Kent State University, 1956.
827. Thomas, E. F. "The Origin and Development of the Society of the Four Arts Library, Palm Beach, Florida." Master's thesis, Florida State University, 1958.
828. Thompson, C. S. "The Darby Library in 1743." *LC* 11 (1943): 15–22.
829. Tolzmann, D. H. "The St. Louis Free Congregation Library: A Study of German-American Reading Interests." *MHR* 70 (1976): 142–61.
830. Topley, H. S. "Libraries." In her *Salem Imprints, 1768–1825*. Salem, Mass.: Essex Institute, 1927.
831. Travous, R. L. "Pioneer Illinois Library." *JISHS* 42 (1949): 446–53.
832. Turrell, G. H. "The Evolution of a Library." *LIF* 15 (1952): 23–25, 33, 38, 47, 54–57.
833. Van Beynum, W. J. "The Book Company of Durham." In *Library History Seminar Number 3*, edited by M. J. Zachert, pp. 73–97. Tallahassee: *JLH*, 1968.
834. ———. "United to Buy Books, a History of the Book-Company of Durham: A Public Library, 1733–1865." Master's thesis, Southern Connecticut State College, 1961.
835. Wallace, D. H. "Reconstruction of Four Philadelphia Eighteenth Century Libraries." *JLH* 1 (1966): 63–65.
836. Ward, T. "The German-Town Road and Its Associations; Part Sixth." *PMHB* 6 (1882): 129–55.
837. Warfel, H. R. "The Phoenix Library." *WPHM* 11 (1928): 69–75.
838. Webber, M. L. "The Georgetown Library Society." *SCHM* 25 (1924): 94–100.
839. Wecter, D. "Instruments of Culture on the Frontier." *YR* 36 (1947): 242–56.
840. Weeks, S. B. "First Libraries in North Carolina." *TA* 5 (October 1891): 10–20.
841. Welborn, E. C. "The Development of Libraries in South Carolina, 1830–1860." Master's thesis, George Peabody College, 1956.
842. ———. "Libraries of South Carolina, 1830–1860." *SEL* 9 (1959): 171–76.
843. Whitehill, W. M. *A Boston Athenaeum Anthology: 1807–1972. Selected from His Annual Reports*. Boston: Boston Athenaeum, 1973.
844. ———. "Portrait Busts in the Library of the Boston Athenaeum." *Antiques* 105 (1973): 1141–56.

845. Wiggin, C. B. "History of the Salem Book Club." *HCEI* 105 (1969): 137–41.
846. ———. "The Kirwan Collection at the Salem Athenaeum with a Biographical Sketch of Richard Kirwan and the History of Acquisition of the Collection." *HCEI* 102 (1966): 26–36.
847. ———. "Salem Athenaeum." *JLH* 3 (1968): 257–60.
848. Wigglesworth, E. "Sketch of the Boston Athenaeum." *AQR* 12 (1839): 149–53.
849. Williams, D. A. "The New Harmony Working Man's Institute." *LQ* 2 (1950): 109–18.
850. Williams, S. R. "The Libraries of Paddy's Run." *POSAHS* 21 (1912): 462–65.
851. Wilson, L. R. "Library Development in North Carolina." *LJ* 48 (1923): 21–26.
852. Winslow, E. "The Boston Athenaeum." *Bostonian* 3 (1895): 227–36.
853. Wolcott, M. D. "The History and Development of the Sandusky Library Association, Sandusky, Ohio." Master's thesis, Kent State University, 1953.
854. Wolf, E., 2d. "The Early Buying Policy of the Library Company of Philadelphia [1735–70]." *WLB* 30 (1955): 316–18.
855. ———. "The First Books and Printed Catalogues of the Library Company of Philadelphia." *PMHB* 78 (1954): 45–70.
856. ———. "Franklin and His Friends Choose Their Books." *PMHB* 80 (1956): 1–36.
857. ———. "Library Company of Philadelphia." *ELIS* 15:1–19.
858. ———. "Some Books of Early English Provenance in the Library Company of Philadelphia." *BC* 9 (1960): 275–84.
859. Woodberry, G. E. "The Salem Athenaeum." In his *The Torch and Other Lectures and Addresses*, pp. 351–57. New York: Harcourt, Brace, and Howe, 1920.
860. Wroth, L. C., and Lewis, W. S. *Redwood Library and Athenaeum: Addresses Commemorating Its 200th Anniversary, 1747–1947.* Newport: Redwood Library, 1947.
861. Wyatt, E. A. "Schools and Libraries in Petersburg, Virginia, Prior to 1861." *TQHGM* 19 (1937): 65–86.

C. Circulating, Sunday School, School District, and YMCA Libraries

862. Adams, L. G. "Sunday School Libraries." *AJ* 6 (1951): 24–26.
863. Bolton, C. K. "Circulating Libraries in Boston, 1765–1865." *PCSM* 11 (1907): 196–208.
864. Brainerd, C. "The Libraries of Young Men's Christian Associations." In U.S. Bureau of Education, *Public Libraries in the United States*

of America . . . , pp. 386–88. Washington, D.C.: Government Printing Office, 1876.
865. Briggs, F. A. "Sunday School Libraries in the 19th Century." *LQ* 31 (1961): 166–77.
866. Cushing, J. D. "The Lancaster Circulating Library." *BNYPL* 64 (1960): 432–36.
867. Cushman, A. B. "A Nineteenth Century Plan for Reading: The American Sunday School Movement." *HB* 33 (1957): 61–71; 159–66.
868. Ditzion, S. "The District School Library, 1835–55." *LQ* 10 (1940): 545–77.
869. Dodge, A. C. "Origins of the School District Library Movement in New York State." Master's thesis, University of Chicago, 1944.
870. Dunning, A. E. *The Sunday School Library.* Boston: Congregational Sunday School & Publishing Society, 1883.
871. Fedder, M. B. "The Origin and Development of the Sunday School Library in America." Master's thesis, University of Chicago, 1951.
872. Fletcher, D. M. "Read a Book and Sin No More: The Early YMCA Libraries." *WLB* 31 (1957): 521–22, 528.
873. Halsell, W. D. "Sunday School Libraries." *MLNews* 37 (1973): 151–53.
874. Hand, M. E. "American Sunday School Library." Master's thesis, Carnegie Institute of Technology, 1950.
875. Held, R. "The Early School-District Library in California." *LQ* 29 (1959): 79–93.
876. Keep, A. B. "Booksellers and Circulating Libraries, 1763–1776." In his *History of the New York Society Library*, pp. 101–11. New York: De Vinne Press, 1908.
877. Kennedy, I. W. "The History of the Pennsylvania Home Teaching Society and Free Circulating Library for the Blind." *OFB* 22 (1923): 29–31.
878. Kraus, J. E. "Libraries of the Young Men's Christian Association in the Nineteenth Century." *JLH* 10 (1975): 3–21.
879. McDonald, M. F. "An Analysis of the American Sunday School Union Publications in the Old Juvenile Collection in the Brooklyn Public Library." Master's thesis, University of North Carolina, 1963.
880. Moore, M. V. "Circulating Libraries in the Southeastern United States, 1762–1842: A Selected Study." Master's thesis, University of North Carolina, 1958. Published: University of Kentucky Press, Microcard Publications, Series B, Number 22.
881. O'Rourke, Sister M. M. "History of the Cathedral Free Circulating Library of New York City (1887–1905)." *CLitW* 25 (1954): 115–19.
882. Patrick, W. R. "A Circulating Library of Antebellum Louisiana." *LHQ* 23 (1940): 131–40.

883. Raddin, G. G. *An Early New York Library of Fiction: With a Checklist of the Fiction in H. Caritat's Circulating Library, no. 1 City Hotel, Broadway, New York, 1804.* New York: H. W. Wilson, 1940.
884. ———. *Hocquet Caritat and the Early New York Literary Scene.* Dover, N.J.: Dover Advance Press, 1953.
885. Richie, J. F. "Railroad Reading Rooms and Libraries in Ohio, 1865–1900." Master's thesis, Kent State University, 1965. Published: ACRL Microcard No. 149.
886. Rush, O. W. "Maine's First Circulating Library." *MLB* 3 (1942): 13–14.
887. Shaffer, E. "The Children's Books of the American Sunday-School Union." *ABC* 17 (1966): 21–28.
888. Shera, J. H. *Foundations of the Public Library: Origins of the Public Library Movement in New England, 1629–1855.* Chicago: University of Chicago Press, 1949.
889. Walter, F. K. "A Poor but Respectable Relation–The Sunday School Library." *LQ* 12 (1942): 731–39.
890. Wheeler, J. T. "Book Sellers and Circulating Libraries in Colonial Maryland." *MHM* 34 (1939): 111–37.
891. Wilcox, H. M. "School District Public Libraries–A Step in Popular Education in the Nineteenth Century with Emphasis on the Period from 1820–1850." Master's thesis, Drexel Institute of Technology, 1953.

V. Public Libraries

American public libraries have drawn more attention from historians than any other aspect of American library history. Jesse Shera, in his essay "Literature of American Library History" (1973, **72**), treats the development of this literature from its antiquarian beginnings to the present, and Sidney Ditzion discusses the philisophical and methodological problems in his paper, "The Research and Writing of American Library History" (1973, **22**). Michael H. Harris, in his *Guide to Research in American Library History* (1974, **38**), presents an annotated list of the master's theses and doctoral dissertations treating the subject. All the above are cited in full in Chapter I of this bibliography.

Early studies of public library history tended to be antiquarian in nature and more interested in description and applause than critical analysis. However, in the 1930's scholars began to call for the application of the critical canons of historical research to public library history. Particularly influential as a stimulus to this new perspective was Arnold Borden's short essay entitled the "Sociological Beginnings of the Library Movement" (1931, **907**). Influenced by Borden's persuasive insistence that libraries must be studied in the context of their coeval culture, a number of classic and still influential studies of public library history were completed by doctoral students at Chicago and Columbia. Most notable of these were Jesse Shera's *Foundations of the Public Library* (1949, **1015**), Sidney Ditzion's *Arsenals of a Democratic Culture* (1947, **924**), and Gwladys Spencer's *The Chicago Public Library* (1943, **1161**).

These works represent such remarkable *tours de force* that they in many ways preempted further substantive work on the subject for nearly twenty years. However, in the late fifties and the sixties a number of new studies, focusing on special aspects of public library history, appeared and provided a basis for a reconsideration of the findings of the earlier work. These new studies approached the subject of public library history from a variety of specialized angles, and taken together they represent a very significant portion of the historiography of the field. For instance, the influence of Andrew Carnegie on the development of the American public library was explored in two excellent monographs, albeit arriving at different conclusions, by George Bobinski (1969, **905**) and David McLeod (1968, **1552**). Similarly, Robert Lee presented a new interpretation of public library service in his *Continuing Education for Adults Through the American Public Library,*

1833-1964 (1966, **982**), which, read with Margaret Monroe's pioneering study of this subject (1963, **993**), revises earlier work in this area.

Other scholars began to investigate public library development in individual states. The most impressive of these studies is Ray Held's history of the public library movement in California, two volumes of which have appeared thus far (1963, **1067**; 1973, **1068**). Another important state has been covered in John Colson's study, "The Public Library Movement in Wisconsin, 1836–1900" (1973, **1547**). Scholars have also focused on the services of librarians to different elements in the community or the relationship of public libraries to other types of libraries. Examples of quality work in this area include Budd Gambee's study of the productive tension which existed between the school and the public library (1973, **942**); Harriet Long's *Public Library Service to Children* (1969, **987**); Elfrieda B. McCauley's study, "Feminine Influence in the Development of Public Libraries in New England" (1971, **763**); Esther Carrier's *Fiction in Public Libraries* (1965, **913**); and recent essays by Haynes McMullen (1976, **990**) and A. P. Marshall (1976, **989**) on public library service to minorities.

A further avenue of approach has been to write the history of individual libraries. Most of the research listed in the bibliography that follows is in this category, but a number of influential studies deserve special mention: Phyllis Dain, *The New York Public Library: A History of Its Founding and Early Years* (1972, **1331**); Clarence Cramer, *Open Shelves and Open Minds: A History of the Cleveland Public Library* (1972, **1408**); Phillip Kalisch, *The Enoch Pratt Free Library: A Social History* (1969, **1204**); Frank Woodford, *Parnassus on Main Street: A History of the Detroit Public Library* (1965, **1282**); and Walter Whitehill, *Boston Public Library: A Centennial History* (1956, **1261**). Students of public library history will want to read these and similar studies in conjunction with the biographies of prominent public librarians, all of which are listed in Chapter XIII of this bibliography. Studies of particular importance are Edward Holley's biography of Charles Evans (1963, **2973**), Joseph Borome's study of Justin Winsor (1950, **3242**), and William Williamson's biography of William Frederick Poole (1963, **3130**).

The provision of a substantial new foundation upon which an interpretation of American public library history could be built, and the emergence of a highly influential revisionist perspective in the writing of American social history generally, stimulated the rise of a revisionist approach to American library history. A number of such studies have appeared recently, but the most important seem to be Dee Garrison, "The Tender Technicians: The Feminization of Public Librarianship" (1973, **948**), and her "Cultural Missionaries: A Study of American Public Library Leaders, 1876–1910" (1973, **945**); Michael H. Harris, "The Purpose of the American Public Library: A Revisionist Interpretation of History" (1973, **956**), and his *The Role of the Public Library in American Life: A Speculative Essay* (1975, **957**); and Michael H. Harris and Gerard Spiegler, "Everett, Ticknor and the

Common Man: The Fear of Societal Instability as the Motivation for the Founding of the Boston Public Library" (1974, **1232**).

This revisionist literature, especially Harris' paper (1973, **956**), provoked a considerable debate, and a number of important critiques of the revisionist studies appeared. The most persuasive of these critiques are Richard Harwell and Roger Michener, "As Public as the Town Pump" (1974, **959**); Evelyn Geller, "Intellectual Freedom: Eternal Principle or Unanticipated Consequence" (1974, **136**); Phyllis Dain, "Ambivalence and Paradox: The Social Bonds of the Public Library" (1975, **919**); and Elaine Fain, "Manners and Morals in the Public Library: A Glance at Some New History" (1975, **28**). Garrison and Harris were invited to respond to Fain's essay, and their papers are printed with hers in the same issue of *Journal of Library History*. This debate continues, and most recent research supports one school or the other.

In conclusion, it is necessary to note the useful but generally brief surveys of public library development in America to be found in Elmer Johnson and Michael H. Harris, *History of Libraries in the Western World* (1976, **156**); Sidney Jackson, *Libraries and Librarianship in the West: A Brief History* (1974, **150**); and Albert Predeek's *A History of Libraries in Great Britain and North America* (1947, **194**). These three items are cited in full in Chapter II of the bibliography.

Public Libraries

A. General Studies

892. Adams, H. B. *Public Libraries and Popular Education*. Albany: University of the State of New York, 1900.

893. Anders, M. E. "The Development of the Public Library Services in the Southeastern States, 1895–1950." Doctoral dissertation, Columbia University, 1958.

894. Anderson, F., comp. *Carnegie Corporation Library Program, 1911–1961*. New York: Carnegie Corp., 1963.

895. "Andrew Carnegie, the Patron Saint of Libraries." *KLAB* 27 (1963): 8–19.

896. Atkins, E. "The Government and Administration of Public Library Service to Negroes in the South." Doctoral dissertation, University of Chicago, 1940.

897. Barker, T. D. *Libraries of the South: A Report on Developments, 1930–1935*. Chicago: American Library Association, 1936.

898. Batchelder, M. L. "Public Library Influence on School Libraries." *LibT* 1 (1953): 271–85.

899. Beddie, J. S. "Libraries in the Twentieth Century." Doctoral dissertation, Harvard University, 1928.

900. Bell, B. L. "Integration in Public Library Service in Thirteen Southern States, 1954–1962." Master's thesis, Atlanta University, 1963.
901. ———. "Public Library Integration in Thirteen Southern States, 1954–1962." *LJ* 88 (1963): 4713–15.
902. Berelson, B., with Ashiem, L. *The Library's Public: A Report of the Public Library Inquiry*. New York: Columbia University Press, 1949.
903. Betancourt, J. A. "Library Service to Puerto Ricans: An Overview." In *Puerto Rican Perspectives*, edited by E. Mapp, pp. 97–103. Metuchen, N.J.: Scarecrow Press, 1974.
904. Bloom, H. "Adult Services: 'The Book That Leads You On.'" *LibT* 25 (1976): 379–98.
905. Bobinski, G. S. *Carnegie Libraries: Their History and Impact on American Public Library Development*. Chicago: American Lirary Association, 1969.
906. Bolton, S. K. "Andrew Carnegie and His Libraries." In her *Famous Givers and Their Gifts*. New York: Crowell, 1896.
907. Borden, A. K. "Sociological Beginnings of the Library Movement." *LQ* 1 (1931): 278–82.
908. Borthwick, H. H. "Trends in Post-War Public Library Architecture." Master's thesis, Carnegie Institute of Technology, 1952.
909. Bostwick, A. E. *The American Public Library*. 4th ed. New York: Appleton, 1929.
910. Brown, E. F. *Bookmobiles and Bookmobile Service*. Metuchen, N.J.: Scarecrow Press, 1967.
911. Byrnes, H. W. "The Library Movement in the United States: Social and Economic Trends Indicating the Purpose and Growth of the Library in a Democracy." *FL* 1 (1935): 48–68.
912. Campbell, H. C. *Public Libraries in the Urban Metropolitan Setting*. London: Bingley, 1973.
913. Carrier, E. J. *Fiction in Public Libraries, 1876–1900*. New York: Scarecrow Press, 1965.
914. Chancellor, J. *The Library in the TVA Adult Education Program*. Chicago: American Library Association, 1937.
915. Collier, F. G. "A History of the American Public Library Movement Through 1880." Doctoral dissertation, Harvard University, 1953.
916. Conant, R. W., ed. *The Public Library and the City*. Cambridge, Mass.: M.I.T. Press, 1965.
917. ———, and Molz, K., eds. *The Metropolitan Library*. Cambridge, Mass.: M.I.T. Press, 1972.
918. Conner, M. *Outline of the History of the Development of the American Public Library*. Chicago: American Library Association, 1931.
919. Dain, P. "Ambivalence and Paradox: The Social Bonds of the Public Library." *LJ* 100 (1975): 261–66.
920. Daniel, H. *Public Libraries for Everyone: The Growth and Devel-*

opment of Library Services in the United States, Especially Since the Passage of the Library Services Act. Garden City, N.Y.: Doubleday, 1961.
921. Davies, D. W. *Public Libraries as Culture and Social Centers: The Origin of the Concept*. Metuchen, N.J.: Scarecrow Press, 1974.
922. Davis, F. C. "The Development of the Traveling Library." Master's thesis, East Texas State College, 1959.
923. Ditzion, S. "The Anglo-American Library Scene: A Contribution to the Social History of the Library Movement." *LQ* 16 (1946): 281–301.
924. ———. *Arsenals of a Democratic Culture: A Social History of the American Public Library Movement in New England and the Middle Atlantic States from 1850 to 1900*. Chicago: American Library Association, 1947.
925. ———. "Opening the People's Library on the Lord's Day." *S&S* 70 (1949): 49–53.
926. ———. "The Public Library Movement in the United States as It Was Influenced by the Needs of the Wage Earner, 1850–1900." Master's thesis, College of the City of New York, 1938.
927. ———. "Social Reform, Education, and the Library, 1850–1900." *LQ* 9 (1939): 156–84.
928. Dix, W. S. "The Library and the American Tradition [Since 1741]." *TLJ* 27 (1951): 60–66.
929. Duane, F. P. "The Carnegie Libraries." *JLH* 5 (1970): 165–70.
930. Duffus, R. L. *Books, Their Place in a Democracy*. Boston: Houghton Mifflin, 1933.
931. ———. *Our Starving Libraries: Studies in Ten American Communities During Depression Years*. Boston: Houghton Mifflin, 1933.
932. Du Mont, R. R. *Reform and Reaction: The Big City Public Library in American Life*. Westport, Conn.: Greenwood Press, 1977.
933. Eberhart, L. "Concepts of the (American) Library's Role in Adult Education, 1926–1951." Master's thesis, University of Wisconsin, 1951.
934. Edwards, E. "The Libraries of the United States of America." In his *Memoirs of Libraries . . .* , vol. 2, pp. 163–242. London, 1859.
935. Epstein, J. S. "History of Urban Main Library Service." *LibT* 20 (1972): 598–624.
936. Esterquest, R. T. "War Attitudes and Activities of American Libraries, 1914–18." *WLB* 15 (1941): 621–36.
937. Fletcher, W. I. *Public Libraries in America*. Columbian Knowledge Series, no. 2. Boston: Roberts Brothers, 1904.
938. ———. "The Public Library Movement." *Cosmo* 18 (1894): 99–106.
939. Franklin, H. R. "Service to the Urban Rank and File." In *A Century of Service: Librarianship in the United States and Canada*, edited by S. L. Jackson et al., pp. 1–19. Chicago: American Library Association, 1976.

940. Frantz, R. W. "A Re-examination of the Influence of Literary Nationalism on the Public Library." *JLH* 1 (1966): 182–86.
941. "Free Town Libraries." In U.S. Bureau of Education, *Public Libraries in the United States of America* . . . , pp. 445–59. Washington, D.C.: Government Printing Office, 1876.
942. Gambee, B. L. "'An Alien Body': Relationships Between the Public Library and the Public Schools, 1876–1920." *Ball State University Library Science Lectures*, First Series (1973): 1–23.
943. Garceau, O. *The Public Library in the Political Process*. New York: Columbia University Press, 1949.
944. Garrison, D. "Cultural Custodians of the Gilded Age: The Public Librarian and Horatio Alger." *JLH* 6 (1971): 327–36.
945. ———. "Cultural Missionaries: A Study of American Public Library Leaders, 1876–1910." Doctoral dissertation, University of California, Irvine, 1973.
946. ———. "Immoral Fiction in the Late Victorian Library." *AQ* 28 (1976): 71–89.
947. ———. "Rejoinder [to Elaine Fain's critique of her work]." *JLH* 10 (1975): 111–16.
948. ———. "The Tender Technicians: The Feminization of Public Librarianship, 1876–1905." *JSocH* 6 (1973): 131–59.
949. Gilman, D. C. *Development of the Public Library in America: An Address Delivered at the Opening of the Cornell University Library . . . 1891*. Ithaca, N.Y.: Cornell University, 1891.
950. Goodknight, J. L. *The Evolution of American Libraries: An Address Delivered at the Dedication of the Carnegie Library Building, Lincoln, Illinois, April 29, 1903*. Lincoln: News-Herald Print, 1903.
951. Green, C. S. "Library Service to the Blind in the United States: Origins and Development to 1931." Master's thesis, University of Chicago, 1967.
952. Green, S. S. *The Public Library Movement in the United States, 1853–1893: From 1876, Reminiscences of the Writer*. Boston: The Boston Book Co., 1919.
953. Haines, H. E. "The Rapid Growth of Public Libraries." *WW* 5 (1903): 3086–90.
954. Handlin, O. "Libraries and Learning." *AtlM* 213 (1964): 103–05.
955. Harris, M. H. "Public Libraries and the Decline of the Democratic Dogma." *LJ* 101 (1976): 2225–30.
956. ———. "The Purpose of the American Public Library: A Revisionist Interpretation of History." *LJ* 98 (1973): 2509–14.
957. ———. *The Role of the Public Library in American Life: A Speculative Essay*. Urbana: University of Illinois Graduate School of Library Science, Occasional paper no. 117, 1975.
958. Harrison, J. L. "Movement for Public Libraries in the United States." *NEM* 10 (1894): 709–22.

959. Harwell, R., and Michener, R. "As Public as the Town Pump." *LJ* 99 (1974): 959–63.
960. Hassenforder, J. *Développement comparé des Bibliothèques Publiques en France, en Grand-Bretagne et aux Etats-Unis dans la Seconde Moitié du XIXe siècle (1850–1914)*. Paris: Cercle de la Librairie, 1967.
961. ———. "Development of Public Libraries in France, the United Kingdom and the United States." *UBL* 22 (1968): 13–19.
962. Henderson, J. D. "County Libraries." *ELIS* 6:254–68.
963. Herdman, M. M. "The Public Library in Depression." Doctoral dissertation, University of Chicago, 1941.
964. ———. "The Public Library in Depression." *LQ* 13 (1943): 310–34.
965. Hurwitz, J. D. "Public Library as 'People's University': An Analytical History of the Concept as a Part of the American Public Library Movement in the Late Nineteenth and Early Twentieth Centuries." Master's thesis, University of Chicago, 1974.
966. Jackson, S. "Tax-Supported Library Service to the People: Why Was 1876–1877 the Nodal Point?" *IntLR* 4 (1972): 417–21.
967. Jevons, S. W. "The Rationale of Free Public Libraries." *CR* 39 (1881): 18–23.
968. Jewett, C. C. *Notices of Public Libraries in the United States of America*. Washington, D.C.: The Smithsonian Institution, 1851.
969. Joeckel, C., and Winslow, A. *A National Plan for Public Library Service*. Chicago: American Library Association, 1948.
970. Johnson, A. S. *The Public Library: A People's University*. New York: American Association for Adult Education, 1938.
971. Johnson, E. D. "Southern Public Libraries in the 1850's: Correcting an Error." *JLH* 4 (1969): 268–70.
972. Johnson, Sister M. I. "The Development of Separate Service for Young People in the Public Libraries of the United States, and Its Implications for Library Schools." Master's thesis, Columbia University, 1940.
973. Kaiser, W. H. "Statistical Trends of Large Public Libraries, 1900–1946." *LQ* 18 (1948): 278–79.
974. Keogh, A. "English and American Libraries: A Comparison." *PubL* 6 (1901): 388–95.
975. Kittle, A. T. "Management Theories in Public Library Administration in the United States, 1925–1955." Doctoral dissertation, Columbia University, 1961.
976. Klopenstein, M. J. "The American Library and Some of Its Benefactors." Master's thesis, Western Reserve University, 1955.
977. Knight, D. M., and Nourse, E. S., eds. *Libraries at Large*. New York: R. R. Bowker, 1969.
978. Koch, T. W. *A Book of Carnegie Libraries*. White Plains, N.Y.: The H. W. Wilson Co., 1917.

979. ———. *Books in the War: The Romance of Library War Service.* Boston: Houghton Mifflin Co., 1919.
980. Kramp, R. S. "The Great Depression: Its Impact on Forty-six Large Public Libraries; An Inquiry Based on Content Analysis of the Published Writings of Their Directors." Doctoral dissertation, University of Michigan, 1975.
981. Learned, W. S. *The American Public Library and the Diffusion of Knowledge.* New York: Harcourt, 1924.
982. Lee, R. E. *Continuing Education for Adults Through the American Public Library, 1833–1964.* Chicago: American Library Association, 1966.
983. Leigh, R. D. *The Public Library in the United States: The General Report of the Public Library Inquiry.* New York: Columbia University Press, 1950.
984. Lester, E. L. "An Analysis of Post-War Trends in the Planning and Design of Public Library Buildings, 1945–1955." Master's thesis, Atlanta University, 1957.
985. Lester, R. M. "The Carnegie Corporation and the Library Renaissance in the South." *WLB* 31 (1956): 244–49.
986. ———. *Carnegie Grants for Library Buildings, 1890–1917.* New York: Carnegie Corp., 1943.
987. Long, H. G. *Public Library Service to Children: Foundation and Development.* Metuchen, N.J.: Scarecrow Press, 1969.
988. Lord, J. W. "The Cosmic World of Childhood: The Ideology of the Children's Librarian, 1900–1965." Doctoral dissertation, Emory University, 1968.
989. Marshall, A. P. "Service to Afro-Americans." In *A Century of Service: Librarianship in the United States and Canada*, edited by S. L. Jackson, et al., pp. 62–78. Chicago: American Library Association, 1976.
990. McMullen, H. "Service to Ethnic Minorities Other than Afro-Americans and American Indians." In *A Century of Service: Librarianship in the United States and Canada*, edited by S. L. Jackson et al., pp. 42–61. Chicago: American Library Association, 1976.
991. Mickelson, P. "American Society and the Public Library in the Thought of Andrew Carnegie." *JLH* 10 (1975): 117–38.
992. Molz, K. "The Public Library: The People's University?" *ASch* 34 (1964): 95–102.
993. Monroe, M. E. *Library Adult Education: The Biography of an Idea.* New York: Scarecrow Press, 1963.
994. Moss, J. R. "A Historical Survey of Ultra-Right Pressure Groups: Their Effect on Public Library Policy, 1950–1967." Master's thesis, East Texas State University, 1968.
995. Munn, R. "Hindsight on the Gifts of Carnegie." *LJ* 76 (1951): 1967–70.

996. Murison, W. J. *The Public Library: Its Origins, Purpose, and Significance.* 2d ed. London: George G. Harrap, 1971.
997. Oehlerts, D. E. "The Development of American Public Library Architecture from 1850 to 1940." Doctoral dissertation, Indiana University, 1975.
998. Olech, J. "Public Library Service to Business, 1904–1964." Master's thesis, Southern Connecticut State College, 1967.
999. Poll, B. "Working People and Their Relationship to the American Public Library: History and Analysis." Master's thesis, University of Washington, 1950.
1000. Poole, W. F. [The Public Library of Our Time] "Address of the President." *LJ* 12 (1887): 311–20.
1001. Powell, S. "Reading Rooms for Children." *PubL* 11 (1897): 125–31.
1002. Predeek, A. "The Idea of the American Library." *LQ* 9 (1939): 445–76.
1003. Prentice, A. E. *The Public Library Trustee: Image and Performance on Funding.* Metuchen, N.J.: Scarecrow, 1973.
1004. Prentis, G. "The Evolution of the Library System." *LQ* 39 (1969): 78–79.
1005. "Public Libraries of Ten Principal Cities." In U.S. Bureau of Education, *Public Libraries in the United States of America . . .* , pp. 837–1009. Washington, D.C.: Government Printing Office, 1876.
1006. Purdy, B. A. "Famous Children's Libraries: A Survey of Five Libraries Devoted Exclusively to Work with Children." Master's thesis, Pratt Institute, 1952.
1007. Quincy, J. P. "Free Libraries." In U.S. Bureau of Education, *Public Libraries in the United States of America . . .* , pp. 389–402. Washington, D.C.: Government Printing Office, 1876.
1008. Rathbone, J. A. "Modern Library Movement." *PubL* 13 (1908): 197–201.
1009. Rees, G. "United States of America." In *Libraries for Children*, pp. 83–138. London: Grafton, 1924.
1010. Root, M. E. S. "An American Past in Children's Work." *LJ* 71 (1946): 547–51; 1422–24.
1011. Rose, E. *The Public Library in American Life.* New York: Columbia University Press, 1954.
1012. Rossel, B. S. *Public Libraries in the Life of the Nation.* Chicago: American Library Association, 1943.
1013. Schick, F. L. "Board-Librarian Relationships in American Public Libraries." Master's thesis, University of Chicago, 1948.
1014. Scudder, H. E. "Public Libraries a Hundred Years Ago." In U.S. Bureau of Education, *Public Libraries in the United States of America . . .* , pp. 2–37. Washington, D.C.: Government Printing Office, 1876.

1015. Shera, J. H. *Foundations of the Public Library: The Origins of the American Public Library Movement in New England 1629–1885.* Chicago: University of Chicago Press, 1949.
1016. ———. "The Public Library in Perspective." In *The Metropolitan Library,* edited by R. W. Conant and K. Molz, pp. 101–22. Cambridge, Mass.: M.I.T. Press, 1972.
1017. Slade, W. A. "As It Was in the Beginning." *PubL* 24 (1924): 293–96.
1018. Sloan, R. M. "The History of the Phonograph Record in the American Public Library: Its Origins and Growth Through 1949." Master's thesis, Western Reserve University, 1950.
1019. Speirs, C. H. "The Effects of Political Censorship in the United States on Public Libraries and Librarians from 1945–1955." Master's thesis, Western Reserve University, 1957.
1020. Spofford, A. R. "The Public Libraries of the United States." *JSS* 2 (1870): 92–114.
1021. Stibitz, M. T. "Relation of the Public Library to Workers' Education, 1918 to 1939." Master's thesis, Columbia University, 1949.
1022. Thompson, C. S. *Evolution of the American Public Library, 1653–1876.* Washington, D.C.: Scarecrow Press, 1952.
1023. Thompson, L. B. "Book Selection Policies and Practices in Public Libraries, 1876–1900." Master's thesis, Catholic University, 1953.
1024. Tyler, M. C. "The Historic Evolution of the Free Public Library in America and Its Functions." *LJ* 9 (1884): 40–47.
1025. Ulrich, C. "The Role of the Library in Public Opinion Formation During World War I." *MinnUb* 2 (1971): 91–104.
1026. Ulveling, R. "The Public Library in the Large Community." In *The Library in the Community,* edited by L. Carnovsky and L. Martin. Chicago: University of Chicago Press, 1944.
1027. Unger, C. P. "School-housed Public Library Revisited." Master's thesis, University of Chicago, 1975.
1028. United States Bureau of Education. *Public Libraries in the United States of America: Their History, Condition and Management. Special Report, Part I.* Washington, D.C.: Government Printing Office, 1876.
1029. Wachtel, L. "State Provisions for the Support of Municipal Public Libraries and Some Comparisons with State Provisions for the Support of Public Schools." *LQ* 3 (1933): 373–89.
1030. Wallace, A. "The Library Movement in the South Since 1899." *LJ* 32 (1907): 253–58.
1031. ———. "The Southern Library Movement." *BALA* 1 (1907): 62–68.
1032. Waples, D. "The Public Library in the Depression." *LQ* 2 (1932): 321–43.
1033. Wellard, J. H. "The Historical Background of the Public Library." In *Book Selection,* pp. 3–68. London: Grafton and Co., 1937.

1034. ———. "Popular Reading and the Origin of the Public Library in America." *LJ* 60 (1935): 185–87.
1035. ———. *The Public Library Comes of Age*. London: Grafton and Co., 1940.
1036. ———. "Trends in the American Public Library Movement During the Nineteenth Century." In *Book Selection*, pp. 47–58. London: Grafton and Co., 1937.
1037. Wellisch, J. B., et al. *The Public Library and Federal Policy*. Westport, Conn.: Greenwood Press, 1974.
1038. Werkley, C. E. *Mister Carnegie's Lib'ary*. New York: American Heritage Press, 1970.
1039. Wight, E. A. "Precursors of Current Public Library Systems." *LQ* 39 (1969): 23–40.
1040. Williamson, C. C. *Andrew Carnegie: His Contribution to the Public Library Movement. A Commemorative Address*. Cleveland: Privately printed, 1920.
1041. Winsor, J. "The Beginnings of Our Public Library System." *LW* 10 (1879): 121–22.
1042. ———. "The Library Movement Thirty Years Ago." *LW* 10 (1879): 330–31.
1043. Wood, M. E. "Libraries as Cultural Centers." *Outlook* 80 (1905): 859–61.
1044. Zimmerman, C. R. "The Public Library and the Political Process." *WLB* 28 (1953): 70–76.

B. Special Studies Arranged by State

ALABAMA

1045. Fonville, E. R. "A History of Public Library Service to Negroes in Bessemer, Alabama." Master's thesis, Atlanta University, 1962.
1046. Grayson, B. R. "The History of Public Library Service for Negroes in Montgomery, Alabama." Master's thesis, Atlanta University, 1965.
1047. Johnson, K. R. "The Early Library Movement in Alabama." *JLH* 6 (1971): 120–32.
1048. Miller, W. T. "Library Service for Negroes in the New South: Birmingham, Alabama, 1871–1918." *AlaL* 27 (1975): 6–8.

ALASKA

1049. Anderson, R. "Alaskan Libraries in 1945." *PNLAQ* 9 (1945): 147–49.
1050. Brady, J. G. "Libraries of Alaska: Historical Library at Sitka." *LJ* 30 (1905): 141–43.
1051. Mauseth, B. J. "A Brief History of the Ketchikan, Alaska, Public

Library, 1901–1956." Master's thesis, University of Washington, 1956.

1052. Stewart, J. "Library Service in Alaska: A Historical Study." Master's thesis, University of Washington, 1957.

ARIZONA

1053. "Public Library Histories." *ArizL* 7 (1950): 1–15.

ARKANSAS

1054. Gates, J. K. "Library Progress in Tax-Supported Institutions in Arkansas, 1924–1949." Master's thesis, Catholic University of America, 1951.
1055. McNeil, C. "History of the Library in Arkansas." Master's thesis, University of Mississippi, 1957.
1056. Tillman, R. H. "The History of Public Library Service to Negroes in Little Rock, Arkansas, 1917–1951." Master's thesis, Atlanta University, 1953.

CALIFORNIA

1057. Benedetti, L. S. "A History of Public Library Service in Menlo Park, California, 1889–1969." Master's thesis, California State University, San Jose, 1969.
1058. Blanford, L. *A History of the Kern County Library*. [Bakersfield?], Calif.: Kern County Historical Society, 1967.
1059. Conmy, P. T. "California Libraries in the 1870's." *CalL* 31 (1970): 37–45.
1060. ———. "Centennial of Oakland Public Library." *CalL* 30 (1969): 42–47.
1061. ———. *The Dismissal of Ina Coolbrith as Head Librarian of Oakland Free Public Library and a Discussion of the Tenure Status of Head Librarians*. Oakland, Calif.: Oakland Public Library, 1969.
1062. ———. *The Organic Structure of the Oakland Public Library: Its History and Development*. Oakland, Calif.: Oakland Public Library, 1969.
1063. ———. "The San Francisco Earthquake and Fire of 1906 and Its Effect upon Libraries." *CalL* 12 (1950): 87–90.
1064. Cooley, L. C. "The Los Angeles Public Library." *HSSCQ* 23 (1941): 5–23.
1065. Eddy, H. G. *County Free Library Organizing in California, 1909–1918: Personal Recollections of Harriet G. Eddy, County Library Organizer, Calif. State Library*. Berkeley: Committee on California Library History, Bibliography and Archives, California Library Association, 1955.

1066. Held, R. "Libraries in California Before the Deluge." *CalL* 28 (1967): 83–93.
1067. ———. *Public Libraries in California, 1849–1878.* Berkeley: University of California Press, 1963.
1068. ———. *The Rise of the Public Library in California.* Chicago: American Library Association, 1973.
1069. Hensley, H. C. "Early Days of the Public Library." *SanDHSQ* 4 (1958): 37–39.
1070. ———. "The Public Reading Room." *SanDHSQ* 7 (1955): 10.
1071. Hyers, F. H. "Brief History of the Los Angeles Public Library." In *Forty-Eighth Annual Report of the Los Angeles Public Library*, pp. 25–78. Los Angeles: The Public Library, 1936.
1072. Irshay, P. C. "The A. K. Smiley Public Library and How It Grew." *CalL* 30 (July 1969): 166–72.
1073. Kendall, H. A. "The Eureka Free Library." In *History of Humboldt County*, edited by L. H. Irvine, pp. 166–70. Los Angeles: Historic Record Co., 1915.
1074. Kirkwood, H. W., et al., comps. *Orange County Free Library, 1921–1965.* Orange, Calif., 1966.
1075. Lichtenstein, J. "San Francisco's Public Library." *SunM* 13 (1904): 163–70.
1076. Los Angeles County Free Library. *History of the Los Angeles County Free Library, 1912–1927.* Los Angeles: The Library, 1927.
1077. Mackenzie, A. D. "The Beginnings of a Library Tradition." *CalL* 14 (1953): 216–18.
1078. Mahoney, B. L. "History of the Marin County Free Library System." Master's thesis, California State University at San Jose, 1972.
1079. Miller, G. C. *The Palo Alto Public Library: Its History and Development.* Palo Alto, Calif., 1929.
1080. Nourse, L. M. "A Comparison of the Establishment and Growth of County Libraries in California and New Jersey as Influenced by Their Respective Legal, Geographical, and Administrative Differences." Master's thesis, Columbia University, 1931.
1081. Steig, L. F. "Notes on the Origins of Public Libraries in California, 1850–1900." *LQ* 22 (1952): 263–69.
1082. Wheeler, J. L. "Ideas Behind the San Diego Public Library." *CalL* 15 (1954): 224–26.

COLORADO

1083. Colorado State Library. *Colorado's Century of Public Libraries.* [Denver?], 1959.
1084. Eastlick, J. T. "Denver Public Library." *ELIS* 6:588–92.

CONNECTICUT

1085. Bergen, E. "History of the Bridgeport Public Library and Reading Room." Master's thesis, Southern Connecticut State College, 1969.
1086. Brophy, E. D. "The History of the Libraries of Windsor, Connecticut." Master's thesis, Southern Connecticut State College, 1974.
1087. Bryan, B. D. "Fairfield Public Library: Antecedents and Development." Master's thesis, Southern Connecticut State College, 1964.
1088. Burke, B. L. "The Development of Libraries in Guilford, Connecticut." Master's thesis, Southern Connecticut State College, 1959.
1089. Clarke, M. *David Wilkinson's Library: One Hundred Years in Hartford, Connecticut, 1866–1966.* Hartford: Trinity College Press, 1966.
1090. DeAngelis, P. "A History of Library Service in Kensington, Connecticut." Master's thesis, Southern Connecticut State College, 1967.
1091. Dexter, F. B. "The First Public Library in New Haven." *PNHCHS* 6 (1900): 301–13.
1092. Giddings, R. L. "The West Hartford Public Library: Its History, Development, and Present Status." Master's thesis, Southern Connecticut State College, 1965.
1093. Hausmann, A. F. "Origin and Development of the New Haven Free Public Library, 1886–1911." Master's thesis, Southern Connecticut State College, 1969.
1094. Hewins, C. M. "The Development of the Public Library in Connecticut." *ConnM* 9 (1905): 161–84.
1095. Lowrey, S. G. R. "A History of Libraries in Madison (East Guilford), Connecticut." Master's thesis, Southern Connecticut State College, 1963.
1096. Miller, M. M. "Public Libraries in Connecticut: Founding and Development of the Public Library at Greenwich, Connecticut." *ConnM* 10 (1906): 490–93.
1097. Mitchell, M. W. "An Historical Study of the Silas Bronson Library of Waterbury, Connecticut." Master's thesis, Southern Connecticut State College, 1966.
1098. New Haven. Free Public Library. *The Free Public Library of New Haven, Conn., Containing a Brief History . . .* New Haven: The Library, 1893.
1099. Norton, C. B., comp. *History of the Scoville Memorial Library.* Salisbury, Conn.: Lakeview Journal Press, 1941.
1100. Stetson, W. "Development of the Free Public Library in New Haven." *ConnM* 10 (1906): 129–38.
1101. Trumbull, J. "Public Libraries in Connecticut: A Presentation of

the Founding and Development of the Otis Library at Norwich." *ConnM* 10 (1906): 345–49.
1102. Waggoner, L. B. "The Development of the Cheshire Public Library." Master's thesis, Southern Connecticut State College, 1965.
1103. Wead, K. H. *Public and School Libraries and the State Board of Education: History [1893–1950], Statistics.* Hartford: Connecticut State Department of Education, 1951.

DELAWARE

1104. Baumgartner, B. "The New Castle County Free Library, 1927–1933." *DH* 13 (1968): 45–56.
1105. Nields, J. P. *The Wilmington Public Library and the New Castle County Free Library: A Historical Sketch.* Wilmington, Del.: The Wilmington Institute, 1943.

DISTRICT OF COLUMBIA

1106. Cook, V. R. "A History and Evaluation of the Music Division of the District of Columbia Public Library." Master's thesis, Catholic University of America, 1952.
1107. DeKaindry, W. "The Washington City Free Library." *RCHS* 16 (1913): 64–95.
1108. Hecht, A. "The Takoma Park Public Library." *RCHS* 66–68 (1969): 318–35.
1109. Johnson, W. D. "Earliest Free Public Library Movement in Washington, 1849–1874." *RCHS* 9 (1906): 9–13.
1110. King, M. L. "Beginnings and Early History of the Public Library of the District of Columbia, 1896–1904." Master's thesis, Catholic University of America, 1953.
1111. Maples, H. L. "The Peabody Library of Georgetown, District of Columbia: A History and Evaluation." Master's thesis, Drexel Institute of Technology, 1952.
1112. Mason, D. D. "The Public Library of the District of Columbia: An Historical Perspective, 1895–1948." *DCL* 20 (1954): 2–5.
1113. Noble, A. D. "Short Survey of the Libraries in the District of Columbia." *DCL* 4 (1933): 70–87.
1114. Williams, M. D. "The Peabody Room in the Georgetown Branch of the D.C. Public Library." *DCL* 24 (1953): 11–16.

FLORIDA

1115. Barfield, I. R. "History of the Miami Public Library." Master's thesis, Atlanta University, 1958.
1116. "The Carnegie Library at Ocala, Florida." *LJ* 42 (1917): 379–81.
1117. Carruth, E., and Monro, I. "Hannibal Square Library [Winter Park, Fla., 1936–52]." *WLB* 26 (1952): 463–65.

1118. Curry, J. L. "History of Public Library Service to Negroes in Jacksonville, Florida." Master's thesis, Atlanta University, 1957.
1119. Gill, S. "The History of the Miami Public Library System, Miami, Florida." Master's thesis, Western Reserve University, 1954.
1120. Mason, P. R. "A History of Public Library Development in Florida." Master's thesis, University of Chicago, 1968.
1121. McCullough, M. W. "The Davis S. Walker Library [Tallahassee]." *Apalachee*, 1946, pp. 13–18.
1122. Neuman, R. "Business Library Service Moves South [to Miami Public]." *LJ* 79 (1954): 2143–45.
1123. Obenaus, K. M. "Private Subscription Built the Indian River County Library." *LJ* 87 (1962): 4353–54.
1124. Patane, J. S. "A History of the Public Library in St. Petersburg, Florida." Master's thesis, Florida State University, 1960.
1125. Perres, M. J. "History and Development of Public Library Service for Negroes in Pensacola, Florida, 1947–1961." Master's thesis, Atlanta University, 1963.
1126. U.S. Works Progress Administration, Florida. *Florida Libraries*. Jacksonville: Works Progress Administration, 1939.
1127. Worley, M. M. "Tampa, Florida, Public Library." Master's thesis, University of Mississippi, 1961.

GEORGIA

1128. Adkins, B. M. "A History of Public Library Service to Negroes in Atlanta, Georgia." Master's thesis, Atlanta University, 1951.
1129. Crittenden, J. L. J. "A History of Public Library Service to Negroes in Columbia, Georgia, 1831–1959." Master's thesis, Atlanta University, 1960.
1130. Daniel, E. C. "Books in Brooks." *GaR* 1 (1947): 242–51.
1131. Fleming, J. B. *199 Years of Augusta's Library: A Chronology (1732–1949)*. Athens: University of Georgia Press, 1949.
1132. Harris, S. M. "Regional Library Development and Service in Georgia." *GaR* 3 (1949): 298–310.
1133. Howard, L. "The Statesboro Regional Library: History, Development and Services." Master's thesis, Florida State University, 1964.
1134. Hutzler, H. C. "History of the Rome, Georgia, Carnegie Library (1911–1961)." Master's thesis, Catholic University of America, 1963.
1135. Jamison, A. H. "Development of the Library in Atlanta." *AHB* 4 (1939): 96–111.
1136. Odom, E. P. *History of the Public Library of Moultrie, Georgia, 1906–1965*. Moultrie: Moultrie–Colquitt County Library, 1966.
1137. Redd, G. L. "A History of Public Library Service to Negroes in Macon, Georgia." Master's thesis, Atlanta University, 1961.

74 Public Libraries

1138. Satterfield, H. C. "History of Highland County District Library." Master's thesis, Kent State University, 1960.

HAWAII

1139. Matsushige, H. "The Library of Hawaii, 1913–1949: A Brief Historical Description." Master's thesis, Pratt Institute, 1951.
1140. Okubo, S. "The Development of Public Library Service in the County of Maui, Territory of Hawaii." Master's thesis, University of Hawaii, 1941.
1141. Ramachandran, R. "Origins of the Carnegie Grant to the Library of Hawaii (1901–1909)." *CaLL* 34 (1973): 44–50.
1142. Tachiata, C. "The History and Development of Hawaii Public Libraries, 1913–1975." Doctoral dissertation, University of Southern California, 1976.

ILLINOIS

1143. Bailey, A. H. "The Antecedents of the Peoria Public Library." In *Contributions to Mid-West Library History*, edited by T. Eaton, pp. 54–105. Champaign: Illini Union Bookstore, 1964.
1144. Berg, V. A. "History of the Urbana Free Library, 1874–1894." Master's thesis, University of Illinois, 1948.
1145. Bostian, I., ed. "Histories of Public Libraries." *IllL* 50 (1968): whole issue.
1146. Bruder, M. "The Chicago Public Library (1873–1952)." *ChiSJ* 33 (1952): 159–62.
1147. Bullock, E. U. "A History of the Geneva Public Library." Master's thesis, Northern Illinois University, 1965.
1148. Burrell, M. R. "A Short History of the Galesburg Ladies' Library Association." In *Contributions to Mid-West Library History*, edited by T. Eaton, pp. 130–153. Champaign: Illini Union Bookstore, 1964.
1149. "Chicago Public Library 100th Anniversary." *IllL* 54 (1972): whole issue.
1150. *The Chicago Public Library, 1873–1923: Proceedings of the Celebration of the Fiftieth Anniversary of the Opening of the Library, January First, Fourth, and Sixth, 1923.* Chicago: The Public Library, 1923.
1151. "Histories of Public Libraries." *IllL* 51 (1969): 357–452.
1152. Hoyne, T. *Historical Sketch of the Origin and Foundation of the Chicago Public Library: Compiled From the Original Documents and Correspondence and Contemporary Publications . . .* Chicago: Beach, Bernard & Co., 1877.
1153. Kimball, C. F. "History of Withers Public Library [Bloomington, Ill.]." *TMCHS* 2 (1903): 224–40.

1154. Kram, R. I. "The Foreign Language Collections of the Chicago Public Library, 1872–1947." Master's thesis, University of Chicago, 1970.
1155. Kratz, E. A. *History of the Champaign Public Library and Reading Room*. [Champaign?], 1926.
1156. Ladenson, A. "Chicago Public Library." *ELIS* 4:530–39.
1157. Mills, F. L., and Hurley, L. J. "A History of Racine Public Library Lectures: 1927–1966." *IllL* 48 (1966): 540–43.
1158. Perry, M. E. "Decatur Public Library, 1901–1951." *IllL* 33 (1951): 350–54.
1159. Prichard, L. G. "A History of the Chicago Public Library." Master's thesis, University of Illinois, 1928.
1160. Sharp, K. "Illinois Libraries: Public Libraries." [University of Illinois] *UnivS* 2, no. 3 (1906): whole issue.
1161. Spencer, G. S. *The Chicago Public Library: Origins and Backgrounds*. Chicago: University of Chicago Press, 1943.
1162. Steuernagel, B. *The Belleville Public Library, 1836–1936: An Historical Sketch*. Belleville, Ill.: News Democrat Journal, 1936.
1163. *The Treasures of All Knowledge: The Official Centennial Publication*. Chicago: Chicago Public Library, 1972.

INDIANA

1164. Beamon, M. "The Origin and Development of the School Services Department of the Indianapolis Public Library." Master's thesis, Indiana University, 1962.
1165. Boyd, F. *A History of Public Library Service in Terre Haute and Vigo County, Indiana, from 1823 to 1966*. Terre Haute: Fairbanks-Vigo County Public Library, 1966.
1166. *A Century of Service, 1873–1973: Historical Highlights of the Indianapolis-Marion County Public Library*. Indianapolis: The Library, 1973.
1167. Constantine, J. R. *The Role of Libraries in the Cultural History of Indiana*. Bloomington: Indiana Library Studies, 1970.
1168. Curless, M. "Library Development in Lagrange County, Indiana." In *Contributions to Mid-West Library History*, edited by T. Eaton, pp. 164–180. Champaign: Illini Union Bookstore, 1964.
1169. Edson, H. "Thanksgiving Day Sermon [at the Indianapolis Public Library 26 November 1868]." In *Indianapolis in the World of Books*, pp. 1–12. Indianapolis: Indianapolis–Marion County Public Library, 1974.
1170. Feaster, D. M. "History of Story Telling in the Indianapolis Public Library." Master's thesis, Western Reserve University, 1951.
1171. Henry, W. E. *Municipal and Institutional Libraries of Indiana: History, Condition, and Management*. Indianapolis, 1904.
1172. Holley, E. G. "The Indianapolis Public Library: A Live Thing in the

Whole Town." In *Indianapolis in the World of Books*, pp. 13–29. Indianapolis: Indianapolis–Marion County Public Library, 1974.

1173. Hull, T. V. "The Origin and Development of the Indianapolis Public Library, 1873–1899." Master's thesis, University of Kentucky, 1956. Published: University of Kentucky Press, Microcard Publications, Series B, Number 2.
1174. Lewis, D. F. "History of the Marion County, Indiana, Library, 1844–1930." Master's thesis, Indiana University, 1954.
1175. McFadden, M. *The Indianapolis Public Library: A Portrait Against the Background of the Past Decade, 1945–1955*. Indianapolis, 1956.
1176. Middleton, E. H., comp. *The First Seventy-Five Years: A Sketch of the Muncie Public Library, 1874–1949*. Muncie, Ind.: Muncie Public Library, 1949.
1177. Peters, O. M. *The Gary Public Library, 1907–1944*. Gary, Ind.: Public Library of Gary, 1945.
1178. Taylor, M. V. "Public Library Commission of Indiana, 1899–1925." Master's thesis, University of Kentucky, 1953. Published: University of Kentucky Press, Microcard Publications, Series B, Number 3.
1179. Walther, L. A. "Legal and Governmental Aspects of Public Library Development in Indiana, 1816–1953." Doctoral dissertation, Indiana University, 1957.
1180. Zimmerman, M. "A History of the South Bend Public Library from 1888–1961." Master's thesis, Catholic University of America, 1962.

IOWA

1181. Blanks, E. W. "The Public Library of Des Moines, Iowa: A History of the First Fifty Years, 1866–1916." Master's thesis, University of Texas, 1967.
1182. Coughlin, B. "History of the Davenport Public Library." Master's thesis, Western Reserve University, 1952.
1183. McGuire, L. P. "A Study of the Public Library Movement in Iowa." *IJHP* 35 (1937): 22–72.
1184. Pease, K. R. "Iowa Public Library Service in Recent History." Master's thesis, University of Chicago, 1968.
1185. Snyder, E. B. "The History and Development of the Music Collection and Department of the Public Library of Des Moines." Master's thesis, Western Reserve University, 1958.

KANSAS

1186. Biby, W. A. "History of the Topeka Free Public Library (1870–1948)." *BSCHS* 2 (1948): 67–78.

1187. Crumpacker, G. F. "Library Legislation and the Library Movement in Kansas." Master's thesis, University of Illinois, 1932.
1188. Gibson, H. B. C. "Wichita and Her Public Libraries." *KHQ* 6 (1937): 387–93.

KENTUCKY

1189. Ridgway, F. H. *Developments in Library Service in Kentucky: A Review*. Berea, Ky.: Berea College Press, 1940.
1190. Wilkins, J. "Blue's 'Colored' Branch: A 'Second Plan' That Became a First in Librarianship." *AL* 7 (1976): 256–57.
1191. Works Progress Administration. *Libraries and Lotteries: A History of the Louisville Free Public Library*. Cynthiana, Ky., 1944.

LOUISIANA

1192. Culver, E. M., and Gittinger, N. M. "A History of the Citizens' Library Movement [1937–53]." *LLAB* 17 (1954): 18–23.
1193. Schultz, F. A. "New Orleans Public Library in the Twentieth Century (1897–1951)." *LLAB* 15 (1952): 78–83.
1194. Smith, R. C. "A Historical Study of Selected Effects of Federal Funding upon Public Libraries in Louisiana, 1956–1973." Doctoral dissertation, Louisiana State University, 1975.
1195. Vaughan, B. "The Shreve Memorial Library [Shreveport, 1923–53]." *LLAB* 16 (1953): 123–25.

MAINE

1196. Hemmer, P. B. "History of the Lewiston Public Library: Lewiston, Maine." Master's thesis, Catholic University of America, 1965.
1197. Scott, K. J. "The Origins of the Public Library in Portland, Maine." Master's thesis, University of Chicago Graduate Library School, 1974.

MARYLAND

1198. Blinkhorn, M. E. "A History of the Bethesda, Maryland, Public Library." Master's thesis, Catholic University of America, 1963.
1199. Castagna, E. "Enoch Pratt Free Library." *ELIS* 8:117–26.
1200. *The Enoch Pratt Free Library at Seventy-Five, 1886–1961: A Retrospective Report*. Baltimore: The Library, 1963.
1201. Enoch Pratt Free Library. Baltimore, Md. *The Enoch Pratt Free Library of Baltimore City: Letters and Documents Relating to Its Foundation and Organization, with the Dedicatory Addresses and Exercises, January 4, 1886*. Baltimore, 1886.
1202. Jackl, W. E. "Station Number Eleven of the Enoch Pratt Free Library." *JLH* 7 (1972): 141–56.
1203. Kahn, R. A. "A History of the Peabody Institute Library, Baltimore,

Maryland, 1857–1916." Master's thesis, Catholic University of America, 1953. Published: Association of College and Research Libraries Microcard, Number 16.

1204. Kalisch, P. A. *The Enoch Pratt Free Library: A Social History.* Metuchen, N.J.: Scarecrow Press, 1969.

1205. ———. "A Parable of Three Branch Libraries: A Social and Historical Analysis of the Waterfront Branches of the Enoch Pratt Free Library, Baltimore, Maryland." In *Library History Seminar Number 4*, edited by H. Goldstein and J. Goudeau, pp. 85–108. Tallahassee: Florida State University School of Library Science, 1972.

1206. Koch, J. V. "The Enoch Pratt Free Library: Its History, Organization, and Service to Readers." Master's thesis, Western Reserve University, 1951.

1207. McMurty, B. B. "The County Public Library: With Special Reference to Maryland and to Prince George's County in Maryland." Master's thesis, Western Maryland College (Westminster), 1947.

1208. Moltenberry, F. "History of Peabody Institute Library: University of the People." In *Approaches to Library History*, edited by J. D. Marshall, pp. 151–64. Tallahassee: *JLH*, 1966.

1209. Morison, N. H. *The Peabody Library*. Baltimore: The Peabody Institute Library, 1954. [First printed, 1871.]

1210. Powell, N. L. "A History of the Washington County, Maryland, Free Library, 1952–65." Master's thesis, Catholic University of America, 1966.

1211. Rice, D. M. "A History of the Silver Springs, Maryland, Public Library from 1931 to 1951." Master's thesis, Catholic University of America, 1961.

1212. Titcomb, M. L., and Holzapfel, M. L. *The Washington County Free Library, 1901–1951.* Hagerstown, Md., 1951.

1213. Uhler, P. R. "A Sketch of the History of the Public Libraries in Baltimore." *LJ* 15 (1890): 334–37.

1214. Wheeler, J. L. "Origin of the Enoch Pratt Library Central Building." *LJ* 71 (1946): 815–16.

MASSACHUSETTS

1215. Baron, M. S. "Evolution of the Springfield, Massachusetts, Public Library, 1796–1912." Master's thesis, Catholic University of America, 1966.

1216. Benton, J. H. *The Working of the Boston Public Library: An Address Before the Beacon Society of Boston, January 2, 1909.* Boston: Rockwell and Churchill Press, 1909.

1217. Buchanan, J. B. "Early Directions of the Boston Public Library and the Genesis of an American Public Library Psychology." Master's thesis, Southern Connecticut State College, 1962.

1218. Bush-Brown, A. *Books, Bass, Barnstable: An Address Delivered at the Centennial Celebration of the Sturgis Library, Barnstable, Massachusetts, August 26, 1967.* Barnstable: Great Marshes Press, 1967.

1219. Cambridge, Mass. Public Library. *1858–1908: History of the Cambridge Public Library, with the Addresses at the Celebration of Its Fiftieth Anniversary, List of Officers, etc.* Cambridge, 1908.

1220. Canavan, M. J. "The Old Boston Public Library, 1656–1747." *PCSM* 12 (1908–09): 116–32.

1221. Carpenter, E. J. "The Story of the Boston Public Library." *NEM* 12 (1895): 737–56.

1222. Cary Memorial Library, Lexington, Mass. "A Century of Service: 1868–1968. [Lexington: Cary Memorial Library, 1968].

1223. Clark, R. B. "History of the Talbot County Free Library, Easton, Massachusetts, 1925–1962." Master's thesis, Catholic University of America, 1963.

1224. Conyngham, M. H. "Forbes Library, Northampton, Massachusetts, 1881–1903." Master's thesis, University of Maryland, 1967.

1225. Fund, C. K. "Boston Public Library Building of 1895." Master's thesis, University of Chicago, 1973.

1226. Gillis, F. J. "Boston Public Library: A Centennial of Service, 1854–1954." *S&S* 79 (1954): 49–53.

1227. Gloucester Lyceum and Sawyer Free Library. *Gloucester Lyceum and Sawyer Free Library, Inc., 1830–1930: The Record of a Century.* Gloucester, 1930.

1228. Green, C. R. "The Jones Library in Amherst." *AGQ* 18 (February 1929): 87–93.

1229. Green, S. S. "Public Libraries." In *History of Worcester County, Massachusetts*, edited by D. H. Hurd, pp. 1491–1509. Philadelphia: J. W. Lewis & Co., 1889.

1230. Haraszti, Z. "A Hundred Years Ago." *MoreB* 23 (1948): 83–89.

1231. ———. "Twenty-five Years of the Treasure Room (of the Boston Public Library, 1930–55)." *BPLQ* 7 (1955): 115–27.

1232. Harris, M. H., and Spiegler, G. "Everett, Ticknor and the Common Man: The Fear of Societal Instability as the Motivation for the Founding of the Boston Public Library." *Libri* 24 (1974): 249–75.

1233. Harrison, J. L. *Forbes Library: The Half Century, 1894–1944.* Northampton: Printed for the Board of Trustees, 1945.

1234. Heard, J. M. *Origins of the Free Public Library System of Massachusetts.* Clinton: Office of the Saturday Courant, 1860.

1235. Hill, L. D. *The Crane Library.* Quincy, Mass.: Published by the Trustees of the Thomas Crane Public Library, 1962.

1236. Hillard, G. S. "History of the Boston Public Library," *AJE* 2 (1856): 203–04.

1237. Hodges, E. J. *A History of the Leominster Public Library. From the Report of the Librarian for 1955: Revised and Amended.* Leominster, Mass.: The Library, 1957.

1238. Jenks, G. A. "The Newton Library." *BCHSP* 3 (1909): 316–31.
1239. Kidder, N. T. *The First Sixty Years of the Milton Public Library, 1870–1931*. Milton, Mass.: Privately printed [Plimpton Press, Norwood], 1932.
1240. Lovett, R. W. "From Social Library to Public Library: A Century of Library Development in Beverly, Massachusetts." *HCEI* 88 (1952): 219–53.
1241. MacDonald, H., and MacDonald, M. *A History of the Lenox Library, Written for Its 100th Anniversary*. Lenox, 1956.
1242. McCord, D. T. W. *As Built with Second Thoughts, Reforming What Was Old: Reflections on the Centennial Anniversary of the Boston Public Library*. Boston: Centennial Commission of Boston Public Library, 1953.
1243. McGowan, O. T. P. "A Centennial History of the Fall River Public Library, 1861–1961." Master's thesis, Catholic University of America, 1964.
1244. Nash, R. "The Society of Printers and the [Boston] Public Library." *MoreB* 20 (1945): 221–26.
1245. Nourse, H. S., comp. "The Free Public Libraries of Massachusetts." In the *Ninth Report of the Free Public Library Commission of Massachusetts, 1899*. Boston, 1899.
1246. Pearl, E. E. "History of the [West Boxford Public] Library from January 14, 1881." *IMPLB* (September 1931): [4–5].
1247. Rand, F. P. *The Field Memorial Library, Comway, Mass.* Boston: The Arakelyan Press, 1907.
1248. Rice, C., ed. *The Field Memorial Library, Comway, Mass.* Boston: The Arakelyan Press, 1907.
1249. Ripley, E. F. *Weston Town Library History, 1857–1957*. Weston, Mass., 1957.
1250. Rolfe, W. J., and Ayer, C. W., comps. *1858–1908: History of the Cambridge Public Library, with the Addresses at the Celebration of Its Fiftieth Anniversary, Lists of Its Officers, etc.* Cambridge, 1908.
1251. Salfas, S. G. "History of the Springfield City Library, 1912–1948." Master's thesis, Southern Connecticut State College, 1969.
1252. Sargent, M. E. F. "The Evolution of the Medford Public Library." *MedHR* 2 (1899): 76–91.
1253. Siebens, C. R. *A Historical Sketch of the Libraries of Cape Cod and Martha's Vineyard and Nantucket*. Hyannis: Patriot Press, 1952.
1254. Steves, N. E. *A History of the Sandwich Public Library*. [Bourne]: Horace C. Pearsons, 1969.
1255. Talcott, M. T. *Athol Public Library, 1882–1972: 90 Years of Service*. [Athol, Mass.: Transcript Press, 1974].
1256. Tietjen, L. M. "A History of Libraries in Old Saybrook." Master's thesis, Southern Connecticut State College, 1975.

1257. Tillinghast, C. B. *The Free Public Libraries of Massachusetts.* Boston, 1891.
1258. Wadlin, H. G. *The Public Library of the City of Boston: A History.* Boston: The Trustees, 1911.
1259. Weis, F. L. *Historical Sketch of the Lancaster Town Library, 1790–1862–1950.* Lancaster, 1950.
1260. Whitehill, W. M. *Boston in the Age of John Fitzgerald Kennedy.* Norman: University of Oklahoma Press, 1966.
1261. ———. *Boston Public Library: A Centennial History, 1854–1954.* Cambridge: Harvard University Press, 1956.
1262. ———. "The Making of an Architectural Masterpiece–The Boston Public Library." *AAJ* 2 (1970): 13–35.
1263. Whitney, J. L. "Incidents in the History of the Boston Public Library." *LJ* 27 (July 1902): 16–24.
1264. Wikander, L. E. *Disposed to Learn: The First Seventy-five Years of the Forbes Library.* Northampton, Mass.: The Trustees of the Forbes Library, 1972.
1265. Wilson, F. A. *The Nahant Public Library: Containing a Brief Sketch of the Public Library Movement, a History of the Nahant Public Library and a Description of the New Library Building.* Linn [sic]: Macfarlane Press, 1895.
1266. Winsor, J. "The Boston Public Library." *SM* 3 (1871): 150–56.
1267. ———. "Libraries in Boston." In *Memorial History of Boston, Including Suffolk County, Massachusetts, 1630–1880,* vol. 4, pp. 279–94. Boston: James Osgood and Co., 1880.
1268. Woodward, D. M.; Hughes, D. E.; and Canavan, B. *Stoughton Public Library: 100 Years, 1874–1974.* [Stoughton?: Stoughton Public Library?, 1974].
1269. Woodwell, R. H. *Amesbury Public Library, 1856–1956.* Amesbury, Mass., 1956.
1270. Worcester, Mass. Free Public Library. *The Fiftieth Anniversary of the Founding of the Worcester Free Public Library, to Dec. 23, 1909.* Worcester: Press of F. S. Blanchard and Co., 1910.

MICHIGAN

1271. Bixby, Mrs. A. F. *Historical Sketches of the Ladies' Library Associations of the State of Michigan.* Compiled and arranged by Mrs. A. F. Bixby and Mrs. A. Howell. Adrian, Mich.: Times and Expositor Steam Print, 1876.
1272. Burich, N.J. "Years of Consolidation and Expansion: A History of the Lansing Public Library from 1930 to 1967." Master's thesis, Kent State University, 1968.
1273. Hamner, P. N. "The Ladies' Library Association of Michigan: A Curious Byway in Library History." Master's thesis, Western Reserve University, 1954.

1274. Helms, C. "The Development of Library Services in Allegan County, Michigan." In *Contributions to Mid-West Library History*, edited by T. Eaton, pp. 106–129. Champaign: Illini Union Bookstore, 1964.
1275. Hoesch, M. J. "A History of the Grosse Pointe Public Library." Master's thesis, Western Reserve University, 1955.
1276. Lonie, C. A. "The Ladies' Library Association of Niles Michigan, as Reported in a Contemporary Newspaper." In *Contributions to Mid-West Library History*, edited by T. Eaton, pp. 154–163. Champaign: Illini Union Bookstore, 1964.
1277. Michigan. Board of Library Commissioners. *Legislative History of Township Libraries in the State of Michigan from 1835 to 1901*. Compiled by L. M. Miller and printed by the order of the Board of Library Commissioners. Lansing: R. Smith Printing Co., 1902.
1278. Thurner, A. W. "How a Library Came to Copper Country [Calument, Mich.]." *WLB* 50 (1976): 608–12.
1279. Ulveling, R. A. "Detroit Public Library." *ELIS* 7:121–28.
1280. Walton, G. M. *Libraries in Michigan: An Historical Sketch in the Year of the Golden Jubilee of the American Library Association, 1876–1926*. Lansing: Michigan State Library, 1926.
1281. "When Culture Came to Kalamazoo." *IMich* 2 (1952): 24–27.
1282. Woodford, F. B. *Parnassus on Main Street: A History of the Detroit Public Library*. Detroit: Wayne State University Press, 1965.

MINNESOTA

1283. Baldwin, C. F. "The Public Library Movement in Minnesota, 1900–1936." *MinnL* 14 (1945): 384–98.
1284. Carlstadt, E. "Public Library Movement in Minnesota, 1849–1900." *MinnL* 14 (1945): 351–63.
1285. Gibson, F. E. "The Effects of the Activities of the Unions in the Minneapolis Public Library on Library Functions and Administrative Processes, and Upon Union Members." Master's thesis, University of Minnesota, 1952.
1286. Lincoln, Sister M. E. "Cultural Significance of the Minneapolis Public Library in Its Origins and Development: A Study in the Relations of the Public Library and American Society." Doctoral dissertation, University of Minnesota, 1958.
1287. Longhway, M. W. *The History of the Library in Wabasha, Minnesota*. [Minneapolis: Division of Library Instruction of the University of Minnesota], 1938.
1288. *Minneapolis Public Library: Fifty Years of Service, 1889–1939*. Minneapolis: The Library, 1939.
1289. Nylander, E. P. "A History of the Duluth Public Library System." Master's thesis, University of Minnesota, 1962.

MISSISSIPPI

1290. Dickey, P. W. "A History of Public Library Service for Negroes in Jackson, Mississippi, 1950–1957." Master's thesis, Atlanta University, 1960.
1291. Green, E. B. "The History and Growth of Lee County Library." Master's thesis, University of Mississippi, 1961.
1292. Gunn, M. H. "History of Jackson Municipal Library, Jackson, Mississippi." Master's thesis, Texas Woman's University, 1965.
1293. Morse, D. B. "The Historical Development and Foreclosure of a Public Library." Master's thesis, University of Mississippi, 1960.
1294. Peebles, M., and Howell, J. B., eds. *A History of Mississippi Libraries*. N.p.: Mississippi Library Association, 1975.
1295. Sparks, E. C. "People with Books: The Services of Northeast Regional Library." Master's thesis, University of Mississippi, 1962.

MISSOURI

1296. Brinton, E. H. "History of Public Libraries in Missouri to 1920." *MLAQ* 11 (1950): 5–7.
1297. Compton, C. H. *Fifty Years of Progress of the St. Louis Public Library, 1876–1926*. St. Louis: St. Louis Public Library, 1926.
1298. ———. *Twenty-five Crucial Years of the St. Louis Public Library, 1927–1952*. St. Louis: The Public Library, 1953.
1299. ———. "An Unfinished Chapter in Missouri Library Legislation." *LQ* 12 (1942): 412–21.
1300. Hoffman, W. H., ed. *Kansas City, Missouri Public Library, 1873–1973: An Illustrated History*. Kansas City: The Kansas City Public Library, 1973.
1301. Swartz, R. G. "The Ozark Regional Library: Its Background and Development, 1947–1965." Master's thesis, University of Chicago, 1968.
1302. Wright, P. B. *Historical Sketch of the Kansas City Public Library, 1911–1936, with Extracts from Annual Reports of Librarian, 1911–1920*. Kansas City, Mo., 1937.

MONTANA

1303. Longworth, R. O. "Glacier County Library [Cut Bank, Mont.]: An Example of Cooperation." *WLB* 29 (1954): 73–74.

NEBRASKA

1304. Lenfest, G. E. "The Development and Present Status of the Library Movement in Nebraska." Master's thesis, University of Illinois, 1931.

NEW HAMPSHIRE

1305. Brennan, J. F. "Peterborough Town Library: The Pioneer Public Library." *GranM* 28 (1900): 281–91.
1306. Fitz, L. "The Library Movement in New Hampshire." *GranM* 15 (November 1893): 349–55.
1307. Irwin, F. T. "The Peterborough Library." *GranM* 60 (May 1928): 213–16.
1308. Lewis, W. P. "New Hampshire Libraries." *GranM* 59 (March 1927): 88–90.
1309. Lord, C. M. *Diary of a Village Library.* Somersworth: New Hampshire Publishing Co., 1971.
1310. Manchester, New Hampshire. City Library. *Seventy-Five Years of the City Library.* Manchester, 1929.

NEW JERSEY

1311. Andrews, F. E. *The Tenafly Public Library: A History, 1891–1970.* Tenafly, N.J.: The Public Library, 1970.
1312. Clark, E. S. *The Orange Public Library: A History of the First Seventy-Five Years, 1883–1958.* [Orange, N.J.: Orange Free Library, 1958].
1313. Doyle, Sister M. A. "A History of the Trenton Free Public Library." Master's thesis, Catholic University of America, 1968.
1314. Gallant, E. F. "The History of the Free Library of Teaneck, New Jersey." Master's thesis, Pratt Institute, 1954.
1315. Hughes, H. L., comp. *Public Libraries in New Jersey, 1750–1850.* N.p.: New Jersey Library Association, 1956.
1316. Lum, L. *As I Remember: A Story of Chatham's Libraries.* Chatham, N.J.: Chatham Free Public Library, 1955.
1317. Newark Public Library. *A Half-Century of Power for Business, 1904–1954.* Newark: Newark Public Library, Business Library, 1954.
1318. ———. *This Is to Be a People's Library: Newark Public Library, 1888–1963.* Newark: The Library, 1963.
1319. O'Brien, Sister M. B. "The History of the Development of a Library Plan for Clark, New Jersey." Master's thesis, Catholic University of America, 1965.
1320. Sabine, J. E. "Antecedents of the Newark Public Library." Doctoral dissertation, University of Chicago, 1946.
1321. [Winser, B.] *Fifty Years [Newark Public Library]: 1889–1939.* [Newark: Public Library of Newark, 1939].

NEW YORK

1322. Alexander, G. L. "Some Notes Toward a History of the New York Public Library Map Room for the Years 1923–1941." *SLAGMDB* (February 1959): 4–7.

1323. Armstrong, C. M., et al. *Development of Library Services in New York State*. Bulletin No. 1376. Albany: State University of New York, Division of Research, 1949.
1324. Barnes, J. W., and Barnes, R. W. "From Books to Multimedia: A History of the Reynolds Library and the Reynolds Audio-Visual Department of the Rochester Public Library." *RH* 36 (1974): 1–38.
1325. Bennett, H. E. "The Jamaica Library Service: Its Foundations and Development." Master's thesis, Southern Connecticut State College, 1966.
1326. Billings, J. S. "New York's Public Library." *LJ* 36 (1911): 233–43.
1327. Breen, M. H. "The Traveling Library Service of the New York Public Library in Richmond and the Bronx: A Descriptive History." Master's thesis, Pratt Institute, 1951.
1328. Bullock, J. Y. "A Resume of the History, Growth, and Development of Library Service to Hospital Patients by the Queens Borough (New York) Public Library." Master's thesis, Atlanta University, 1962.
1329. Cole, G. W. "Early Library Development in New York State (1809–1900)." *BNYPL* 30 (1926): 849–57, 917–25.
1330. Cutter, C. A. "Buffalo Public Library in 1893: An Excursion in the Land of Dreams." *LJ* 8 (1883): 211–17.
1331. Dain, P. *The New York Public Library: A History of Its Founding and Early Years*. New York: New York Public Library, 1972.
1332. Dalphin, M. "Library Beginnings in Westchester County." *WCHSB* 15 (1939): 73–80.
1333. Davis, J. M. "Chemung County Library: Past, Present, and Future." Master's thesis, Pratt Institute, 1954.
1334. Eisner, J. "Development of Public Libraries and Library Legislation in New York State." *NYLAB* 9 (1961): 13–17.
1335. Fannin, G. M. "A Resume of the History, Growth and Development of the Story Hour in the New York Public Library." Master's thesis, Atlanta University, 1958.
1336. Fess, M. R. *The Grosvenor Library and Its Times*. Buffalo: Grosvenor Reference Division of the Buffalo and Erie County Public Library, 1956.
1337. Flick, H. M. "Milestones in Library Development in New York State." *Bookmark* 24 (1965): 201–03.
1338. Franklin, W. D. "A Historical Study of Library Development in New York State Compared with That in Catskill, N.Y." Master's thesis, State University of New York at Albany, 1965.
1339. Garnett, R. "New York and Its Three Libraries." *NAR* 193 (1911): 850–60.
1340. Goldberg, A. *The Buffalo Public Library: Commemorating Its First Century of Service to the Citizens of Buffalo, 1836–1936*. Buffalo: The Library, 1937.

1341. Goldstein, D. "The Library for the Blind of the New York Public Library." Master's thesis, Drexel Institute of Technology, 1953.
1342. Gore, D. J. "The Schomberg Collection and Its Catalog: A Historical Sketch." Master's thesis, University of North Carolina, 1963.
1343. Haywood, W. C. *Who Uses the Public Library: A Survey of the Patrons of the Circulation and Reference Departments of the New York Public Library.* Chicago: University of Chicago Press, 1938.
1344. Hisz, E. "History of the Theatre Collection, New York Public Library at Lincoln Center." Master's thesis, Long Island University, 1969.
1345. Howard, J. G. "Portfolio of Plans for the New York Public Library: Placed Second in a Competition 1897." *A&E* 113 (1933): 33–37.
1346. Jacobson, B. "History of the New York Public Library for the Blind and Physically Handicapped, 1895–1969." Master's thesis, Long Island University, 1971.
1347. Lydenberg, H. M. *History of the New York Public Library: Astor Lenox and Tilden Foundation.* New York: New York Public Library, 1923.
1348. ———. "New York Libraries (1848–1950): The Long View." *SL* 41 (1950): 169–71, 242–45.
1349. Mamaroneck, N.Y. Free Library. *The Story of the Mamaroneck Free Library, 1922–1947.* Mamaroneck, 1947.
1350. McKelvey, B., ed. *The History of Rochester Libraries.* New York: Rochester Historical Society, 1937.
1351. ———. "The Semi-Centennial of the Rochester Public Library." *RH* 23 (1961): 1–24.
1352. McVee, M. F. "Public Library Contributions to Formal Adult Education Programs in Small Cities of New York State." Master's thesis, State University of New York at Albany, 1958.
1353. Moran, I. S. "Brooklyn Public Library–75 Years Young." *LHR* 1 (1974): 55–82.
1354. New York Public Library. *After One Hundred Years: An Account of the Partnership Which Has Built and Sustained the New York Public Library, 1848–1948.* [New York: The Library, 1948].
1355. ———. "Dedication of the New York Public Library Building, May 23, 1911." *RASHPS* 17 (1912): 317–42.
1356. ———. *Municipal Reference Library: 50th Anniversary, 1913–1963.* New York: New York Public Library, 1963.
1357. ———. "Proceedings at the New Building of the New York Public Library, Astor, Lenox and Tilden Foundation, Tuesday, May 23, 1911." *BNYPL* 15 (1911): 327–48.
1358. ———. Board of Trustees. "Progress of the New York Public Library, 1896–1906." *BNYPL* 10 (1906): 343–57.
1359. Nichols, B. B. "Westchester Library System: The History and Evaluation of a Program of Service." Master's thesis, Southern Connecticut State College, 1969.

1360. Overton, J. M. "The Children's Library of Westbury (Long Island): Its First Twenty-five Years [1924–49]." *HB* 25 (1949): 451–66.
1361. Peer, S. *The First Hundred Years: A History of the Cornell Public Library, Ithaca, New York, and the Cornell Library Association, 1864–1964.* Ithaca: The Library, 1969.
1362. Rogers, F. *The Story of a Small Town Library: The Development of the Woodstock, N.Y., Library.* Woodstock: Overlook Press, 1974.
1363. Rollins, O. H. "The Hepburn Libraries of the St. Lawrence Valley." Master's thesis, Western Reserve University, 1960. Published: University of Kentucky Press, Microcard Publications, Series B, Number 44.
1364. *Seventeen Years of Service of the Rochester Public Library, 1912–1928.* Rochester: Rochester Public Library, 1929.
1365. Shirley, N. "A Survey of Library Development in Hudson, N.Y." Master's thesis, State University of New York at Albany, 1963.
1366. Utica, New York. Public Library. *Utica Public Library, 1893–1908.* Utica: The Library, 1909.
1367. Wong, R. "A History of the Chatham Square Branch of the New York Public Library." Master's thesis, Pratt Institute, 1955.
1368. Young, B. A. "A Historical Study of the Countee Cullen Regional Branch Library of the New York Public Library System: Its Inception, Trends, Developments." Master's thesis, Southern Connecticut State College, 1969.

NORTH CAROLINA

1369. Aldrich, W. L. B. "The History of Public Library Service to Negroes in Salisbury, North Carolina, 1937–1963." Master's thesis, Atlanta University, 1964.
1370. Ballance, P. S., comp. *The First Fifty Years of Public Library Service in Winston-Salem, 1906–1956.* Winston-Salem: Public Library of Winston-Salem and Forsyth County, North Carolina, n.d.
1371. Batten, S. S. "The History of the Johnson County Public Library System, 1941–1951." Master's thesis, University of North Carolina, 1960.
1372. Cooke, A. M. "A History of the Public Library in Murphy, North Carolina." Master's thesis, Florida State University, 1962.
1373. Eury, W. "The Citizen's Library Movement in North Carolina." Master's thesis, George Peabody College for Teachers, 1951.
1374. Flournoy, M. W. *A Short History of the Public Library of Charlotte and Mecklenburg County, Charlotte, North Carolina.* Charlotte: Public Library of Charlotte and Mecklenburg County, 1952.
1375. Gardner, O. M. *The Significance of the Citizen's Library Movement.* Raleigh: North Carolina Library Association, 1929.
1376. Garrison, B. S. "A History of the Concord Public Library of Con-

cord, North Carolina." Master's thesis, University of North Carolina, 1965.
1377. Hoover, A. R. "History of the Carnegie Library of Charlotte and Mecklenburg County, North Carolina, 1903–1920." Master's thesis, University of North Carolina, 1968.
1378. Hunter, C. P. "A History of the Olivia Raney Library, 1899–1959." Master's thesis, University of North Carolina, 1964.
1379. Memory, M. W. "A History of the Randolph Public Library, 1935–1967." Master's thesis, University of North Carolina, 1968.
1380. Moore, B. L. "A History of Public Library Service to Negroes in Winston-Salem, North Carolina, 1927–1951." Master's thesis, Atlanta University, 1961.
1381. Murphy, S. B. "The History of the Rockingham County Library, 1930–1955." Master's thesis, University of North Carolina, 1956.
1382. Scoggin, R. B. "The Development of Public Library Services in Chowan, Tyrrell and Washington Counties." Master's thesis, University of North Carolina, 1967.
1383. Stewart, W. L. "A History of the High Point, North Carolina, Public Library." Master's thesis, University of North Carolina, 1963.
1384. Taylor, J. "Public Library Legislation in the State of North Carolina, 1897–June 30, 1956." Master's thesis, University of North Carolina, 1958. Published: University of Kentucky, Microcard Publications, Series B, Number 29.
1385. Van Oesen, E. "Public Library Extension in North Carolina and the WPA [1932–42]." *NCHR* 29 (1952): 379–99.
1386. Whedbee, M. M. "A History of the Development and Expansion of Bookmobile Service in North Carolina, 1923–1960." Master's thesis, University of North Carolina, 1962.

NORTH DAKOTA

1387. Brudvig, G. L. "Development of Public Library Service in North Dakota." *NDHQ* 31 (1963): 61–66.
1388. ———. "Public Libraries in North Dakota: The Formative Years, 1880–1920." Master's thesis, University of Minnesota, 1962.

OHIO

1389. Antrim, Mrs. S. *The County Library: The Pioneer County Library (the Brumback Library of Van Wert County, Ohio) and the County Library Movement in the United States . . .* Van Wert: The Pioneer Press, 1914.
1390. Arthur, A. W. "A History of the Warder Public Library, Springfield, Ohio." Master's thesis, Kent State University, 1955.
1391. Barnett, L. F. "A History of the Akron Public Library, 1874–1942." Master's thesis, Kent State University School of Library Science, 1974.

1392. Battles, F. M. "An Account of the Development of the Public Library Movement in Ohio, with Special Reference to Some Outstanding Libraries." Master's thesis, University of Illinois, 1928.
1393. Baughman, R. O. "Fifty-three Years of Progress: Public Libraries in Lima, Ohio, 1855–1908." Master's thesis, Western Reserve University, 1954.
1394. Blair, J. *Akron Public Library–One Hundred Years of Service, 1874–1974*. Akron: Friends of Akron–Summit County Public Library, 1974.
1395. Bollenbacher, B. "Cleveland Public Library." *ELIS* 5:197–205.
1396. ———, and Long, F. *The Proud Years, 1869–1969: A Pictorial History of the Cleveland Public Library*. Cleveland: The Library, 1970.
1397. Boone, H. H. "A History of the Salem (Ohio) Public Library." Master's thesis, Kent State University, 1962. Published: University of Kentucky Press, Microcard Publications, Series B, Number 53.
1398. Bowden, C. N. "The History of Lane Public Library, Hamilton, Ohio." Master's thesis, Western Reserve University, 1955.
1399. Bradley, N. B. "The Development of Service to Children in the Cleveland Public Library, with Special Reference to Perkins Library." Master's thesis, Western Reserve University, 1951.
1400. Brookover, B. "A History of the Leonard Case Library, Cleveland, Ohio, 1846–1941." Master's thesis, Western Reserve University, 1957.
1401. Burton, A. S. "The Cuyahoga County (Ohio) Library System: A History." Master's thesis, Western Reserve University, 1952.
1402. Butrick, M. W. "History of the Foreign Literature Department of the Cleveland Public Library, 1925–1972." Master's thesis, Kent State University, 1974.
1403. Buzzard, R. A. "History of Bookmobile Service, Dayton Public Library, Dayton, Ohio." Master's thesis, Western Reserve University, 1953.
1404. Cincinnati. Public Library. *A Decade of Service, 1930–1940*. Cincinnati: Public Library of Cincinnati and Hamilton County, 1941.
1405. Clarke, J. H. "The Public Library." In *A History of Cleveland, Ohio*, edited by S. P. Orth. Chicago: S. J. Clarke Publishing Co., 1910.
1406. Collins, L. T. "A History of the East Cleveland Public Library." Master's thesis, Western Reserve University, 1951.
1407. Copeland, E. F. "A History of the Carnegie West Branch of the Cleveland Public Library." Master's thesis, Western Reserve University, 1954.
1408. Cramer, C. H. *Open Shelves and Open Minds: A History of the Cleveland Public Library*. Cleveland: Western Reserve University Press, 1972.
1409. Crammer, J. C. "History and Development of Library Services in

the Township of Hudson, Summit County, Ohio." Master's thesis, Kent State University, 1950.

1410. Dax, E. R. "Land Public Library's First 100 Years." *OLAB* 36 (1966): 6–10.

1411. Eckert, C. J. "A History of the New Philadelphia–Tuscarawas County (Ohio) District Library." Master's thesis, Western Reserve University, 1955.

1412. Elias, W. D. "History of the Reed Memorial Library, Ravenna, Ohio." Master's thesis, Kent State University, 1961.

1413. Faries, E. "History of Libraries in Ohio." *OLAB* 31 (1961): 3–6.

1414. Fleischer, M. L. "A History of the Rocky River Public Library." Master's thesis, Western Reserve University, 1954.

1415. Forney, D. J. "The History of the East Palestine Public Library." Master's thesis, Western Reserve University, 1954.

1416. Galbreath, C. B. *The Library Movement in Ohio.* Columbus, 1909.

1417. ———, comp. *Sketches of Ohio Libraries.* Columbus: F. J. Heer, 1902.

1418. Gooch, R. E. "History of the Birchard Public Library and the Sandusky County Extension Service." Master's thesis, Western Reserve University, 1957.

1419. Goodale, G. "History of the Portage County Library, Ohio." Master's thesis, Western Reserve University, 1951.

1420. Greene, J. T. "A History and Description of the Literature Division of the Cleveland Public Library." Master's thesis, Western Reserve University, 1954.

1421. Harshfield, L. "The Wagnall's Memorial." Master's thesis, Western Reserve University, 1957.

1422. Havron, H. J. "A History of Library Service in Crawford County, Ohio." Master's thesis, Kent State University, 1969.

1423. Hazeltine, R. E. "The History of Birchard Library, Freemont, Ohio, 1847–1950." Master's thesis, Western Reserve University, 1950.

1424. Heim, H. R. "A History of the Lepper Library of Lisbon, Ohio." Master's thesis, Kent State University, 1965.

1425. Hibbs, J. E. "A History of the Toledo Public Library." *NWOQ* 46 46 (1974): 72–116.

1426. Hopkins, L. "The Development of the Local History and Genealogy Division of the Toledo Public Library." Master's thesis, Western Reserve University, 1957.

1427. Ingalls, M. E. "The History and Description of the Philosophy and Religion Division of the Cleveland Public Library." Master's thesis, Western Reserve University, 1954.

1428. Lewis, M. E. "A History of the Mount Vernon, Ohio, Public Library, 1888–1949." Master's thesis, Western Reserve University, 1950.

1429. MacCampbell, B. B. "History of the Kent, Ohio, Free Library." Master's thesis, Western Reserve University, 1950.

1430. Meshot, G. V. "A History of the Hubbard Public Library." Master's thesis, Western Reserve University, 1949.
1431. Metz, C. A. "The Brumback Library of Van Wert County." *OEM* 61 (1912): 202–05.
1432. Moss, Mrs. F. C. B. "The Evolution of the Sandusky Free Library." *FP* 13 (1900): 658–67.
1433. Murray, K. "History of the Development of Bookmobile Service, Hamilton County, Ohio." Master's thesis, Western Reserve University, 1951.
1434. Murray, M. E. "The Branch Library: A Mirror of Its Community, with Case Histories of Several Branches of the Cleveland Public Library." Master's thesis, Western Reserve University, 1951.
1435. Mutschler, H. F. "The Ohio Public Library and State Aid." Master's thesis, Western Reserve University, 1952.
1436. Nagy, M. C. "History and Relationship of the Rice Branch Library to Its Hungarian Patrons." Master's thesis, Western Reserve University, 1952.
1437. Nestleroad, R. "A History of Fifty Years of Library Service: Napoleon Public Library, Napoleon, Ohio." Master's thesis, Western Reserve University, 1956.
1438. Nolan, C. "The History of the County Library in Ohio." Master's thesis, Western Reserve University, 1949.
1439. Pardee, H. L. *A Story of the Akron Public Library, 1834–1942*. Akron: Published by the Library, 1943.
1440. Phillips, V. "Fifty-six Years of Service to the Foreign-born by the Cleveland Public Library." Master's thesis, Western Reserve University, 1957.
1441. Reed, M. M. "History of the Lakewood Public Library, Lakewood, Ohio: The First Twenty-five Years, 1913–1938." Master's thesis, Western Reserve University, 1959.
1442. Ring, D. F. "The Cleveland Public Library and the WPA: A Study in Creative Partnership." *OH* 84 (1975): 158–64.
1443. Rodstein, F. M. "The East 79th Street Branch of the Cleveland Public Library: An Historical Overview, 1909–1970." Master's thesis, Kent State University, 1971.
1444. Ryberg, H. T. "Warren Public Library: A History." Master's thesis, Western Reserve University, 1957.
1445. Schryver, N. E. "A History of the Business Information Bureau of the Cleveland Public Library." Master's thesis, Western Reserve University, 1950.
1446. Shamp, B. K. "The Music Section of the Cleveland Public Library." Master's thesis, Western Reserve University, 1954.
1447. Sheffield, H. G. "A Report on the History and Development of the Library for the Blind of the Cleveland Public Library." Master's thesis, Western Reserve University, 1951.
1448. Shewmaker, J. D. "History of the Willoughby Public Library, Wil-

loughby, Ohio." Master's thesis, Western Reserve University, 1953.
1449. Silver, R. A. "A Description and History of the Foreign Literature Division of the Cleveland Public Library." Master's thesis, Western Reserve University, 1953.
1450. Somerville, S. A. "A Brief History of the Public Libraries of Mentor, Ohio." Master's thesis, Kent State University, 1962. Published: University of Kentucky Press, Microcard Publications, Series B, Number 59.
1451. Spaulding, V. A. "A History of the Two Public Libraries in Mentor, Ohio." Master's thesis, Western Reserve University, 1950.
1452. Stratton, G. W. "History of the Solon Public Library." Master's thesis, Kent State University, 1972.
1453. Szkudlarek, M. E. "Historical Development of Work with Children in the Toledo Public Library." Master's thesis, Western Reserve University, 1954.
1454. Thomas, M. E. "History of Public Library Service in Jackson County, Ohio." Master's thesis, Kent State University, 1963.
1455. Toledo Public Library. *The Toledo Public Library: A Century of Progress, 1838–1938.* Toledo, 1938.
1456. Vandemark, P. "The Cleveland Public Library: 1869–1969." *WLB* 43 (1969): 728–33.
1457. Weis, L. A. "The History of Children's Work at Akron Public Library in Akron, Ohio." Master's thesis, Western Reserve University, 1951.
1458. Weller, J. M. "160 Years of Library Service to Cincinnati and Hamilton County." In *Contributions to Mid-West Library History*, edited by T. Eaton, pp. 1–53. Champaign: Illini Union Bookstore, 1964.
1459. Wine, E. "The Development of the Dayton Public Library, Dayton, Ohio, 1900–1957." Master's thesis, Western Reserve University, 1958.
1460. Yockey, R. "The Winged Bequest: An Account of the Cleveland Public Library's Service to the Incapacitated." Master's thesis, Western Reserve University, 1949.
1461. Young, M. J. "The Akron Public Library, 1942–1957." Master's thesis, Western Reserve University, 1958.

OKLAHOMA

1462. Henke, E. M. "The History of Public Libraries in Oklahoma." Master's thesis, University of Oklahoma, 1954.

OREGON

1463. Anderson, K. E. *Historical Sketch of the Library Association of Portland, 1864–1964.* [Multnomah County Library]. Portland, 1964.
1464. Barrett, M. "History of Oregon Public Libraries." Master's thesis, University of Oregon, 1940.
1465. Kirchem, C. E. "Library Development in Clackamas County, Oregon." Master's thesis, University of Washington, 1952.
1466. *Public Library Buildings in Oregon, 1905–1955.* Portland: Oregon State Library, 1955.

PENNSYLVANIA

1467. Ambler, B. H. "History of the Children's Department of the Free Library of Philadelphia, 1898–1953." Master's thesis, Drexel Institute of Technology, 1956.
1468. Barker, J. W. "The History and Development of the Monessen Public Library, Monessen, Pennsylvania." Master's thesis, Western Reserve University, 1953.
1469. Diana, J. P. "History of the Osterhout Free Library, 1889–1961." Master's thesis, Marywood College (Scranton, Penn.), 1961.
1470. Di Pietro, L. N. "The Free Library of Philadelphia: Its Formation and Early Physical Growth from 1891 to 1917." Master's thesis, Drexel Institute of Technology, 1952.
1471. Doms, K. "Free Library of Philadelphia." *ELIS* 9:105–11.
1472. Egolf, J. L. "A History of the Bethlehem Public Library, Bethlehem, Pennsylvania, 1901 to 1954." Master's thesis, Drexel Institute of Technology, 1955.
1473. Girvin, C. M. "The Allentown Free Library: A History of Its Growth and Services." Master's thesis, Drexel Institute of Technology, 1954.
1474. Heizmann, L. J. *The Library That Would Not Die: The Turbulent History of the Reading Public Library.* Reading, Penn.: Reading Eagle Press, 1971.
1475. Keim, A. "The History of Cambria Free Library, Johnstown, Pennsylvania, 1925–1951." Master's thesis, Drexel Institute of Technology, 1952.
1476. Klugiewicz, E. "Short History of the Erie (Penn.) Public Library." Master's thesis, Western Reserve University, 1953.
1477. Lingfelter, M. R. *Books on Wheels.* New York: Funk and Wagnalls, 1938.
1478. Martin Memorial Library, York, Pennsylvania. *The Founding and the Establishment of the Martin Memorial Library of York, Pennsylvania, and Its Founder, Wilton Daniel Martin, with the Program of Presentation of the Library to the Public of York and York County.* York, Penn., 1935.

1479. Mathews, E. L. "Public Libraries of Pennsylvania." *PLN* 14 (1934): 402–07.
1480. Meyer, W. P. "A History of the Reading, Pennsylvania, Public Library, and Its Services to the Community, 1898–1952." Master's thesis, Drexel Institute of Technology, 1953.
1481. Montgomery, T. L. "A Survey of Pennsylvania Libraries." *PLN* 6 (1913): 45–59.
1482. Munn, R. "Books Alive Since '95: Celebrating Fifty Years of Library Service to the People of Pittsburgh." *CarnM* 19 (1945): 99–103.
1483. ———. "Carnegie Library of Pittsburgh." *ELIS* 4:207–11.
1484. ———. *Carnegie Library of Pittsburgh: A Brief History and Description.* Pittsburgh: Carnegie Library of Pittsburgh, 1968.
1485. Philadelphia City Institute. *The One Hundredth Anniversary of the Philadelphia City Institute: A Branch of the Free Library of Philadelphia.* [Philadelphia, 1952].
1486. Philadelphia Free Library. *Decade of Growth, 1951–1960: The Free Library of Philadelphia.* Philadelphia, 1961.
1487. Potera, E. J. "History of the Back Mountain Memorial Library, Dallas, Pennsylvania." Master's thesis, Marywood College (Scranton, Penn), 1969.
1488. Shaffer, E. "The Rare Book Department, Free Library of Philadelphia." *PBSA* 64 (1970): 1–11.
1489. Smith, M. H. "Three Rural Libraries of Chester County, Pennsylvania: A Historical Survey of Their Development and Services to the Community." Master's thesis, Drexel Institute of Technology, 1950.
1490. Tuck, R. S. "Evolution of the Chester County Library: A History." Master's thesis, Drexel Institute of Technology, 1954.
1491. Whitney, E. M. "History of the Morristown (Penn.) Public Library." Master's thesis, Drexel Institute of Technology, 1955.
1492. Winger, A. K. "History of the Huntingdon County Library, Huntingdon, Pennsylvania, 1935–1953." Master's thesis, Drexel Institute of Technology, 1954.

RHODE ISLAND

1493. Foster, W. E. *The First Fifty Years at the Providence Public Library, 1878–1928.* Providence: Providence Public Library, 1928.
1494. [Gardner, H. B.]. *The History and Present Need of the Providence Public Library.* Providence: Livermore and Knight Co., 1926.
1495. Harding, Sister M. F. "A History of the Providence Public Library, Providence, Rhode Island, from 1878 to 1960." Master's thesis, Catholic University of America, 1964.
1496. Koopman, H. L. "Library Progress in Rhode Island." *LJ* 31 (1906): conf. no. 10–17.

1497. Palmer, H. R. "The Libraries of Rhode Island." *NEM* 22 (1900): 478–500.
1498. Sherman, S. C. *The First Ninety Years of the Providence Public Library, 1878–1968*. Providence, 1968.

SOUTH CAROLINA

1499. Bowers, C. W. "The History and Development of the Newberry County (South Carolina) Library." Master's thesis, University of South Carolina, 1942.
1500. Jarrell, P. H. "The Development of the County Library System in South Carolina from 1929 to 1943." Master's thesis, University of North Carolina, 1955.
1501. Orlando, P. "The Rocky Bottom, South Carolina, Transient Camp Library." Master's thesis, Southern Connecticut State College, 1960.
1502. Stringfellow, K. "History of Chester County Library." *SCL* 5 (1960): 19–21.

SOUTH DAKOTA

1503. Crouch, M. L. "The Library Movement in South Dakota with Special Reference to Some Outstanding Libraries." Master's thesis, University of Illinois, 1930.
1504. "Histories of South Dakota Libraries by Their Librarians." *SDLB* 49 (1963): whole issue.

TENNESSEE

1505. Buck, J. P. "A History of the Library Resources of Putnam County." Master's thesis, Tennessee Polytechnic Institute, 1961.
1506. Govan, J. F. "The History of the Chattanooga Public Library, 1905–1950." Master's thesis, Emory University, 1955.
1507. Hansbrough, I. C. "Public Library Service to Negroes in Knoxville, Tennessee." Master's thesis, Atlanta University, 1959.
1508. Hoffman, R. P. "A History of Public Library Services to Negroes in Memphis, Tennessee." Master's thesis, Atlanta University, 1955.
1509. McCrary, M. E. "A History of Public Library Service to Negroes in Nashville, Tennessee, 1916–1958." Master's thesis, Atlanta University, 1959.
1510. Moore, Mrs. J. T. "The First Century of Library History in Tennessee, 1813–1913." *PETHS* 16 (1944): 3–21.

TEXAS

1511. Allen, D. L. "The Kemp Public Library: A History, 1896–1963." Master's thesis, University of Texas, 1965.

1512. Barnes, G. S. "A History of Public Library Service to Negroes in Galveston, Texas, 1904–1955." Master's thesis, Atlanta University, 1957.
1513. Bradshaw, L. M. "Dallas Public Library." *ELIS* 6:407–17.
1514. Cody, N. B. "Historical Development of Public Libraries in Gregg County, Texas." Master's thesis, East Texas State College, 1959.
1515. Downing, M. "The W.P.A. and the Acquisition of the Fort Worth Public Library Building, 1933–1939." *TL* 27 (1965): 126–32.
1516. Fulton, S. "Waxahachie's Sims Library, One of the State's Oldest." *TL* 37 (1975): 119–128.
1517. Gillespie, R. C. "La Retama Public Library: Its Origin and Development, 1909–1952." Master's thesis, University of Texas, 1953.
1518. Jeffress, I. P. "The Friends of the Seguin Guadalupe County Public Library: History and Analysis, 1954–66." Master's thesis, University of Texas, 1967.
1519. Lee, R. E. "Texas Library Development: Its Relation to the Carnegie Movement, 1898–1915." Master's thesis, University of Texas, 1959.
1520. Mason, L. G. "The Founding of the Beaumont, Texas, Public Library, 1850–1926." Master's thesis, Texas State College, 1951.
1521. Smith, M. H. K. "A History of the Libraries of Bonham, Texas." Master's thesis, East Texas State College, 1963.
1522. Suhler, S. A. "The Austin Public Library, 1926–1956." Master's thesis, University of Texas, 1959.
1523. Swogetinsky, B. A. "A Study of Censorial Demands on Texas Libraries, 1952–1957." Master's thesis, University of Texas, 1967.
1524. Teague, A. H. "Carnegie Library Building Grants to Texas Communities: A Brief Account and a Comparison." Master's thesis, University of Texas, 1967.
1525. Wales, B. "Through Many Generations . . . Rosenburg Library's First 50 Years [Galveston, 1900–1954]." *TLJ* 30 (1954): 200–02.
1526. Woodman, J. "The Fort Worth Public Library [1892–1952]." *JrH* 3 (1953): 29–30.
1527. Wyche, B. "Free Public Libraries in Texas: Ten Years Growth, 1899–1909." *TL* 31 (1969): 88–89.

VERMONT

1528. Coolidge, Mrs. O. H. "A Golden Anniversary: The Founding and the History of the Rutland Free Library." *VLB* 31 (1936): 54–56.
1529. Ellis, M. "The History of the Brookfield Library." *VQ* 18 (1950): 29–32.
1530. Johnson, L. B. "The Kimball Public Library [Randolph, Vt.]." *Vermonter* 8 (1903): 300–03.

1531. Vermont. Free Public Library Commission. *Libraries in Vermont* . . . Montpelier, 1938.

VIRGINIA

1532. Brandt, B. S. "The Alexandria, Virginia, Library: Its History, Present Facilities, and Future Program." Master's thesis, Catholic University of America, 1950.
1533. Elliott, M. E. "The Development of Library Service in Fairfax County, Virginia, Since 1939." Master's thesis, Drexel Institute of Technology, 1951.
1534. Hoover, F. R. "The Rockingham Public Library, 1928–1947." *MadQ* 8 (1948): 74–85.
1535. Moyers, J. C. "History of the Rockingham Public Library, Harrisonburg, Virginia." Master's thesis, University of North Carolina, 1959.

WASHINGTON

1536. Brass, L. J. *Eighty Years of Service: A History of the Children's Department, Seattle Public Library*. Seattle: Seattle Public Library, 1971.
1537. Hake, S. D. "A History of Library Development in Kittitas County, Washington." Master's thesis, University of Washington, 1953.
1538. Johns, H. "The Founding of the Longview [Washington] Public Library." *PNLAQ* 15 (1951): 116–22.
1539. Newson, H. E. "Fort Vancouver Regional Library: A Study of the Development of Public Library Service in Clark and Skamania Counties, Washington." Master's thesis, University of Washington, 1954.
1540. Orr, M. F. "Development of the Walla Walla Public Library." Master's thesis, University of Washington, 1953.
1541. Pitcher, P. M. "A Historical Study of Library Development in Chelan County, Washington." Master's thesis, University of Washington, 1952.
1542. Strother, J. V. "The Development and the Adequacy of the Library as an Institution in the State of Washington." Master's thesis, University of Washington, 1938.
1543. Wallace, W. S. "Founding the Public Library in Yakima." *PNQ* 45 (1954): 95–101.
1544. Ward, B. A. "A History of Public Library Development in Whitman County, Washington." Master's thesis, University of Washington, 1960.

WEST VIRGINIA

1545. Wade, B. A. "History of the Waitman Barbe Public Library of Morgantown, West Virginia, 1926–1956." Master's thesis, Western Reserve University, 1957.
1546. White, A. W. "The Public Library Movement in West Virginia." Master's thesis, Columbia University, 1935.

WISCONSIN

1547. Colson, J. "The Public Library Movement in Wisconsin, 1836–1900." Doctoral dissertation, University of Chicago, 1973.
1548. ———. "'Public Spirit' at Work: Philanthropy and Public Libraries in Nineteenth-Century Wisconsin." *WMH* 59 (1976): 192–209.
1549. Ela, J. *Free and Public*. Madison: Madison Public Library, 1974.
1550. "History of the Wisconsin Library Commission." *WisLB* 5 (1909): 287–89.
1551. Lester, C. B. "The Library Movement in Wisconsin." In *Wisconsin: Its History and Its People*, edited by M. M. Quaife, vol. 2, pp. 411–32. Chicago: S. J. Clark Publishing Co., 1924.
1552. MacLeod, D. I. *Carnegie Libraries in Wisconsin*. Madison: Published for the Department of History, University of Wisconsin, by the State Historical Society of Wisconsin, 1968.
1553. Malone, E. G. "The Madison Free Library Since the Ulveling-Rutzen Survey of 1951." Master's thesis, University of Wisconsin, 1958.
1554. Mills, F. L., and Hurley, L. J. "History of Racine Public Library Lectures: 1927–1966." *IllL* 48 (1966): 540–43.
1555. Saucerman, K. "A Study of the Wisconsin Library Movement, 1850–1900." Master's thesis, University of Wisconsin, 1944.
1556. Stearns, L. E., ed. "Wisconsin Supplement." *LJ* 21 (1896): 171–94.
1557. Wisconsin Free Library Commission. *Free Traveling Libraries in Wisconsin: The Story of Their Growth, Purposes and Development; With Accounts of a Few Kindred Movements*. Madison: Wisconsin Free Library Commission, 1897.

WYOMING

1558. Hayden, E. C. "Teton County Library: Its Birth and Growth, Jackson, Wyoming." *WLR* 10 (1954): 2–4.

VI. Academic Libraries

The significant historical literature pertaining to America's academic libraries consists primarily of research originally undertaken in doctoral study. Although several monographs exist, much research remains only in dissertation form or in condensed journal articles.

For more than forty years Louis Shores' pioneering work *Origins of the American College Library, 1638–1800* (1934, **1623**) has been the starting point for scholars seeking an overview of the colonial beginnings. The appendices and bibliography are still useful, though the latter is now dated. Other work has sought to build on this foundation on both chronological and topical bases.

Chronologically, Joe Kraus has developed some of the same general material as Shores, but in much more specific detail. His dissertation, "Book Collections of Five Colonial College Libraries: A Subject Analysis" (1960, **1599**), has yielded several printed articles on the subject and has inspired the author to further work in the analysis of collections. Howard Clayton attempted to carry the story further in his "The American College Library: 1800–1860" (1968, **1573**). Much earlier W. N. C. Carlton reviewed the end of this period in his "College Libraries in the Mid-Nineteenth Century" (1907, **1571**). Kenneth Brough has dealt with the period 1876 to 1946 in his *Scholar's Workshop: Evolving Conceptions of Library Service* (1953, **1566**), which treats four major research libraries–Harvard, Yale, Columbia, and Chicago–in great detail. The recent anthology, *Libraries for Teaching, Libraries for Research: Essays for a Century*, edited by Richard D. Johnson (Chicago: American Library Association, 1977), consists of articles published in *College and Research Libraries* during 1976. These appear individually in this chapter.

Several major efforts illustrate the topical approach within the chronological framework. Thomas Harding documented a major ingredient to developing academic libraries in his *College Literary Societies* (1971, **1588**), which treats the period to 1876. J. Periam Danton's *Book Selection and Collections: A Comparison of German and American University Libraries* (1963, **1575**) offers insightful observations on research collections from the nineteenth-century acceleration to the mid-twentieth century. A final example of the topical studies is the dissertation by Neil Radford, "The Carnegie Corporation and the Development of American College Libraries, 1928–1941" (1972, **1615**).

Individual college and university libraries have attracted the attention of an unusual number of students as topics for master's and doctoral studies. Naturally not all are of high quality with respect to analysis and interpretive judgment. Most of them treat a limited period of time, often corresponding to one librarian's tenure. Collegiate institutions have generally been subjected to study by master's candidates, while major research libraries have appealed to more serious students. The latter group includes dissertations by Roscoe Rouse on the Baylor University Library (1962, **1940**), Kenneth Peterson on the University of California at Berkeley's Library (1968, **1650**), Haynes McMullen on the University of Chicago Library (1949, **1697**), Winifred Linderman on the Columbia University Library (1959, **1844**), Wayne Yenawine on the University of Illinois Library (1955, **1704**), Mildred Lowell on Indiana University Library (1957, **1707**), Russell Bidlack on the University of Michigan Library (1954, **1812**), James Skipper on the Ohio State University Library (1960, **1890**), Louis Moloney on the University of Texas Library (1970, **1939**), C. C. Gorchels on the University of Washington Library (1971, **1956**), and Robert Munn on the University of West Virginia Library (1962, **1960**).

Aside from Peterson's *The University of California Library at Berkeley, 1900–1945* (1970, **1650**), these dissertations have remained unpublished in monograph form, though related journal articles appear from time to time. Other university presses have published histories of local libraries, such as John Jennings's *The Library of the College of William and Mary in Virginia, 1693–1793* (1968, **1949**), Harry Clemons's *The University of Virginia Library* (1954, **1945**), and J. Orin Oliphant's *The Library of Bucknell University* (1962, **1910**).

As the foundational studies of individual libraries continue to grow in number, one will not be surprised to see more general, "second generation" studies appear. One early example of this type is Benjamin Powell's "The Development of Libraries in Southern State Universities to 1920" (1946, **1612**), which also offers some comparisons with northern universities. A later example is Robert Brundin's "Changing Patterns of Library Service in Five California Junior Colleges, 1907–1967" (1970, **1645**).

Other sources lead to depth and breadth in printed materials. The biography section of this bibliography includes titles dealing with academic libraries which should be considered. Richard Harwell's article "College Libraries" in the *Encyclopedia of Library and Information Science* (1971, **1590**) provides a fresh overview with provocative insights for research. The *Encyclopedia* also includes numerous lengthy entries for individual academic and research libraries.

Academic Libraries

A. General Studies

1559. Almy, P. "Background and Development of the Junior College Library." *LibT* 14 (1965): 123–31.
1560. Andrews, T. "Trends in College Library Buildings." Master's thesis, University of Chicago, 1945.
1561. Armour, A. W., ed. "College Library Routine a Century Ago." *ACJ* 3 (January 1951): 26–29.
1562. Back, H. "The Snows of Yesteryear." *CRL* 30 (1969): 301–06.
1563. Barous, T. R. *Carnegie Corporation and College Libraries, 1938–1943.* New York: Carnegie Corporation, 1943.
1564. Bishop, W. W. *Carnegie Corporation and College Libraries, 1929–1938.* New York: Carnegie Corporation, 1938.
1565. Boll, J. J. "Library Architecture 1800–1875: A Comparison of Theory and Buildings with Emphasis on New England College Libraries." Doctoral dissertation, University of Illinois, 1961.
1566. Brough, K. J. *Scholar's Workshop: Evolving Conceptions of Library Service.* Urbana: University of Illinois Press, 1953.
1567. Brumbaugh, W. D. "Developmental Aspects of Film Library Centers in Selected Colleges and Universities from 1942–1951." *SE* 4 (1953): 65–69.
1568. Bryant, D. W. "The Changing Research Library." *HLB* 22 (1974): 365–73.
1569. Buchanan, L. B. "Library Buildings of Teachers' Colleges, 1932–1942." Master's thesis, Columbia University, 1944.
1570. Buchanan, R. E. "The Development and Function of a Research Library, 1922–46." *CRL* 8 (1947): 294–97.
1571. Carlton, W. N. C. "College Libraries in the Mid-Nineteenth Century." *LJ* 32 (1907): 479–86.
1572. Church, F. E. "A Historical Survey of the Libraries in a Group of State Normal Schools Prior to 1900." Master's thesis, Columbia University, 1931.
1573. Clayton, H. "The American College Library: 1800–1860." *JLH* 3 (1968): 129–37.
1574. "College Libraries." In U.S. Bureau of Education, *Public Libraries in the United States of America . . .* , pp. 60–126. Washington, D.C.: Government Printing Office, 1876.
1575. Danton, J. P. *Book Selection and Collections: A Comparison of German and American University Libraries.* New York: Columbia University Press, 1963.
1576. Doherty, F. X. "The New England Deposit Library History and Development." *LQ* 18 (1948): 245–54.
1577. Downs, R. B. "The Growth of Research Collections." *LibT* 25 (1976): 55–80.

1578. ———. "The Role of the Academic Librarian, 1876–1976." *CRL* 37 (1976): 491–502.
1579. ———. "Status of Academic Librarians in Retrospect." In *A Case for Faculty Status for Academic Librarians*, edited by L. C. Branscomb, pp. 111–18. Chicago: American Library Association, 1970.
1580. Dunlap, C. R. "Organizational Patterns in Academic Libraries, 1876–1976." *CRL* 37 (1976): 395–407.
1581. Edelman, H., and Tatum, G. M. "The Development of Collections in American University Libraries." *CRL* 37 (1976): 222–45.
1582. Erickson, E. W. *College and University Library Surveys, 1938–1952*. Chicago: American Library Association, 1961.
1583. Evans, L. H. "Research Libraries in the War Period, 1939–45." *LQ* (1947): 241–62.
1584. Gelfand, M. A. "A Historical Study of the Evaluation of Libraries in Higher Institutions by the Middle States Association of Colleges and Secondary Schools." Doctoral dissertation, New York University, 1960.
1585. Gilchrist, D. B. "The Evolution of College and University Libraries." *BALA* 20 (1926): 293–99.
1586. Gossage, W. "The American Library College Movement to 1968: The Library as Curriculum and Teaching with Books." *ELB* 18 (1975): 1–21.
1587. Guild, R. A. "The College Library." *LJ* 10 (1885): 216–21.
1588. Harding, T. S. *College Literary Societies*. Brooklyn: Pageant-Poseidon, 1971.
1589. ———. "College Literary Societies: Their Contribution to the Development of Academic Libraries, 1815–76." *LQ* 29 (1959): 1–26; 29 (1959): 94–112.
1590. Harwell, R. "College Libraries in 1876." *ELIS* 5:269–81.
1591. Holley, E. G. "Academic Libraries in 1876." *CRL* 37 (1976): 15–47.
1592. Johnson, E. R. "The Development of the Subject-Divisional Plan in American University Libraries." Doctoral dissertation, University of Wisconsin, 1974.
1593. Jones, H. G. "Archival Training in American Universities, 1938–1968." *AAr* 31 (1968): 135–54.
1594. Kansfield, N. J. "The Origins of Protestant Theological Seminary Libraries in the United States." Master's thesis, University of Chicago, 1970.
1595. Kaplan, L. "The Midwest Inter-Library Center, 1949–1964." *JLH* 10 (1975): 291–310.
1596. Kaser, D. "A Century of Academic Librarianship as Reflected in the Literature." *CRL* 37 (1976): 110–27.
1597. Knoer, Sister M. M. A. "A Historical Survey of the Libraries of Certain Catholic Institutions of Learning in the United States." Master's thesis, University of Illinois, 1930.

1598. Kraus, J. W. "The Book Collections of Early American College Libraries." *LQ* 43 (1973): 142–59.
1599. ———. "Book Collections of Five Colonial College Libraries: A Subject Analysis." Doctoral dissertation, University of Illinois, 1960.
1600. Kulp, A. C. "The Historical Development of Storage Libraries in America." Master's thesis, University of Illinois, 1953. Published: Association of College and Research Libraries Microcard, Number 12.
1601. Leach, S. "The Growth Rates of Major Academic Libraries: Rider and Purdue Reviewed." *CRL* 37 (1976): 531–42.
1602. Lemke, D. H. "Origins, Structures and Activities of Five Academic Library Consortia." Doctoral dissertation, Indiana University, 1975.
1603. Lowell, M. H. "College and University Library Consolidations." Master's thesis, University of Chicago, 1939.
1604. Martens, A. "A Study of the History and Development of the Protestant Theological Seminary Library Movement in the United States." Master's thesis, Southern Connecticut State College, 1958.
1605. McElderry, S. "Readers and Resources: Public Services in Academic and Research Libraries, 1876–1976." *CRL* 37 (1976): 408–20.
1606. Metcalf, K. D. "Six Influential Academic and Research Librarians." *CRL* 37 (1976): 332–45.
1607. Miller, L. A. "Changing Patterns of Circulation Services in University Libraries." Doctoral dissertation, Florida State University, 1971.
1608. Muller, R. H. "College and University Library Buildings, 1929–1949." *CRL* 12 (1951): 261–65.
1609. Orne, J. "Academic Library Buildings: A Century in Review." *CRL* 37 (1976): 316–31.
1610. Orr, R. S. "Financing and Philanthropy in the Building of Academic Libraries Constructed Between 1919 and 1958." Master's thesis, Western Reserve University, 1959.
1611. Powell, B. E. "Collection Development in Southeastern Libraries Since 1948." *SEL* 24 (1975): 59–67.
1612. ———. "The Development of Libraries in Southern State Universities to 1920." Doctoral dissertation, University of Chicago, 1946.
1613. ———. "Southern University Libraries During the Civil War." *WLB* 31 (1956): 250–54, 259.
1614. Radford, N. A. "Academic Library Surveys Prior to 1930." *JLH* 8 (1973): 150–58.
1615. ———. "The Carnegie Corporation and the Development of American College Libraries, 1928–1941." Doctoral dissertation, University of Chicago, 1972.

1616. Reynolds, H. M. "University Library Buildings in the United States, 1890–1939." Master's thesis, University of Illinois, 1946.
1617. ———. "University Library Buildings in the United States, 1890–1939." *CRL* 14 (1953): 149–57.
1618. Rothstein, S. "From Reaction to Interaction: The Development of the North American University Library." *CLJ* 29 (1972): 111–15.
1619. ———. "Service to Academia." In *A Century of Service: Librarianship in the United States and Canada*, edited by S. L. Jackson et al., pp. 79–109. Chicago: American Library Association, 1976.
1620. Rouse, R. "The Libraries of Nineteenth Century College Societies." In *Books in America's Past*, edited by D. Kaser, pp. 26–42. Charlottesville: University of Virginia, 1966.
1621. Schorr, A. E. "Library-College and Its Critics Since 1965: A Bibliographic Essay." *PNLAQ* 40 (1975): 4–11.
1622. Shiflett, O. L. "The Origins of American Academic Librarianship, 1876–1923." Doctoral dissertation, Florida State University, 1976.
1623. Shores, L. *Origins of the American College Library, 1638–1800.* New York: Barnes and Noble, 1934.
1624. Skelley, G. T. "Characteristics of Collections Added to American Research Libraries, 1940–1970: A Preliminary Investigation." *CRL* (1975): 52–60.
1625. Smith, J. C. "Patterns of Growth in Library Resources in Certain Land-Grant Universities." Doctoral dissertation, University of Illinois, 1964.
1626. Stanford, E. B. "Federal Aid for Academic Library Construction." *LJ* 99 (1974): 112–15.
1627. Storie, C. P. "The American College Society Library and the College Library." *CRL* 6 (1945): 240–48.
1628. ———. "What Contributions Did the American College Society Library Make to the History of the American College Library?" Master's thesis, Columbia University, 1938.
1629. Strauss, L. H. "The Liberal Arts College Library, 1929–1940: A Comparative Interpretation of Financial Statistics of Sixty-Eight Representative and Twenty Selected Liberal Arts College Libraries." Master's thesis, University of Chicago, 1942.
1630. Stevens, N. D. "Three Early Academic Library Surveys." *CRL* 30 (1969): 498–505.
1631. Stewart, N. "Sources for the Study of American College Library History, 1800–1876." *LQ* 13 (1943): 227–31.
1632. Thompson, L. S. "The Historical Background of Departmental and Collegiate Libraries." *LQ* 12 (1942): 49–74.
1633. ———. "University Libraries and the Future of Scholarship in the South [1920–50]." *SAQ* 50 (1951): 192–98.
1634. Thurber, E. "American Agricultural College Libraries, 1862–1900." *CRL* 6 (1945): 346–52.

1635. ———. "The Library of the Land-Grant College, 1862–1900." Master's thesis, Columbia University, 1928.
1636. Tuttle, H. W. "From Cutter to Computer: Technical Services in Academic and Research Libraries, 1876–1976." *CRL* 37 (1976): 421–51.
1637. Veit, F. "Library Service to College Students." *LibT* 25 (1976): 361–78.
1638. Wadsworth, R. W. "Notes on the Development of Music Collections in American Academic Libraries." Master's thesis, University of Chicago, 1943.
1639. Wallace, J. O. "Newcomer to the Academic Scene: The Two-Year College Library/Learning Center." *CRL* 37 (1976): 503–13.
1640. Weber, D. C. "A Century of Cooperative Programs Among Academic Librarians." *CRL* 37 (1976): 205–21.
1641. Wilson, L. R. *The Emergence of the College Library: An Address by Dr. Louis R. Wilson.* New York: Carnegie Corporation of New York, 1931.
1642. Winsor, J. "The Development of the Library." *LJ* 19 (1894): 370–75.
1643. Yueh, N. N. "The Development of Library Collections at Former State Teacher Education Institutions: 1920–1970, with Special Consideration of Six New Jersey State Colleges." Doctoral dissertation, Columbia University, 1974.

B. Special Studies Arranged by State

ARIZONA

1644. Heisser, W. A. "A Historical Survey of the Phoenix College Library: Phoenix, Arizona, 1925–1957." Master's thesis, Arizona State College, 1958.

CALIFORNIA

1645. Brundin, R. E. "Changing Patterns of Library Service in Five California Junior Colleges, 1907–1967." Doctoral dissertation, Stanford University, 1970.
1646. Coney, D., and Michel, J. G. "The Berkeley Library of the University of California: Some Notes on Its Formation." *LibT* 15 (1966): 286–302.
1647. Hansen, R. W. "The Stanford University Library: Genesis 1891–1906." *JLH* 9 (1974): 138–58.
1648. Laudine, Sister M. "The Honnold Library of Claremont College: Its History and Services, 1952–1961." Master's thesis, Immaculate Heart College, 1961.

1649. Paul, G. N. "The Development of the Hoover Institution on War, Revolution and Peace Library, 1919–1944." Doctoral dissertation, University of California, 1974.
1650. Peterson, K. G. *The University of California Library at Berkeley, 1900–1945*. Berkeley: University of California Press, 1970.
1651. Powell, L. C. "From Private Collection to Public Institution: The William Andrews Clark Memorial Library." *LQ* 20 (1950): 101–08.
1652. Smith, D. "History of the University of California Library to 1900." Master's thesis, University of California, 1930. Published: Association of College and Research Libraries Microcard, Number 21.

COLORADO

1653. Wilson, E. H. "A Century with Friends of the [University of Colorado] Libraries." *ON* 16 (1976): 1–8.

CONNECTICUT

1654. Bassett, J. S. "The Trinity College Library." *TA* 16 (1905): 273–79.
1655. Bryant, L. M., and Patterson, M., comps. "The List of Books Sent by Jeremiah Dummer." In *Papers in Honor of Andrew Keogh, Librarian of Yale University*, edited by M. C. Withington, pp. 421–92. New Haven: Privately printed, 1938.
1656. Clarke, M. G. M. *David Watkinson's Library: One Hundred Years in Hartford, Connecticut, 1866–1966*. Hartford: Trinity College Press, 1966.
1657. Colla, Sister M. B. "A History of the Pope Pius XII Library, St. Joseph College, West Hartford, Connecticut, 1932–1962." Master's thesis, Catholic University of America, 1964.
1658. Fuller, H. M. "Bishop Berkeley as a Benefactor of Yale." *YULG* 28 (1953): 1–18.
1659. Gilman, D. C. "Bishop Berkeley's Gifts to Yale College [1733]." *PNHCHS* 1 (1865): 147–70.
1660. Hegel, R. "Some Libraries of Yale's Old Campus." *JNHCHS* 17 (1968): 117–52.
1661. Kennett, Sister M. E., F.S.E "Annhurst College Library, South Woodstock, Connecticut, 1941–1967." Master's thesis, Southern Connecticut State College, 1968.
1662. Keogh, A. "Bishop Berkeley's Gift of Books in 1733." *YULG* 8 (1933): 1–26.
1663. Powers, Z. J. "A Yale Bibliophile in European Book Shops." In *Papers in Honor of Andrew Keogh, Librarian of Yale University*, edited by M. C. Withington, pp. 373–422. New Haven: Privately printed, 1938.

1664. Pratt, A. S. "The Books Sent from England by Jeremiah Dummer to Yale College." In *Papers in Honor of Andrew Keogh, Librarian of Yale University*, edited by M. C. Withington, pp. 7–44. New Haven: Privately printed, 1938.
1665. ———. *Isaac Watts and His Gift of Books to Yale College*. Yale University Library Miscellanies, II. New Haven: Yale University Library, 1938.
1666. ———, and Keogh, A. "The Yale Library of 1742." *YULG* 15 (1940): 29–40.
1667. Rider, F. "The Growth of American College and University Libraries . . . and Wesleyan's." *ABooks* 11 (September 1940): 1–11.
1668. Troxell, G. M. "Bookplates of the Yale Libraries, 1780–1846." In *Papers in Honor of Andrew Keogh, Librarian of Yale University*, edited by M. C. Withington, pp. 145–56. New Haven: Privately printed, 1938.
1669. Wing, D. G., and Johnson, M. L. "The Books Given by Elihu Yale in 1718." *YULG* 13 (1939): 46–47.

DELAWARE

1670. Able, A. H., and Lewis, W. D. "The Library Story (1833–1953)." *DN* 26 (1953): 77–91.
1671. Bauersfeld, S. H. "The Growth and Development of the University of Delaware Library, Newark, Delaware, 1833–1965." Master's thesis, Catholic University of America, 1967.

DISTRICT OF COLUMBIA

1672. Chamberlain, L. C. "Georgetown University Library, 1789–1937." Master's thesis, Catholic University of America, 1962.
1673. Duncan, A. M. "History of Howard University Library, 1867–1929." Master's thesis, Catholic University, 1951. Published: Association of College and Research Libraries Microcard, Number 42.
1674. Pendell, L. "Gallaudet College Library [since 1876]." *DCL* 28 (1957): 4–8.
1675. Reason, J. "The Howard University Libraries (1867–1953)." *DCL* 24 (1953): 8–12.

FLORIDA

1676. Adams, K. B. "The Growth and Development of the University of Florida Libraries, 1940–1958." Master's thesis, Catholic University of America, 1959.
1677. Axford, H. W. "Florida Atlantic University Library." *ELIS* 8:545–57.

1678. Hansen, A. M. "Rollins College Library." In *In Pursuit of Library History*, edited by J. D. Marshall, pp. 63–64. Tallahassee: Florida State University Library School, 1961.
1679. Husselbee, M. V. "History of the University of Miami Libraries, 1928–1960." Master's thesis, University of North Carolina, 1962.
1680. Shaw, B. "University of Florida's Chinsegut Hill Library." *LJ* (1956): 1118–20.
1681. Smith, C. A. "Stetson University Library." In *In Pursuit of Library History*, edited by J. D. Marshall, p. 65. Tallahassee: Florida State University Library School, 1961.

GEORGIA

1682. English, T. H. "Emory University Library." *ELIS* 8:34–43.
1683. LaBoone, E. "A History of the University of Georgia Library." Master's thesis, University of Georgia, 1955.
1684. Satterfield, V. "College Libraries in Georgia." *GHQ* 25 (1941): 16–38.
1685. ———. "The History of College Libraries in Georgia as Interpreted from the Study of Seven Selected Libraries." Master's thesis, Columbia University, 1936.

HAWAII

1686. Kittelson, D. "University of Hawaii Library, 1920–1941." *HLAJ* 30 (1973): 16–26.

ILLINOIS

1687. Archer, H. R. "Some Aspects of the Acquisition Program at the University of Chicago: 1892–1928." Doctoral dissertation, University of Chicago, 1954.
1688. Clancy, Sister M. M. "An Historical Survey of the Rosary College Library." Master's thesis, Rosary College, 1964.
1689. Dorf, A. T. "The University of Chicago Libraries: A Historical Note." *LQ* 4 (1934): 185–97.
1690. Gwynn, S. E. "University of Chicago Library." *ELIS* 4:542–59.
1691. Heckman, M. L. "A History of the Library of Bethany Biblical Seminary, Chicago, Illinois." Master's thesis, University of Chicago, 1963.
1692. Jackson, W. *The Development of Library Resources at Northwestern University [1920–49]*. Urbana: University of Illinois Graduate School of Library Science, Occasional Paper Number 26, 1957.
1693. Johnson, E. C. "A History of the Theological Book Collection in the Library of Augustana College and Theological Seminary." Master's thesis, University of Chicago, 1957.

1694. Krueger, H. E. "History of the Carroll College Library." Master's thesis, University of Chicago, 1943.
1695. Lundean, J. W. "History of the Library of the Chicago Lutheran Theological Seminary of Maywood, Illinois." Master's thesis, University of Chicago, 1967.
1696. Maxfield, D. K., ed. "College and University Libraries in Illinois." *IllL* 33 (1951): 175–79, 208–10, 264–67, 373–75, 418–21, 462–64.
1697. McMullen, C. H. "The Administration of the University of Chicago Libraries, 1892–1898." Doctoral dissertation, University of Chicago, 1949.
1698. ———. "Administration of the University of Chicago Libraries, 1892–1928." *LQ* 22 (1952): 325–34; 23 (1953): 23–32.
1699. Miller, A. H. "The Harriet Monroe Modern Poetry Library: Origins and Growth to 1960." Master's thesis, University of Chicago, 1968.
1700. Ratcliffe, T. E. "Development of the Buildings, Policy, Collections of the University of Illinois Library to Urbana, 1895–1940." Master's thesis, University of Illinois, 1949.
1701. Sexton, M. M. "The Cavagna Library at the University of Illinois." *PBSA* 19 (1925): 66–72.
1702. Sharp, K. "Illinois Libraries: College, Institutional and Special Libraries; Public School Libraries by Counties." [University of Illinois] *UnivS* 2, no. 6 (1906): whole issue.
1703. Wilcox, L. E. "History of the University of Illinois Library, 1868–1897." Master's thesis, University of Illinois, 1931.
1704. Yenawine, W. S. "The Influence of Scholars on Research Library Development at the University of Illinois." Doctoral dissertation, University of Illinois, 1955.

INDIANA

1705. Alexander, W. A. "The Indiana University Library." In *History of Indiana University*, edited by B. D. Myers, vol. 2, pp. 597–611. Bloomington: Indiana University, 1952.
1706. Lind, L. R. "Early Literary Societies at Wabash College." *IMH* 42 (1946): 173–76.
1707. Lowell, M. H. "Indiana University Libraries, 1829–1942." Doctoral dissertation, University of Chicago, 1957.
1708. ———. "Indiana University Libraries, 1829–1942." *CRL* 22 (1961): 423–29, 462–64.
1709. *The Roy O. West Library, Dedicated October 20, 1956*. Greencastle, Ind.: DePauw University, 1956.
1710. Springer, N. P. "The Mennonite Historical Library at Goshen College." *MenQR* 25 (1951): 296–319.

1711. Stanley, E. L. "The Earlham College Library: A History of Its Relation to the College, 1847–1947." Master's thesis, University of Illinois, 1947.

IOWA

1712. Slavens, T. P. "A History of the Drake University Libraries." Master's thesis, University of Minnesota, 1962.

KANSAS

1713. Kansas State Teachers College. Emporia. *A Memorial to a Great American* [the William Allen White Library]. Emporia, [1952?].
1714. Stephens, H. H. "A Study of the Growth and Development of the Library of Kansas State Teachers College, Emporia, 1875–1930." Master's thesis, Kansas State Teachers College, 1935.

KENTUCKY

1715. Brunner, J. E. "The History of the University of Louisville Libraries." Master's thesis, University of North Carolina, 1953. Published: Association of College and Research Libraries Microcard, Number 60.
1716. Bull, J. "The Samuel M. Wilson Library." *RKSHS* 47 (1949): 52–54.
1717. McMullen, H. "College Libraries in Ante-Bellum Kentucky." *RKSHS* 60 (1962): 106–33.
1718. Scott, E. "The History and Influence of the Old Library of Transylvania University." Master's thesis, University of Kentucky, 1929.
1719. Thompson, L. W. "Books at the University of Kentucky." *FCHQ* 24 (1950): 58–65.
1720. Transylvania University. *The Transylvania Library*. Lexington: The University, 1948.

LOUISIANA

1721. Green, C. W. "History of the Louisiana State University Libraries [1860–1952]." *LLAB* 15 (1952): 110–15.
1722. Knighten, L. "A History of the Library of Southwestern Louisiana Institute, 1900–1948." Master's thesis, Columbia University, 1949.

MAINE

1723. Herrick, M. D., and Rush, N. O. "Early Literary Societies and Their Libraries in Colby College, 1824–78." *CRL* 6 (1944): 58–63.
1724. Michener, R. "Rivals and Partners: Early Literary Societies at Bowdoin College." *JLH* 10 (1975): 214–30.

1725. Rush, N. O. *The History of College Libraries in Maine.* Worcester, Mass.: Clark University Library, 1946.

MARYLAND

1726. "Age of Discovery." *JHAM* 2 (1950): 17–23.
1727. Brisco, R. "A History of the Library of the University of Maryland, 1813–1938." *UMSMB* 23 (1938): 44–57.
1728. Brown, A. W. "The Phoenix: A History of the St. John's College Library." *MHM* 65 (1970): 413–29.
1729. Dutrow, K. E., ed. "Histories of the College Libraries in Maryland." *ML* 27 (1961): 4–16.
1730. Falley, E. W. "Goucher College Library, 1919–1929." *GAQ* 7 (1929): 30–34.
1731. Goodwillie, M. C. "The Friends of the Library, 1931–1949." *JHAM* 37 (1949): 126–29.
1732. Greer, J. J. "A History of the Library of Woodstock College of Baltimore County, Maryland, from 1869 to 1957." Master's thesis, Drexel Institute of Technology, 1957.
1733. Griswold, A. M. "A History of the Columbia Union College Library, Takoma Park, Maryland, 1904–1954." Master's thesis, Catholic University of America, 1964.
1734. Hoff, A. "A History of the Library of Western Maryland College." Master's thesis, Drexel Institute of Technology, 1954.
1735. Kirby, M. B. "A History of the Goucher College Library, Baltimore, Maryland, 1885–1949." Master's thesis, Catholic University, 1952. Published: Association of College and Research Libraries Microcard, Number 26.
1736. Klein, S. J. "The History and Present Status of the Library of St. John's College, Annapolis." Master's thesis, Catholic University of America, 1952.
1737. Nichols, M. E. "Historical Survey of the Library of the College of Notre Dame of Maryland." Master's thesis, Catholic University of America, 1957.
1738. Ownings, V. B. "A History of the Library of Morgan State College from 1867 to 1939." Master's thesis, Catholic University, 1952.
1739. Roddy, Sister R. "A History of Saint Joseph College Library, 1902–1955." Master's thesis, Catholic University of America, 1956.
1740. Williams, R. V. "George Whitefield's Bethesda: The Orphanage, the College and the Library." In *Library History Seminar Number 3*, edited by M. J. K. Zachert, pp. 47–72. Tallahassee: *JLH*, 1968.

MASSACHUSETTS

1741. [Adams, T. R.]. *A Brief Account of the Origins and Purpose of the Chapin Library at Williams College.* Williamstown, 1956.

1742. Bentinck-Smith, W. *Building a Great Library: The Coolidge Years at Harvard*. Cambridge: Harvard University Library, 1976.
1743. Birkhoff, G. "The George David Birkhoff Mathematical Library (1888–1954)." *HLB* 9 (1955): 282–84.
1744. Bolton, C. K. "Harvard University Library: A Sketch of Its History and Its Benefactors." *NEM* 9 (1892): 433–49.
1745. Briggs, W. B. "Sundry Observations upon Four Decades of Harvard College Library." *CHSP* 27 (1941): 29–41.
1746. Broderick, J. H. "The Robbins Library of Philosophy (1906–55)." *HLB* 9 (1955): 415–17.
1747. Brown, H. M. "Wellesley College Library: An Historical Sketch." *BSL* 49 (1959): 1–5.
1748. Bryant, D. W., and Williams, E. E. "The Harvard Library in the 1960's." *HLB* 15 (1967): 82–98.
1749. Buck, P. *Libraries and Universities*. Cambridge: Harvard University Press, 1964.
1750. Cadbury, H. J. "Bishop Berkeley's Gifts to the Harvard Library." *HLB* 7 (1953): 73–87, 196–207.
1751. ———. "Harvard College Library and the Libraries of the Mathers." *PAAS* 50 (1940): 20–48.
1752. ———. "John Harvard's Library." *PCSM* 34 (1943): 353–77.
1753. ———. "Religious Books at Harvard." *HLB* 5 (1951): 159–80.
1754. Coleman, E. E. "Copyright Deposit at Harvard (1783–90)." *HLB* 10 (1956): 135–40.
1755. Cook, R. U. "The Library of the Department of Architecture [Harvard University, 1893–1952]." *HLB* 6 (1952): 263–69.
1756. Coolidge, A. C. "The Harvard College Library." *HGM* 24 (1915): 23–31.
1757. Cutter, C. A. "Harvard College Library." *NAR* 107 (1868): 568–93.
1758. Davison, A. T. "The Isham Memorial Library [Harvard University Library, 1932–52]." *HLB* 6 (1952): 376–80.
1759. Elkins, K. C., ed. "Foreshadowings of Lamont: Proposals in the Nineteenth Century." *HLB* 8 (1954): 41–53.
1760. ———. "The Harvard Library and the Northeastern Boundary Dispute [1828–52]." *HLB* 6 (1952): 255–63.
1761. ———. "President Elliot and the Storage of 'Dead' Books." *HLB* 8 (1954): 299–312.
1762. Engley, D. B. "The Emergence of the Amherst College Library, 1821–1911." Master's thesis, University of Chicago, 1947.
1763. Goodhue, A. "The Reading of Harvard Students, 1770–1781, as Shown by the Records of the Speaking Club." *HCEI* 63 (1937): 107–29.
1764. Grieder, E. M. "The Littauer Center Library: A Few Notes on Its Origins." *HLN* 4 (1942): 97–104.
1765. "Harvard College Library, 1638–1938." *HLN* 19 (1939): 207–90.

1766. Hickman, R. W. "The Physics Libraries of Harvard University (1884–1956)." *HLB* 10 (1956): 356–66.
1767. Hoffleit, D. "The [Phillips] Library of the Harvard College Observatory [1845–1950]." *HLB* 5 (1951): 102–11.
1768. James, J. W. "History and Women at Harvard: The Schlesinger Library." *HLB* 16 (1968): 385–99.
1769. Jones, F. N. "The Libraries of the Harvard Houses." *HLB* 2 (1948): 362–77.
1770. Kraus, J. W. "The Harvard Undergraduate Library of 1773." *CRL* (1961): 247–52.
1771. Lane, W. C. "The Harvard College Library, 1877–1928." In *The Development of Harvard University Since the Inauguration of President Eliot, 1869–1929*, edited by S. E. Morison, pp. 608–31. Cambridge: Harvard University Press, 1930.
1772. ———. "Justin Winsor's Administration of the Harvard Library, 1877–1897." *HGM* 6 (1897): 182–88.
1773. ———. "New Hampshire's Part in Restoring the Library and Apparatus of Harvard College After the Fire of 1764." *PCSM* 25 (1922–24): 24–33.
1774. ———. "The Sojourn of the Harvard Library in Concord, Massachusetts, 1775–1776." In *Essays Offered to Herbert Putnam by His Colleagues and Friends on His Thirtieth Anniversary as Librarian of Congress, 5 April 1929*, edited by W. W. Bishop and A. Keogh, pp. 275–87. New Haven: Yale University Press, 1941.
1775. *The Library of Mount Holyoke College: 1837–1968*. [South Hadley, Mass.: Mount Holyoke College Library, 1968].
1776. Lovett, R. W. "Harvard College and the Supply of Textbooks." *HLB* 4 (1950): 114–22.
1777. ———. "Harvard Union Library, 1901–1948." *HLB* 2 (1948): 230–37.
1778. ———. "The Hasty Pudding Club Library, 1808–1948." *HLB* 2 (1940): 393–401.
1779. ———. "Pecuniary Mulets and the Harvard Library [1650–1949]." *HLB* 3 (1949): 288–94.
1780. ———. "The Undergraduate and the Harvard Library, 1877–1937." *HLB* 1 (1947): 221–37.
1781. McNiff, P. J. "A Century of College Libraries in Massachusetts." *MassLAB* 41 (1951): 24–26.
1782. Metcalf, K. D. "Administrative Structure of the Harvard University Library." *HLB* 7 (1953): 5–18.
1783. ———. "The Finances of the Harvard University Library." *HLB* 7 (1953): 333–48.
1784. ———. "Harvard's Book Collections." *HLB* 5 (1951): 51–62, 209–20.
1785. ———. "Problems of Acquisition Policy in a University Library." *HLB* 4 (1950): 98–115.

1786. ———. "Spatial Growth in the Harvard Library, 1638–1947." *HLB* 2 (1948): 98–115.
1787. ———. "Spatial Growth in University Libraries." *HLB* 1 (1947): 133–54.
1788. ———. "The Undergraduate and the Harvard Library, 1765–1877." *HLB* 1 (1947) 29–51.
1789. ———. "The Undergraduate and the Harvard Library, 1937–1947." *HLB* 1 (1947): 288–305.
1790. ———. "Vital Statistics of the Harvard University Library, 1937–1955." *HLB* 10 (1956): 119–29.
1791. Munn, J. B. "The Child Memorial Library [Harvard University 1892–1951]." *HLB* 6 (1952): 110–18.
1792. Porritt, R. K. "The Radcliffe College Library After Seventy-Five Years." *HLB* 9 (1955): 335–49.
1793. Potter, A. C. "Catalogue of John Harvard's Library." *PCSM* 21 (1919): 190–230.
1794. ———. *Descriptive and Historical Notes on the Library of Harvard University*. 4th ed. Cambridge: Library of Harvard University, 1934.
1795. Robbins, C. "Library of Liberty–Assembled for Harvard College by Thomas Hollis of Lincoln's Inn." *HLB* 5 (1951): 5–23, 181–96.
1796. Roberts, E. D. *A Brief History of the Wellesley College Library*. Wellesley, Mass., 1936.
1797. Seybolt, R. F. "Student Libraries at Harvard, 1763–1764." *PCSM* 28 (1930–33): 449–61.
1798. Shepley, H., and Metcalf, K. D. "The Lamont Library." *HLB* 3 (1949): 5–30.
1799. Smith, M. B. "The Founding of the Memorial Hall Library, Andover." *HCEI* 79 (1943): 246–55.
1800. Swan, M. W. S. "Professor Longfellow, Scandinavian Book Buyer." *HLB* 4 (1950): 359–73.
1801. Sweeney, J. L. "A Place for Poetry: The Woodberry Poetry Room in Widener and Lamont [1931–53]." *HLB* 8 (1954): 65–73.
1802. Terrell, D. "History of the Dumbarton Oaks Research Library of Harvard University, 1940–1950." Master's thesis, Catholic University of America, 1954.
1803. Wang, S. Y. "Harvard-Yenching Library: Harvard University, History and Development." Master's thesis, Southern Connecticut State College, 1967.
1804. Williams, E. E. "Harvard University Library." *ELIS* 10:317–73.
1805. Winthrop, R. C. "Reminiscences of a Night Passed in the Library of Harvard College." *MHSP* 2 ser., 3 (1886–87): 216–18.
1806. Work, R. L. "Ninety Years of Professor Agassiz's Natural History Library." *HLB* 6 (1952): 202–18.

MICHIGAN

1807. Abbott, J. C. "Raymond Cazallis Davis and the University of Michigan General Library, 1877–1905." Doctoral dissertation, University of Michigan, 1957.

1808. Adams, R. G. *The Whys and Wherefores of the William L. Clements Library: A Brief Essay on Book Collecting as a Fine Art.* Ann Arbor: University of Michigan Press, 1931.

1809. Bidlack, R. E. "Book Collection of the Old University of Michigan." *MAQR* 64 (1958): 100–13.

1810. ———. "Four Early Donors of Books to the University of Michigan." *MAQR* 65 (1958): 110–22.

1811. ———. *Nucleus of a Library: A Study of the Book Collection of the University of Michigan and the Personalities Involved in Its Acquisition, 1837–1845.* Ann Arbor: University of Michigan Department of Library Science, 1962.

1812. ———. "The University of Michigan General Library: A History of Its Beginnings, 1837–1852." Doctoral dissertation, University of Michigan, 1954.

1813. Bishop, W. W. "The University [of Michigan] Library's Bookplates [1915–30]." *MAQR* 57 (1951): 348–50.

1814. Michigan. University. Library. *University of Michigan Library, 1905–1912: A Brief Review by the Librarian.* Ann Arbor: Ann Arbor Press, 1912.

1815. Oddon, Y. "Une Bibliothèque Universitaire aux États-Unis; la Bibliothèque de l'Université de Michigan." *RDB* 38 (1928): 129–55.

1816. Towne, J. E. *A History of the Michigan State University Library, 1855–1959.* Rochester, N.Y.: Association of College and Research Libraries, 1961. ACRL Microcard, Number 34.

MINNESOTA

1817. Fortin, C. C. "A History of the St. Thomas College Library." Master's thesis, University of Minnesota, 1951.

1818. Miller, V. P. "A History of the Library of Gustavus Adolphus College, St. Peter, Minnesota." Master's thesis, University of Minnesota, 1961.

1819. Roloff, R. W. "St. John's University Library: A Historical Evaluation." Master's thesis, University of Minnesota, 1953. Published: Association of College and Research Libraries Microcard, Number 34.

1820. Walter, F. L. "Notes on the Beginning of a Midwest University Library." In *Essays Offered to Herbert Putnam by His Colleagues ...*, edited by W. W. Bishop and A. Keogh, pp. 510–19. New Haven: Yale University Press, 1929.

MISSISSIPPI

1821. Nichols, M. E. "Early Development of the University of Mississippi Library." Master's thesis, University of Mississippi, 1957. Published: Association of College and Research Libraries Microcard, Number 111.

MISSOURI

1822. Carlin, O. R. *History of William Jewell College Library, 1854–1939*. Liberty, Mo.: William Jewell College Press, 1940.
1823. Hoyer, M. "The History of Automation in the University of Missouri Library, 1947–1963." Master's thesis, Indiana University, 1965. Published: Association of College and Research Libraries Microcard Number 166.
1824. Severance, H. O. *History of the Library of the University of Missouri*. Columbia: University of Missouri, 1928.

NEW HAMPSHIRE

1825. *The Isaiah Thomas Donation [to the Library of Dartmouth College]*. Hanover, N.H.: Dartmouth College Library, 1949.
1826. Morin, R. W. "Dartmouth College Libraries." *ELIS* 6:428–34.

NEW JERSEY

1827. Gapp, K. S. "The Theological Seminary Library [Princeton 1811–1953]." *PULC* 15 (1954: 90–100.

NEW YORK

1828. Allan, J. M. "The Library of Hamilton College, Clinton, New York from January, 1763 to January, 1963: The Development of an American Liberal Arts College." Thesis submitted for Fellowship of the Library Association, 1968. 4 vols. bibl. (Available from Hamilton College.)
1829. Berthel, J. "Their Wine Will Warm: An Appreciation of the Bancroft Bequest." *CLC* 1 (1952): 12–16.
1830. Bogart, R. E. "College Library Development in New York State During the 19th Century." Master's thesis, Columbia University, 1948.
1831. Bonnell, A. H. "Columbia University Libraries." *ELIS* 5:362–70.
1832. Butler, N. M. "The Libraries of Columbia." *CUQ* 27 (1935): 1–5.
1833. Canfield, J. H. "The Library." In *A History of Columbia University, 1735–1904: Published in Commemoration of the One Hundred and Fiftieth Anniversary of the Founding of King's College*. New York: Columbia University Press, 1904.
1834. Emberman, A. "The History of the Vassar College Library, 1861–1968." Master's thesis, University of Chicago, 1969.

1835. Gilchrist, D. B. "A History of the University of Rochester Libraries." *RHSP* 16 (1937): 101–34.
1836. ———. "The Rush Rhees Library at the University of Rochester." *LJ* 56 (1931): 343–46.
1837. Hamlin, T. F. "The Avery Architectural Library of Columbia University [1890]." *ASLHM* 24 (1953): 261–81.
1838. Harris, G. W. *Twenty-five Years of the Annals of the Cornell University Library, 1868–1893*. Ithaca: Cornell University Library, 1893.
1839. Hayes, C. D. "The History of the University of Rochester Libraries –120 Years." *URLB* 25 (1970): 59–112.
1840. Jones, H. D. "Brooklyn College Library: A Profile." *LACUNYJ* 1 (1972): 24–28.
1841. Jones, R. "A History of the Library of Teachers College, Columbia University, 1887–1952." Master's thesis, Drexel Institute of Technology, 1953. Published: Association of College and Research Libraries Microcard, Number 39.
1842. Kato, Mother A. "A History of Brady Memorial Library, Manhattanville College of the Sacred Heart: Purchase, New York, 1841–1957." Master's thesis, Catholic University of America, 1959.
1843. Keep, A. B. "The Library of King's College." *CUQ* 13 (1911): 275–84.
1844. Linderman, W. B. "History of the Columbia University Library, 1876–1926." Doctoral dissertation, Columbia University, 1959.
1845. Severance, H. O. "The Columbia Library, 1866–1892." *MHR* 7 (July 1913): 232–36.
1846. Shepherd, G. F. "Cornell University Libraries." *ELIS* 6:167–81.
1847. Slavens, T. P. "The Acquisition of the Van Ess Collection by Union Theological Seminary." In *Library History Seminar no. 3 Proceedings, 1968*, edited by M. J. Zachert, pp. 26–34. Tallahassee: *JLH*, 1968.
1848. ———. "The Development of the Library of Union Theological Seminary in the City of New York." *LHR* 1 (1974): 84–93.
1849. ———. "The Library of Union Theological Seminary in the City of New York, 1836 to the Present." Doctoral dissertation, University of Michigan, 1965.
1850. Thorpe, J. "Pioneering in the Pre-Olin Day." *CULB* 183 (1973): 13–17.

NORTH CAROLINA

1851. Adams, C. M. "Woman's College Library, the University of North Carolina." *CRL* 14 (1953): 135–39.
1852. Bahnsen, J. C. "Collections in the University of North Carolina Library Before 1830." *CRL* 20 (1959): 125–29.

1853. Battle, M. E. "A History of the Carnegie Library at Johnson C. Smith University." Master's thesis, University of North Carolina, 1960.
1854. Breedlove, J. P. "Duke University Library, 1840–1940: A Brief Account with Reminiscences." *Library Notes: A Bulletin Issued by the Friends of the Duke University Library.* no. 30 (1955): whole issue.
1855. Cranford, J. P. "The Documents Collection of the University of North Carolina Library from Its Beginning Through 1963." Master's thesis, University of North Carolina, 1965.
1856. Diaz, A. J. "A History of the Latin American Collection of the University of North Carolina Library." Master's thesis, University of North Carolina, 1956.
1857. Eaton, J. D. "A History and Evaluation of the Hanes Collection in the Louis R. Wilson Library, University of North Carolina." Master's thesis, University of North Carolina, 1957.
1858. Farrow, M. H. "The History of Guilford College Library, 1837–1955." Master's thesis, University of North Carolina, 1959. Published: Association of College and Research Libraries Microcard, Number 120.
1859. Halmos, D. M. "The Hancock Library of Biology and Oceanography." *CRL* 15 (1954): 29–32.
1860. Heindel, S. W. "A History of the Institute of Government Library of the University of North Carolina." Master's thesis, University of North Carolina, 1965.
1861. Holder, E. J. "A History of the Library of the Woman's College of the University of North Carolina, 1892–1945." Master's thesis, University of North Carolina, 1955. Published: Association of College and Research Libraries Microcard, Number 86.
1862. Leonard, H. V. "The Divinity School Library: The Historical Background Since 1850." *LNDUL* (1973): 19–42.
1863. List, B. T. "The Friends of the University of North Carolina Library, 1932–1962." Master's thesis, University of North Carolina, 1965.
1864. Moore, G. G. "The Southern Historical Collection in the Louis Round Wilson Library of the University of North Carolina from the Beginning of the Collection Through 1948." Master's thesis, University of North Carolina, 1958.
1865. Nicholson, J. M. "A History of the Wake Forest College Library, 1878–1946." Master's thesis, University of North Carolina, 1954. Published: Association of College and Research Libraries Microcard, Number 78.
1866. Orr, A. P. "A History and Analysis of the Freshman Library Instruction Program Presented at the University of North Carolina." Master's thesis, University of North Carolina. 1958. Published: Association of College and Research Libraries Microcard, Number 125.

1867. Pearsall, T. F. "History of the North Carolina Agricultural and Technical College Library." Master's thesis, Western Reserve University, 1955.
1868. Perkins, T. E. "The History of Elon College Library, 1890–1957." Master's thesis, University of North Carolina, 1962.
1869. Powell, B. E. "Duke University Library." *ELIS* 7:314–23.
1870. Pugh, J. F. "The History of the Library of the University of North Carolina." *UNCM* 44 (1914): 207–13.
1871. Tarlton, S. M. "The Development of the Library of Charlotte College, 1946–July 1, 1965." Master's thesis, University of North Carolina, 1966.
1872. Wilson, L. R. "First Book in the Library of the First State University." *CRL* 22 (1961): 35–39.
1873. ———. *The Library of the First State University: A Review of Its Past and a Look at Its Future.* Chapel Hill: University of North Carolina Library, 1960.

OHIO

1874. Adam, C. "Kent State University Library." Master's thesis, Kent State University, 1950.
1875. Barnett, M. F. "A History of the Baldwin-Wallace College Library, 1913–1964." Master's thesis, Kent State University, 1967.
1876. Baughman, N. C. "A History of the Otterbein College Library." Master's thesis, Western Reserve University, 1955.
1877. Belanger, M. D. "The Library That Letters Built." *OLAB* 46 (1976): 10–12.
1878. Bobinski, G. S. "A Brief History of the Libraries of Western Reserve University, 1826–1952." Master's thesis, Western Reserve University, 1952. Published: Association of College and Research Libraries Microcard, Number 50.
1879. Clinefeller, R. W. "A History of Bierce Library of the University of Akron." Master's thesis, Kent State University, 1956.
1880. Harper, J. R. "A History of Mount Union College Library." Master's thesis, Kent State University, 1968.
1881. Hopper, O. C. "History of the Ohio State University Library, 1910–1925." In *History of the Ohio State University*, edited by T. C. Mendenhall, vol. 2. Columbus: Ohio State University Press, 1926.
1882. Irwin, M. "History of the Ohio Wesleyan University Library, 1844–1940." Master's thesis, University of California, 1941.
1883. Mathews, Brother S. G. "Marian Library of the University of Dayton: Origin and Development." Master's thesis, Western Reserve University, 1952.

1884. Meyers, J. K. "A History of the Antioch College Library, 1850–1929." Master's thesis, Kent State University, 1963. Published: Association of College and Research Libraries Microcard, Number 150.
1885. Mount Union College. *The History of the Mount Union College Library, 1854–1955: With Summary Reports of the Library for the Years 1920–1955, by Robert E. Stauffer, Librarian, 1920–1955.* Alliance: Mount Union College, 1956.
1886. Saviers, S. H. "The Literary Societies and Their Libraries at Hiram College." Master's thesis, Kent State University, 1958.
1887. Schink, R. J. "A History of the Youngstown University and Its Library." Master's thesis, Western Reserve University, 1956.
1888. Schoyer, G. *History of the Ohio State University Libraries: 1870–1970.* Columbus: Ohio State University Libraries, 1970.
1889. Silva, Sister M. F. C. "A History of the Ursuline College Library, Cleveland, Ohio, 1922–1957." Master's thesis, Western Reserve University. Published: Association of College and Research Libraries Microcard, Number 108.
1890. Skipper, J. E. "The Ohio State University Library, 1873–1913." Doctoral dissertation, University of Michigan, 1960.
1891. Stein, J. H. "The Development of the Hiram College Library from the Literary Societies Which Formed Its Nucleus." Master's thesis, Kent State University, 1950.
1892. Tucker, J. S. "Oberlin College Library, 1833–1885." Master's thesis, Western Reserve University, 1953. Published: Association of College and Research Libraries Microcard, Number 45.
1893. Vermilya, N. C. "A History of the Otterbein College Library." Master's thesis, Western Reserve University, 1955. Published: Association of College and Research Libraries Microcard, Number 58.
1894. Zafren, H. C. "The Hebrew Union College Library." *SL* 47 (1956): 314–17.

OREGON

1895. Carlson, W. H. "History and Present Status of the Centralization of the Libraries of the Oregon State System of Higher Education (1931–53)." *CRL* 14 (1953): 414–17.
1896. Sheldon, H. D. *The University of Oregon Library, 1882–1942.* [Eugene]: University of Oregon Library, [1943?].

PENNSYLVANIA

1897. Armstrong, E. V. *The Story of the Edgar Fahs Smith Memorial Collection in the History of Chemistry.* Philadelphia: University of Pennsylvania, 1937.
1898. Cheney, E. P. "The Henry C. Lea Library." *LC* 1 (1933): 4–5.

1899. David, C. W. "The University Library in 1886." *LC* 18 (1952): 72–76.
1900. Davidson, J. S. "Literary Society Libraries at Muhlenberg College [1867–1912]." *CRL* 16 (1955): 183–86.
1901. Dunaway, W. F. "Library." In *History of the Pennsylvania State College*, pp. 356–62. State College: Pennsylvania State College, 1946.
1902. Earnshaw, J. "A History of the Henry Lea Library at the University of Pennsylvania." Master's thesis, Drexel Institute of Technology, 1955.
1903. Girvin, A. G. "The Albright Alumni Memorial Library." Master's thesis, Drexel Institute of Technology, 1954.
1904. Jones, S. B. "The Early Years of the University [of Penn.] Library." *Library Chronicle: Bicentennial Issue Published in Memory of the Founding of the University of Pennsylvania Library, 1750* 17 (1950): 8–22.
1905. Kraft, Sister M. I. "A History of the Library of Chestnut Hill College: Pennsylvania, 1890–1965." Master's thesis, Catholic University of America, 1967.
1906. McFarland, M. M. "History of the Development of Bucknell University Library, Lewisburg, Pennsylvania." Master's thesis, Drexel Institute of Technology, 1955.
1907. McTaggart, J. B. "The History of the Eastern Baptist Theological Seminary Library, 1925–1953." Master's thesis, Drexel Institute of Technology, 1954.
1908. Meyerend, M. H. "A History and Survey of the Fine Arts Library of the University of Pennsylvania from Its Founding to 1953." Master's thesis, Drexel Institute of Technology, 1955.
1909. Nehlig, M. E. "The History and Development of the Drexel Institution Library, 1892–1914." Master's thesis, Drexel Institute of Technology, 1952.
1910. Oliphant, J. O. *The Library of Bucknell University*. Lewisburg, Penn.: Bucknell University Press, 1962.
1911. Osborne, J. T. "The Ursinus College Library, 1869–1953." Master's thesis, Drexel Institute of Technology, 1954.
1912. Phillips, J. W. "The Sources of the Original Dickinson College Library." *PennH* 14 (1947): 108–17.
1913. Richardson, E. R. "The La Salle College Library, Philadelphia, 1930–1953." Master's thesis, Drexel Institute of Technology, 1953.
1914. Shellem, J. J. "The Archibishop Ryan Memorial Library of St. Charles Borromeo Seminary, Overbrook, Pennsylvania." *ACHS* 75 (1964): 53–55.
1915. Shinn, M. E. "Sine Quibus Non: The University of Pennsylvania Librarians." *LC* 17 (1950): 23–29.

1916. Smith, D. J. "The Early History of the Library of Allegheny College, Meadville, Pennsylvania." Master's thesis, Western Reserve University, 1953. Published: Association of College and Research Libraries Microcard, Number 61.
1917. ———. "Early Libraries in Crawford County." *WPHM* 40 (1957): 251–76. (Allegheny College, French Creek, Meadville.)
1918. Tauber, M. "A Brief History of the Library of Temple University." *TUN* 14 (1934): 5.
1919. Thompson, C. S. "The Gift of Louis XVI." *LC* 2 (1934): 37–48, 60–67.
1920. Valentine, Sister M. "Holy Family College Library: The First Decade." Master's thesis, Marywood College (Scranton, Penn.), 1956.
1921. Wagner, L. F. "A Descriptive History of the Library Facilities of Lafayette College, Easton, Pennsylvania, 1826–1941." Master's thesis, Catholic University of America, 1951. Published: Association of College and Research Libraries Microcard, Number 27.
1922. Wolf, E. 2d. "Some Books of Early New England Provenance in the 1823 Library of Allegheny College." *PAAS* 73 (1963): 13–44.

RHODE ISLAND

1923. Adams, T. R. "John Carter Brown Library." *ELIS* 3:378–82.
1924. Chase, E. *The Library: Rhode Island School of Design*. Providence, 1942.
1925. Graniss, R. "The John Carter Brown Library and Its Catalogue." *LJ* 45 (1920): 67–69.
1926. Jonah, D. A. "Brown University Library." *ELIS* 3:382–408.
1927. Van Hoesen, H. B. *Brown University Library: The Library of the College or University in the English Colony of Rhode Island and Providence Plantations in New England in America [1767–1782]*. Providence: Privately printed, 1938.
1928. Winship, G. P. *The John Carter Brown Library: A History*. Providence, 1914.
1929. Wroth, L. C. *The John Carter Brown Library in Brown University, Providence, Rhode Island*. Providence: Privately printed, 1936.

SOUTH CAROLINA

1930. Everhart, F. B. "The South Carolina College Library: Background and Beginning." *JLH* 3 (1968): 221–41.
1931. Green, E. L. "The Library of the University of South Carolina." *USCB* 7 (1906): 1–22.

TENNESSEE

1932. Atkins, E. "A History of Fisk University Library and Its Standing in Relation to the Libraries of Other Comparable Institutions." Master's thesis, University of California, 1936.

1933. Duncan, R. B. "A History of the George Peabody College Library, 1785–1910." Master's thesis, George Peabody College for Teachers, 1940.
1934. McClary, B. H., ed. "Not for the Moment Only: Edward Berts to Mary Percival, February 18, 1886." *THQ* 24 (1965): 54–62.

TEXAS

1935. Barker, E. C. "To Whom Credit Is Due." *SHQ* 54 (July 1950): 6–12.
1936. Clark, J. B. "The Odyssey of a University Library, 1869–1968." *JLH* 5 (1970): 119–32.
1937. Cochran, M. A. "The University of Texas Package Loan Library, 1914–1954." Master's thesis, University of Texas, 1956.
1938. Lee, J. B. "A History of the Library of Texas College of Arts and Industries, 1925–1955." Master's thesis, University of Texas, 1958.
1939. Moloney, L. C. "A History of the University Library at the University of Texas, 1833–1934." Doctoral dissertation, Columbia University, 1970.
1940. Rouse, R. "A History of the Baylor University Library, 1845–1919." Doctoral dissertation, University of Michigan, 1962.
1941. ———. "The Two Libraries of Baylor University." In *Approaches to Library History*, edited by J. D. Marshall, pp. 128–40. Tallahassee: *JLH*, 1966.
1942. Sitter, C. L. "The History and Development of the Rare Books Collections of the University of Texas Based on Recollections of Miss Fannie Ratchford." Master's thesis, University of Texas, 1966.

VERMONT

1943. White, R. A. "The Library That Saved a University [of Vermont]." *JLH* 1 (1966): 66–69.

VIRGINIA

1944. Byrd, R. E. "The Tracy W. McGregor Library (University of Virginia, 1936–48)." *AB* 2 (1948): 973–74.
1945. Clemons, H. *The University of Virginia Library*. Charlottesville: University of Virginia Library, 1954.
1946. Cometti, E., ed. *Jefferson's Ideas on a University Library: Letters from the Founder of the University of Virginia to a Boston Bookseller*. Charlottesville: Tracy W. McGregor Library, University of Virginia, 1950.
1947. Edsall, M. H. "History of the Library of the Protestant Episcopal Theological Seminary in Virginia, 1823–1955." Master's thesis, Catholic University of America, 1955.
1948. Hudson, J. P. "A History of the Roanoke College Library, 1842–1959." Master's thesis, University of North Carolina, 1963.

1949. Jennings, J. M. *The Library of the College of William and Mary in Virginia, 1693–1793*. Charlottesville: Published for the Earl Swenn Library by the University Press of Virginia, 1968.
1950. ———. "Notes on the Original Library of the College of William and Mary in Virginia, 1693–1705." *PBSA* 41 (1947): 239–67.
1951. O'Neal, W. B. *Jefferson's Fine Arts Library for the University of Virginia, with Additional Notes on Architectural Volumes Known to Have Been Owned by Jefferson*. Charlottesville: University of Virginia Press, 1956.
1952. Servies, J. A. "Notes on William and Mary Library History." In *In Pursuit of Library History . . .* , edited by J. D. Marshall, pp. 60–62. Tallahassee: Florida State University School of Library Science, 1961.
1953. Tyler, L. G. "Library of the College of William and Mary." WMQ 19 (1910): 48–51.
1954. *1928 Catalogue of the Library of the University of Virginia*. Reproduced in facsimile with an introduction by W. H. Peden. Charlottesville: Printed for the Alderman Library of the University of Virginia, 1945.

WASHINGTON

1955. Bauer, H. C. "Books at the University of Washington." *PacS* 3 (1949): 63–72.
1956. Gorchels, C. C. "Land-grant University Library: The History of the Library of Washington State University, 1892–1946." Doctoral dissertation, Columbia University, 1971.
1957. Potter, J. C. "The History of the University of Washington Library." Master's thesis, University of Washington, 1954. Published: Association of College and Research Libraries Microcard, Number 56.

WEST VIRGINIA

1958. Amos, A. "A History of Robert F. Kidd Library." Master's thesis, Western Reserve University, 1953.
1959. Harris, V. "Library Development in Five Denominational Colleges in West Virginia." Master's thesis, Western Reserve University, 1952.
1960. Munn, R. F. "West Virginia University Library, 1867–1917." Doctoral dissertation, University of Michigan, 1962.
1961. Powell, R. A. "A History of the Fairmont State College Library, 1867–1967." Master's thesis, Kent State University, 1967.

WISCONSIN

1962. Cain, S. M. *History of Harold G. Andersen Library at Wisconsin State University–Whitewater.* Whitewater, 1968.

1963. Hubbard, C. L. "History of Wisconsin State College, Oshkosh, Library: September 1871–August 1953." Master's thesis, Drexel Institute of Technology, 1954.

1964. Krueger, H. E. "History of the Carroll College Library." Master's thesis, University of Chicago, 1943.

1965. Towne, J. E. "President [Charles Kendall] Adams and the University [of Wisconsin] Library [1893–1902]." *WMH* 35 (1952): 257–61.

VII. School Libraries

Much work remains to be done on the history of school libraries in America. However, the building blocks for broadly conceived interpretive studies do appear to be available, and if the time is not yet ripe for the writing of such histories, it should be here soon. A number of short surveys of school library development are available in the papers by Rosemae W. Campbell (1953, **1975**), Henry L. Cecil and Willard A. Heaps (1940, **1977**), T. J. Cole (1959, **1978**), Mabel Smith (1967, **2031**), C. A. Stolt (1971, **2033**), Carolyn I. Whitenack (1956, **2040**), and Azile Woffard (1940, **2042**). These syntheses offer a starting point for those who would write the much needed general studies of school libraries. A recent and well-documented overview is found in Sarah Fenwick's "Library Service to Children and Young People" (1976, **1987**).

Much of the most promising work on school libraries has focused on special aspects of school library development, such as school library growth during a particular period or the relationship between school libraries and other kinds of libraries. Examples of important work in this category are Gerald Alvey's study of storytelling (1974, **1969**); Budd Gambee's studies of the tension existing between school and public libraries in the early stages of school library development (1973, **1991**) and his paper on the standards for school media programs of 1920 (1970, **1992**); Gene D. Lanier's dissertation on modern school libraries (1968, **2007**); Dawson E. Lemley's dissertation on the development and evaluation of administrative policies in school libraries (1949, **2008**); Harriet Long's study of the development of children's services in public libraries, which has much to say about school libraries (1969, **2009**); and Julia W. Lord's imaginative study of the children's librarian which reflects on the development of the school librarian (1968, **2011**).

Finally, as the user of this chapter of the bibliography will notice, a good deal of work has been done on school library development in various parts of the country. Taken together, these studies provide important information on school library history. Most important of these studies are Frederic D. Aldrich on school libraries in Ohio (1959, **1968**); Ann E. Hall on school libraries in California (1974, **1997**); Frances E. Hammit on school libraries in Indiana, Illinois, and Wisconsin (1948, **1999**); Sister M. Constance Melvin on school library development in Pennsylvania (1962, **2015**; 1966, **2016**); and Margaret I. Rufsvold's work on school libraries in the South (1933, **2024**).

School Libraries

1966. Abraham, M. L. "Development of Public School Libraries in Pennsylvania." *PLMN* 14 (1934): 411–13.
1967. Adams, R. T. "A History of School Libraries in Connecticut, 1948–1967." Master's thesis, Southern Connecticut State College, 1968.
1968. Aldrich, F. D. *The School Library in Ohio with Special Emphasis on Its Legislative History*. New York: Scarecrow Press, 1959.
1969. Alvey, G. R. "The Historical Development of Organized Storytelling to Children in the United States." Doctoral dissertation, University of Pennsylvania, 1974.
1970. Barr, J. L. C. "The Immigrant in Children's Fictional Books Recommended for American Libraries, 1883–1939." Doctoral dissertation, Indiana University, 1976.
1971. Bell, D. "History of School Libraries in Connecticut, 1839–1860." Master's thesis, Southern Connecticut State College, 1964.
1972. Branyan, B. M. "Outstanding Women Who Promoted the Concept of the Unified School Library and Audiovisual Programs, 1950 through 1975." Doctoral dissertation, Southern Illinois University, 1977.
1973. Briggs, M. I. "The Development of Public School Libraries in Minnesota, 1861–1938." Master's thesis, University of Chicago, 1945.
1974. Burge, N. T. "Development of High School Libraries in North Carolina, 1900–1947." Master's thesis, George Peabody College for Teachers, 1948.
1975. Campbell, R. W. "The Development of Public School Librarianship in the United States." Master's thesis, Colorado College, 1953.
1976. Carroll, F. C. "School Library Development in Indiana." Master's thesis, University of Illinois, 1929.
1977. Cecil, H. L., and Heaps, W. A. *School Library Service in the United States: An Interpretive Survey*. New York: H. W. Wilson, 1940.
1978. Cole, T. J. "Origin and Development of School Libraries." *PJE* 37 (1959): 87–92.
1979. Cookston, J. S. "Development of Louisiana Public School Libraries, 1929–1965." Doctoral dissertation, Louisiana State University, 1971.
1980. Daughtrey, J. A. "A Content Analysis of Periodical Literature Relating to the Certification of Librarians, 1906–1952." Master's thesis, Atlanta University, 1954.
1981. Davidge, I. B. "Development of the Public School Library." *LJ* 63 (1927): 680–82.
1982. Dengler, T. P. "The Public Library in School Library Service, Madison, Wisconsin, 1902–1953." Master's thesis, University of Chicago, 1967.

1983. Donaldson, L. L. "A Decade and a Half with the School Libraries of Texas." Master's thesis, Texas State College for Women, 1954.
1984. ———. "Decade and a Half with Texas School Libraries." *TLJ* 30 (1954): 203–06.
1985. Dunkley, G. C. "Development of Public School Libraries in Virginia with Emphasis on the Period 1958–1959 Through 1963–1964." Master's thesis, University of North Carolina, 1965.
1986. Feeney, R. B. "The History and Development of the Library in the Public Schools of Houston, Texas." Master's thesis, Texas State College for Women, 1954.
1987. Fenwick, S. I. "Library Service to Children and Young People." *LibT* 25 (1976): 329–60.
1988. Foster, P. M. "An Historical and Descriptive Study of the Bellevue Public School Library System and of Its Administrative Pattern with Implications for the Future." Master's thesis, University of Washington, 1959.
1989. Galloway, M. L. "The Historical Development and Present Status of Public High School Libraries in Kentucky: 1908 to 1950." Master's thesis, Columbia University, 1951.
1990. ———. "The Historical Development and Present Status of Public School Libraries in Kentucky, 1908–1950." [University of Kentucky Department of Education] *EB* 20 (1952): 5–121.
1991. Gambee, B. L. "An Alien Body: Relationships Between the Public Library and the Public Schools, 1876–1920." In *Ball State University Library Science Lectures*, First series, pp. 1–23. Muncie, Ind.: Department of Library Science, Ball State University, 1973.
1992. ———. "Standards for School Media Programs, 1920: A Lesson from History." *AL* 1 (1970): 483–85.
1993. Gaston, M. "Greenville High School: Mississippi's Oldest School Library." *MLNews* 37 (1973): 29–30.
1994. Gates, E. S. "The Library-School Council of Wethersfield, Connecticut." Master's thesis, Southern Connecticut State College, 1964.
1995. Geller, E. "Somewhat Free: Post-Civil War Writing for Children." *WLB* 51 (1976): 172–76.
1996. Greenman, E. D. "The Development of Secondary School Libraries." *LJ* 38 (1913): 183–89.
1997. Hall, A. E. "Public Elementary and Secondary School Library Development in California, 1850–1966." Doctoral dissertation, Columbia University, 1974.
1998. Hall, E. "Wisconsin High School Library Housing, 1935–1940." Master's thesis, Columbia University, 1941.
1999. Hammitt, F. E. "School Library Legislation in Indiana, Illinois, and Wisconsin: A Historical Study." Doctoral dissertation, University of Chicago, 1948.
2000. Henne, F. "The Basic Need in Library Service for Youth and Children." *LQ* 25 (1955): 37–46.

2001. Holden, O. "The History of Library Service in Austin Public Schools." Master's thesis, University of Texas, 1962.
2002. Hoyle, N. E. "A Study of the Development of Library Service in the Public Schools of Virginia." Master's thesis, Columbia University, 1938.
2003. Huggins, M. A. "High School Libraries in North Carolina: A Study of their Origin, Development, and Present Status." Master's thesis, University of North Carolina, 1929.
2004. Jackson, C. O. "Service to Urban Children." In *A Century of Service: Librarianship in the United States and Canada*, edited by S. L. Jackson et al., pp. 20–41. Chicago: American Library Association, 1976.
2005. Johnson, M. H. "The History and Development of Instructional Materials Centers in School Libraries." Master's thesis, Atlanta University, 1969.
2006. Lane, M. "The Development of Library Service to Public Schools in New Jersey." Master's thesis, Columbia University, 1938.
2007. Lanier, G. D. "The Transformation of School Libraries into Instructional Materials Centers." Doctoral dissertation, University of North Carolina, 1968.
2008. Lemley, D. E. "The Development and Evaluation of Administrative Policies and Practices in Public School Library Service as Evidenced in City School Surveys, 1907–1947." Doctoral dissertation, University of Pittsburgh, 1949.
2009. Long, H. G. *Public Library Service to Children: Foundation and Development*. Metuchen, N.J.: Scarecrow Press, 1969.
2010. Lopez, M. D. "Children's Libraries: Nineteenth Century American Origins." *JLH* 11 (1976): 316–42.
2011. Lord, J. W. "The Cosmic World of Childhood: The Ideology of the Children's Librarian, 1900–1965." Doctoral dissertation, Emory University, 1968.
2012. Loyola, Sister M. "School Library: A History." *CSJ* 53 (1952): 43–45.
2013. Lunnon, B. S. "Dade's Libraries: The Nation's Best." *FEd* 42 (1965): 19–21.
2014. Lynch, D. N. *Libraries and Library Service for Children in Brooklyn to 1914*. Brooklyn, 1948.
2015. Melvin, Sister M. C. "A History of School Libraries in Pennsylvania." Doctoral dissertation, University of Chicago, 1962.
2016. ———. "A History of State Administration and Public School Libraries in Pennsylvania." In *Approaches to Library History*, edited by J. D. Marshall, pp. 106–18. Tallahassee: *JLH*, 1966.
2017. Noonan, M. Z. "The Development of Libraries in the Chicago Public Elementary Schools." Master's thesis, De Paul University, 1953.

2018. Powell, S. "Early Libraries for Children." In *The Childrens' Library: A Dynamic Factor in Education*, pp. 33–46. New York: H. W. Wilson, 1917.
2019. Pratt, C. "San Jacinto Unified School & Library: A History." *CSL* 47 (1976): 11–16.
2020. Pratt, S. M. "The Library of St. Stephen's Episcopal School, Austin, Texas, 1950–60." Master's thesis, University of Texas, 1961.
2021. Rathbone, J. A. "Co-operation Between Libraries and Schools: An Historical Sketch." *LJ* 26 (1901): 187–91.
2022. Rayward, W. B. "What Shall They Read? A Historical Perspective." *WLB* 51 (1976): 146–53.
2023. Redding, B. N. "The Developmental History of the Elementary School Libraries in Guilford County, North Carolina." Master's thesis, University of North Carolina, 1957.
2024. Rufsvold, M. I. "Library Service to Schools in the South Since 1900." Master's thesis, George Peabody College for Teachers, 1933.
2025. Rukus, A. T. "History of School Libraries in Connecticut, 1917–1947." Master's thesis, Southern Connecticut State College, 1968.
2026. Sasse, M. "Invisible Women: The Children's Librarian in America." *LJ* 98 (1973): 213–17.
2027. Scudder, H. E. "School Libraries." *AtlM* 72 (1893): 678–81.
2028. Seth, O. C. "Development of School Library Standards in Texas." Master's thesis, University of Texas, 1961.
2029. Singer, A. R. "History of School Libraries in Connecticut, 1871–1916." Master's thesis, Southern Connecticut State College, 1966.
2030. Skaar, M. O. "Public School Libraries in Wisconsin: A Historical Study of School Libraries Under the Supervision of the State Department of Public Instruction." Master's thesis, Columbia University, 1938.
2031. Smith, M. "Development of the Elementary School Library." Master's thesis, University of Mississippi, 1967.
2032. Songer, F. H. "Development of Public School Libraries in Georgia, 1890–1950." Master's thesis, University of North Carolina, 1955.
2033. Stolt, C. A. "Schools and School Libraries Over Two Centuries: The Presidential Address at the Annual Conference of the School Library Association on 30th December, 1970." *SchL* 19 (1971): 15–23, 101–07.
2034. Thomassen, C., ed. "Illinois School Libraries: History and Development." *IllL* 50 (1968): 853–958.
2035. Tinklepaugh, D. K. "School Libraries in New York State: Their History from 1890 to 1930." Master's thesis, Columbia University, 1937.

2036. Van Allen, S. J. "A History of the Elementary School Library in New York State." Master's thesis, State University of New York at Albany, 1958.
2037. Vaughan, J. E. "Grammar School Library in the Late Seventeenth Century." *SchL* 10 (1961): 511–12.
2038. Wenger, E. M. "The Development of Brooklyn School Library, 1940–1950, in Relation to Other Cuyahoga County Library Standards." Master's thesis, Western Reserve University, 1953.
2039. Wesson, J. J. "The High School Library in Mississippi." Master's thesis, University of Mississippi, 1931.
2040. Whitenack, C. I. "Historical Development of the Elementary School Library." *IllL* 38 (1956): 143–49.
2041. Wofford, A. "The History and Present Status of School Libraries in South Carolina, 1868–1938." Master's thesis, Columbia University, 1938.
2042. ———. "School Library Evolution." *PDK* 22 (1940): 283–88.

VIII. State Libraries

Most of the work on state library history to date has focused on the development of individual state libraries or aspects of the development of individual libraries. This work represents the beginning of what, hopefully, will become further regional or national studies of state library development in the United States. At this point one can only single out a few works of major importance from the many useful, but generally limited, studies listed here. Examples are the fine study of the New York State Library written by Cecil R. Roseberry (1970, **2090**) and the excellent dissertations on the Indiana State Library by Larry Barr (1976, **2044**), the Michigan State Library by John Larsen (1967, **2077**), the Louisiana State Library by Harriet Stephenson (1957, **2097**), and the Ohio State Library by M. M. Vannorsdall (1974, **2103**).

State Libraries

2043. Babylon, E. R. "History of the North Carolina Library Commission." Master's thesis, University of North Carolina, 1954.

2044. Barr, L. J. "The Indiana State Library, 1825–1925." Doctoral dissertation, Indiana University, 1976.

2045. Barrett, M. A. "Development of Library Extension in New Mexico." Master's thesis, Western Reserve University, 1958. Published: Association of College and Research Libraries Microcard, Number 97.

2046. Bird, M. F. "History of the Demonstration Program of the Illinois State Library." Master's thesis, University of Chicago, 1952.

2047. Bliss, R. P. *A History of the Pennsylvania State Library*. Harrisburg: Printed for the Pennsylvania Library Association by the Telegraph Press, 1937.

2048. Brown, C. C. "History of the New Hampshire State Library." Master's thesis, Southern Connecticut State College, 1969.

2049. Burnett, P. M. "The Development of State Libraries and Library Extension Service in Arizona and New Mexico." *LQ* 35 (1965): 31–51.

2050. Byrnes, H. W. "State Library Commission Observes Its Fiftieth Anniversary, 1907–1957." *NDLNN* 39 (Winter 1957): 1–3.

2051. Cahill, A. M. "19th Century Library Innovation: The Division of Library Extension from 1890 to 1940." *BSL* 55 (1965): 7–12.
2052. Capozzi, M. R. "A History of Maryland State Library Agencies, 1902–1945." Master's thesis, Catholic University of America, 1966.
2053. Chalker, W. J. "The Historical Development of the Florida State Library, 1845–1959." Master's thesis, George Peabody College for Teachers, 1951.
2054. Cochran, M. A. "The University of Texas Package Loan Library, 1914–1954." Master's thesis, University of Texas, 1956.
2055. Conmy, P. T. "California's Ex-Officio State Librarians, 1850–1861." *NNCL* 69 (1974): 247–57.
2056. Coover, R. W. "A History of the Maryland State Library, 1827–1939." Master's thesis, Catholic University of America, 1956.
2057. ———. *A History of the Maryland State Library, 1827–1939 (With a Summary of Events from 1939–1959)*. Washington, D.C., 1959.
2058. Culver, E. M. "Louisiana State Library [and Its Predecessors, 1909–53]." *LLAB* 16 (1953): 18–20, 41–48.
2059. Currier, L. G. "The Lengthened Shadow: Essae M. Culver and the Louisiana State Library [1925–58]." *BALA* 53 (1959): 35–37.
2060. Dixon, M., and Gittinger, N. *The First Twenty-five Years of the Louisiana State Library, 1925–1950*. Baton Rouge: The Library, 1950.
2061. Drury, J. W. *The Kansas Traveling Library Commission: An Administrative History*. Lawrence: University of Kansas, Governmental Research Center, 1965.
2062. Esbin, M. "Old Capitol Library: Its History, Contents, and Restoration." *AnI* 42 (1975): 523–40.
2063. Flack, H. E. "History and Growth of Legislative Reference Libraries." *SL* 32 (1941): 294–97.
2064. Galbreath, C. B. "The State Library and the Public Schools." *OEM* 46 (1897): 468–72.
2065. Gibson, T. J. "The Texas State Library [Since 1839]." *TLJ* 28 (1952): 84–91.
2066. *A Gift From the State to Oregonians: A Half Century of Reading in Oregon, 1905–1955*. Salem: Oregon State Library, 1955.
2067. Gillis, M. R. "California State Library: Its Hundred Years (1850–1950)." *CLB* 11 (1949): 55–57.
2068. Godard, G. S. "A Brief Summary of the Activities of the Connecticut State Library." In *Essays Offered to Herbert Putnam by His Colleagues and Friends on His Thirtieth Anniversary as Librarian of Congress, 5 April 1929*, edited by W. W. Bishop and A. Keogh, pp. 172–77. New Haven: Yale University Press, 1929.
2069. ———. "Development of the State Library." *CBJ* 1 (1927): 319–29.
2070. Handy, C. H. "The Connecticut State Library, 1851–1936." Master's thesis, Southern Connecticut State College, 1965.

2071. Hintz, C. W. E. "Oregon State Library: Its First Fifty Years." *PNLAQ* 29 (1955): 15–19.
2072. Homes, H. A. "State and Territorial Libraries." In U.S. Bureau of Education, *Public Libraries in the United States of America . . .* , pp. 292–311. Washington, D.C.: Government Printing Office, 1876.
2073. Howard, L. "The Statesboro Regional Library: History, Development and Services." Master's thesis, Florida State University, 1964.
2074. Jamsen, E. "Michigan State Library: Its First Hundred Years." *MichL* 32 (1966): 8–11.
2075. "John M. Bernhisel and the Territorial Library." *UHQ* 24 (1956): 359–62.
2076. Kunkle, H. J. "A Historical Survey of the Extension Activities of the California State Library with Particular Emphasis on Its Role in Rural Library Development, 1850–1966." Doctoral dissertation, Florida State University, 1969.
2077. Larsen, J. C. "A Study in Service: The Historical Development of the Michigan State Library and Its Territorial Predecessor, the Legislative Council Library, 1828–1941." Doctoral dissertation, University of Michigan, 1967.
2078. ———. "The Ventriloquist and the State Library: The Vattemare Correspondence." *MichL* 36 (1970): 6–7.
2079. Levine, L. E. "The Assembly Legislative Reference Service: A Short History." *CalL* 28 (1967): 107–11.
2080. MacKay, M. B. "South Dakota State Library Commission." *SDLB* 49 (1963): 5–9.
2081. MacKinney, G. "A Century of Library Development of the Pennsylvania State Library." *PLN* 14 (1934): 407–11.
2082. "Massachusetts Division of Library Extension, Executive Staff, 1890–1965." *BSL* 55 (1965): 15–16.
2083. McNitt, E. U. "Short History of the Indiana State Library." *LO* 10 (1931): 21–30.
2084. *Michigan State Library, 1828–1928, One Hundred Years*. Lansing: Michigan State Library, 1928.
2085. Moore, M. D. "The Tennessee State Library in the Capitol (1853–1953)." *THQ* 12 (1953): 3–22.
2086. New York State Library. *New York State Library, 1818–1918: A Souvenir of the Visit of the ALA July 6, 1918, Commemorating the 100th Anniversary of the Founding of the Library*. Albany: The Library, 1918.
2087. Peace, W. K. "A History of the Texas State Library with Emphasis on the Period from 1930 to 1958." Master's thesis, University of Texas, 1959.

2088. Phelps, D. J. "Organization and Development of the Alaska Department of Library Service, 1955–1959." Master's thesis, University of Utah, 1960.
2089. Richards, E. S. "Fifty Years with the Library Commission for the State of Delaware." Master's thesis, Drexel Institute of Technology, 1951.
2090. Roseberry, C. R. *A History of the New York State Library*. Albany: New York State Library, 1970.
2091. Ryan, D. T. "The State Library and Its Founder." *POSAHS* 38 (1919): 98–114.
2092. Settlemire, C. L. "The Tennessee State Library, 1854–1923." Master's thesis, George Peabody College for Teachers, 1951.
2093. Simmons, B. S. "In Retrospect: Audiovisual Services in the Illinois State Library." *IllL* 49 (1967): 106–17.
2094. Smith, C. E. "The Growth of the Service of the Ohio State Traveling Library." Master's thesis, University of Cincinnati, 1936.
2095. Smith, C. "Books for People, 1817–1967." *WWO* 31 (December 1967): 22–27.
2096. ———. "The State Library–150 Years." *OLAB* 38 (1968): 4–7.
2097. Stephenson, H. S. "History of the Louisiana State Library, Formerly Louisiana Library Commission." Doctoral dissertation, Louisiana State University, 1957.
2098. Strother, J. V. "The Development and the Adequacy of the Library as an Institution in the State of Washington." Master's thesis, University of Washington, 1938.
2099. Taylor, M. V. "The Public Library Commission of Indiana, 1899–1925." Master's thesis, University of Kentucky, 1953.
2100. Thomas, M. A. "The Delaware State Archives: 1931–1951." Master's thesis, Drexel Institute of Technology, 1952.
2101. Thornton, E. M. *The Georgia State Library, 1926–1935*. Atlanta: Stein Printing Co., State Printers, 1936.
2102. VanMale, J. E. "A History of Library Extension in Colorado, 1890–1930." Master's thesis, University of Denver, 1940.
2103. Vannorsdall, M. M. "The Development of Library Services at the State Level in Ohio, 1817–1896." Doctoral dissertation, University of Michigan, 1974.
2104. Vloebergh, H. E. "A History of the New York State Library from 1818 to 1905." Master's thesis, Catholic University of America, 1956. Published: Association of College and Research Libraries Microcard, Number 83.
2105. Wilson, L. R. "North Carolina Library Commission, 1909–1949." *NCL* 8 (1949): 7–10.
2106. Winfrey, D. H. "The Texas State Library: Its History and Service to the People of Texas." *TL* 28 (1966): 12–22.
2107. Wright, L. M. "Iowa's Oldest Library." *IJHP* 38 (1940): 408–28.

IX. Special Libraries

A. General Studies

Defining a special library has always proven difficult for librarians. For the purposes of this bibliography we have included, in addition to a short list of general studies, citations to six kinds of special libraries: private research libraries; historical society, museum, and institute libraries; business and industrial libraries; law libraries; medical libraries; and government libraries. Our attempt to keep the repetition of entries to a minimum has forced us to make certain compromises. For instance, departmental libraries of university and public libraries are not covered here but rather are cited in the public and academic library sections of the bibliography. However, exceptions to this rule come in the cases of law and medical libraries; for these libraries we include all references in this part of the list. Finally, while state libraries are certainly government libraries, the extent of the literature on state libraries seemed to justify organizing that material as a separate part of the bibliography. Those seeking a general overview of special library development should begin with A. W. John's book on the subject (1968, **2117**), which provides a useful, historical summary. More recently, two interpretive assessments have appeared in papers by Elin B. Christianson (1976, **2113**) and Angelina Martinez (1976, **2119**).

B. Private Research Libraries

A number of important private research libraries have been treated in some detail by historians. Among the most significant are the studies by J. Christian Bay on the Crerar Library (1945, **2134**); Clarence B. Brigham (1958, **2137**) and Clifford K. Shipton (1949, **2176**) on the American Antiquarian Society Library; Giles E. Dawson (1949, **2146**), Stanley King (1950, **2154**), Dorothy Mason et al. (1969–70, **2165**), and Louis B. Wright (1968, **2187**) on the Folger Library; William E. Lingelbach (1946, **2158**; 1953, **2157**) on the American Philosophical Society Library; Guy Marco (1966, **2164**) and Lawrence Towner (1970, **2182**) on the Newberry Library; and John E. Pomfret (1969, **2170**) and Robert O. Schad (1931, **2174**) on the Huntington Library. Users of this bibliography should also consult the sections on private libraries and biography, both of which contain material relating to the rise of some of the privately endowed research libraries. Further, presidential libraries are cited in the section on government libraries.

C. *Historical Society, Museum, and Institute Libraries*

Only a few of the nation's many historical society and museum libraries have been covered by historians. However, a number of informative studies are available, mostly articles and master's theses, and they are listed in this section of the bibliography.

D. *Business and Industrial Libraries*

A limited number of studies have focused on the business and industrial libraries. The standard study is Anthony T. Kruzas's excellent book, *Business and Industrial Libraries in the United States, 1820–1940* (1965, **2237**). Some provocative new work is underway, however, and one example is Victor Jelin's controversial study of the intellectual origins of the modern industrial library (1970, **2235**).

E. *Law Libraries*

Law libraries have been the focus of a substantial number of studies. Especially important as general interpretive frameworks for the study of law libraries are Christine A. Brock's "Law Libraries and Librarians: A Revisionist History" (1974, **2250**), Maurice L. Cohen et al. on the historical development of the American lawyer's library (1968, **2253**), and Michael H. Harris's study of the lawyer's library on the frontier (1972, **284**). In addition to the studies of individual law libraries listed here, users will also find citations to correctional institution libraries, such as the works by Ruth E. Johnson (1959, **2266**) and Austin H. MacCormick (1970, **2270**). For articles and books dealing with the individual lawyer's library, especially in early America, see the section of this bibliography devoted to private libraries.

F. *Medical Libraries*

A large number of individual medical libraries have been treated by historians. There are also a number of important general works available, such as Virginia Donley's chronology of medical library development (1957, **2302**), Albert Huntington's survey of the early development of medical libraries (1904, **2321**), Thomas Keys's essay on private medical libraries (1958, **298**), and Marjorie Wannarka's history of medical library collections in public libraries (1968, **2348**). The nation's leading medical library–the National Li-

138 Special Libraries

brary of Medicine—has been the subject of a good deal of research, and this material is covered in the section of the bibliography dealing with government libraries.

G. Government Libraries

Many major and minor government libraries have been studied by librarians. The most important of this work centers on the Library of Congress. Dozens of studies have been written on the Library of Congress, but the standard overview is David Mearns's book (1947, **2419**). The leading authority on the Library of Congress's history presently working in the field is John Y. Cole, and his recent essay (1976, **2377**) is particularly valuable. Users should also consult the biography section of the bibliography for studies of librarians like Ainsworth Spofford and Herbert Putnam, both of whom figured prominently in the rise of the Library of Congress.

Special Libraries

A. General Studies

2108. Adkinson, B. W. "Federal Government's Support of Information Activities." *Basis* 2 (1976): 25–26.
2109. Becker, J. "The Rich Heritage of Information Science." *Basis* 2 (1976): 9–13.
2110. Brodman, E. "Scientists as Librarians: A Historical Review." *LIS* 9 (1971): 105–13.
2111. ———. "The Special Library: The Mirror of Its Society." In *Approaches to Library History*, edited by J. D. Marshall, pp. 32–48. Tallahassee: *JLH*, 1966.
2112. Brown, R. E. "History of Special Libraries in Denver, Colorado, 1861–1953." Master's thesis, University of Chicago, 1955.
2113. Christianson, E. B. "Special Libraries: Putting Knowledge to Work." *LibT* 25 (1976): 399–416.
2114. Dana, J. C. "The Evolution of the Special Library." *SL* 5 (1914): 70–76.
2115. Edward, J. P. "An Information Science Chronology in Perspective." *Basis* 2 (1976): 51–56.
2116. Jelin, V. "The Instrumental Use of Libraries: A Study of the Intellectual Origins of the Modern Industrial Libraries in Nineteenth Century America." *Libri* 20 (1970): 15–28.
2117. Johns, A. W. *Special Libraries: Development of the Concept, Their Organization, and Their Services*. Metuchen, N.J.: Scarecrow Press, 1968.

2118. Langner, M. C. "User and User Services in Science Libraries, 1945–1965." *LibT* 23 (1974): 7–30.
2119. Martinez, A. "Services to Special Clienteles." In *A Century of Service: Librarianship in the United States and Canada*, edited by S. L. Jackson et al., pp. 110–28. Chicago: American Library Association, 1976.
2120. McMullen, H. "Special Libraries in Antebellum Kentucky." *RKSHS* 59 (1961): 29–46.
2121. Mullins, L. S. "The Rise of Map Libraries in America During the Nineteenth Century." *SLAGMDB* 63 (1966): 2–11.
2122. Ristow, W. W. "The Emergence of Maps in Libraries." *SL* 58 (1967): 400–19.
2123. Salton, G. "Computers and Information Science." *Basis* 2 (1976): 19–21.
2124. Schultz, C. K., and Garwig, P. L. "History of the American Documentation Institute–A Sketch." *AmD* 20 (1969): 152–60.
2125. Shera, J. H. "Two Centuries of American Librarianship." *Basis* 2 (1976): 39–40.
2126. Smith, M. J. "American Battleship Libraries." *LO* 24 (1973): 335–38.
2127. Stevens, E. L. "One Hundred and Ten Years of Special Library Service in Honolulu." *SL* 52 (1961): 143–47.
2128. Varner, Sister C. "The Development of Special Libraries in St. Paul and Minneapolis, Minnesota, 1849–1949." Master's thesis, University of Chicago, 1950.
2129. West, E. K. "A History of the Bibliographic Center for Research: Rocky Mountain Region, 1942–1966." Master's thesis, Long Island University, 1970.
2130. Yanchisin, D. A. "For Carolina's Sake–A Case History in Special Librarianship." *JLH* 9 (1971): 41–71.
2131. Zachert, M. J. "American Special Libraries: Eighteenth Century Ancestors." In *Approaches to Library History*, edited by J. D. Marshall, pp. 141–50. Tallahassee: *JLH*, 1966.

B. Private Research Libraries

2132. Adams, F. B. *An Introduction to the Pierpont Morgan Library*. New York: In Conjunction with New York Times Foundation, 1964.
2133. Baker, C. H. C. "Our Founder's Foresight." *HLQ* 12 (1949): 331–38.
2134. Bay, J. C. *The John Crerar Library, 1895–1944: An Historical Report* . . . Chicago: John Crerar Library, 1945.
2135. Bliss, C. S. "The Huntington Library." *AB* 5 (1950): 697–98.
2136. Boyce, G. K. "The Pierpont Morgan Library, 1883–1951." *LQ* 22 (1952): 21–35.

2137. Brigham, C. B. *50 Years of Collecting Americana for the Library of the American Antiquarian Society, 1908–1958*. Worcester, Mass.: Antiquarian Society, 1958.
2138. Budington, W. S. "'To Enlarge the Sphere of Human Knowledge': The Role of the Independent Research Library." *CRL* 37 (1976): 299–315.
2139. Burstyn, H. L. "The Salem Philosophical Library: Its History and Importance for American Science." *HCEI* 96 (1960): 169–206.
2140. Camp, D. N. "Institute Libraries of New Britain, Connecticut." *ConnM* 9 (1905): 781–94.
2141. Carpenter, E. H. "Three Rare Book Libraries in Southern California." *CalL* 14 (1953): 224–26, 255.
2142. Chinard, G. "Adventures in a Library." *NLB* 2 (1952): 223–28.
2143. Couch, C. R. "The DeGolyer Foundation Library." Master's thesis, University of Texas, 1967.
2144. Cowles, L. H. "The First Century of the Library of the New Britain Institute." Master's thesis, Western Reserve University, 1951.
2145. Davidson, H. L. "The Lilly Library–76 Years." *SL* 57 (1966): 391–94.
2146. Dawson, G. E. "The Resources and Policies of the Folger Shakespeare Library [1885–1949]." *LQ* 19 (1949): 178–85.
2147. Dillon, R. "Adolph Sutro Finds a Librarian." *JLH* 2 (1967): 225–34.
2148. ———. "A Peek at Sutro Library." *BCCQNL* 17 (1952): 27–32.
2149. Edwards, A. "The Library of the American Antiquarian Society." *MM* 9 (1916): 3–17.
2150. Fisher, H. H. "The Hoover Library on War, Revolution and Peace." *PBSA* 33 (1939): 107–15.
2151. Franklin Typographical Society, Boston. *A Sketch of the History of the Franklin Typographical Society, and of Its Library, Read Before the Society at Its April Meeting, by the Librarian*. Boston: H. W. Dutton & Son, 1860.
2152. Gladeck, A. A. "The Library of the Franklin Institute." Master's thesis, Drexel Institute of Technology, 1953. Published: Association of College and Research Libraries Microcard, Number 37.
2153. Hilker, E. W. "The Franklin Institute Library." *PLAB* 23 (1967): 98–104.
2154. King, S. *Recollections of the Folger Shakespeare Library*. [Ithaca]: Published for the Trustees of Amherst College by the Cornell University Press, 1950.
2155. Knachel, P. A. "Folger Shakespeare Library." *ELIS* 8:582–91.
2156. Law, R. A. "Two Texas Libraries." *TR* 5 (1920): 349–57.
2157. Lingelbach, W. E. "The American Philosophical Society Library from 1942 to 1952, with a Survey of Its Historical Background [Since 1743]." *PAPS* 97 (1953): 471–92.
2158. ———. "The Library of the American Philosophical Society [1743]." *WMQ* 3 (1946): 48–69.

2159. Lydenburg, H. M. "The Ecology of the Pierpont Morgan Library and Its First Director." In *Studies in Art and Literature for Belle la Costa Greene*, edited by D. E. Miner, pp. 6–9. Princeton: Princeton University Press, 1954.
2160. ———. "Footnotes on the Astor Library's History from George Templeton Strong's Diary." *BNYPL* 58 (1954): 167–73.
2161. Marchman, W. P. *The Hayes Memorial*. Columbus: Ohio State Archaeological and Historical Society, 1950.
2162. ———. "The Hayes Memorial Library [Fremont, Ohio]." *ACJ* 3 (October 1950): 8–10.
2163. ———. "The Rutherford B. Hayes Library." *CRL* 17 (1956): 224–27.
2164. Marco, G. "Beginnings of the Newberry Library Music Collection: Background and Personal Influences." In *Approaches to Library History*, edited by J. D. Marshall, pp. 165–81. Tallahassee: *JLH*, 1966.
2165. Mason, D. E.; Flower, E.; and Knachel, P. "The Folger Shakespeare Library in Washington, D.C.: A Brief History." *RCHS* (1969–70): 346–70.
2166. McLean, P. T. "The Hoover Institute and Library (1914–19)." *LQ* 19 (1949): 235–49.
2167. Myers, A. "Washington Irving and the Astor Library." *BNYPL* 72 (1968): 378–99.
2168. Pierpont Morgan Library. New York. *The First Quarter Century of the Pierpont Morgan Library (1924–48): A Retrospective Exhibition in Honor of Belle la Costa Greene* . . . New York, 1949.
2169. ———. *The Pierpont Morgan Library: Review of the Activities and Major Acquisitions of the Library, 1941–1948; With a Memoir of John Pierpont Morgan and the Pierpont Morgan Library, 1913–1943*. New York, 1950.
2170. Pomfret, J. E. *The Henry E. Huntington Library and Art Gallery: From Its Beginnings to 1969*. San Marino: Huntington Library, 1969.
2171. ———. "The Huntington Library: Fifteen Years of Growth, 1951–1966." *CHSQ* 45 (1966): 241–57.
2172. ———. "Publishing at the Huntington Library, 1928–54." *CRL* 15 (1954): 388–92.
2173. Sahlin, N. G. "Our Institute's Library 1929–51." *ASIB* 7 (1952): 24–29.
2174. Schad, R. O. *Henry Edwards Huntington, the Founder and the Library*. Cambridge, Mass.: Harvard University Press, 1931.
2175. ———. "A Quarter Century at the Huntington Library." *BCCQNL* 17 (1972): 75–80.
2176. Shipton, C. K. "America's First Research Library." *LJ* 74 (1949): 89–90.
2177. Spell, L. M. "The Sutro Library." *HAHR* 29 (1949): 452–54.

2178. Stinson, D. "The Winston Churchill Memorial and Library in the United States." *JLH* 8 (1973): 70–77.
2179. Stoneman, R. E. "The Libraries of the Art Institute of Chicago." *IllL* 35 (1953): 348–50.
2180. Thomas, E. F. "The Origin and Development of the Society of the Four Arts Library, Palm Beach, Florida." Master's thesis, Florida State University, 1958.
2181. Towner, L. "The Newberry Library: A Research Opportunity in Library History." In *Library History Seminar Number 3*, edited by M. J. Zachert, pp. 1–16. Tallahassee: *JLH*, 1968.
2182. ———. *An Uncommon Collection of Uncommon Collections: The Newberry Library*. Chicago: The Newberry Library, 1970.
2183. Waldeck, F. "Adolph Sutro's Lost Library." *CRL* 18 (1957): 19–22.
2184. Wheatland, H. "Historical Sketch of the Philosophical Library at Salem, with Notes." *HCEI* 4 (1862): 175–81, 271–82.
2185. William L. Clements Library. *History of the William L. Clements Library, 1923–1973: Its Development and Its Collections*. Ann Arbor: University of Michigan, 1973.
2186. Wright, L. B. "The Folger Library as a Research Institute [1932–51]." *CRL* 13 (1952): 14–17.
2187. ———. *The Folger Library: Two Decades of Growth, an Informal Account*. Charlottesville: University Press of Virginia, 1968.
2188. ———. "More Than a Library." *ASch* 2 (1933): 366–70.

C. Historical Society, Museum, and Institute Libraries

2189. Bettie, Sister P. M. "Growth and Development of the Library Collection at the Marine Historical Association." Master's thesis, Southern Connecticut State College, 1969.
2190. Bishop, C. "The Museum of Modern Art Film Library, 1935–55." In *Educational Film Society Primer*, edited by C. Starr, pp. 56–61. Forest Hills, N.Y.: American Federation of Film Societies, 1956.
2191. Chenery, F. L. "The Library of the Church Historical Society." *HMPEC* 28 (1959): 187–90.
2192. Coats, N. M. "The Academy's John Shepard Wright Memorial Library." *PIAS* 63 (1954): 248–52.
2193. Cooper, M. K. "The Founding of the Martha Kinney Cooper Ohioana Library." *Ohioana* 2 (1959): 75–76, 114.
2194. Currier, M. "The Peabody Museum Library." *HLB* 3 (1949): 94–101.
2195. Dennis, A. W. "The Library of Massachusetts Historical Society." *MM* 3 (1910): 225–39.
2196. Duniway, D. C. "The Administration of Six Selected State Historical Society Libraries: A Historical Study." Master's thesis, University of California, 1939.

2197. Gilreath, J. W. "The Formation of the Western Reserve Historical Society's Shaker Collection." *JLH* 8 (1973): 133–42.
2198. Green, S. A. "Formation and Growth of the Society's Library." *PMHS* 8 (1892–94): 312–44.
2199. Halmos, D. "The Building of a Library." *Coranto: Journal of the Friends of Libraries of the University of Southern California* 5 (1967): 3–12; 5 (1968): 27–33; 6 (1969): 13–18.
2200. Harris, A. W. "Cass Gilbert's Old Library Building: The Eugene C. Barker Texas History Center, 1910–1960." *SHQ* 64 (1960): 1–13.
2201. Heskin, M. K. "The Philadelphia Commercial Museum Library, 1896–1952." Master's thesis, Drexel Institute of Technology, 1952.
2202. Hicham, J. S. "Memorial Genealogical Library (Oklahoma) Daughters of the American Revolution (1925–50)." *CO* 28 (1950): 292–98.
2203. Homes, H. A., et al. "Historical Society Libraries in the United States." In U.S. Bureau of Education, *Public Libraries in the United States of America* . . . , pp. 312–77. Washington, D.C.: Government Printing Office, 1876.
2204. Hook, A. "Resources of the Library of the Historical and Philosophical Society of Ohio." *BHPSO* 14 (1956): 105–21.
2205. Hudson, Ohio, Library and Historical Society. *"Open the Books If You Wish to be Free": A Commemorative Book Published . . . on the Occasion of the Opening of the Enlarged Historical House.* Hudson, Ohio: Hudson Library and Historical Society, 1954.
2206. Jerabek, E. "Library of the Minnesota Historical Society." *MinnL* 18 (1956): 204–07.
2207. King, D. M. "Minnesota Historical Society Library, a Treasure House of Information." *MinnL* 17 (1953): 227–30.
2208. Lea, J. "History of the Tennessee Historical Society." *AHM* 6 (1901): 354–56.
2209. Lenhart, J. M. "The Historical Library at the Central Bureau of the Catholic Central Verein in St. Louis, Mo., Founded in 1913 by F. P. Kenkel." *SJR* 49 (1957): 348–52, 384–87; 50 (1957): 24–27.
2210. Libby, D. C. "The Library of the Chicago Historical Society: A Study." Master's thesis, University of Chicago, 1948.
2211. Miller, R. C. "The California Academy of Sciences and the Early History of Science in the West." *CHSQ* 21 (1942): 363–71.
2212. Moore, Mrs. J. T. "The Tennessee State Historical Society, 1849–1918." *THQ* 3 (1944): 195–225.
2213. Pease, M. E. "The Illinois Historical Survey Library, University of Illinois [1909–54]." *IllL* 36 (1954): 298–301.
2214. Pressing, K. L. "The Library of the Historical Society of Delaware." Master's thesis, Drexel Institute of Technology, 1954.
2215. Putnam, L. A. "The Library of the Field Museum of Natural History." Master's thesis, University of Chicago, 1971.

2216. Scriven, M. "Chicago Historical Society." *IllL* 35 (1953): 158–60.
2217. Sims, E. E. "The Allen Memorial Art Museum Library, Oberlin, Ohio: A Study." Master's thesis, Western Reserve University, 1952.
2218. Skidmore, W. L. "A History of the Peninsula (Ohio) Library and Historical Society, 1941–1967." Master's thesis, Kent State University, 1967.
2219. Smail, H. A. "A History of the Eleanor Squire Memorial Library of the Garden Center of Greater Cleveland." Master's thesis, Western Reserve University, 1955.
2220. Thwaites, R. G. "Wisconsin State Historical Society Library. *LJ* 16 (1891): 203–07.
2221. Towne, J. E. "The Inception of the Library Building for the State Historical Society of Wisconsin, 1893–1900." *WMH* 39 (1956): 73–75.
2222. Wainwright, N. B. *One Hundred and Fifty Years of Collecting by the Historical Society of Pennsylvania, 1824–1974.* Philadelphia: Historical Society of Pennsylvania, 1974.
2223. Waldron, R. K. "A History of the Library of the State Historical Society of Colorado, 1879–1940." Master's thesis, University of Denver, 1950.
2224. Walker, M. H. "The Library of the Western Reserve Historical Society." Master's thesis, Kent State University, 1952.
2225. Welch, E. W. "A Library Grows Up." *JISHS* 50 (1957): 176–89.
2226. Wolf, N. E. "The Library of the Genealogical Society of Pennsylvania, 1892–1952." Master's thesis, Drexel Institute of Technology, 1953.

D. Business and Industrial Libraries

2227. Archer, H. R. "The Lakeside Press Library." *BCCQNL* 20 (1954): 12–19.
2228. Axelrod, H. B. "The History, Development and Organization of the New York Times Library, and Contributions of the Times to Scholarship." Master's thesis, Southern Connecticut State College, 1965.
2229. Benjamin, H. C. "The Library of the Industrial Relations Sections [of the Department of Economic and Social Institutions]." *PULC* 15 (1954): 151–55.
2230. Bogardus, J. "Business Libraries and Collections." *ELIS* 3:530–53.
2231. Brown, J. V. "History of the Industrial Relations Research Libraries." Master's thesis, Western Reserve University, 1958.
2232. Handy, D. N. *The First Sixty Years: The Story of the Insurance Library Association of Boston, Incorporated December 28, 1887; an Historical Sketch.* Boston, 1947.

2233. Harris, J. F. "The Newspaper Library: Its History, Function, and Value with Special Reference to the New York Herald Tribune." Master's thesis, Southern Connecticut State College, 1959.
2234. Huleatt, R. S. "The Stone and Webster Library, 1900–1970." *SL* 61 (1970): 374–76.
2235. Jelin, V. "Instrumental Use of Libraries: A Study of the Intellectual Origins of the Modern Industrial Libraries in Nineteenth Century America." *Libri* 20 (1970): 15–28.
2236. Joannes, E. "A Fifty-Year Old Technical Library." *SL* 30 (1939): 254–57.
2237. Kruzas, A. T. *Business and Industrial Libraries in the United States, 1820–1940*. New York: Special Libraries Association, 1965.
2238. Langner, M. C. "User and User Services in Science Libraries: 1945–1965." *LibT* 23 (1974): 7–30.
2239. Laubach, H. "Library Service to Business, Labor and Industry: Its Development in Libraries at Princeton, Akron, and Pittsburgh." Master's thesis, Carnegie Institute, 1952.
2240. Leasure, M. F. "A History of the Libraries of the Baltimore and Ohio Railroad Company." Master's thesis, Drexel Institute of Technology, 1954.
2241. Lopez, M. D. "Books and Beds: Libraries in Nineteenth and Twentieth Century American Hotels." *JLH* 9 (1974): 196–221.
2242. Schmutz, C. A. "Standard and Poor's Corporation Library [New York]." *SL* 45 (1954): 147–50.
2243. Skeen, J. R. "The Origin and Influence of Major Technical Libraries in Philadelphia." *JFrI* 250 (1950): 381–90.
2244. Strable, E. G. "The Origin, Development and Present Status of Advertising Agency Libraries in the United States." Master's thesis, University of Chicago, 1954.
2245. Tilghman, G. "Seaboard Air Line Railway Free Traveling Library System." *SEL* 10 (1960): 126–29.

E. Law Libraries

2246. Arnold, J. H. "The Harvard Law Library." *HBM* 16 (1906): 230–41.
2247. ———. "The Harvard Law Library and Some Account of Its Growth." *LLJ* 5 (1912): 17–25.
2248. Bade, E. S. "Quo Vadimus?" *JLE* 2 (1949): 41–52.
2249. Berry, W. J. C. *Association of the Bar of the City of New York: The First Quarter-Century of Its Library*. New York: Privately printed, [1895?].
2250. Brock, C. A. "Law Libraries and Librarians: A Revisionist History; or More Than You Ever Wanted to Know." *LLJ* 67 (1974): 325–61.
2251. Brooks, R. E. "The Yale University Law School Library: Its History,

Organization and Development, 1824 to 1962." Master's thesis, Southern Connecticut State College, 1965.
2252. Clarke, O. "The Library of the Supreme Court of the United States." *LLJ* 31 (1938): 89–102.
2253. Cohen, M. L.; Wolf, E.; and Jeffery, W. "Historical Development of the American Lawyer's Library." *LLJ* 61 (1968): 440–62.
2254. Coyte, D. E. "A History of the University of Louisville School of Law Library, 1846–1966." Master's thesis, University of North Carolina, 1968.
2255. Cropper, M. S. "An Analysis of the Literature of Law Library Administration, 1936–1968." Master's thesis, Atlanta University, 1969.
2256. Elliot, L. M. "History of the Law Library." In *A Century of Legal Education*, edited by R. H. Wettach. Chapel Hill: University of North Carolina Press, 1947.
2257. "The First Step Towards a Public Law Library." *IMH* 32 (1936): 274–76.
2258. Gholdson, E. "The Cincinnati Law Library." *LLJ* 13 (1921): 75–79.
2259. Ginnell, F. W. "A Brief History of the Social Law Library." *MLR* 10 (1925): 48–53.
2260. Griswold, S. B. "Law Libraries." In U.S. Bureau of Education, *Public Libraries in the United States of America* . . . , pp. 161–70. Washington, D.C.: Government Printing Office, 1876.
2261. Hench, M. "The Library of the Supreme Court of the United States." Master's thesis, Drexel Institute of Technology, 1951.
2262. Holloway, D. P. "History of the Akron Law Library, with Special Attention to Pertinent Legislation." Master's thesis, Kent State University, 1962.
2263. Hudon, E. G. "The Library Facilities of the Supreme Court of the United States: A Historical Study." Master's thesis, Catholic University of America, 1956. Published: Association of College and Research Libraries Microcard, Number 84.
2264. ———. "The Supreme Court of the United States: A History of Its Books and Library [1812–1956]." *FBJ* 19 (1959): 185–99.
2265. ———. "U.S. Supreme Court Library: An Account of Its Development and Growth." *LLJ* 59 (1966): 166–76.
2266. Johnson, R. E. "Libraries in Correctional Institutions." Master's thesis, Western Reserve University, 1959.
2267. Johnston, G. A. "Our Predecessors and Their Achievements." *LLJ* 49 (1956): 138–47.
2268. Lathrop, O. C. "History of Michigan Law Libraries and Their Relation to General Libraries in Michigan." *LLJ* 16 (1923): 15–23.
2269. "Libraries in Prisons and Reformatories." In U.S. Bureau of Education, *Public Libraries in the United States of America* . . . , pp. 218–29. Washington, D.C.: Government Printing Office, 1876.

2270. MacCormick, A. H. *A Brief History of Libraries in American Correctional Institutions.* [Chicago: Association of Hospital and Institutional Libraries Division, American Library Association], 1970.
2271. Marke, J. J. "The Mills Memorial Library of the School of Law of New York University." *SL* 45 (1954): 107–10.
2272. Peterson, L. "Law Libraries of New England, 1946–1955." *LLJ* 49 (1956): 198–203.
2273. Petty, W. E. "The History of the Ohio Penitentiary Library." Master's thesis, Western Reserve University, 1949.
2274. Pound, R. "The Harvard Law Library (1829–1951).' *HLB* 5 (1951): 290–303.
2275. Price, O. M. "Legal Education During the Past Fifty Years as Reflected in the Changing Character of Law Library Acquisitions." *UFLR* 6 (1953): 221–30.
2276. Proctor, M. M. "Historical Survey of the Law School Library of Texas Southern University, Houston, Texas." Master's thesis, Catholic University of America, 1966.
2277. Pulling, A. C. "The Harvard Law School Library [1817–1949]." *LLJ* 43 (1950): 1–11.
2278. Roalfe, W. R., and Schwerin, K. "The Elbert H. Gary Law Library of Northwestern University (1859–1953)." *LLJ* 46 (1953): 219–34.
2279. Russy, E. N. de. "The Library Company of the Baltimore Bar Since 1940." *ML* 35 (1969): 15–17.
2280. Truman, L. S. *The Louisville Law Library, 1839–1912.* Louisville: Smith and Dugan, 1912.
2281. U.S. Library of Congress. *Centennial of the Law Library, 1832–1932: An Exhibit of Books, Prints, and Manuscripts in Honor of the Supreme Court of the United States, and the American Bar Association on the Occasion of the Laying of the Cornerstone of the Supreme Court Building, October 13, 1932.* Washington, D.C.: U.S. Government Printing Office, 1931.
2282. Williamson, R. *The Law Library in the Capitol, Washington, D.C.* Washington, D.C.: J. Byrne and Co., 1929.

F. Medical Libraries

2283. Adams, S. "The Army Medical Library and Other Medical Libraries of the Nation (1836–1947)." *CRL* 9 (1948): 126–32.
2284. ———, and McCarn, D. B. "From Fasciculus to On-Line Terminal: One Hundred Years of Medical Indexing [National Library of Medicine]." In *Communication in the Service of American Health . . . A Bicentennial Report from the National Library of Medicine*, pp. 14–25. Bethesda, Md., 1976.

2285. ———. "The Way of the Innovator: Notes Toward a Prehistory of MEDLARS." *MLAB* 60 (1972): 523–33.
2286. Alessios, A. B. "Library Work with the Blind [1892–1948]." *WLB* 23 (1949): 369–75.
2287. Allen, A. W. "The Doctor and His Books." *NEJM* 249 (1953): 320–22.
2288. Baird, V. M. "Books and the Doctor in Nineteenth-Century Texas: Some Early Attempts to Establish Medical Libraries." *MLAB* 56 (1968): 428–34.
2289. Balkema, J. A. "A History of the Robert Lefevre Memorial Library at the New York University College of Medicine." Master's thesis, Drexel Institute of Technology, 1958.
2290. Bell, W. J. "The Old Library of the Pennsylvania Hospital." *MLAB* 60 (1972): 543–50.
2291. Bernier, B. R. "A History of the Art Collection of the National Library of Medicine." Master's thesis, University of North Carolina, 1962.
2292. Billings, J. S. "Medical Libraries in the United States." In U.S. Bureau of Education, *Public Libraries in the United States of America . . .* , pp. 171–82. Washington, D.C.: Government Printing Office, 1876.
2293. Brodman, E. *The Development of Medical Bibliography*. N.p.: Medical Library Association, 1954.
2294. ———; MacDonald, M. R.; and Rogers, F. B. "The National Medical Library: The Survey and Ten Years Progress." *MLAB* 42 (1954): 439–46.
2295. Chadwick, J. *The Medical Libraries of Boston: A Report Read at the First Annual Meeting of the Boston Medical Library Association, Held on Oct. 3, 1876.* Cambridge, Mass.: Riverside Press, 1876.
2296. ———. "Medical Libraries, Their Development and Use." *BMSJ* 134 (1896): 101–04.
2297. Clymer, B. F. "The History of the Division of Health Affairs Library of the University of North Carolina." Master's thesis, University of North Carolina, 1959.
2298. Coffman, C. "The Dental-Pharmacy Library: A Short History." *TULB* 1 (1948): 9–10.
2299. Cunning, E. T. "A History of Jefferson Medical College Library, 1898–1973." Master's thesis, Drexel Institute of Technology, 1954.
2300. Dean-Throckmorton, J. "History of the Iowa State Medical Library." *ISMSJ* 29 (1939): 472–75.
2301. Denton, G. B. "The Beginnings and Growth of Dental Libraries." *SL* 30 (1940): 403–06.
2302. Donley, V. "A Chronology of Medical Libraries in the United States with Some Bibliographic Notes Pertaining to Their Early History." Master's thesis, Western Reserve University, 1957.

2303. Draper, W. "Medical Libraries of New York State." *NYSJM* 57 (1957): 584–94.
2304. Farlow, J. W. *The History of the Boston Medical Library*. Norwood, Mass.: Plimpton, 1918.
2305. Farr, L. M. "The History of the Buncombe County Medical Library [1935–53]." *NCMJ* 15 (1954): 87–89.
2306. *The First Catalogue of the Library of the Surgeon General's Office, Washington, 1840*. Facsimile copy. Washington, D.C.: National Library of Medicine, 1961.
2307. Fisher, C. P. "An Account of the Library of the College of Physicians of Philadelphia." *TCPP* 28 (1906): 291–302.
2308. Freund, C. E. "The Library of the College of Physicians of Philadelphia." Master's thesis, Drexel Institute of Technology, 1951.
2309. Fry, A., and Adams, S. "Medical Library Architecture in the Past Fifty Years [1911–57]." *MLAB* 45 (1957): 471–79.
2310. Fulton, J. F. "History of the Yale Medical Libraries." *MLAB* 34 (1946): 184–88.
2311. ———; Kilgour, F. G.; and Stanton, M. E. *Yale Medical Library: The Formation and Growth of Its Historical Library*. New Haven: Associates of the Yale Medical Library, 1962.
2312. Henkle, H. H. "The History of Medical Libraries of Chicago." *ICSJ* 40 (1963): 611–19.
2313. Holt, A. C. "The Library at the Harvard Medical School, 1847 and 1947." *HLB* 2 (1948): 32–43.
2314. Hume, E. E. "The Army Medical Library of Washington and Its Collection of Early Ketuckiana." *KMJ* 38 (1940): 258–67.
2315. ———. "The Army Medical Library of Washington, D.C.: the Largest Medical Library That Has Ever Existed." *Isis* 26 (1937): 423–47.
2316. ———. "Buildings for the Army Medical Library." *MS* 80 (1937): 45–53.
2317. ———. "The Celebration of the Centenary of the Army Medical Library, 1836–1936." *JHAM* 34 (1936): 107–35.
2318. ———. "Garrison and the Army Medical Library, 1891–1930." *BHM* 5 (1937): 301–46.
2319. ———. "The History and the Work of the Army Medical Library." *Science* 85 (1937): 207–10.
2320. ———. "The Story of the Army Medical Library." *VMM* 67 (1940): 261–72.
2321. Huntington, A. T. "The Medical Library Movement in the United States." *MLHJ* 2 (1904): 119–28.
2322. Johns Hopkins University. *The William H. Welch Medical Library of Johns Hopkins University: An Account of Its Origin and Development, Together With a Description of the Building and an Account of the Exercises Held on the Occasion of the Dedication of the Library and the Inauguration of the Chair of the His-*

tory of Medicine at the Johns Hopkins University, Baltimore, Maryland, October 17 and 18, 1929.* Baltimore: Williams and Wilkins, 1929.
2323. Jones, H. W. "The Centenary of the Army Medical Library." *MS* 80 (1937): 1–4.
2324. Keen, W. W. "The Library of the College of Physicians of Philadelphia." *NatH* 20 (1920): 283–85.
2325. Keys, T. E. "Sir William Osler and the Medical Library." *MLAB* 49 (1961): 24–41, 127–48.
2326. Kilgour, F. G. *The Library of the Medical Institute of Yale College and Its Catalogue of 1865.* [New Haven]: Yale University Press, 1960.
2327. Koudelka, J. B. "A History of the Johns Hopkins Medical Libraries, 1889–1935." Master's thesis, Catholic University of America, 1963.
2328. Lage, L. C.; Miller, L. B.; and Washburn, D. "Dental, Nursing, and Pharmaceutical Libraries, 1947–1957." *MLAB* 45 (1957): 371–77.
2329. *The Making of a Library: Extracts and Letters, 1934–1941, of Harvey Cushing, Arnold C. Klebs, [and] John F. Fulton. Presented to John Fulton by His Friends on His Sixtieth Birthday, 1 November 1959.* New Haven, [1959].
2330. Marshall, M. "A History of Dental Libraries in the United States: With Sketches of Important Dental Libraries in Canada and Foreign Countries." *MLAB* 26 (1937): 86–99.
2331. McColl, M. C. "Evans Dental Library, University of Pennsylvania: History and Service." Master's thesis, Drexel Institute of Technology, 1955.
2332. Morris, D. A. "Medical Books Used by Physicians and Medical Students in the United States, 17th–19th Centuries." Master's thesis, Western Reserve University, 1957.
2333. Nonacs, M. "The Kornhauser Memorial Medical Library: Its History and Development." Master's thesis, University of Texas, 1966.
2334. O'Malley, C. D. "The Barkan Library of the History of Medicine and Natural Science Books: An Account of Its Development." *SMB* 9 (1952): 145–55.
2335. Packard, F. R. "The Earliest Medical Library in the United States (Pennsylvania Hospital, Philadelphia)." *VMM* 60 (1933): 139–44.
2336. Ray, F. K. "New York State Medical Library, Established Thirty-one Years Ago." *AMAn* 43 (1922): 320–35.
2337. RePass, E. W. "A History of the Library of the Medical Society of the City and County of Denver (1893–1948)." *MLAB* 39 (1951): 128–34.
2338. Schullman, D. M., and Rogers, F. "The National Library of Medicine." *LQ* 28 (1958): 1–17, 95–121.

2339. Sevy, B. "Temple University School of Medicine Library 1910–1954." Master's thesis, Drexel Institute of Technology, 1955.
2340. Simmons, C. M. "Centennial of Lloyd Library: A Century of Contribution to the Pharmaceutical, Botanical and Biological Sciences, 1864–1964." *Lloydia* 27 (1964): 141–47.
2341. ———. "Lloyd Library: Pharmacy in Cincinnati [1864–1953]." *SL* 45 (1954): 70–73.
2342. Spivak, C. D. "The Medical Libraries in the U.S." *PMJ* 2 (1898): 817–58.
2343. Thomas, E. H. "A History of the National Institutes of Health Library, 1901–1954." Master's thesis, Catholic University of America, 1956.
2344. Thompson, K. S. "America's Oldest Medical Library: The Pennsylvania Hospital (1762–1950)." *MLAB* 44 (1956): 428–30.
2345. Titley, J. "The Library of the Louisville Medical Institute, 1837–1846." *MLAB* 52 (1964): 353–69.
2346. Van Ingen, P. "The Library Without a Home." *AcaB* 1 (Fall 1948): 2–7.
2347. Wannarka, M. B. "History of a Medical Collection Housed in the Denver Public Library, 1893–1899." *RMMJ* 64 (1967): 55–57.
2348. ———. "Medical Collections in Public Libraries of the United States: A Brief Historical Study." *MLAB* 56 (1968): 1–14.
2349. Waring, J. I. "The Library of the Medical Society of South Carolina (1791–1949)." *MLAB* 38 (1950): 253–60.
2350. Warner, H. J. "A History of the New York State Medical Library." Master's thesis, State University of New York at Albany, 1967.
2351. Weakley, M. E. "The Origin and History of the Medical Library of the University of Virginia School of Medicine, 1825–1962." Master's thesis, University of North Carolina, 1966.
2352. Webster, J. P. "The Story of a Plastic Surgery Library." *CLC* 1 (Fall 1951): 9–17.
2353. Wilson, W. J. "Early Plans for a National Medical Library." *MLAB* 42 (1954): 426–34.

G. Government Libraries

2354. Adkins, M. T. "Growth of a Great National Library, 1800–1889." *MAH* 22 (1889): 229–33.
2355. Alder, C. "The Smithsonian Library." In *The Smithsonian Institution, 1846–1896: The History of Its First Half Century*, edited by G. B. Goode, pp. 265–302. Washington, D.C., 1897.
2356. Ashley, F. W. "Three Eras in the Library of Congress." In *Essays Offered to Herbert Putnam by His Colleagues and Friends on His Thirtieth Anniversary as Librarian of Congress, 5 April, 1929,*

edited by W. W. Bishop and A. Keogh, pp. 57–67. New Haven: Yale University Press, 1929.
2357. Baatz, W. Y. "Library Service in the Veterans Administration (1921–49)." *LQ* 19 (1949): 166–77.
2358. Barnett, C. R. "Government Libraries–Old and New." *SL* 9 (1918): 214–19.
2359. Basler, R. P. *The Muse and the Librarian*. Westport, Conn.: Greenwood Press, 1974.
2360. Belanger, S. E. "History of the Library of the Marine Biological Laboratory, 1888–1973." *JLH* 10 (1975): 255–63.
2361. Berthold, A. M. "The Library of the Department of State." *LQ* 28 (1958): 27–37.
2362. Billings, J. S. "The Influence of the Smithsonian Institution Upon the Development of Libraries, the Organization and Work of Societies, and the Publication of Scientific Literature in the United States." In *The Smithsonian Institution, 1846–1896: The History of Its First Half Century*, edited by G. B. Goode, pp. 815–22. Washington, D.C.: 1897.
2363. Bishop, W. W. *Library of Congress*. Chicago: American Library Association Publishing Board, 1911.
2364. ———. "Thirty Years of the Library of Congress, 1899–1929." In *Essays Offered to Herbert Putnam by His Friends and Colleagues on His Thirtieth Anniversary as Librarian of Congress, 5 April 1929*, edited by W. W. Bishop and A. Keogh, pp. 24–34. New Haven: Yale University Press, 1929.
2365. ———. "Thirty Years of the Library of Congress, 1899 to 1929." *LJ* 54 (1929): 379–87.
2366. Breisacher, R. "A History and Survey of the Library of the National Bureau of Standards." Master's thesis, Catholic University of America, 1953.
2367. Brinkley, C. "Army Post Library Service: An Inquiry into Its Origin and Development, Present Organization, and Future." Master's thesis, University of Washington, 1952.
2368. Bromiley, F. "The History and Organization of the Franklin D. Roosevelt Library, Hyde Park, New York." Master's thesis, Western Reserve University, 1959. Published: Association of College and Research Libraries Microcard, Number 117.
2369. Burnette, P. J. "The Army Library." *LQ* 27 (1957): 23–37.
2370. Clapp, V. W. "The Library of Congress and the Other Scholarly Libraries of the Nation [1800–1947]." *CRL* 9 (1948): 116–25.
2371. Cole, G. L. "Presidential Libraries." *JL* 4 (1972): 115–29.
2372. Cole, J. Y. "Ainsworth Spofford and the National Library." Doctoral dissertation, George Washington University, 1971.
2373. ———. "For Congress and the Nation: The Dual Nature of the Library of Congress." *QJLC* 32 (1975): 118–38.

2374. ———. "Of Copyright, Men and a National Library." *QJLC* 28 (1971): 114–36.
2375. ———. "L.C. and ALA, 1876–1901." *LJ* 98 (1973): 2965–70.
2376. ———. "The Library of Congress in the Nineteenth Century: An Informal Account." *JLH* 9 (1974): 222–40.
2377. ———. "The National Libraries of the United States and Canada." In *A Century of Service: Librarianship in the United States and Canada*, edited by S. L. Jackson et al., pp. 243–59. Chicago: American Library Association, 1976.
2378. ———. "The National Monument for a National Library: Ainsworth Rand Spofford and the New Library of Congress, 1871–1897." *RCHS* 48 (1973): 468–507.
2379. ———. "Smithmeyer and Pelz: Embattled Architects of the Library of Congress." *QJLC* 29 (1972): 282–307.
2380. Colkel, M. B., and Preston, E. H. "Local History and Genealogical Reference Section, Library of Congress." *AG* 17 (1940): 65–68.
2381. Commons, E. "The Libraries of the Department of Health, Education, and Welfare [Since 1947]." *LQ* 27 (1957): 173–86.
2382. Connor, R. D. W. "The Franklin D. Roosevelt Library." *AAr* 3 (1940): 81–92.
2383. Cylke, F. K. "Federal Libraries." *ELIS* 8:371–87.
2384. Dale, D. C. *The United Nations Library: Its Origin and Development*. Chicago: American Library Association, 1970.
2385. Diamond, I. S. "The Library of the U.S. Treasury Department." *LQ* 27 (1957): 83–87.
2386. Evans, L. H. "The Strength by Which We Live." *BALA* 44 (1950): 339–45.
2387. Ford, W. C. "A Division of Manuscripts." In *Essays Offered to Herbert Putnam by His Friends and Colleagues on His Thirtieth Anniversary as Librarian of Congress, 5 April 1929*, edited by W. W. Bishop and A. Keogh. New Haven: Yale University Press, 1929.
2388. Fry, B. M.; Warheit, I. A.; and Randall, G. E. "The Atomic Energy Commission Library System: Its Origin and Development (1946–49)." *CRL* 11 (1950): 5–9.
2389. Gabriel, R. H. "The Library of Congress and American Scholarship." *BALA* 44 (1950): 349–51.
2390. Gartland, H. J. "The Veterans Administration Medical Library Program, 1946–1956." *MLAB* 45 (1957): 389–98.
2391. Giandonato, R. M. H. "Connecticut Agricultural Experiment Station Library, 1875–1950." *SL* 41 (1950): 352–58, 370.
2392. Goff, F. R. "Early Library of Congress Bookplates." *QJLC* 26 (1969): 55–61.
2393. ———. "Oldest Library in Washington: The Rare Book Division of the Library of Congress." *RCHS* (1971): 322–45.

2394. Goldman, S. "History of the United States Weather Bureau Library." Master's thesis, Catholic University of America, 1959.
2395. Gondos, V. "The Movement for a National Archives of the United States, 1906–1926." Doctoral dissertation, American University, 1971.
2396. Goodrum, C. A. *The Library of Congress*. New York: Praeger Publishers, 1974.
2397. Greathouse, C. H. "Development of Agricultural Libraries." In *Yearbook of the United States Department of Agriculture, 1899*, pp. 491–512. Washington, D.C.: Government Printing Office, 1900.
2398. Gropp, A. E. "The Library of Congress and the Hispanic-American Field." *BALA* 44 (1950): 358–59.
2399. Hill, D. *Libraries of Washington*. Chicago: American Library Association, 1936.
2400. Howard, P. "The Department of Interior Library System." *LQ* 27 (1957): 38–46.
2401. Johnston, W. D. *The History of the Library of Congress, 1800–1864*. Washington, D.C.: Government Printing Office, 1904.
2402. ———. "The Smithsonian Institution and the Plans for a National Library." In his *History of the Library of Congress, 1800–1864*, pp. 403–506. Washington, D.C.: Government Printing Office, 1904.
2403. Jones, H. G. *The Records of a Nation*. New York: Atheneum, 1969.
2404. Junior Service League, Independence, Mo. *The Harry S. Truman Library in Historic Independence*. [Independence, 1957].
2405. Kaula, N. "175 Years of the Library of Congress." *HLS* 14 (1975): 244–46.
2406. Lacy, D. M. "The Library of Congress: A Sesquicentenary Review 1800–1950." *LQ* 20 (1950): 157–79, 235–58.
2407. Lacy, M. G. "The Library of the U.S. Department of Agriculture and Its Branches." *LJ* 46 (1921): 493–95.
2408. LaMontagne, L. E. "Jefferson and the Library of Congress." In his *American Library Classification: With Special Reference to the Library of Congress*, pp. 27–62. Hamden, Conn.: Shoestring Press, 1961.
2409. Lloyd, D. D. "The Harry S. Truman Library." *AAr* 18 (April 1955): 99–110.
2410. Lord, M. E. "The Library of Congress." *BALA* 44 (1950): 346–48.
2411. Lorenz, J. G., et al. "The Library of Congress Abroad." *LibT* 20 (1972): 548–76.
2412. Luckett, G. R. "A History of the United States Naval Academy Library, 1845–1907." Master's thesis, Catholic University of America, 1951.
2413. MacLeish, A. "The American Experience: The Hispanic Foundation in the Library of Congress." *BPAU* 73 (1939): 621–34.

2414. ———. "The Reorganization of the Library of Congress, 1939–44." *LQ* 14 (1944): 277–315.
2415. Marley, S. B. "Newspapers and the Library of Congress." *QJLC* 32 (1975): 207–37.
2416. McCoy, D. R. "The Beginnings of the Franklin D. Roosevelt Library." *Prologue* 7 (1975): 136–50.
2417. McDonough, J. "Justin Smith Morrill and the Library of Congress." *VH* 35 (1967): 141–50.
2418. Mearns, D. C. "The First White House Library (1801–11)." *DCL* 24 (1953): 2–7.
2419. ———. *The Story Up to Now: The Library of Congress, 1800–1946.* Washington, D.C., 1947.
2420. ———. "Virginia in the History of the Library of Congress, or Mr. Jefferson's Other Seedlings." *VLB* 16 (1951): 1–4.
2421. Mohrhardt, F. E. "The Library of the United States Department of Agriculture [Since 1862]." *LQ* 27 (1957): 81–82.
2422. Mood, F. "The Continental Congress and the Plan for a Library of Congress in 1782–1783: An Episode in American Cultural History." *PMHB* 72 (1948): 3–24.
2423. Morrisey, M. "Historical Development and Organization of the Federal Library Committee." *DLQ* 6 (1970): 207–31.
2424. Mugridge, D. H. "Thomas Jefferson and the Library of Congress." *WLB* 18 (1944): 608–11.
2425. Mumford, L. Q. "Bibliographic Developments at the Library of Congress." *Libri* 17 (1967): 294–304.
2426. North, N. "O.A.E.S.L.: A History of the Library of the Ohio Agricultural Experiment Station at Wooster, Ohio." Master's thesis, Western Reserve University, 1953.
2427. Putnam, H. "A National Library for the United States." *Bookman* 15 (1902): 52–57.
2428. Rhees, W. J. *The Smithsonian Institution: Documents Relative to Its Origin and History, 1835–1887.* Washington, D.C.: Government Printing Office, 1901.
2429. Salamanca, L. *Fortress of Freedom: The Story of the Library of Congress.* Philadelphia: Lippincott, 1942.
2430. Schmeckebier, L. F. *The Government Printing Office: Its History, Activities, and Organization.* Baltimore: Johns Hopkins Press, 1925.
2431. Schwartz, A. E. "American Libraries Abroad: U.S. Military Libraries." *LibT* 20 (1972): 527–37.
2432. Scott, C. D. "The History and Present Status of the Library of the United States Tariff Commission." Master's thesis, Catholic University of America, 1955. Published: Association of College and Research Libraries Microcard, Number 53.
2433. Smith, L. E. "The Library List of 1783: Being a Catalogue of Books, Composed and Arranged by James Madison, and Others, and Rec-

ommended for the Use of Congress on January 24, 1783." Doctoral dissertation, Claremont Graduate School, 1969.
2434. Smith, R. C. "The Hispanic Foundation in the Library of Congress." *BPAU* 73 (1939): 625–34.
2435. Snapp, E. "The Acquisition of the Vollbehr Collection of Incunabula for the Library of Congress." *JLH* 10 (1975): 152–61.
2436. Solberg, T. "A Chapter in the Unwritten History of the Library of Congress from January 17–April 5, 1899." *LQ* 9 (1939): 285–98.
2437. Spofford, A. R., et al. "Libraries of the General Government." In U.S. Bureau of Education, *Public Libraries in the United States of America . . .* , pp. 252–78. Washington, D.C.: Government Printing Office, 1876.
2438. ———. "The Relation Between the Smithsonian Institution and the Library of Congress." In *The Smithsonian Institution, 1846–1896: The History of Its First Half Century*, edited by G. B. Goode, pp. 823–32. Washington, D.C., 1897.
2439. Steele, H. M. "The Library of the United States Department of Labor, Washington, D.C. [1917–50]." *SL* 41 (1950): 93–97.
2440. Stevens, M. H. "Enough Fathom Long Swine." *LLJ* 42 (1949): 1–11.
2441. Stillman, M. E. "The United States Air Force Library Service: Its History, Organization and Administration." Doctoral dissertation, University of Illinois, 1966.
2442. Story, J. "A National Library: Mr. Justice Story Speaks. A Letter Edited by Mortimer D. Schwartz and John Hogan." *JLE* 8 (1955): 328–30.
2443. Sturdevant, E. "The Walter Reed Army Medical Center Library [Since 1928]." *DCL* 28 (1957): 3–10.
2444. Taylor, R. M. *History of the North Carolina Supreme Court Library [July 1, 1969]*. St. Paul: West Publishing Co., 1969.
2445. Thomas, M. A. "The Delaware State Archives: 1931–1951." Master's thesis, Drexel Institute of Technology, 1952.
2446. U.S. Library of Congress. Map Division. *The Services and Collections of the Map Division (1897–1951)*. Washington, D.C.: Library of Congress, 1951.
2447. ———. Rare Book Division. *The Rare Books Division: A Guide to Its Collections and Services*. Washington, D.C.: Library of Congress, 1950.
2448. U.S. National Agricultural Library. Associates. *The National Agricultural Library: A Chronology of Its Leadership and Attainments, 1839–1973*. [Beltsville, Md.]: Associates of the National Agricultural Library, [1974].
2449. Vance, J. T. "The Centennial of the Law Library of Congress." *ABAJ* 18 (1931): 597–99.
2450. Vought, S. W. "The Library of the Federal Office of Education." *PJE* 12 (1934): 21–25.
2451. Vrooman, F. "Our National Library." *Arena* 36 (1906): 278–85.

2452. Waserman, M. J. "Historical Chronology and Selected Bibliography Relating to the National Library of Medicine." *MLAB* 60 (1972): 551–58.
2453. Washburn, W. E. "The Influence of the Smithsonian Institution on the Intellectual Life in Mid-Nineteenth Century Washington." *RCHS* 1963–65 (1966): 96–121.
2454. Willis, D. E. "The History and Present Status of the Library of the United States Geological Survey." Master's thesis, Catholic University of America, 1953.
2455. Zabel, J. M. "Prison Libraries." *SL* 67 (1976): 1–7.

X. Education for Librarianship

If one excludes ephemeral journal articles, the historical literature of education for librarianship divides rather neatly into printed primary sources and scholarly dissertations, without much in between. The research studies have usually been confined to chronological segments or to single aspects of the field.

Several works set the framework for more intensive studies. Gerald Bramley's *A History of Library Education* (1969, **2460**), while focusing on British efforts, devotes several chapters to the American scene. Robert Downs contributed "Education for Librarianship in the United States and Canada" to initiate the published conference proceedings entitled *Library Education: An International Survey* (1968, **2481**). The single most insightful piece on the topic remains Louis R. Wilson's "Historical Development of Education for Librarianship in the United States" in *Education for Librarianship* (1949, **2533**). Though dated now, its summaries and hypotheses are provocative. Donald Davis presents a chronological outline and overview in the *Library Trends* centennial issue (1976, **2477**). Carl White's brief study, *A Historical Introduction to Library Education: Problems and Progress to 1951* (1976, **2529**), is an interpretive review of the formative period.

Bibliographical coverage of the printed sources, as well as some of the manuscript collections, is nearly complete because of several doctoral dissertations completed between 1959 and 1969 which treat the period from before 1887 to 1960. Three are now published monographs. Sarah Vann's *Training for Librarianship Before 1923* (1961, **2524**) is the most heavily documented from primary sources and provides complete coverage to the celebrated Williamson Report. Charles Churchwell continued the chronology in his "Education for Librarianship in the United States: Some Factors Which Influenced Its Development Between 1919 and 1939" (1966), published as *The Shaping of American Library Education* (1975, **2472**). C. Edward Carroll's *The Professionalization of Education for Librarianship* (1970, **2471**) deals primarily with the years 1940 to 1960.

The most significant document remains Charles C. Williamson's *Training for Library Service* (1923), a report for the Carnegie Corporation which has been reprinted and has received textual study and analysis by Sarah Vann as *The Williamson Reports of 1921 and 1923* (1971, **2526**) and *The Williamson Reports: A Study* (1971, **2525**).

While a number of surveys of library education have historical interest as contemporary documents, several have survived the test of time to be landmarks of their periods, such as Ernest J. Reece's *The Curriculum in Library Schools* (1936, **2511**), Joseph L. Wheeler's *Progress and Problems in Education for Librarianship* (1946, **2528**), and "The Future of Library Education" conference reported in the *Journal of Education for Librarianship* (summer 1962).

Individual schools, particularly the older and more prominent ones, have been the subject of occasional commemorative volumes, such as those covering the school at Columbia: *School of Library Economy of Columbia College, 1887–1889: Documents for a History* (1937, **2473**) and Ray Trautman's *History of the School of Library Service, Columbia University* (1954, **2523**). A special aspect of library education is treated in Donald Davis's *The Association of American Library Schools, 1915–1968: An Analytical History* (1974, **2476**).

Finally, those interested in this subject should also see the biography section of the bibliography for the studies of library educators like Melvil Dewey and Katharine Sharp.

Education for Librarianship

2456. "Accredited Library School Histories." *LJ* 62 (1937): 24–35.
2457. Adrian, J. M. "A History of the Library Science Department of East Texas State College." Master's thesis, East Texas State College, 1959.
2458. Asheim, L. E. "Education for Librarianship." *LQ* 25 (1955): 76–90.
2459. Blazek, R. "The Place of History in Library Education." *JLH* 9 (1974): 193–95.
2460. Bramley, G. *A History of Library Education.* New York: Archon, 1969.
2461. Burgess, R. S. "Education for Librarianship–U.S. Assistance." *LibT* 20 (1972): 515–26.
2462. Cain, S. M. *History of the Library Science Department, Wisconsin State University, Whitewater.* Whitewater, Wis.: Wisconsin State University, 1967.
2463. Callaham, B. E. "The Carnegie Library School of Atlanta, 1905–1925." Master's thesis, Emory University, 1961.
2464. ———. "The Carnegie Library School of Atlanta." *LQ* 37 (1967): 49–79.
2465. Campion, A. L. "Education for Special Librarians in the United States and Canada in 1946 and 1952." Master's thesis, Drexel Institute of Technology, 1953.
2466. Cantrell, C. H. "Education for Librarianship, 1900–1925." *AlaL* 2 (1951): 7–11.
2467. Carnovsky, L. "Changing Patterns in Librarianship: Implications for Library Education." *WLB* 41 (1967): 484–91.

160 Education for Librarianship

2468. ———. "The Evaluation and Accreditation of Library Schools." *LQ* 37 (1967): 333–47.
2469. ———, and Swanson, D. R. "The University of Chicago Graduate Library School." *ELIS* 4:540–42.
2470. Carroll, C. E. "History of Library Education." In *The Administrative Aspects of Education for Librarianship: A Symposium*, edited by M. B. Cassata and H. L. Totten, pp. 2–28. Metuchen, N.J.: Scarecrow Press, 1975.
2471. ———. *The Professionalization of Education for Librarianship, with Special Reference to the Years 1940–1960*. Metuchen, N.J.: Scarecrow Press, 1970.
2472. Churchwell, C. D. *The Shaping of American Library Education*. Chicago: American Library Association, 1975.
2473. Columbia University. School of Library Service. *School of Library Economy of Columbia College, 1887–1889: Documents for a History*. New York: Columbia University School of Library Service, 1937.
2474. Danton, J. P. "Doctoral Study in Librarianship in the United States." *CRL* 20 (1959): 435–53+
2475. Davenport, F. B. "A History of the Western Reserve University Library School, 1904–1954." Master's thesis, Western Reserve University, 1956.
2476. Davis, D. G. *The Association of American Library Schools, 1915–1968: An Analytical History*. Metuchen, N.J.: Scarecrow Press, 1974.
2477. ———. "Education for Librarianship." *LibT* 25 (1976): 113–34.
2478. Debons, A. "Education in Library and Information Science." *ELIS* 7:414–74.
2479. Doane, G. H. "Library School Heritage." *WisLB* 52 (1956): 184–86.
2480. Doe, J. "The Development of Education for Medical Librarianship." *MLAB* 37 (1949): 213–20.
2481. Downs, R. B. "Education for Librarianship in the United States and Canada." In *Library Education: An International Survey*, edited by L. E. Bone, pp. 1–20. Champaign: University of Illinois Graduate School of Library Science, 1968.
2482. Dubois, P. Z. *Education for Librarianship at Kent State University*. Kent: Kent State University, 1971.
2483. Emert, F. A. "Trends in Thought on the Training of Special Librarians from the Beginning of the Special Libraries Association in 1909 Through 1950." Master's thesis, Western Reserve University, 1952.
2484. Evans, G. E. "An Historical Note Relating to Library Degrees and the Two Year Program." *JEL* 11 (1971): 308–24.
2485. Evraiff, L. A. K. "A Survey of the Development and Emerging Patterns in the Preparation of School Librarians." Doctoral dissertation, Wayne State University, 1969.

2486. Fleischer, M. B. "Credentials Awarded Through August, 1961, by Agencies Presently or Formerly Approved or Accredited by the American Library Association." Master's thesis, University of Texas, 1963.
2487. Galvin, T. J. "The Accreditation Controversy: An Essay in Issues and Origins." *JEL* 10 (1969): 11–27.
2488. Garrison, G. "Drexel University Graduate School of Library Science." *ELIS* 7:302–05.
2489. Goggin, M. K. "University of Denver Graduate School of Librarianship." *ELIS* 6:592–95.
2490. Goldstein, H. "Florida State University School of Library Science." *ELIS* 8:561–66.
2491. Grotzinger, L. A. "The University of Illinois Library School, 1893–1942." *JLH* 2 (1967): 129–41.
2492. Howe, H. E. "Two Decades of Education for Librarianship." *LQ* 12 (1942): 447–70.
2493. Illinois, University. Library School. *Fifty Years of Education for Librarianship: Papers Read at the University of Illinois Library School, 1943*. Urbana: University of Illinois Press, 1943.
2494. James, M., and Kalp, M. E. "The Association of American Library Schools, 1915–1924." *AALSNL* 9 (1957): 8–13.
2495. Jones, H. E. "Archival Training in American Universities, 1938–1968." *AAr* 31 (1968): 135–54.
2496. Jordan, M. "Events in the Development of Education for Medical Librarianship in the Last Decade." *MLAB* 45 (1957): 341–60.
2497. Khurshid, A. "Intellectual Foundations of Library Education." *IntlR* 8 (1976): 3–21.
2498. Kortendick, J. J. "Catholic University of America, Graduate Department of Library Science." *ELIS* 4:319–22.
2499. Kunkle, J. "The California State Library School." *JEL* 12 (1972): 232–39.
2500. Lawson, V. "Emory University Division of Librarianship." *ELIS* 8: 28–34.
2501. "Library Education at Madison: The University of Wisconsin Library School." *WisLB* 71 (1975): 332–38.
2502. Linderman, W. B. "Columbia University, School of Library Science." *ELIS* 5:370–90.
2503. Lohrer, M. A. "The Teacher-Librarian Training Program, 1900–1944." Master's thesis, University of Chicago, 1944.
2504. Luther, K. *The Teaching of Cataloging and Classification at the University of Illinois Library School [1893–1949]*. Urbana: University of Illinois Library School Occasional Paper No. 5, 1957.
2505. Mitchell, S. B. "The Pioneer Library School in Middle Age." *LQ* 20 (1950): 272–88.
2506. Norton, F. "Five Decades of Library Education in the South." *LLAB* 14 (1951): 5–12.

2507. Nehlig, M. E. "The History and Development of the Drexel Institute Library School, 1892–1914." Master's thesis, Drexel Institute of Technology, 1952.
2508. Nesbitt, E. "Training of Children's Librarians: History and Implications." *BNYPL* 60 (1966): 605–10.
2509. Osburn, H. "A History of the Library Science Department of the Millersville State Teachers College, Millersville, Pennsylvania." Master's thesis, Drexel Institute of Technology, 1955.
2510. Penland, P. R. "Accrediting Library Schools: A Study of the Background and Problems." Master's thesis, University of Michigan, 1955.
2511. Reece, E. J. *The Curriculum in Library Schools*. New York: Columbia University Press, 1936.
2512. Reed, S. R. "The Curriculum of Library Schools Today: A Historical Overview." In *Education for Librarianship: The Design of the Curriculum of Library Schools*, edited by H. Goldhor, pp. 19–45. Urbana: University of Illinois Graduate School of Library Science, 1971.
2513. ———. "Feast or Famine." *LIS* 9 (1971): 61–83.
2514. Roden, C. B. "An Essay in Retrospection [University of Chicago Graduate Library School]." *LQ* 12 (1942): 659–65.
2515. Roper, F. W. "A Comparative Analysis of Programs in Medical Library Education in the United States, 1957–1971." Doctoral dissertation, Indiana University, 1971.
2516. Rothstein, S. "Issues, Decisions, and Continuing Debate: The History of American Library Education, 1870–1970." In *Workshop on Education for Librarianship*, pp. 3–11. Edmonton, Alta.: University of Alberta, 1970.
2517. Schenk, R. K. "Highlights in the History of the Library School of the University of Wisconsin." *WisLB* 52 (1956): 187–90.
2518. Shera, J. H. "Case Western Reserve University School of Library Science." *ELIS* 4:220–28.
2519. Singleton, M. E. "Reference Teaching in the Pioneer Library Schools, 1883–1903." Master's thesis, Columbia University, 1942.
2520. Stallmann, E. L. *Library Internships: History, Purpose, and a Proposal*. Urbana: University of Illinois Graduate School of Library Science Occasional Paper No. 37, 1957.
2521. Stanbery, G. W. "History of the Carnegie Library School: Through Its First Fifty Years." Master's thesis, Carnegie Institute, 1951.
2522. Tai, Tse-Chien. *Professional Education for Librarianship*. New York: Wilson, 1925.
2523. Trautman, R. L. *A History of the School of Library Service, Columbia University*. New York: Columbia University, 1954.
2524. Vann, S. K. *Training for Librarianship Before 1923: Education for Librarianship Prior to the Publication of Williamson's Report on*

Training for Library Service. Chicago: American Library Association, 1961.
2525. ———. *The Williamson Reports: A Study.* Metuchen, N.J.: Scarecrow Press, 1971.
2526. ———, ed. *The Williamson Reports of 1921 and 1923 . . .* Metuchen, N.J.: Scarecrow Press, 1971.
2527. Webb, D. A. "Local Efforts to Prepare Library Assistants and Librarians in Texas from 1900 to 1942." Doctoral dissertation, University of Chicago, 1963.
2528. Wheeler, J. L. *Progress and Problems in Education for Librarianship.* New York: Carnegie Corporation, 1946.
2529. White, C. M. *A Historical Introduction to Library Education: Problems and Progress to 1951.* Metuchen, N.J.: Scarecrow Press, 1976.
2530. Wicklzer, A. F. "Education for Librarianship: A Brief History, 1886–1953." Master's thesis, Western Reserve University, 1953.
2531. Wiesner, J. "A Brief History of Education for Librarianship [1887–1954]." *Education* 74 (1954): 173–77.
2532. Wilson, L. R. "Challenge of Library Literature to Education for Librarianship, 1923–1953." In *Challenges to Librarianship,* edited by L. Shores, pp. 125–40. Tallahassee: Florida State University, 1953.
2533. ———. "Historical Development of Education for Librarianship in the United States." In *Education for Librarianship,* edited by B. Berelson, pp. 44–59. Chicago: American Library Association, 1949.
2534. Wing, M. J. "A History of the School of Library Science of the University of North Carolina: The First Twenty-five Years." Master's thesis, University of North Carolina, 1958. Published: Association of College and Research Libraries Microcard, Number 119.
2535. Wisconsin Library School Association. "Some Interesting History." *WisLB* 20 (1924): 53–56.
2536. Wisconsin University Library School. *Directory of Graduates for Twenty-five Classes, 1907–1931.* Madison: Wisconsin University Library School, 1931.
2537. Wyer, J. I. "The New York State Library School, 1887–1926." *LJ* 62 (1937): 5–10.

XI. Library Associations

Besides the official organs of the various organizations and the general library press, the printed materials dealing with library associations have generally consisted of brief historical surveys and criticisms of library associations in general and works treating individual library associations. The latter may in turn be divided into anniversary or commemorative pieces and scholarly treatises. A noteworthy exception to the above generalization is the *Library Trends* issue (January 1955, **2568**), edited by David H. Clift, "Library Associations in the United States and the British Commonwealth." The editor's lead article, "Associations in the United States," provides the best historical survey and coverage of the printed literature.

Although the American Library Association has dominated historical coverage, several insightful articles have evaluated associations as a group. Among these are Peter Conmy and Caroline M. Coughlin's study (1976, **2575**), Ralph E. Ellsworth's "Critique of Library Associations in America" (1961, **2594**), and Eli M. Oboler's "Library Associations: Their History and Influence" (1967, **2649**).

The American Library Association is the subject of several works fulfilling different purposes. Edward G. Holley's *Raking the Historic Coals* (1967, **2616**) provides documents and commentary relating to the 1876 meeting which resulted in the formation of the association, and Sister M. A. J. O'Loughlin has studied the same meeting in detail (1971, **2650**). George B. Utley's *Fifty Years of the American Library Association* (1926, **2685**) carries the story forward in summary fashion, while Arthur Young has written a detailed study of ALA activities during World War I (1976, **2699**). Dennis V. Thomison's dissertation, "The History and Development of the American Library Association, 1876–1957" (1973, **2678**), is projected for publication in revised form by the association.

While other associations may likewise be studied through the library press, they are the subject of fewer serious works. Some have issued special summaries, such as *Special Libraries Association: Its First Fifty Years, 1909–1959* (1959, **2644**) and J. F. Ballard's "The Past History of the Medical Library Association, Inc." (1948, **2552**). Commemorative articles abound in association media.

Few doctoral dissertations are widely known and fewer have found their way into print; yet the corpus of histories is growing. Mehl's history of the American Theological Library Association (1973, **2639**); Charles Hale's study of the Association of College and Research Libraries (1976, **2609**),

McGowan's study of the Association of Research Libraries (1972, **2637**), and Davis's analysis of the Association of American Library Schools (1972) have been the subject of considerable scholarly interest. Only Donald Davis's *The Association of American Library Schools, 1915–1968* (1974, **2583**) has been published to date. A considerable number of national, regional, and state, as well as specialized associations, have received attention in master's theses, and they are listed in the following bibliography.

Library Associations

2538. Abrahamson, D. "The Louisiana Library Association: Its History [1909–1952]." *LLAB* 15 (1952): 66–74.

2539. Allen, M. E. *History of the Connecticut School Library Association*. [Hartford?]: The Connecticut School Library Association, 1958.

2540. American Library Association. *Division of Cataloging and Classification in Retrospect: A History of the Division of Cataloging and Classification of the American Library Association, 1900–1950*. Chicago: American Library Association, 1950.

2541. Anders, M. E. "Southeastern Library Association, 1920–1950." *SEL* 6 (1956): 9–39, 68–81.

2542. ———. "State Library Associations in the Southeast [nine states, 1897–1950]." *SEL* 2 (1952): 7–24.

2543. ———. *The Tennessee Valley Library Council, 1940–1949: A Regional Approach to Library Planning*. Atlanta: The Southeastern Library Association, 1960.

2544. Anderson, I. T., and Osborne, G. E. "The History of the Committee on Libraries of the American Association of Colleges of Pharmacy (1933–53)." *MLAB* 41 (1953): 414–18.

2545. Annan, G. L. "The Medical Library Association in Retrospect, 1937–1967." *MLAB* 55 (1967): 379–89.

2546. Archer, N. W. "The Georgia Library Association: The First Forty Years." Master's thesis, Emory University, 1962.

2547. Ayrault, M. S., and Vann, S. K. "RTSD . . . After Twenty Years." *LRTS* 20 (1976): 303–14.

2548. "A Backward Glance: 1957–72." *AS* 9 (1972): 30–36.

2549. Baker, F. "History of the Northern Section." *BCSLA* 20 (1949):13–14.

2550. Baldwin C. F. "Minnesota Library Association, 1900–1942." *MinnL* 13 (1942): 327–30.

2551. Ball, A. D. "District of Columbia Library Association." *ELIS* 7:241–42.

2552. Ballard, J. F. "The Past History of the Medical Library Association, Inc." *MLAB* 36 (1948): 227–41.

2553. Ballou, R. O. *A History of the Council on Books in Wartime, 1942–1946*. New York: The Council, 1946.

2554. Bennett, H. H. "Delaware Library Association." *ELIS* 6:543–46.
2555. Bennett, J. D. "An Anniversary." *DCL* 26 (1955): 7–10.
2556. Bennett, J. P. "The Music Library Association, 1931–1956." Master's thesis, Western Reserve University, 1957.
2557. Bowerman, G. F. "The District of Columbia Library Association: Semicentennial Notes." *DCL* 15 (1944): 9–10.
2558. Bowker, R. R. "Seed Time and Harvest–The Story of the ALA." *BALA* 20 (1926): 355–56.
2559. Brewster, E., and Houk, J. "Colorado Library Association." *ELIS*: 5:355–56.
2560. Brigham, H. O. "The Special Libraries Association–A Historical Sketch." *LJ* 54 (1929): 337–40.
2561. ———; Cox, M., and twenty former presidents of the SLA. "Remembrance of Things Past." *SL* 40 (1949): 134–44.
2562. Browning, W. "The Development of the Association of Medical Librarians." *MLAB* 9 (1919): 1–5.
2563. Brunton, D. W. "California Library Association." *ELIS* 3:649–53.
2564. Carlson, W. H. "The Washington Library Association, 1931–55: A Review Article." *PNQ* 48 (1957): 25–26.
2565. Chapman, M. L. "Florida Library Association." *ELIS* 8:557–61.
2566. Clement, E. G. "Audiovisual Concerns and Activities in the American Library Association, 1924–1975." Doctoral dissertation, Indiana University, 1975.
2567. Clift, D. H. "Associations in the United States." *LibT* 3 (1955): 221–37.
2568. ———, ed. "Library Associations in the United States and British Commonwealth." *LibT* 3 (1955): 219–329.
2569. Cohn, W. L. "An Overview of ARL Directors, 1933–1973." *CRL* 37 (1976): 137–44.
2570. Colburn, E. B. "In Retrospect: RTSD, 1957–67." *LRTS* 11 (1967): 5–10.
2571. "The CONGREGATIONAL Library Association: Its Origins and Objects." *CQ* 1 (1859): 70–73.
2572. Conmy, P. T. "CLA's Library History Chapter: Why History?" *CalL* 33 (1972): 205–09.
2573. ———. "The Centennial of the American Library Association and Togetherness." *CLW* 46 (1975): 338–41.
2574. ———. "Centennial and Bi-Centennial: American Library Association and the United States." *OakL* 2 (1973): 1–7.
2575. ———, and Coughlin, C. M. "The Principal Library Associations." In *A Century of Service: Librarianship in the United States and Canada*, edited by S. L. Jackson et al., pp. 260–80. Chicago: American Library Association, 1976.
2576. Connecticut Library Association. *The Connecticut Library Association: Its History and Its Members*. Hartford, 1947.
2577. Consolata, Sister M. "History of the Catholic Library Association."

CLW 36 (1965): 526–27, 611–12; 37 (1965–66): 104–08, 192–94, 257–59, 482–83, 530–31, 591–92; 38 (1966–67): 266–67, 388–89, 441–43; 39 (1967–68): 220–21, 352–53, 518–19, 591–92, 651–52; 40 (1968): 186–88, 243–44.

2578. Council of National Library Associations. *The American Book Center for War Devastated Libraries, Inc., 1944–1948: A Report*. New York, 1953.

2579. Countryman, G. A. "Early History of the Minnesota Library Association, 1891–1900." *MinnL* 13 (1942): 322–26.

2580. Dana, J. C. "Special Libraries Association Chronology: 1909–1949." *SL* 40 (1949): 125–35.

2581. Dane, C. "A Chapter in the History of ALA: The Publishing Board, 1909–1915." *IllL* 36 (1954): 186–89.

2582. Davis, D. G. "An Assessment of AALS." *JEL* 13 (1973): 155–68.

2583. ———. *The Association of American Library Schools, 1915–1968: An Analytical History*. Metuchen, N.J.: Scarecrow Press, 1974.

2584. ———. *Comparative Historical Analysis of Three Associations of Professional Schools*. Urbana: University of Illinois Graduate School of Library Science Occasional Paper No. 115, 1974.

2585. Deale, H. V. "MALC's Second Decade: Commitment to Communication." *CRL* 36 (1975): 143–51.

2586. Debagh, J. "A History of the Hawaii Library Association, 1921–1974." *HLAJ* 31 (1974): 11–13.

2587. DiCanio, F. "The Chicago Association of Law Libraries, 1945–1955." *LLJ* 49 (1956): 204–08.

2588. Dick, E. J. "Educational Film Library Association (EFLA)." *ELIS* 7:481–86.

2589. Donovan, M. J. "Presidential Addresses to the Medical Library Association, 1890–1965: A Thematic Analysis." Master's thesis, Catholic University of America, 1968.

2590. Dyer, J. R. "Centennial of the St. Louis Law Library Association." *MBJ* 9 (1938): 265–66.

2591. Easterly, A. "The Tennessee Library Association's First Fifty Years, 1902–1951." Master's thesis, George Peabody College for Teachers, 1954.

2592. Elliot, C. A. "The U.S. Bureau of Education: Its Role in Library History, 1876." In *Library History Seminar Number 3*, edited by M. J. Zachert, pp. 98–111. Tallahassee: *JLH*, 1968.

2593. Elliott, E. M. "Federal Relations of the American Library Association, 1930–1940." Master's thesis, University of Chicago, 1946.

2594. Ellsworth, R. E. "Critique of Library Associations in America." *LQ* 31 (1961): 382–400.

2595. Emert, F. A. "Trends in Thought on the Training of Special Librarians from the Beginning of the Special Libraries Association in 1909 Through 1950." Master's thesis, Western Reserve University, 1952.

2596. Estes, D. E. "Georgia Library Association." *ELIS* 9:383–86.
2597. Ferguson, E. "Council of National Library Associations." *ELIS* 6: 229–35.
2598. Fitzgerald, W. A. "From Birth to Maturity in a Quarter of a Century." *CLW* 27 (1956): 260–65.
2599. Fleischer, M. B. "Credentials Awarded Through August, 1961, by Agencies Presently or Formerly Approved or Accredited by the American Library Association." Master's thesis, University of Texas, 1963.
2600. Folmer, F. "As Others See Us: The Background." *TLJ* 30 (1954): 107–13.
2601. Foreman, C. "An Analysis of Publications Issued by the American Library Association, 1907–1957." Master's thesis, University of Texas, 1959.
2602. Foster, W. E. "Five Men of '76." *BALA* 20 (1926): 312–23.
2603. Francis, W. W. "Margaret Charlton and the Early Days of the Medical Library Association." *MLAB* 25 (1936): 58–63.
2604. Frost, J. "The Library Conference of '53." *JLH* 2 (1967): 154–60.
2605. "A Further Remembrance of Things Past: SLA's Sixty Years, 1909/1969." *SL* 60 (1969): 535–58.
2606. Gillies, M. "The Wyoming Library Association: An Historical Footnote [1913–17]." *WLR* 8 (1952): 1–7.
2607. Glasier, G. G. "Beginnings of the American Association of Law Libraries (1906–11)." *LLJ* 43 (1950): 147–59.
2608. Golter, P. "The Arizona State Library Association–Twenty-five Years: 1926–1951." *ArizL* 8 (1951): 4–10.
2609. Hale, C. "Association of College and Research Libraries." Doctoral dissertation, Indiana University, 1976.
2610. Harris, M. H. "'An Idea in the Air'–How the ALA Was Born." *LAR* 78 (1976): 302–04.
2611. Heckel, J. W. "American Association of Law Libraries: Charter Members, Officers, and Meeting Places, 1906–1956." *LLJ* 49 (1956): 225–31.
2612. Hendrickson, R. M. "The Rio Grande Chapter of the Special Libraries Association." Master's thesis, University of Texas, 1962.
2613. "History of the Wisconsin Library Association." *WisLB* 5 (1909): 76–79.
2614. Hoffman, J. "The Alabama Library Association, 1904–39: A History of Its Organization, Growth and Contribution to Library Development." Master's thesis, Florida State University, 1962.
2615. Holley, E. G. "ALA at 100." In *ALA Yearbook*, pp. 1–32. Chicago: American Library Association, 1976.
2616. ———, ed. *Raking the Historic Coals: The ALA Scrapbook of 1876.* Beta Phi Mu Chapbook no. 8 [Chicago: Lakeside Press], 1967.
2617. ———. "Who We Were: Profiles of the American Librarian at the Birth of the Professional Association, 1876." *ALib* 7 (1976): 323–26.

2618. James, M., and Kalp, M. E. "The Association of American Library Schools, 1915–1924." *AALSNL* 9 (1957): 8–13.
2619. Jamieson, J. A. *Books for the Army: The Army Library Service in the Second World War.* New York: Columbia University Press, 1950.
2620. Johns, H. *Twenty-five Years of the Washington Library Association.* [Palo Alto, Calif.]: Pacific Books, [1956].
2621. Johnson, B. "The California Library Association, 1895–1906: Years of Experimentation and Growth." *CalL* 37 (1976): 24–29.
2622. Kell, B. F. "An Analysis of Texas Library Association Membership and Officers, 1902–1956." Master's thesis, University of Texas, 1956.
2623. Kraus, J. W. "The Progressive Librarians' Council." *LJ* 97 (1972): 2551–54.
2624. Langdell, M. E. "W.L.A. Through Fifty Years." *WisLB* 37 (1941): 98–101.
2625. Leverette, S., and Elliott, L. "History of the Carolina–South Eastern Chapter (of the American Association of Law Libraries), 1937–1955." *LLJ* 49 (1956): 180–85.
2626. Maddox, L. J. "Trends and Issues in American Librarianship as Reflected in the Papers and Proceedings of the American Library Association, 1876–1885." Doctoral dissertation, University of Michigan, 1958.
2627. Maggetti, M. T. "The Medical Library Association: Its History and Activities, 1898–1953." Master's thesis, Drexel Institute of Technology, 1955.
2628. Magrath, Sister G. "Library Conventions of 1853, 1876, and 1877." *JLH* 8 (1973): 52–69.
2629. Marion, G. E. "Resume of the Association's Activities, 1910–1915." *SL* 5 (1915): 143–46.
2630. ———. "The Special Libraries Association." *LJ* 45 (1920): 294–304.
2631. Marke, J. J. "The Law Library Association of Greater New York (LLAGNY), 1938–1956." *LLJ* 49 (May 1956): 186–90.
2632. Massman, V. F. "From Out of a Desk Drawer: The Beginnings of ALA Headquarters." *BALA* 63 (1969): 475–81.
2633. McClaren, D. N. "The First Ten Years of the Teenage Library Association of Texas, 1949–1959." Master's thesis, University of Texas, 1966.
2634. McCord, J. L. V. "History of the District of Columbia Library Association, 1894–1930." *DCL* 1 (1930): 67–74.
2635. McDaniel, W. B. "Notes on the Association's Interests and Activities as Reflected in the Bulletin, 1911–1941." *MLAB* 30 (1941): 72–79.
2636. ———. "A Salute to Some Milestones, Detours, and Dead-Ends in the History of the [Medical Library] Association Since 1898." *MLAB* 45 (1957): 461–65.

2637. McGowan, F. M. "The Association of Research Libraries, 1932–1962." Doctoral dissertation, University of Pittsburgh, 1972.
2638. McGregor, J. W. "History of the American Association of Law Libraries from 1906 to 1942." Master's thesis, University of Chicago, 1963.
2639. Mehl, W. R. "The Role of the American Theological Library Association in Protestant Theological Libraries and Librarianship, 1947–1970." Doctoral dissertation, Indiana University, 1973.
2640. Michelson, A. I. "The American Merchant Marine Library Association–Its History and Functions." Master's thesis, Western Reserve University, 1950.
2641. Miltimore, C. "Later Days of the Florida Library Association." *FLB* 1 (May 1, 1927): 3–9.
2642. *The Mississippi Library Association: A History, 1909–1968.* N.p.: The Mississippi Library Association, 1968.
2643. Mitchell, A. C. "Special Libraries Association: A Brief History [1909–50]." *SL* 43 (1952): 162–64.
2644. ———, ed. *Special Libraries Association: Its First Fifty Years, 1909–1959.* New York: Special Libraries Association, 1959.
2645. Moore, M. R. "Southern Association, State and Local Leadership for Library Service in Texas Schools." Master's thesis, University of Texas, 1955.
2646. Morroni, J. R. "The Music Library Association, 1931–1961." Master's thesis, University of Chicago, 1968.
2647. Munford, W. A. "The American Library Association and the Library Association: Retrospect, Problems, and Prospects." *Advances in Librarianship* 7 (1977): 145–76.
2648. Neal, P. "Library Problems, 1876–1886: An Analysis of 'Notes and Queries' in 'Library Journal' and 'Proceedings of the American Library Association.'" Master's thesis, Carnegie Institute of Technology, 1954.
2649. Oboler, E. M. "Library Associations: Their History and Influence." *DLQ* (1967): 255–62.
2650. O'Loughlin, Sister M. A. J. "Emergence of American Librarianship: A Study of Influence Evident in 1876." Doctoral dissertation, Columbia University, 1971.
2651. Perham, M. "Reference Section, a Short History." *WisLB* 57 (1961): 160–64+.
2652. Pond, P. "Development of a Professional School Library Association: American Association of School Librarians." *SMQ* 5 (1976): 12–18.
2653. Poole, W. F. "Conference of Librarians: Address of the President." *LJ* 11 (1886): 199–204.
2654. Potter, H. "Great Beginnings–the Southern Section (1915–49)." *BCSLA* 20 (1949): 15–16.
2655. Prassel, M. A. "Some Notes Toward a History of the Texas Library

Association, 1902–1909." Master's thesis, University of Texas, 1967.
2656. Prime, L. M. "The Medical Library Association: Aims, Activities, and a Brief History." *MLAB* 40 (1952): 30–36.
2657. Rathbone, J. A. "The Association of American Library Schools." *LJ* 40 (1915): 302–03.
2658. Roper, D. F. "The American Library Association Subscription Books Committee and Its Influence on Encyclopedia Publishing, 1930–1938." Master's thesis, Florida State University, 1960.
2659. Ross, Sister M. C. "A Study of the Catholic Library Association Based on Presidential Addresses Made During the Years, 1931–1956." Master's thesis, University of Texas, 1958.
2660. Rothe, B. M. "The Law Librarians Society of Washington, D.C., 1939–1955." *LLJ* 49 (1956): 191–97.
2661. Samuels, C. "The American Library Association and the Field of Reprint Publishing, 1924–1965: Some Aspects of History." *RB* 12 (1967): 2–11.
2662. Saniel, I. "A Quarter Century of the Philippine Library Association." *BPLA* 1 (1965): 1–12.
2663. Schultz, C. K. "ASIS: Notes on Its Founding and Development." *Basis* 2 (1976): 49–51.
2664. Schunk, R. J. "The First National Library Conference in Minnesota." *MinnL* (1954): 293–301.
2665. Schwartz, B. "The Role of the American Library Association in the Selection of Archibald MacLeish as Librarian of Congress." *JLH* 9 (1974): 241–64.
2666. Seabrook, M. "A History of the District of Columbia Library Association, 1894–1954." Master's thesis, Catholic University of America, 1957.
2667. Shelton, W. "History of the New Mexico Library Association." *NMLB* 6 (1937): 3–6.
2668. Shera, J. H. "Failure and Success: Assessing a Century." *LJ* 100 (1976): 281–88.
2669. Shove, R. H. "AALS Before 1915." *JEL* 1 (1960): 81–86.
2670. Smith, C. W. "The Early Years of the P.N.L.A." *PNLAQ* 12 (1948): 130–35; 13 (1949): 70–76, 107–13.
2671. Sparks, C. G. "Presidential Addresses Made to the American Library Association, 1876–1951: A Content Analysis." Master's thesis, University of Texas, 1952. Published: Association of College and Research Libraries Microcard, Number 131.
2672. Steinbarger, H. "What Is Past Is Prologue: Development of the Middle Atlantic States Regional Area Conference." *DCL* 21 (1949): 3–8.
2673. Stevens, W. F. *The Keystone State Library Association, 1901–1915.* N.p.: Printed by Order of the Executive Committee, 1916. Supplement (1916–22) pub. 1923.

2674. Sullivan, P. "Library Associations." *LibT* 25 (1976): 135–52.
2675. Thomison, D. "The A.L.A. Goes West: The 1891 San Francisco Conference." *CalL* 37 (1976): 31–35.
2676. ———. "The A.L.A. and Its Missing Presidents." *JLH* 9 (1974): 362–67.
2677. ———. "F.D.R., the ALA, and Mr. MacLeish." *LQ* 42 (1972): 390–98.
2678. ———. "The History and Development of the American Library Association, 1876–1957." Doctoral dissertation, University of Southern California, 1973.
2679. Tower, E. B. "The Story of the A.M.M.L.A." *SL* 14 (1923): 69–72.
2680. Troxel, W. "The Medical Library Association, 1947–1957." *MLAB* 45 (1957): 378–85.
2681. Turner, H. M. "Conference of Eastern College Librarians." *ELIS* 7: 338–45.
2682. Tuttle, M. L. "A History of the American Theological Library Association." Master's thesis, Emory University, 1961.
2683. Utley, G. B. "American Library Institute: A Historical Sketch." *LQ* 16 (1946): 152–59.
2684. ———. "Early Days of the Florida Library Association." *FLB* 1 (May 1, 1927): 1–2.
2685. ———. *Fifty Years of the American Library Association*. Chicago: American Library Association, 1926.
2686. ———. *The Librarians Conference of 1853: A Chapter in American Library History*. Chicago: American Library Association, 1951.
2687. Walker, M. J. D. "The Southwestern Library Association, 1922–1954." Master's thesis, University of Texas, 1959.
2688. Whalum, C. G. "A Content Analysis of the American Library Association Presidential Inaugural Addresses, 1940–64." Master's thesis, Atlanta University, 1969.
2689. White, L. W. "Some Highlights of the ILA's Past." *IllL* 51 (1969): 190–99.
2690. Whitman, J. B. "History of the Western North Carolina Library Association." *NCL* 32 (1974): 15–17.
2691. Wilcox, B. H. *The Wisconsin Library Association, 1891–1966*. Madison: Wisconsin Library Association, 1966.
2692. Wilgus, A. C. "The Interamerican Bibliographical and Library Association, 1930–1950." *IARB* 1 (1951): 6–11.
2693. Willet, M. M. "A History and Survey of the Nassau County Library Association Union Catalog." Master's thesis, Drexel Institute of Technology, 1955.
2694. Williams, Sister M. L. "History and Description of the Baltimore Archdiocesan Library Council." Master's thesis, Catholic University of America, 1960.
2695. Wilson, B. "History of AHIL." *AHILQ* 8 (1968): 48–54.

2696. Wilson, L. R. "North Carolina Library Association, 1904–1909." *NCL* 13 (1954): 2–7.
2697. Wilt, M. R. "Catholic Library Association." *ELIS* 4:312–17.
2698. Winser, M. C. "John Cotton Dana and the Special Libraries Association, 1909–14." *SL* 50 (1959): 208–11.
2699. Young, A. P. "The American Library Association in World War I: Services, Ideology, and Consequences." Doctoral dissertation, University of Illinois, 1976.

XII. Special Aspects of American Librarianship

This chapter of the bibliography contains materials which relate to special aspects of American library history and which seem to justify categorization. It is broken into three sections: (A) International Relations, (B) Cataloging and Classification, and (C) Reference Work.

A. International Relations

The area of comparative librarianship and the study of U.S. influence abroad overlap, and thus the student interested in this aspect of American library history will want to begin investigation with an examination of J. Periam Danton's recent handbook, *The Dimensions of Comparative Librarianship* (1973, **2707**). Two further studies by Danton are classics in the area of American relations with foreign library interests: *Book Selection and Collection: A Comparison of German and American University Libraries* (1963, **2706**) and *United States Influence on Norwegian Librarianship, 1890–1940* (1957, **2708**). Two recent essays on American contact with foreign librarianship are by Boyd Rayward (1976, **2721**) and Vivian D. Hewitt (1976, **2714**).

A number of very useful more specialized studies are also available, and important examples would include William Warner Bishop's recollections of international relations (1949, **2859**); Beverly Brewster's study of American overseas library technical assistance from 1940 to 1970 (1976, **2703**); Margaret Chapman's study of American ideas in German librarianship (1971, **2704**); Budd L. Gambee's works on the American librarian at foreign library conferences (1967, **2711**; 1972, **2712**); Norman Horrocks's dissertation on the Carnegie Corporation's impact on Australian library development (1971, **2715**); and Yukihisa Suzuki's study of American influence on the development of Japanese libraries from 1860 to 1941 (1974, **2729**).

Users of this section should also consult the part of the bibliography dealing with the American Library Association, as well as the biography section, for materials relating to this subject.

B. Cataloging and Classification

Cataloging and classification in the United States have garnered a considerable amount of attention from historians. As a result, many important surveys of the field exist, and a significant number of substantive studies of special aspects of the subject have also appeared to date. Among the most impressive of the general interpretive studies are those by Leo E. LaMontagne (1953, **2776**), Charles Martel (1926, **2781**), Vivian D. Palmer (1963, **2788**), David C. Weber (1964, **2808**), and Wyllis E. Wright (1953, **2812**). Also of note is a recent series of papers, all published in 1976, on cataloging and classification by Kathryn Henderson (**2767**), Doralyn Hickey (**2769**), Suzanne Massonneau (**2782**), Barbara Markuson (**2780**), Ann Schabas (**2795**), and Edith Scott (**2797**).

Nearly every element of the development of cataloging and classification in this country has been studied, although much remains to be done. Examples of the work completed to date are the studies by Nancy P. Bates on the classification of maps (1954, **2736**); Russell E. Bidlack (1957, **2738**), John P. Comaromi (1976, **2741**), Benjamin A. Custer (1971, **2746**), and Eugene F. Graziano (1959, **2756**) on the Dewey Decimal Classification; William Carlson (1952, **2739**), John M. Dawson (1967, **2748**), James R. Hunt (1964, **2771**), and Velva J. Osborn (1944, **2786**) on various aspects of cooperative cataloging; Sarah Corcoran (1936, **2743**), Jim Ranz (1964, **2791**), Mary B. Ruffin (1935, **2793**), and Richard H. Shoemaker (1960, **2801**) on the printed book catalog; Martha M. Evans (1969, **2753**), J. C. M. Hanson (1929, **2762**), Leo E. LaMontagne (1961, **2775**), and Alpheus L. Walter (1952, **2807**) on the Library of Congress system; Ruth M. Heiss on card catalogs (1938, **2765**); Donald J. Lehnus on famous catalogers and their writings (1974, **2777**); and James A. Servies on Thomas Jefferson's contributions to cataloging and classification (1950, **2799**).

Users of this bibliography will also note a number of studies of the cataloging and classification systems of individual libraries, large and small, in the United States. Finally, the biographies of figures important to the development of cataloging and classification in the United States, such as Jewett, Dewey, Cutter, J. C. M. Hanson, and Esther Peircy, should be examined—these are listed in the biography section.

C. Reference Work

Reference work in American libraries has received some attention from historians, and a number of broadly conceived and carefully researched studies are available to scholars wishing to investigate this aspect of librarianship. The most impressive of these are the studies by Louis Kaplan on reference services in American libraries from 1876 to 1893 (1947, **2816**; 1952, **2817**) and Samuel Rothstein's widely hailed studies of reference service, especially his *The Development of Reference Services Through Academic Traditions, Public Library Practice and Special Librarianship* (1955, **2824**). In addition to the other studies focused specifically on reference service listed in this section of the bibliography, users should examine the histories of major academic and public libraries, which frequently contain information on reference work in those libraries, and the biographies of librarians who figured prominently in the development of reference services, such as John Cotton Dana and John Shaw Billings.

Special Aspects of Librarianship

A. International Relations

2700. Au, C. "American Impact on Modern Chinese Library Development." Master's thesis, University of Chicago, 1964.
2701. Bixler, P. "The Charity of Books." *LibT* 20 (1972): 478–99.
2702. Bone, L. E. "The American Library in Paris: Fifty Years of Service." *ALib* 1 (1970): 279–83.
2703. Brewster, B. *American Overseas Library Technical Assistance, 1940–1970.* Metuchen, N.J.: Scarecrow Press, 1976.
2704. Chapman, M. "American Ideas in the German Public Libraries: Three Periods." *LQ* 41 (1971): 35–53.
2705. Collett, J. "American Libraries Abroad: United States Information Agency Activities." *LibT* 20 (1972): 538–47.
2706. Danton, J. P. *Book Selection and Collections: A Comparison of German and American University Libraries.* New York: Columbia University Press, 1963.
2707. ———. *The Dimensions of Comparative Librarianship.* Chicago: American Library Association, 1973.
2708. ———. *United States Influence on Norwegian Librarianship, 1890–1940.* Berkeley: University of California Press, 1957.
2709. Donovan, D. G. "Library Development and the U.S. Consultant Overseas." *LibT* 20 (1972): 506–14.
2710. Gambee, B. L. "Best Foot Forward: Representation of American Librarianship at World's Fairs, 1853–1904." In *Library History Seminar Number 3,* edited by M. J. Zachert, pp. 137–74. Tallahassee: *JLH,* 1968.
2711. ———. "The Great Junket: American Participation in the Conference of Librarians, London, 1877." *JLH* 22 (1967): 9–44.
2712. ———. "The Role of American Librarians at the Second International Library Conference, London, 1897." In *Library History Seminar Number 4,* edited by H. Goldstein and J. Goudeau, pp. 52–85. Tallahassee: Florida State University School of Library Science, 1972.
2713. Glazier, K. M. "United States Influence on Canadian Universities and Their Libraries." *CRL* 28 (1967): 311–16.
2714. Hewitt, V. D. "Services to Library Life Abroad." In *A Century of Service: Librarianship in the United States and Canada,* edited

Special Aspects of American Librarianship 177

by S. L. Jackson et al., pp. 321–40. Chicago: American Library Association, 1976.
2715. Horrocks, N. "Carnegie Corporation of New York and Its Impact on Library Development in Australia: A Case Study of Foundation Influence." Doctoral dissertation, University of Pittsburgh, 1971.
2716. Kildal, A. "American Influence on European Librarianship." LQ 7 (1937): 196–210.
2717. Liebaers, H. "Books, Libraries, Librarians–European and American Style." JLH 8 (1973): 18–22.
2718. Lorenz, J. G., et al. "The Library of Congress Abroad." LibT 20 (1972): 548–76.
2719. Parker, J. A. "The Books Across the Sea Library in the United States: Its Establishment, Purposes, and Operation." Master's thesis, Pratt Institute, 1955.
2720. Poste, L. I. "The Development of U.S. Protection of Libraries and Archives in Europe During World War II." Doctoral dissertation, University of Chicago, 1958.
2721. Rayward, W. B. "Librarianship in the New World and Old: Some Points of Contact." LibT 25 (1976): 209–26.
2722. Rochester, M. "American Influence on New Zealand Librarianship, as Facilitated by the Carnegie Corporation of New York." Doctoral dissertation, University of Wisconsin, 1976.
2723. Schwartz, A. E. "American Libraries Abroad: U.S. Military Libraries." LibT 20 (1972): 557–91.
2724. Siggins, J. A. "American Influence on Modern Japanese Library Development." Master's thesis, University of Chicago, 1969.
2725. Steig, L. F. "American Librarians Abroad, 1946–1965." LQ 38 (1968): 315–22.
2726. Stroup, E. W. "The American Hauser and Their Libraries: An Historical Sketch and Evaluation." JLH 4 (1969): 239–52.
2727. Sullivan, P. "The International Relations Program of the American Library Association." LibT 20 (1972): 577–91.
2728. Sussman, J. *United States Information Service Libraries*. Urbana: University of Illinois Graduate School of Library Science, 1973.
2729. Suzuki, Y. "American Influence on the Development of Library Services in Japan, 1860–1941." Doctoral dissertation, University of Michigan, 1974.
2730. Thompson, S. O. "The American Library in Paris: An International Development in the American Library Movement." LQ 34 (1964): 179–90.
2731. Vosper, R. "A Century Abroad." CRL 37 (1976): 514–30.
2732. Werdel, J. A., and Adams, S. "U.S. Participation in World Information Activities." Basis 2 (1976): 45–48.
2733. Williamson, I. R. "The Development of the United States Collec-

tion, Department of Printed Books, British Museum." *JAmS* 1 (1967): 79–86.
2734. Wormann, C. D. "Aspects of International Library Cooperation, Historical and Contemporary." *LQ* 38 (1968): 340–42.

B. *Cataloging and Classification*

2735. Albrecht, T. J. "Evidence of an Early Union Catalog in Texas." *TL* 35 (1973): 204–06.
2736. Bates, N. P. "The History of the Classification and Cataloging of Maps as Shown in Printed Book Catalogues from Sixteen United States Libraries Issued from 1827 through 1907." Master's thesis, University of North Carolina, 1954. Published: University of Kentucky Press, Microcard Publications, Series B, Number 15.
2737. Batty, D. "Dewey Abroad: The International Use of the Dewey Decima Classification." *QJLC* 33 (1976): 300–10.
2738. Bidlack, R. E. "The Coming Catalogue of Melvil Dewey's Flying Machine: Being the Historical Background of the A.L.A. Catalog." *LQ* 27 (1957): 137–60.
2739. Carlson, W. H. "Cooperation: An Historical Review and a Forecast." *CRL* 13 (1952): 5–13.
2740. Chevalier, S. A. "The History of the Catalogue Department." *MoreB* 2 (1927): 215–19.
2741. Comaromi, J. P. *The Eighteen Editions of the Dewey Decimal Classification.* Albany, N.Y.: Forest Pines, 1976.
2742. ———. "Knowledge Organized Is Knowledge Kept: The Dewey Decimal Classification, 1873–1976." *QJLC* 33 (1976): 311–31.
2743. Corcoran, S. R. "A Study of Cataloging Practice Through 1830 as Shown in Printed Book Catalogs of Six Libraries of the City of New York." Master's thesis, Columbia University, 1936.
2744. Currier, M. "Cataloguing at Harvard in the Sixties." *HLN* 4 (1942): 67–73.
2745. Currier, T. F. "Cataloging and Classification at Harvard, 1878–1938." *HLN* 29 (1939): 232–42.
2746. Custer, B. A. "Dewey Decimal Classification." *ELIS* 7:128–42.
2747. Davis, E. R. "Author vs. Title: A Historical Treatment of the Conflict Over Choice of Entry for Serials Issued by Corporate Bodies." Master's thesis, University of Chicago, 1973.
2748. Dawson, J. M. "A History of Centralized Processing." *LRTS* 11 (1967): 28–32.
2749. Devlin, E. "The Development of the Catalogue of the University of Pennsylvania Library (1829–1955)." *LC* 22 (1956): 19–28.
2750. Dunkin, P. S. "Criticisms of Current Cataloging Practice (1941–(1956)." *LQ* 26 (1956)L 286–302.

2751. Edlund, P. "A Monster and a Miracle: The Cataloging Distribution of the Library of Congress, 1901–1976." *QJLC* 33 (1976): 383–421.
2752. Evans, L. H. "History and the Problem of Bibliography." *CRL* 7 (1946): 195–205.
2753. Evans, M. M. "A History of the Development of Classification K (Law) at the Library of Congress." *LLJ* 63 (1969): 25–39.
2754. Frarey, C. J. "Subject Heading Revision by the Library of Congress, 1941–1950." Master's thesis, Columbia University, 1951. Published: Association of College and Research Libraries Microcard, Number 15.
2755. Gore, D. J. "The Schomberg Collection and Its Catalog: A Historical Sketch." Master's thesis, University of North Carolina, 1963.
2756. Graziano, E. E. "Hegel's Philosophy as a Basis for the Dewey Classification Schedule." *Libri* 9 (1959): 45–52.
2757. ———. "The Philosophy of Hegel as Basis for the Dewey Decimal Classification Schedule." Master's thesis, University of Oklahoma, 1955.
2758. Grove, P. S. "The Bibliographic Organization of Nonprint Media." In *Nonprint Media in Academic Libraries*, edited by P. S. Grove, pp. 1–51. Chicago: American Library Association, 1975.
2759. Hagler, R. "The Development of Cataloging Rules for Nonbook Materials." *LRTS* 9 (1975): 268–78.
2760. Hanson, E. R. "Cataloging and the American Library Association, 1876–1956." Doctoral dissertation, University of Pittsburgh, 1974.
2761. ———, and Dailey, J. E. "Catalogs and Cataloging." *ELIS* 4:242–305.
2762. Hanson, J. C. M. "The Library of Congress and Its New Catalogue." In *Essays Offered to Herbert Putnam*, edited by W. W. Bishop and A. Keogh, pp. 178–94. New Haven: Yale University Press, 1929.
2763. ———. "The Subject Catalogs of the Library of Congress." *BALA* 3 (1909): 385–97.
2764. Heisey, T. M. "Early Catalog Code Development in the United States, 1876–1908." *JLH* 11 (1976): 218–48.
2765. Heiss, R. M. "The Card Catalog in Libraries of the United States Before 1876." Master's thesis, University of Illinois, 1938.
2766. ———. "The Card Catalog in Libraries of the United States Before 1876." *CCY* 8 (1939): 125–26.
2767. Henderson, K. L. "'Treated with a Degree of Uniformity and Common Sense': Descriptive Cataloging in the United States–1876–1975." *LibT* 25 (1976): 227–72.
2768. Hensel, E. M. "History of the Catalog Department of the University of Illinois Library." Master's thesis, University of Illinois, 1936.
2769. Hickey, D. J. "Subject Analysis: An Interpretive Survey." *LibT* 25 (1976): 273–92.

2770. Hitchcock, J. E. "The Yale Library Classification." *YULG* 27 (1953): 95–109.
2771. Hunt, J. R. "The Historical Development of Processing Centers in the United States." *LRTS* 8 (1964): 54–59.
2772. Immroth, J. P. "Library of Congress Classification." *ELIS* 15:93–200.
2773. Kebabian, B. "Bibliographic Quiddling." *LRTS* 11 (1967): 397–404.
2774. Kipp, L. J., and Thomas, A. T. "The Creation of a Cataloging Economy: The Typing Section of the Widener Library [1892–1950]." *HLB* 5 (1951): 112–16.
2775. LaMontagne, L. E. *American Library Classification: With Special Reference to the Library of Congress.* Hamden, Conn.: Shoestring Press, 1961.
2776. ———. "Historical Background of Classification." In *Subject Analysis of Library Materials,* edited by M. Tauber, pp. 16–28. New York: Columbia University Press, 1953.
2777. Lehnus, D. J. *Milestones in Cataloging: Famous Catalogers and Their Writings, 1835–1969.* Littleton, Col.: Libraries Unlimited, 1974.
2778. Leidecker, K. F. "The Debt of Melvil Dewey to William Torrey Harris." *LQ* 15 (1945): 139–42.
2779. Leonard, L. E. *Cooperative and Centralized Cataloging and Processing: A Bibliography, 1850–1967.* Urbana: University of Illinois Graduate School of Library Science Occasional Paper Number 93, 1968.
2780. Markuson, B. E. "Bibliographic Systems, 1945–1976." *LibT* 25 (1976): 311–28.
2781. Martel, C. "Cataloging: 1876–1926." *BALA* 20 (1926): 492–98.
2782. Massonneau, S. "Technical Services and Technology: The Bibliographical Imperative." In *A Century of Service: Librarianship in the United States and Canada,* edited by S. L. Jackson et al., pp. 192–207. Chicago: American Library Association, 1976.
2783. Monrad, A. M. "Historical Notes on the Catalogues and Classifications of the Yale University Library." In *Papers in Honor of Andrew Keogh, Librarian of Yale University,* edited by M. C. Withington, pp. 251–84. New Haven: Privately printed, 1938.
2784. Nelson, C. A. "The 'A.L.A.' Library Catalog, 1876–1894 [a poem]." *LJ* 19 (1894): 134.
2785. Nyhom, A. W. "The Final Solution to the Problem of Cataloging: A Note on the Contribution of Agnes M. Cole, 1873–1956." *WLB* 31 (1957): 247–49.
2786. Osborn, V. J. "A History of Cooperative Cataloging in the United States." Master's thesis, University of Chicago, 1944.
2787. Oswald, J. F. "The Development of the Medical Subject Heading." Master's thesis, Drexel Institute of Technology, 1955.

2788. Palmer, V. D. "A Brief History of Cataloging Codes in the United States, 1852–1949." Master's thesis, University of Chicago, 1963.
2789. Pette, J. "The Development of Authorship Entry and the Formulation of Authorship Rules as Found in the Anglo-American Code." *LQ* 6 (1936): 270–99.
2790. Pitkin, G. M. *Serials Automation in the United States: A Bibliographic History.* Metuchen, N.J.: Scarecrow Press, 1976.
2791. Ranz, J. *The Printed Book Catalogue in American Libraries, 1723–1900.* Chicago: American Library Association, 1964.
2792. Reddie, J. N. "Author Headings of the Official Publications of the State of Ohio, 1900–1957." Master's thesis, Kent State University, 1958.
2793. Ruffin, M. B. "Some Developments Toward Modern Cataloging Practice in University Libraries as Exemplified in the Printed Book Catalogs of Harvard and Yale Before 1876." Master's thesis, Columbia University, 1935.
2794. Saracevic, T. "Intellectual Organization of Knowledge: The American Contribution." *Basis* 2 (1976): 16–17.
2795. Schabas, A. H. "Technical Services and Technology: Technological Advance." In *A Century of Service: Librarianship in the United States and Canada,* edited by S. L. Jackson et al., pp. 208–20. Chicago: American Library Association, 1976.
2796. Schley, R. "Cataloging in the Libraries of Princeton, Columbia, and the University of Pennsylvania Before 1876." Master's thesis, Columbia University, 1946.
2797. Scott, E. "The Evolution of Bibliographic Systems in the United States, 1876–1945." *LibT* 25 (1976): 293–310.
2798. Selmer, M. L. "Map Cataloging and Classification Methods: A Historical Survey." *SLAGMDB* (March 1976): 7–12.
2799. Servies, J. A. "Thomas Jefferson and His Bibliographic Classification." Master's thesis, University of Chicago, 1950.
2800. Shera, J. H., and Egan, M. E. *The Classified Catalog: Basic Principles and Practices.* Chicago: American Library Association, 1956.
2801. Shoemaker, R. H. "Some 20th Century Book Catalogs: Their Purposes, Format, and Production Techniques." *LRTS* 9 (1960): 197–210.
2802. Stevenson, G. "The Historical Context: Traditional Classification Since 1950." *DLQ* 10 (1974): 11–20.
2803. Straka, M. "A Historical Review of the Cataloging Department of the Columbia University Libraries: 1883–1950." Master's thesis, Columbia University, 1951.
2804. Tate, E. L. "International Standards: The Road to the Universal Bibliographic Control." *LRTS* 20 (1976): 16–24.
2805. Tauber, M. F. "Board on Cataloging Policy and Research: Review of Its Work, 1951–1956." *JCC* 12 (1956): 229–33.

2806. Thackston, F. V. "The Development of Cataloging in the Libraries of Duke University and the University of North Carolina from Their Establishment to 1953." Master's thesis, University of North Carolina, 1959. Published: Association of College and Research Libraries Microcard, Number 124.

2807. Walter, A. L. "Fifty Years Young: Library of Congress Cards." *CRL* 13 (1952): 305–08.

2808. Weber, D. C. "The Changing Character of the Catalog in America." In *Library Catalogs: Changing Dimensions*, edited by R. F. Strout, pp. 20–33. Chicago: University of Chicago Press, 1964.

2809. Wilkins, M. J. "History and Evaluation of Subject Heading Approach in Medicine: A Study of Certain Medical Indexes Published in the United States." Master's thesis, Catholic University of America, 1955.

2810. Willet, M. M. "A History and Survey of the Nassau County Library Association Union Catalog." Master's thesis, Drexel Institute of Technology, 1955.

2811. Wright, W. E. "The Anglo-American Cataloging Rules: A Historical Perspective." *LRTS* 20 (1976): 36–47.

2812. ———. "The Subject Approach to Knowledge: Historical Aspects and Purposes." In *Subject Analysis of Library Materials*, edited by M. Tauber, pp. 8–15. New York: Columbia University Press, 1953.

C. Reference Work

2813. Adams, E. M. "A Study of Reference Librarianship in the American College: 1876–1955." Master's thesis, East Texas State Teachers College, 1956.

2814. Dunn, A. "The Nature and Functions of Readers' Advisory Service as Revealed by a Survey of the Literature of the Field from 1935–1950." Master's thesis, Western Reserve University, 1950.

2815. Gambee, B. L., and Gambee, R. R. "Reference Services and Technology." In *A Century of Service: Librarianship in the United States and Canada*, edited by S. L. Jackson et al., pp. 169–91. Chicago: American Library Association, 1976.

2816. Kaplan, L. "Early History of Reference Service in the United States." *LibR* 11 (1947): 286–90.

2817. ———. *The Growth of Reference Service in the United States from 1876 to 1891*. Chicago: Association of College and Research Libraries, 1952.

2818. ———. "Reference Services in University and Special Libraries Since 1900." *CRL* 19 (1958): 217–20.

2819. McBride, M. "Reference Service for Congress Before 1915." Master's thesis, Drexel Institute of Technology, 1955.

2820. Perrins, B. C. "Business and Industrial Reference Service by Academic Libraries, 1900-1965." Master's thesis, Southern Connecticut State College, 1967.
2821. Phelps, R. B. "Reference Services in Public Libraries: The Last Quarter Century." *WLB* 32 (1957): 281-85.
2822. Rothstein, S. "The Development of the Concept of Reference Service in American Libraries, 1850-1900." *LQ* 23 (1953): 1-15.
2823. ———. "The Development of Reference Services in American Research Libraries." Doctoral dissertation, University of Illinois, 1954.
2824. ———. *The Development of Reference Services Through Academic Traditions, Public Library Practice and Special Librarianship.* Chicago: American Library Association, 1955.
2825. Short, O. C. "Development of the Municipal Reference Service in the Bureau of the Census." *SL* 28 (1937): 364-65.
2826. Thompson, M. C. "History of the Reference Department of the University of Illinois Library." Master's thesis, University of Illinois, 1942.

XIII. Biographies of Librarians and Library Benefactors

The literature of American library biography follows a pattern familiar to students of American history, though successive stages appear to have come much later in library history.

Among the earliest writing, one finds relatively brief tributes to library leaders on the occasion of their death or retirement. Examples of this genre are the tributes of the Newberry Library to William Frederick Poole (1895, **3129**); the New York Public Library to John Shaw Billings, edited by F. H. Garrison (1915, **2847**); and the Library of Congress to Herbert Putnam by D. C. Mearns (1956, **3139**).

As the first generation of American library leaders passed, the profession showed concern that their contributions and personalities not be forgotten. Following World War I the American Library Association launched its American Library Pioneers series, which over a thirty-year span included seven small biographical works: H. W. Lydenberg on John Shaw Billings (1924, **2851**), R. K. Shaw on Samuel Swett Green (1926, **2995**), W. P. Cutter on Charles Ammi Cutter (1931, **2922**), Linda A. Eastman on William Howard Brett (1940, **2881**), Chalmers Hadley on John Cotton Dana (1943, **2932**), Fremont Rider on Melvil Dewey (1944, **2956**), and Joseph A. Boromé on Charles Coffin Jewett (1951, **3039**). Several projected volumes did not see completion, but an omnibus volume concluded the series with short sketches of eighteen librarians. Edited by E. M. Danton, it appeared as *Pioneering Leaders in Librarianship* (1953, **2831**).

Autobiographies have been few in librarianship. Several brief reminiscences have appeared as articles in journals or as commemorative pieces. One of very few real autobiographies is the informative and engaging one written by Arthur E. Bostwick, *A Life with Men and Books* (1939, **2872**); his successor at St. Louis, Charles H. Compton, tried to do the same in his *Memories of a Librarian* (1954, **2910**), with less success. The memoirs of Sidney B. Mitchell were published posthumously in 1960 (**3100**). Two recently retired statesmen in the profession have tried to recount their experiences for another generation—Lawrence Clark Powell in *Fortune and Friendship: An Autobiography* (1968, **3131**) and Louis Shores in *Quiet World: A Librarian's Crusade for Destiny* (1975, **3165**).

Full-length, completely documented scholarly biographies have begun to appear in comparative abundance only since about 1960. Most of these efforts originated as doctoral dissertations in library schools and a large percentage have not appeared in print. One of the earliest published studies was E. M. Fleming's biography of R. R. Bowker (1952, **2879**). A decade later Martha Boaz published her brief life of Althea Warren (1962, **3210**). The year 1963 saw publication of two outstanding biographies: Edward Holley's study of Charles Evans (**2973**) and William L. Williamson's biography of William Frederick Poole (**3130**). Both were candidates for a single ALA award and marked a new direction in library biography. Other works appeared in the following decade—Laurel A. Grotzinger's on Katharine Sharp (1966, **3157**), Maurice F. Tauber's on Louis R. Wilson (1967, **3236**), C. H. Baumann's on Angus Snead Macdonald (1972, **3079**), and J. D. Rhodehamel and R. F. Wood's on Ina Coolbirth (1973, **2911**)—to name some noteworthy examples. A recent scholarly biography of a major library figure is Peggy Sullivan's study of Carl H. Milam (1976, **3097**).

Many master's theses on librarians and professionally related individuals exist in libraries and are often the sole source of collected material on their subjects, frequently local, state, or regional figures. More lamentable is the limited availability of scholarly biographical studies which have not yet received editing for formal publication. Some of the following are in various stages of preparation, but all are unpublished at present. Among the subjects treated are Justin Winsor by Joseph A. Boromé (1950, **3242**), William Warner Bishop by C. G. Sparks (1967, **2868**), Charles C. Williamson by Paul A. Winckler (1968, **3225**), J. C. M. Hanson by Edith Scott (1970, **3015**), Ainsworth R. Spofford by John Y. Cole (1971, **3177**), and Charles Ammi Cutter by Francis Miksa (1974, **2928**).

Other approaches to biography exist in addition to full-scale works. From time to time interpretive articles treat influential library figures, such as Sidney Ditzion's "The Social Ideas of a Library Pioneer: Joseph Nelson Larned, 1836–1913" (1943, **3058**). Other useful introductions occur in commemorative volumes or *festschriften*, such as those pieces scattered through the early pages of *Essays Offered to Herbert Putnam* (1929, **3135**). A related type of work is the selected anthology which allows the subject to speak for himself, such as *Champion of a Cause: Essays and Addresses on Librarianship* by Archibald MacLeish (1971, **3082**).

A new type of biographical study is represented by the projected Heritage of Librarianship Series, which will attempt in single volumes devoted to one person to include an interpretive essay on the significance of the particular leader, a selected anthology of the subject's writings, and a bibliography of works by and about the subject. The first volumes to appear are those on Charles Coffin Jewett (1975, **3041**) and Ainsworth Spofford (1975, **3175**), with futher volumes planned on Cutter, Dewey, Winsor, and Poole.

An ultimate stage in library biography may be retrospective biography. Students have found "A Library Hall of Fame" (*LJ* 76 [March 15, 1951]: 466–72) helpful for the forty sketches included. But it was hardly a reference work. Library historians have drawn heavily from articles in the *National Cyclopedia of American Biography, Dictionary of American Biography, Notable American Women,* and *Encyclopedia of Library and Information*

Science and have been able to glean the bare essentials from the successive current biographical directories of American librarians issued since 1933. The maturation of library biography may well be symbolized by the forthcoming *Dictionary of American Library Biography,* which is a joint effort of library historians and others to provide in one volume biographical coverage of about three hundred library-related figures in America. It will certainly become the starting place for the second century of biographical study in librarianship.

Biographies of Librarians and Library Benefactors

Arranged by Subject

ADAMS, CHARLES KENDALL

2827. Towne, J. E. "Charles Kendall Adams and the First University Library Building (Ann Arbor) (1881–1833)." *MichHM* 37 (June 1953): 129–44.

ADAMS, RANDOLPH GREENFIELD

2828. Adams, R. G. "The Credo of the Late Director of the Wm. L. Clements Library, as Historian, Librarian and Bibliophile." *MAQR* 57 (1951): 310–17.
2829. Storm, C. "Randolph Greenfield Adams: 1892–1951." *AB* 7 (1951): 1097–98.
2830. University of Michigan. William L. Clements Library. *A Bibliography of Randolph G. Adams with an Introductory Memoir.* Ann Arbor: Published for the Clements Library Associates, 1962.

ANDREWS, CLEMENT WALKER

2831. Brown, C. H. "Clement Walker Andrews, 1858–1930." In *Pioneering Leaders in Librarianship,* First Series, edited by E. M. Danton, pp. 1–12. Chicago: American Library Association, 1953.

ASKEW, SARAH B.

2832. Severns, H. "Sarah B. Askew, 1863–1942." In *Pioneering Leaders in Librarianship,* First Series, edited by E. M. Danton, pp. 13–21. Chicago: American Library Association, 1953.

ASPLUND, JULIA BROWN

2833. Honea, A. B. "Julia Brown Asplund: New Mexico Librarian, 1875–1958." Master's thesis, University of Texas, 1967.

BALDWIN, CLARA FRANCES

2834. Countryman, G. A. "Clara F[rances] Baldwin [1871–1951]." *MinnL* 16 (1951): 291–92.

BALLARD, JAMES FRANCIS

2835. McDaniel, W. B. "James Francis Ballard, 1878–1955." *MLAB* 44 (1956): 92–97.
2836. Spector, B. "James Francis Ballard, 1878–1955." *JHMAS* 11 (1956): 339–41.

BARRETTE, LYDIA MARGARET

2837. Barrette, L. M. *There Is No End*. New York: Scarecrow Press, 1961.

BAY, J. CHRISTIAN

2838. Bay, J. C. *The Fortune of Books: Essays, Memories and Prophecies of a Librarian*. Chicago: Walter M. Hill, 1941.
2839. Taylor, K. L. *J. Christian Bay at Seventy: A Review and a Bibliography*. Chicago: Crerar Library, 1941.

BEALS, RALPH A.

2840. "Ralph A. Beals." *BNYPL* 59 (1955): 3–15.

BECKLEY, JOHN

2841. Berkeley, E., and Berkeley, D. S. "The First Librarian on Congress: John Beckley." *QJLC* 32 (1975): 83–110.
2842. ———. *John Beckley: Zealous Partisan in a Nation Divided*. Philadelphia: American Philosophical Society, 1973.

BEER, WILLIAM

2843. Kraus, J. W. *William Beer and the New Orleans Libraries, 1891–1927*. Chicago: Association of College and Research Libraries, 1952.

BERTRAM, JAMES

2844. Bobinski, G. S. "James Bertram and Alvin S. Johnson: The Important but Little Known Figures in Library History." In *Library*

History Seminar Number 3, edited by M. J. Zachert, pp. 35–46. Tallahassee: *JLH*, 1968.

BILLINGS, JOHN SHAW

2845. Bradway, F. "Bibliography of the Writings of John Shaw Billings." In *Selected Papers of John Shaw Billings*, compiled by F. B. Rogers, pp. 285–300. Chicago: Medical Library Association, 1965.
2846. Cummings, M. M. "Books, Computers, and Medicine: Contributions of a Friend of Sir William Osler." *MedH* 10 (1966): 130–37.
2847. Garrison, F. H., ed. *John Shaw Billings: A Memoir*. New York: New York Public Library, 1915.
2848. Griffith, T. J. "High Points in the Life of Dr. John Shaw Billings." *IMH* 30 (1934): 325–30.
2849. Hasse, A. R. "Bibliography of the Writings of John Shaw Billings, 1861–1913." In *John Shaw Billings: A Memoir*, edited by F. H. Garrison. New York: New York Public Library, 1915.
2850. Hurd, H. M. "Dr. John Shaw Billings, Bibliographer and Librarian." *MLAB* 5 (1915–16): 35–40.
2851. Lydenberg, H. M. *John Shaw Billings: Creator of the National Medical Library and Its Catalogue, First Director of the New York Public Library*. Chicago: American Library Association, 1924.
2852. ———. "John Shaw Billings and the New York Public Library." *BHM* 6 (1938): 377–86.
2853. *Memorial Meeting in Honor of the Late Dr. John Shaw Billings, April 25, 1913*. New York: New York Public Library, 1913.
2854. Mitchell, S. W. "Biographical Memoir of John Shaw Billings." *Science* 38 (1913): 827–33.
2855. Rogers, F. B. "The Life of John Shaw Billings." In *The Selected Papers of John Shaw Billings*, compiled by F. B. Rogers, pp. 11–13. Chicago: Medical Library Association, 1965.

BISHOP, WILLIAM WARNER

2856. Bishop, W. W. "The American Library Association: Fragments of Autobiography (1896–1918)." *LQ* 19 (1949): 36–45; 21 (1951): 35–41.
2857. ———. *Backs of Books and Other Essays in Librarianship*. Baltimore: Williams and Wilkins Co., 1926.
2858. ———. "College Days, 1889–93: Fragments of Autobiography." *MAQR* 54 (1948): 340–52.
2859. ———. "International Relations: Fragments of Autobiography." *LQ* 19 (1949): 270–84.
2860. ———. "The Library of Congress, 1907–15: Fragments of Autobiography." *LQ* 18 (1948): 1–23.

2861. ———. "Princeton, 1902–07: Fragments of Autobiography." *LQ* 16 (1946): 211–24.
2862. ———. "Rome and Brooklyn, 1889–1902: Fragments of Autobiography." *LQ* 15 (1945): 324–38.
2863. ———. "Some Chicago Librarians of the Nineties: Fragments of Autobiography." *LQ* 14 (1944): 339–48.
2864. ———. "Some Recollections of William Lawrence Clements and the Formation of His Library." *LQ* 18 (1948): 185–91.
2865. Kaser, D. "William Warner Bishop: Contributions to a Bibliography." *LQ* 26 (1956): 52–60.
2866. Lydenberg, H. M., and Keogh, A., eds. *William Warner Bishop: A Tribute*. New Haven: Yale University Press, 1941.
2867. Mohrhardt, F. E. "Dr. William Warner Bishop (1871–1955): Our First International Librarian." *WLB* 32 (1957): 207–15.
2868. Sparks, C. G. "William Warner Bishop." Doctoral dissertation, University of Michigan, 1967.

BLUE, THOMAS FOUNTAIN

2869. Wright, L. T. "Thomas Fountain Blue, Pioneer Librarian, 1866–1935." Master's thesis, Atlanta University, 1955.

BOOTH, MARY JOSEPHINE

2870. Lawson, R. W. "Mary Josephine Booth: A Lifetime of Service, 1904–1945." Doctoral dissertation, Indiana University, 1975.

BOSTWICK, ARTHUR ELMORE

2871. Boromé, J. A. "Bibliography of Arthur Elmore Bostwick, 1860–1942." *BB* 18 (1944): 62–66.
2872. Bostwick, A. E. *A Life with Men and Books*. New York: H. W. Wilson, 1939.
2873. Cunningham, L. L. "Contributions of Arthur Elmore Bostwick to the Library Profession." Master's thesis, Indiana University, 1962.
2874. Doud, M. "Arthur E. Bostwick, 1860–1942." In *Pioneering Leaders in Librarianship*, First Series, edited by E. M. Danton, pp. 22–33. Chicago: American Library Association, 1953.
2875. ———. "Recollections of Arthur E[lmore] Bostwick." *WLB* 27 (1953): 818–25.

BOWERMAN, GEORGE F.

2876. Bowerman, G. F. *Some Memories, 1868–1956*. N.p.: Privately printed, 1956.
2877. ———. "Some Reminiscences by Dr. George F. Bowerman, Chief Librarian, D.C. Public Library, 1904–1940." *DCL* 26 (1955): 3–7.

BOWKER, RICHARD ROGERS

2878. Ferguson, M. J. "Richard Rogers Bowker, 1848–1933." In *Pioneering Leaders in Librarianship*, First Series, edited by E. M. Danton, pp. 34–47. Chicago: American Library Association, 1953.
2879. Fleming, E. M. *R. R. Bowker: Militant Liberal*. Norman: University of Oklahoma Press, 1952.
2880. Landau, R. A. "Richard Rogers Bowker." *ELIS* 3:148–55.

BRETT, WILLIAM HOWARD

2881. Eastman, L. A. *Portrait of a Librarian: William Howard Brett*. Chicago: American Library Association, 1940.
2882. Vitz, C. "William Howard Brett." *ELIS* 3:260–69.
2883. "William Howard Brett: In Memoriam." *LJ* 43 (1918): 793–807.

BRIENTNALL, JOSEPH

2884. Bloore, S. "Joseph Brientnall, First Secretary of the Library Company." *PMHB* 59 (1935): 42–56.

BRIGHAM, JOHNSON

2885. Wright, L. M. "Johnson Brigham–Librarian." *Palimpsest* 33 (1952): 225–56.

BROWN, CHARLES HARVEY

2886. Crawford, H. "Bibliography of Charles Harvey Brown. *CRL* 8 (1947): 380–84.

BUFFINGTON, WILLIE LEE

2887. Carr, L. D. "The Reverend Willie Lee Buffington's Life and Contributions to the Development of Rural Libraries in the South." Master's thesis, Atlanta University, 1958.

BULLEN, HENRY LEWIS

2888. Mallison, D. W. "Henry Lewis Bullen and the Typographic Library and Museum of the American Type Founders Company." Doctoral dissertation, Columbia University, 1976.

BUTLER, PIERCE

2889. "Bibliography of Pierce Butler." *LQ* 22 (1952): 165–69.
2890. Pargellis, S. M. "Pierce Butler [Born 1886]–A Biographical Sketch." *LQ* 22 (1952): 170–73.
2891. Wilson, L. R. "Pierce Butler, 1886–1953." *NCL* 11 (1953): 70.

BUTLER, SUSAN DART

2892. Bolden, E. E. M. "Susan Dart Butler–Pioneer Librarian." Master's thesis, Atlanta University, 1959.

CANFIELD, JAMES HULME

2893. Fisher, D. C. "A Librarian's Creed: James Hulme Canfield." *CLC* 2 (1952): 2–12.

CAREY, MARIAM E.

2894. Jones, P. "Miriam E. Carey, 1858–1937." In *Pioneering Leaders in Librarianship*, First Series, edited by E. M. Danton, pp. 48–60. Chicago: American Library Association, 1953.

CARLSON, WILLIAM HUGH

2895. Carlson, W. H. *In a Grand and Awful Time*. Corvallis: Oregon State University Press, 1967.

CARLTON, WILLIAM N. C.

2896. Carlton, W. N. C. "After Forty Years (1893–1933): Some Memories and Reflections." *MLCB* 23 (1933): 43–48.

CARNEGIE, ANDREW

2897. Belfour, S. "Andrew Carnegie." *ELIS* 4:192–200.
2898. Ollé, J. "Andrew Carnegie: The 'Unloved Benefactor.'" *LW* 70 (1969): 255–62.
2899. Wall, J. F. *Andrew Carnegie*. New York: Oxford University Press, 1970.

CARNOVSKY, LEON

2900. Haygood, W. C. "Leon Carnovsky: A Sketch." *LQ* 38 (1968): 422–28.
2901. "Leon Carnovsky: A Bibliography." *LQ* 38 (1968): 429–41.

CASSEL, ABRAHAM HARLEY

2902. Heckman, M. L. "Abraham Harley Cassel: Nineteenth-Century American Book Collector." Doctoral dissertation, University of Chicago, 1971.

CHARLETON, MARGARET

2903. Francis, W. W. "Margaret Charleton and the Early Days of the Medical Library Association." *MLAB* 25 (1936): 58–63.

CLARK, GEORGE THOMAS

2904. Conmy, P. T. "George Thomas Clark, the California Library Association's Illustrious Number Two." *CalL* 27 (1976): 5–13.

CLEMENTS, WILLIAM L.

2905. Maxwell, M. N. F. "Anatomy of a Book Collector: William L. Clements and the Clements Library." Doctoral dissertation, University of Michigan, 1971.
2906. ———. *Shaping a Library: William L. Clements as Collector.* Amsterdam: N. Israel, 1973.

CLIFT, DAVID

2907. "Two Decisive Decades–1952–1972: Special Issue Honoring David Clift." *ALib* 3 (1972): 701–815*i*.

COGSWELL, JOSEPH GREEN

2908. Ticknor, A. E. *Life of Joseph Green Cogswell, as Sketched in his Letters.* Cambridge, Mass., 1874.

COLELAZER, HENRY

2909. Bidlack, R. E. "Henry Colelazer, the University of Michigan's First Librarian: Custodian of a Handful of Books." *MAQR* 62 (1956): 157–71.

COMPTON, CHARLES H.

2910. Compton, C. H. *Memories of a Librarian.* St. Louis, 1954.

COOLBRITH, INA

2911. Rhodehamel, J. D., and Wood, R. F. *Ina Coolbrith: Librarian and Laureate of California.* Provo: Brigham Young University Press, 1973.

COULTER, EDITH M.

2912. Parker, W. E. "Chronological List of the Writings of Edith M. Coulter." *CalL* 24 (1963): 103–04.
2913. Powell, L. C. *The Example of Miss Edith M. Coulter.* Sacramento: California Library Association, 1969.

COUNTRYMAN, GRATIA ALTA

2914. Dyste, M. C. "Gratia Alta Countryman, Librarian." Master's thesis, University of Minnesota, 1965.

CRERAR, JOHN

2915. Goodspeed, T. W. *John Crerar.* Chicago: The John Crerar Library, 1939.

CRONIN, JOHN W.

2916. Clapp, V. B., and Welsh, W. J., eds. "The Age of Cronin: Aspects of the Accomplishment of John W. Cronin, Library of Congress, 1925–1968." *LRTS* 12 (1968): 385–405.

CRUNDEN, FREDERICK MORGAN

2917. Bostwick, A. E. *Frederick Morgan Crunden: A Memorial Bibliography.* St. Louis, 1924.
2918. Doane, B. "Frederick M[organ] Crunden [1847–1911]." *WLB* 29 (1955): 446–49, 452.

CULVER, ESSAE M.

2919. Currier, L. G. "The Lengthened Shadow: Essae M. Culver and the Louisiana State Library]1925–58]." *BALA* 53 (1959): 35–37.

CURRIER, THOMAS FRANKLIN

2920. Roxas, S. A. "Thomas Franklin Currier." *ELIS* 6:375–79.

CURRY, ARTHUR RAY

2921. Winship, S. G. "Arthur Ray Curry: A Biography." Master's thesis, University of Texas, 1966.

CUTTER, CHARLES AMMI

2922. Cutter, W. P. *Charles Ammi Cutter.* Chicago: American Library Association, 1931.
2923. Foster, W. E. "Charles Ammi Cutter: A Memorial Sketch." *LJ* 28 (1903): 697–703.
2924. Horiuchi, I. "Charles Ammi Cutter." *LIS* 10 (1972): 187–94.
2925. Immroth, J. P. "Charles Ammi Cutter." *ELIS* 6:380–87.
2926. Little, A. E. "Charles Ammi Cutter, Librarian at Forbes Library, Northampton, Massachusetts, 1894–1903." Master's thesis, University of North Carolina, 1962.
2927. Miksa, F., ed. *Charles Ammi Cutter: Library Systematizer.* Littleton, Colo.: Libraries Unlimited, 1977.
2928. ———. "Charles Ammi Cutter." Doctoral dissertation, University of Chicago, 1974.
2929. Morse, C. R. "A Biographical, Bibliographical Study of Charles Ammi Cutter, Librarian." Master's thesis, University of Washington, 1961.

DANA, JOHN COTTON

2930. Cohen, L. G. "John Cotton Dana's Library Services for Children in Springfield, Massachusetts." Master's thesis, Southern Connecticut State College, 1966.
2931. Dana, J. C. *Suggestions*. Boston: F. W. Faxon Co., 1921.
2932. Hadley, C. *John Cotton Dana: A Sketch*. Chicago: American Library Association, 1943.
2933. Hauserman, D. D. "John Cotton Dana: The Militant Minority of One." Master's thesis, New York University, 1965.
2934. *John Cotton Dana [1856–1929], the Centennial Convocation: Addresses by Arthur T. Vanderbilt and L. Quincy Mumford, with a Prefatory Note by James E. Bryan*. New Brunswick, N.J.: Rutgers University Press, 1957. 61, [2]p. bibliog. (p. 57).
2935. Johnson, H., and Winser, B. "Bibliography: John Cotton Dana, Author." *LQ* 7 (1937): 68–98.
2936. Lansberg, W. R. "John Cotton Dana, 1856–1929." *WLB* 31 (1957): 542.
2937. Sabine, J. "John Cotton Dana." *ELIS* 6:417–23.

DANTON, J. PERIAM

2938. *J. Periam Danton: A Bibliography*. Berkeley: School of Librarianship, University of California, 1976.

DAVID, CHARLES WENDELL

2939. Riggs, J. B. *Charles Wendell David: Scholar, Teacher, Librarian*. Philadelphia: Union Catalogue of the Philadelphia Metropolitan Area, Inc., 1965.

DAVIS, RAYMOND CAZALLIS

2940. Abbott, J. C. "Raymond Cazallis Davis and the University of Michigan General Library, 1877–1905." Doctoral dissertation, University of Michigan, 1957.

DEWEY, MELVIL

2941. Burger, B. "He Lived as If He Were Always Catching Trains: Melvil Dewey." *NCLife* 5 (Spring 1951): 26–28, 43.
2942. Dawe, G. *Melvil Dewey: Seer, Inspirer, Doer, 1851–1931*. Lake Placid, N.Y.: Lake Placid Club, 1932.
2943. Ferguson, M. J. "'Diamond' Dewey." *DCL* 11 (1951): 2–4.
2944. Frost, J. E. "Wakers and Shakers." *AlaL* 27 (1975): 2–5.
2945. Grotzinger, L. A. "Melvil Dewey: The 'Sower.'" *JLH* 3 (1968): 313–28.
2946. Gunjal, S. R. "Melvil Dewey and His Achievements." *HLS* 4 (1965): 39–45.

2947. Harlow, N. "Who's Afraid of Melvil Dewey?" *PNLAQ* 31 (1966): 10–17.
2948. Hassenforder, J. "Trois Pionniers des Bibliothèques Publiques, Edward Edwards, M. Dewey, Eugene Morel: Étude Biographique Comparée." *EeB* 11 (1964): 11–40.
2949. Horiuchi, I. "Melvil Dewey." *LIS* 12 (1974): 143–53.
2950. Jast, L. S. "Recollections of Melvil Dewey." *LibR* 31 (1934): 285–90.
2951. Kennedy, R. F. "Who Was Melvil Dewey?" *IndL* 8 (1953): 8–13.
2952. Kumar, P. S. G. "Dewey and Ranganathan: A Perspective." *HLS* (1973): 163–68.
2953. Linderman, W. B. "Melvil Dewey." *ELIS* 7:142–60.
2954. MacLeod, R. D. "Melvil Dewey and His Famous School." *LibR* 35 (1960): 479–84.
2955. Rayward, W. B. "Melvil Dewey and Education for Librarianship." *JLH* 3 (1968): 297–312.
2956. Rider, F. *Melvil Dewey*. Chicago: American Library Association, 1944.
2957. Rockwood, R. H. "Melvil Dewey and Librarianship." *JLH* 3 (1968): 329–41.
2958. Takeuchi, S. "Dewey in Florida." *JLH* 1 (1966): 127–32.
2959. Trautman, R. "Melvil Dewey and the 'Wellesley Half Dozen.'" *CLC* 3 (1954): 9–13.
2960. Williamson, C. C. "Melvil Dewey, Creative Librarian." In *Fifty Years of Education for Librarianship*. Papers Presented at the Celebration of the Fiftieth Anniversary of the University of Illinois Library School, 2 March 1943, pp. 1–8. Urbana: University of Illinois Press, 1943.

DOE, JANET

2961. "A Bibliography of Janet Doe." *MLAB* 45 (1957): 281–84.

DORAN, ELECTRA COLLINS

2962. Holingsworth, V. "Memories of a Great Librarian–Electra Collins Doren [1861–1927]." *WLB* 28 (1954): 782–87.

DOWNS, ROBERT BINGHAM

2963. Gunning, C. "Publications of Robert B. Downs." In *Research Librarianship: Essays in Honor of Robert B. Downs*, edited by J. Orne, pp. 141–62. New York: R. R. Bowker, 1971.
2964. Suen, M. T. "Robert Bingham Downs and Academic Librarianship." Master's thesis, Southern Connecticut State College, 1967.

DRAPER, LYMAN COPELAND

2965. Hesseltine, W. B. *The Story of Lyman Copeland Draper*. Madison: The State Historical Society of Wisconsin, 1954.
2966. Thwaites, R. G. "Lyman Copeland Draper—A Memoir." *WSHSC* 12 (1892): 1–19.

DUNKIN, PAUL S.

2967. Carnovsky, R. F. "Paul S. Dunkin." *LRTS* 12 (1968): 447–49.

EAMES, WILBERFORCE

2968. Paltsits, V. H. "Wilberforce Eames, American Bibliographer." *BNYPL* 59 (1955): 505–19.

EASTMAN, LINDA ANNE

2969. Phillips, C. O. "Linda Anne Eastman: Librarian." Master's thesis, Western Reserve University, 1953.
2970. Wright, A. E. "Linda A. Eastman: Pioneer in Librarianship." Master's thesis, Kent State University, 1952.

EDMUNDS, JOHN

2971. Clapp, V. W., and First, E. W. "A.L.A. Member No. 13: A First Glance at John Edmunds." *LQ* 26 (1956): 1–22.

ELLIOTT, LESLIE ROBINSON

2972. Benson, S. H. "Leslie Robinson Elliott: His Contribution to Theological Librarianship." Master's thesis, University of Texas, 1965.

EVANS, CHARLES

2973. Holley, E. G. *Charles Evans: American Bibliographer*. Urbana: University of Illinois Press, 1963.

EVANS, LUTHER

2974. Sittig, W. J. "Luther Evans: Man for a New Age." *QJLC* 33 (1976): 251–67.

FELLOWS, DORKAS

2975. Getchell, M. W. "Dorkas Fellows, Cataloger and D.C. Editor." *CCH* 8 (1940): 14–19.

FLETCHER, WILLIAM ISAAC

2976. Bobinski, G. S. "William Isaac Fletcher: An Early American Library Leader." *JLH* 5 (1970): 101–18.

FLEXNER, JENNIE M.

2977. Johnston, E. "Jennie M. Flexner, 1882–1944." In *Pioneering Leaders in Librarianship*, First Series, edited by E. M. Danton, pp. 61–73. Chicago: American Library Association, 1953.

FOGARTY, JOHN E.

2978. Healey, J. S. *John E. Fogarty: Political Leadership for Library Development*. Metuchen, N.J.: Scarecrow Press, 1974.

FOIK, PAUL J.

2979. Bresie, M. "Paul J. Foik, C.S.C., Librarian-Historian." Master's thesis, University of Texas, 1964.

FOSTER, WILLIAM EATON

2980. Sherman, C. E. "William E[aton] Foster [1851–1930]: Liberal Librarian." *WLB* 30 (1956): 449–53, 467.

FRANKLIN, LOUISE

2981. Pettigrew, C. L. "Louise Franklin: The Education of a Texas Librarian." Master's thesis, University of Texas, 1967.

FREEDLEY, GEORGE R.

2982. Correll, L. "American Theatre Librarianship: Focus on Leadership of George R. Freedley." *JLH* 6 (1971): 317–26.

GAY, FRANK BULTER

2983. Kerr, R. A. "Frank Butler Gay (1856–1934)–Bibliophile." *TCLG* 1 (February 1955): 18–21.

GEROULD, JAMES THAYER

2984. Heyl, L. "James Thayer Gerould: Some Recollections of an Association." *PULC* 14 (1953): 91–93.

GILLET, CHARLES RIPLEY

2985. Slavens, T. P. "Incidents in the Librarianship of Charles Ripley Gillet." *JLH* 4 (1969): 321–29.

GILLIS, JAMES L.

2986. Brewitt, T. R. "James L. Gillis, 1857–1917." In *Pioneering Leaders in Librarianship*, First Series, edited by E. M. Danton, pp. 74–84. Chicago: American Library Association, 1953.
2987. "James L. Gillis Centennial." *CalL* 18 (1957): 220–38.
2988. Mumm, B., and Ottley, A. "James L. Gillis in Print." *NNCL* 42 (1957): 654–58.

GILLIS, MABEL RAY

2989. Conmy, P. T. "Mabel Ray Gillis, California State Librarian: The Fulfillment of the Destiny of Inheritance." *NNCL* 63 (1968): 284–94.
2990. Warren, A. "Mabel Ray Gillis." *CalL* 12 (1952): 196–99, 224.

GOODRICH, NATHANIEL L.

2991. Goodrich, N. L. "Report on 38 Years." *DCLB* 5 (April 1950): 35–40.

GOODWIN, JOHN EDWARD

2992. Powell, L. C. "John E. Goodwin, Founder of the UCLA Library: An Essay Toward a Biography." *JLH* 6 (1971): 265–74.
2993. Salinas, A. "John Edward Goodwin: University Librarian." Master's thesis, University of Texas, 1966.

GRAHAM, BESSIE

2994. Campbell, M. M. "Bessie Graham, Bibliophile." Master's thesis, Texas State College for Women, 1953.

GREEN, SAMUEL SWETT

2995. Shaw, R. K. *Samuel Swett Green*. Chicago: American Library Association, 1926.

GRIFFIN, ETTA JOSSELYN

2996. Stevenson, V. F. *Etta Josselyn Griffin: Pioneer Librarian for the Blind*. Washington, D.C.: National Library for the Blind, 1959.

GROTHAUS, JULIA

2997. Drummond, D. R. "Julia Grothaus, San Antonio Librarian." Master's thesis, University of Texas, 1964.

GUNTER, LILLIAN

2998. Nichols, I. C., and Nichols, M. I. "Lillian Gunter and Texas County Legislation, 1914–1919." *JLH* 8 (1973): 11–17.
2999. Nichols, M. I. "Lillian Gunter: Pioneer Texas County Librarian, 1870–1926." Master's thesis, University of Texas, 1958.

HADLEY, CHALMERS

3000. "In Memory of Chalmers Hadley." *GP* 33 (1958): 1–30.

HAINES, HELEN E.

3001. Haines, H. E. "Through Time's Bifocals." *CalL* 12 (1950): 85–86, 114–15.
3002. Harlan, R. D. "Helen E. Haines." *ELIS* 10:278–84.
3003. Hyers, F. H. "Helen E. Haines." *BB* 20 (1951): 129–31.
3004. Sive, M. R. "Helen E. Haines, 1872–1961: An Annotated Bibliography." *JLH* 5 (1970): 146–64.

HALLIDIE, ANDREW SMITH

3005. Kahn, E. M. "Andrew Hallidie as Writer and Speaker." *CHSQ* 25 (1946): 1–16.
3006. ———. "Andrew Smith Hallidie." *CHSQ* 19 (1970): 144–56.
3007. Mood, F. "Andrew S. Hallidie and Librarianship in San Francisco, 1868–79." *LQ* 16 (1946): 202–10.

HAMMOND, GEORGE P.

3008. Farquhar, F. P. P. "George P. Hammond's Publications." In *G.P.H.: An Informal Record of George P. Hammond and His Record in the Bancroft Library*, pp. 83–106. Berkeley: University of California, 1965.

HANSON, JAMES C. M.

3009. Bishop, W. W. "J. C. M. Hanson and International Cataloging." *LQ* 4 (1934): 165–68.
3010. Butler, P. "Bibliography of James C. M. Hanson." *LQ* 4 (1934): 131–35.
3011. Dorf, A. T. "The University of Chicago Libraries [and J. C. M. Hanson]: A Historical Note." *LQ* 4 (1934): 185–97.
3012. Hanson, J. C. M. *What Became of Jens? A Study in Americanization Based on the Reminiscences of J. C. M. Hanson, 1864–1943*. Edited by O. M. Hovde. Decorah, Iowa: Luther College Press, 1974.

3013. McMullen, H. "J. C. M. Hanson, 1864–1943." In *Pioneering Leaders in Librarianship*, First Series, edited by E. M. Danton, pp. 85–96. Chicago: American Library Association, 1953.
3014. Scott, E. "J. C. M. Hanson." *ELIS* 10:304–11.
3015. ———. "J. C. M. Hanson and His Contribution to Twentieth Century Cataloging." Doctoral dissertation, University of Chicago, 1970.
3016. Starr, H. K. "Mr. Hanson and His Friends." *LQ* 4 (1934): 329–33.

HARRIS, THADDEUS MASON

3017. Frothingham, N. L. "Memoir of Thaddeus Mason Harris." *CMHS* ser. 4, 2 (1854): 130–55.
3018. Hawthorne, N. "The Ghost of Dr. Harris." *LivA* 224 (1900): 345–49.

HARRIS, WILLIAM TORREY

3019. Leidecker, K. F. *Yankee Teacher: The Life of William Torrey Harris.* New York: Philosophical Library, 1946.

HARRISON, ALICE S.

3020. Herring, B. G. U. "Alice S. Harrison, Pioneer School Librarian, 1882–1967." Master's thesis, University of Texas, 1968.

HART, GILBERT

3021. Hutchinson, V. L. "Gilbert Hart (1828–1912), the Man and His Library." *VQ* 20 (1952): 108–12.

HASSE, ADELAIDE ROSALIA

3022. Childs, J. B. "Adelaide Rosalia Hasse." *ELIS* 10:373–77.

HENRY, EDWARD ATWOOD

3023. Kuhlman, A. F. "Edward Atwood Henry." *BB* 20 (1952): 153–54.

HEWINS, CAROLINE MARIA

3024. Dekenis, A. "Caroline Maria Hewins: Pioneer in the Development of Library Service for Children." Master's thesis, Southern Connecticut State College, 1959.
3025. Miller, B. M., ed. *Caroline M. Hewins: Her Book.* Boston: Horn Book, 1954.
3026. Root, M. E. S. "Caroline Maria Hewins, 1846–1926." In *Pioneering Leaders in Librarianship*, First Series, edited by E. M. Danton, pp. 97–107. Chicago: American Library Association, 1953.

HICKS, FREDERICK G.

3027. "Bibliography of Books and Articles by Frederick G. Hicks." *LLJ* 37 (1944): 19–24.
3028. Roalfe, W. R. "Frederick G. Hicks [1875–1956]: Scholar-Librarian." *LLJ* 50 (May 1957): 88–98.

HOLMES, THOMAS JAMES

3029. Keys, T. E. "Thomas James Holmes, Bibliographer, Bookbinder, and Librarian 1875–1959." *MLAB* 47 (1959): 325–29.

HOOLE, WILLIAM STANLEY

3030. Hoole, M. D. "William Stanley Hoole, Student-Teacher-Librarian-Author." Master's thesis, Florida State University, 1958.

HOWLAND, ARTHUR CHARLES

3031. Setton, K. M. "Arthur Charles Howland (1869–1952)." *LC* 18 (1952): 77–79.

HUTCHINS, FRANK AVERY

3032. Kent, A. E. "Frank Avery Hutchins: Promoter of 'The Wisconsin Idea.'" *WLB* 30 (1955): 73–77.

IDESON, JULIA BEDFORD

3033. McSwain, M. B. "Julia Bedford Ideson, Houston Librarian, 1880–1945." Master's thesis, University of Texas, 1966.

ISOM, MARY FRANCES

3034. Johansen, D. O. *The Library and the Liberal Tradition.* Corvallis: Friends of the Library, Oregon State College, 1959.
3035. Kingsbury, M. E. "'To Shine in Use': The Library and War Service of Oregon's Pioneer Librarian, Mary Frances Isom." *JLH* 10 (1975): 22–34.
3036. Van Horne, B. "Mary Frances Isom: Creative Pioneer in Library Work in the Northwest." *WLB* 33 (1959): 409–16.

JACKSON, WILLIAM ALEXANDER

3037. Jackson, W. A. *Records of a Bibliographer: Selected Papers.* Cambridge, Mass.: Harvard University Press, 1967.

JEFFERSON, THOMAS

3038. Adams, R. G. "Thomas Jefferson, Librarian." In his *Three Americanists . . .* , pp. 69–96. Philadelphia: University of Pennsylvania Press, 1939.

JEWETT, CHARLES COFFIN

3039. Boromé, J. A. *Charles Coffin Jewett (1816–68).* Chicago: American Library Association, 1951.

3040. Guild, R. A. "Memorial Sketch of Professor Charles Coffin Jewett." *LJ* 12 (1887): 507–11.

3041. Harris, M. H., ed. *The Age of Jewett: Charles Coffin Jewett and American Librarianship, 1841–1868.* Littleton, Colo.: Libraries Unlimited, 1975.

3042. ———. "An 1845 Overture to the Librarian's Creed: Farsighted Bibliophile Promotes the Free Flow of Information." *ALib* 6 (1975): 404.

3043. Trask, W. B. "Charles Coffin Jewett." *NEHGR* 22 (1868): 365–66.

JONES, SAMUEL MINOT

3044. Walker, C. S. *Samuel Minot Jones: The Story of an Amherst Boy.* Amherst, Mass.: [The Jones Library], 1922.

JOSEPHSON, AKSEL G. S.

3045. Foos, D. D. "Aksel G. S. Josephson, 1860–1944, Precursor." In *Library History Seminar Number 4,* edited by H. Goldstein and J. Goudeau, pp. 195–202. Tallahassee: Florida State University School of Library Science, 1972.

KAISER, JOHN BOYNTON

3046. Newark, N.J., Free Public Library. *An Annotated Bibliography of the Writings of John Boynton Kaiser, Published 1911 to 1958: Prepared on the Occasion of His Retirement as Director, April 15, 1943–July 2, 1958, of the Newark Public Library.* Newark: Newark Public Library, 1958.

KELSO, TESSA

3047. Geller, E. "Tessa Kelso: Unfinished Hero of Library Herstory." *ALib* 6 (1975): 347.

KEOGH, ANDREW

3048. Babb, J. T. "Andrew Keogh: His Contribution to Yale [1899–1938]." *YULG* 29 (1954): 47–60.

3049. Rollins, C. P. "Andrew Keogh (November 14, 1869–February 13, 1953)." *YULG* 28 (1954): 139–43.

KEPPEL, FREDERICK P.

3050. Wilson, L. R. "Frederick P. Keppel, 1875–1943." *LQ* 14 (1944): 55–56.

KERR, WILLIS H.

3051. Kerr, W. H. "My Life with Books." *CalL* 13 (1952): 203–04, 236.

KEYS, THOMAS EDWARD

3052. Keys, T. E. "Past Presidents I Have Known." *MLAB* 63 (1975): 49–59, 216–22.

KIDDER, IDA ANGELINE

3053. Carlson, W. H. "Ida Angeline Kidder: Pioneer Western Land-Grant Librarian." *CRL* 29 (1968): 217–23.

KINGSBURY, MARY A.

3054. Clark, M. B. "Mary A. Kingsbury, Pioneer." *WLB* 26 (1951): 50–51.

KOCH, THEODORE WESLEY

3055. Snyder, F. B. *Theodore Wesley Koch: An Address.* Evanston: Northwestern University Press, 1941.

KUHLMAN, AUGUSTUS FREDERICK

3056. Matthews, J. P. "A. F. Kuhlman—A Bibliographic View." *SEL* 11 (1961): 313–18.

LARNED, JOSEPHUS NELSON

3057. Ditzion, S. "Josephus Nelson Larned, 1836–1913." In *Pioneering Leaders in Librarianship,* First Series, edited by E. M. Danton, pp. 108–19. Chicago: American Library Association, 1953.
3058. ———. "The Social Ideas of a Library Pioneer: Josephus Nelson Larned, 1836–1913." *LQ* 13 (1943): 112–31.
3059. Young, B. "Josephus Nelson Larned and the Public Library Movement." *JLH* 10 (1975): 323–40.

LEE, MOLLY HUSTON

3060. Moore, R. N. "Molly Huston Lee: A Profile." *WLB* 49 (1975): 432–39.

LEGLER, HENRY EDWARD

3061. Field, P. I., and Warren, A. "Henry Edward Legler, 1861–1917." In *Pioneering Leaders in Librarianship,* First Series, edited by E. M. Danton, pp. 120–29. Chicago: American Library Association, 1953.

LENNOX, JAMES

3062. Stevens, H. *Recollections of James Lennox and the Formation of His Library.* New York: New York Public Library, 1951.

LEYPOLDT, FREDERICK

3063. Beswick, J. W. *The Work of Frederick Leypoldt: Bibliographer and Publisher.* New York: R. R. Bowker, 1942.

LOGASA, HANNAH

3064. Pulling, H. A. "Hannah Logasa." *BB* 22 (September–December 1956): 1–3.

LONGFELLOW, HENRY WADSWORTH

3065. Johnson, C. L. "Henry W. Longfellow, Librarian [Bowdoin College, 1829–35]." *CRL* 15 (1954): 425–29.
3066. Michener, R. "Henry Wadsworth Longfellow: Librarian of Bowdoin College, 1829–1835." *LQ* 43 (1973): 215–26.

LOUGHRAN, VERNON

3067. Loughran, V. "Pioneering in Platte County, or the Exciting Adventure of a Library Extension Worker." *WLR* 11 (June 1956): 9–13.

LOWE, JOHN ADAMS

3068. O'Flynn, M. E. "John Adams Lowe: Administrator and Library Planner." Master's thesis, Drexel Insitute of Technology, 1955.

LUDINGTON, FLORA BELL

3069. Johnson, M. "Flora Bell Ludington: A Biography and Bibliography." *CRL* 25 (1964): 377–79.

LUMMIS, CHARLES FLETCHER

3070. Gordon, D. "Aggressive Librarian: Charles Fletcher Lummis." *WLB* 45 (1970): 399–405.
3071. ———. *Charles F. Lummis: Crusader in Corduroy.* Los Angeles: Cultural Assets Press, 1972.

LYDENBURG, HARRY MILLER

3072. Fulton, D., gen. ed. *Bookman's Holiday: Notes and Studies Gathered in Tribute to Harry Miller Lydenburg.* New York: New York Public Library, 1943.

MCCARTHY, CHARLES

3073. Casey, M. "Charles McCarthy's 'Idea': A Library to Change Government." *LQ* 44 (1974): 29–41.
3074. Donnan, E., and Stock, L. F., eds. "Letters: Charles McCarthy to J. Franklin Jameson." *WMH* 33 (September 1949): 64–86.
3075. Fitzpatrick, E. A. *McCarthy of Wisconsin.* New York: Columbia Univesity Press, 1944.
3076. Plunkett, H. "McCarthy of Wisconsin: The Career of an Irishman Abroad as It Appeals to an Irishman at Home." *NC* 77 (1915): 1335–47.

MCCLUNG, CALVIN MORGAN

3077. Mellen, G. F. "Calvin Morgan McClung and His Library." *THM* 7 (1921): 3–26.

MCDIARMID, ERRETT WEIR

3078. McCulley, K. M. "Dr. Errett Weir McDiarmid's Application of His Philosophy of Library Administration in the University of Minnesota Library, 1943–1951." Master's thesis, University of North Carolina, 1963.

MACDONALD, ANGUS SNEAD

3079. Baumann, C. H. *Agnus Snead Macdonald.* Metuchen, N.J.: Scarecrow Press, 1972.

MaCLEISH, ARCHIBALD

3080. Benco, N. L. "Archibald MacLeish: The Poet Librarian." *QJLC* 33 (1976): 233–49.
3081. Goldschmidt, E. "Archibald MacLeish: Librarian of Congress." *CRL* 30 (1969): 12–24.
3082. ———, ed. *Champion of a Cause: Essays and Addresses on Librarianship by Archibald MacLeish.* Chicago: American Library Association, 1971.

MAGRUDER, PATRICK

3083. Gordon, M. K. "Patrick Magruder: Citizen, Congressman, Librarian of Congress." *QJLC* 32 (1975): 154–71.

MANN, HORACE

3084. Downs, R. B. "Books and Libraries." In *Horace Mann: Champion of Public Schools*, pp. 58–68. Boston: Twyne Publishing, 1974.
3085. Jones, E. K. "Horace Mann and the Early Libraries of Massachusetts." *MassLAB* 27 (1937): 19–21.
3086. King, C. S. "Horace Mann's Influence on South American Libraries." *HEQ* 1 (1961): 16–26.

MANN, MARGARET

3087. Grotzinger, L. "The Proto-feminist Librarian at the Turn of the Century: Two Studies." *JLH* 10 (1975): 195–213.
3088. Shaw, D. R. "Life and Work of Margaret Mann." Master's thesis, Drexel Institute of Technology, 1950.
3089. Wead, E. "Margaret Mann–A Bibliography." *CCY* 7 (1938): 15–18.

MARTIN, MARY P.

3090. Wetzel, N. P. "Mary P. Martin and the Canton Public Library, 1884–1928: A Study in Library Leadership." Master's thesis, Kent State University, 1969.

MAZE, ADELE HENRY

3091. Maze, A. H. "Librarian Tells of 35 Years' Service in South Oak Park." *IllL* 36 (1954): 137–39.

MEEHAN, JOHN SILVA

3092. McDonough, J. "John Silva Meehan: A Gentleman of Amiable Manners." *QJLC* 33 (1976): 3–28.

METCALF, KEYES D.

3093. Williams, E. E. "The Metcalf Administration, 1937–1955, and Keyes D. Metcalf: A Bibliography of Published Writings." *HLB* 17 (1969): 113–42.

MILAM, CARL HASTINGS

3094. Dale, D. C., ed. *Carl H. Milam and the United Nations Library*. Metuchen, N.J.: Scarecrow Press, 1976.
3095. Danton, E. M. "Carl Hastings Milam." *BALA* 53 (1959): 753–62.
3096. Fontaine, E. O. "People and Places of the Milam Era." *BALA* 58 (1964): 363–71.
3097. Sullivan, P. *Carl H. Milam and the American Library Association*. New York: H. W. Wilson, 1976.
3098. Wilson, L. R. "Carl H. Milam." *LJ* 70 (1945): 331–33.

MILLER, CHARLES

3099. Miller, C. "'Exit Smiling' Reflections Culled from the Autobiography of Charles Miller, Librarian of the Mercantile Library of St. Louis (ca. 1890)." *MHSB* 6 (October 1949): 44–52.

MITCHELL, SIDNEY B.

3100. Mitchell, S. B. *The Memoirs of Sidney B. Mitchell: Librarian-Teacher-Gardener*. Berkeley: California Library Association, 1960.
3101. Powell, L. C. "Mitchell of California." *WLB* 28 (1954): 778–81, 790.
3102. Rosenberg, B. "Sidney B. Mitchell Bibliography." In Mitchell's *The Memoirs of Sidney B. Mitchell, Librarian-Teacher-Gardener*, pp. 245–63. Berkeley: California Library Association, 1960.

MONTI, MINNE SWEET

3103. Hershey, F. E. "Minne Sweet Monti: Her Life and Influence." Master's thesis, Western Reserve University, 1957.

MOORE, ANNE CARROLL

3104. Akers, N. M. "Anne Carroll Moore: A Study of Her Work With Children's Libraries and Literature." Master's thesis, Pratt Institute, 1951.
3105. Poor, A. M. "Anne Carroll Moore: The Velvet Glove of Librarianship." Master's thesis, Southern Connecticut State College, 1966.
3106. Power, L. S. "Recollections of Anne Carroll Moore (Children's Librarian in New York Since 1906)." *BNYPL* 60 (1956): 623–27.
3107. Strang, M. "Good Labor of Old Days." *BNYPL* 60 (1956): 537–50.

MORSCH, LUCILE

3108. Wheeler, J. L. "Lucile Morsch." *JCC* 7 (1951): 73–75.

MUDGE, ISADORE GILBERT

3109. Evans, A. P. "God Almighty Hates a Quitter." *CLC* 2 (1952): 13–18.

MUMFORD, LAWRENCE QUINCY

3110. Powell, B. E. "Lawrence Quincy Mumford: Twenty Years of Progress." *QJLC* 33 (1976): 269–87.
3111. Rogers, R. D. "LQM of LC." *BB* 25 (1968): 161–65.

OBERLY, EUNICE ROCKWOOD

3112. Allen, J. M. "Eunice Rockwood Oberly, 1878–1921." In *Pioneering Leaders in Librarianship*, First Series, edited by E. M. Danton, pp. 130–40. Chicago: American Library Association, 1953.

OBOLER, ELI MARTIN

3113. Oboler, E. M. "Twenty Years an Idaho Librarian: A Personal Report." *IL* 21 (July 1969): 95–99.

OWEN, THOMAS MCADORY

3114. Ketchersid, A. L. "Thomas McAdory Owen: Archivist." Master's thesis, Florida State University, 1961.

PARGELLIS, STANLEY

3115. Krummel, D. W. "The Writings of Stanley Pargellis." In *Essays in History and Literature Presented by Fellows of the Newberry Library to Stanley Pargellis*, edited by H. Bluhm, pp. 221–31. Chicago: The Newberry Library, 1965.
3116. Pargellis, S. M. "On Being a Librarian." *AmO* 40 (1953): 3–8.

PATTEN, FRANK CHAUNCY

3117. Jordan, M. "Frank Chauncy Patten: The Galveston Years." Master's thesis, University of Texas, 1966.

PAYLORE, PATRICIA

3118. Paylore, P. "The Chief Librarian and Book Knowledge." *CRL* 15 (1954): 313–16.

PEARSON, EDMUND LESTER

3119. Durnell, J. "An Irrepressible Deceiver." *PNLAQ* 36 (1971): 17–23.
3120. Hyland, L. "An Interpretation of Edmund Lester Pearson–Librarian Extraordinary, to Which Is Added a Bibliography of His Works." Master's thesis, Carnegie Institute of Technology, 1952.
3121. Pearson, E. L. *The Librarian: Selections from the Column of That Name*, edited by J. B. Durnell and N. D. Stevens. Metuchen, N.J.: Scarecrow Press, 1976.
3122. ———. *The Library and the Librarian: A Selection of Articles from the Boston Evening Transcript and Other Sources*. Woodstock, Vt.: The Elm Tree Press, 1910.

PERSONS, FREDERICK TORREL

3123. Babcock, F. K. "Frederick Torrel Persons and Church Architecture." *AmCAB* 2 (1951): 3–14.

PIERCE, CORNELIA MARVIN

3124. Brisley, M. A. "Cornelia Marvin Pierce: Pioneer in Library Extension." Master's thesis, University of Chicago, 1967.
3125. ———. "Cornelia Marvin Pierce: Pioneer in Library Extension." *LQ* 38 (1968): 125–53.

PIERCY, ESTHER J.

3126. Dunkin, P. S., ed. "Studies in Memory of Esther J. Piercy, Editor, *Library Resources and Technical Services*, 1957–1967." *LRTS* 11 (1967): 259–384; 12 (1967): 389–498.

POLK, MARY

3127. Lopez, L. L. "Mary Polk–Library Pioneer." *JPL* 3 (1970): 61–72.
3128. Perez, C. B. "Mary Polk: Library Pioneer." *LM* 2 (1931): 24–26.

POOLE, WILLIAM FREDERICK

3129. "Publications of William Frederick Poole." In *Memorial Sketch of Dr. William Frederick Poole*, pp. 29–34. Chicago: Newberry Library, 1895.
3130. Williamson, W. L. *William Frederick Poole and the Modern Library Movement*. New York: Columbia University Press, 1963.

POWELL, LAWRENCE CLARK

3131. Powell, L. C. *Fortune and Friendship: Autobiography*. New York: R. R. Bowker, 1968.
3132. Rosenberg, B. *Checklist of the Published Writings of Lawrence Clark Powell*. Los Angeles: University of California, 1966.

POWER, EFFIE LOUISE

3133. Becker, M. B. "Effie Louise Power: Pioneer in the Development of Library Services for Children." Master's thesis, Western Reserve University, 1950.

PUTMAN, HERBERT

3134. Bay, J. C. "Herbert Putnam, 1861–1955." *Libri* 6 (1957): 201–07.
3135. Countryman, G. A. "Mr. Putnam and the Minneapolis Public Library." In *Essays Offered to Herbert Putnam by His Colleagues and Friends on His Thirtieth Anniversary as Librarian of Congress, 5 April 1929*, edited by W. W. Bishop and A. Keogh, pp. 5–9. New Haven: Yale University Press, 1929.
3136. Dickinson, A. D. "Recollections of Herbert Putnam." *WLB* 30 (1955): 311–15.
3137. Jones, H. D. "Herbert Putnam: [A Bibliography]." In *Herbert*

Putnam, 1861–1955: A Memorial Tribute, pp. 53–80. Washington, D.C.: Library of Congress, 1956.

3138. Krieg, C. J. "Herbert Putnam's Philosophy of Librarianship." Master's thesis, Long Island University, 1971.

3139. Mearns, D. C. "Herbert Putnam and His Responsible Eye." In *Herbert Putnam, 1861–1955: A Memorial Tribute*, pp. 1–52. Washington, D.C.: Library of Congress, 1956.

3140. ———. "Herbert Putnam: Librarian of the U.S." *DCL* 26 (1955): 22–24.

3141. ———. "Herbert Putnam, Librarian of the United States–the Minneapolis Years." *WLB* 29 (1954): 59–63.

3142. Waters, E. N. "Herbert Putnam: The Tallest Little Man in the World." *QJLC* 33 (1976): 151–75.

RAINES, CALDWELL WALTON

3143. Christie, C. C. "Caldwell Walton Raines, 1839–1906: Historian and Librarian." Master's thesis, University of Texas, 1966.

RANCK, SAMUEL H.

3144. Wheeler, J. L. "Samuel H. Ranck." *MichL* 7 (1941): 6.

RATCHFORD, FANNIE ELIZABETH

3145. Wiley, A. N. "Fannie Elizabeth Ratchford." *TLJ* 27 (1951): 15–19.

RATHBONE, JOSEPHINE ADAMS

3146. Fenneman, N. "Recollections of Josephine Adams Rathbone." *WLB* 23 (1949): 773–74.

RICE, PAUL NORTH

3147. Lydenburg, H. M. "Paul North Rice: The Man and the Librarian." *BNYPL* 57 (1953): 389–91.

RICHARDSON, ERNEST CUSHING

3148. Branscomb, L. C. "A Bio-bibliographic Study of Ernest Cushing Richardson, 1860–1939." Doctoral dissertation, University of Chicago, 1954.

3149. ———. "Ernest Cushing Richardson, 1860–1939." In *Pioneering Leaders in Librarianship*, First Series, edited by E. M. Danton, pp. 141–52. Chicago: American Library Association, 1953.

ROBBINS, THOMAS

3150. Harlow, T. R. "Thomas Robbins, Clergyman, Book Collector, and Librarian." *PBSA* 61 (1967): 1–11.

ROCKWELL, WILLIAM WALKER

3151. Slavens, T. P. "William Walker Rockwell and the Development of the Union Theological Seminary Library." *JLH* 11 (1976): 26–43.

ROGAN, OCTAVIA R.

3152. Banks, K. "Octavia R. Rogan, Texas Librarian." Master's thesis, University of Texas, 1963.

ROWELL, JOSEPH CUMMINGS

3153. Kurts, B. *Joseph Cummings Rowell, 1853–1938.* Berkeley: University of California Press, 1940.

SANDERS, MINERVA

3154. Smith, E. "Minerva Sanders, 1837–1912." In *Pioneering Leaders in Librarianship*, First Series, edited by E. M. Danton, pp. 153–64. Chicago: American Library Association, 1953.

SCHEUBER, JENNIE SCOTT

3155. Taylor, R. N. "Jennie Scott Scheuber: An Approach to Librarianship." Master's thesis, University of Texas, 1968.

SCHICK, MARY ELIZABETH

3156. Standlee, M. W. "The Book Lady." *MS* 111 (1952): 44–49.

SHARP, KATHARINE LUCINDA

3157. Grotzinger, L. A. *The Power and the Dignity: Librarianship and Katharine Sharp.* Metuchen, N.J.: Scarecrow Press, 1966.
3158. Howe, H. E. "Katharine Lucinda Sharp, 1865–1914." In *Pioneering Leaders in Librarianship*, First Series, edited by E. M. Danton, pp. 165–72. Chicago: American Library Association, 1953.

SHERA, JESSE HAUK

3159. Ruderman, L. P. "Jesse Shera: A Bio-Bibliography." Master's thesis, Kent State University, 1968.

SHIRLEY, WAYNE

3160. Marshall, J. D. "As I Remember Wayne Shirley." *JLH* 9 (1974): 293.
3161. Rush, N. O. "Wayne Shirley, 1900–1973: An Appreciation." *JLH* 9 (1974): 294–95.
3162. Shirley, W. "An American Librarian's Heritage." *FSUS* 12 (1953): 141–56.
3163. Shores, L. "Wayne Shirley: In Memoriam." *JLH* 9 (1974): 291–92.

SHORES, LOUIS

3164. Marshall, J. D. *Louis Shores: A Bibliography*. Tallahassee: Beta Phi Mu, Gamma Chapter. Florida State University Library School, 1964.
3165. Shores, L. *Quiet World: A Librarian's Crusade for Destiny*. Hamden, Conn.: Archon, 1975.

SHORTESS, LOIS F.

3166. Theriot, B. C. "A Study of the Contributions of Lois F. Shortess to Louisiana's Public School Library Development." Master's thesis, University of Southwestern Louisiana, 1968.

SHULER, ELLIS WILLIAM

3167. Trent, R. M. "Ellis William Shuler and the (Southern Methodist) University Libraries (1915–50)." *F&L* 21 (1953): 10–12.

SIBLEY, JOHN LANGDON

3168. Peabody, A. P. *Memoire of John Langdon Sibley*. Cambridge, Mass.: John Wilson & Son, 1886.
3169. Shipton, C. K. "John Langdon Sibley, Librarian." *HLB* 9 (1955): 236–61.

SKINNER, MARK

3170. Utley, G. B. "An Early 'Friend' of Libraries [Mark Skinner]." *LQ* 12 (1942): 725–30.

SMITH, CHARLES W.

3171. Gershevsky, R. H. "Charles W. Smith, 1877–1956: An Affectionate Tribute." *PNLAQ* 20 (1956): 156–57.

SMITH, HENRY PRESERVED

3172. Slavens, T. P. "The Librarianship of Henry Preserved Smith, 1913–1925." In *Library History Seminar Number 4*, edited by H. Goldstein and J. Goudeau, pp. 183–94. Tallahassee: Florida State University School of Library Science, 1972.

SOHIER, ELIZABETH PUTNAM

3173. Wellman, H. C. "Elizabeth Putnam Sohier, 1847–1926." In *Pioneering Leaders in Librarianship*, First Series, edited by E. M. Danton, pp. 173–78. Chicago: American Library Association, 1953.

SPOFFORD, AINSWORTH RAND

3174. *Ainsworth Rand Spofford, 1825–1908: A Memorial Meeting at the Library of Congress.* New York: Printed for the District of Columbia Library Association by the Webster Press, 1909.
3175. Cole, J. Y., ed. *Ainsworth Rand Spofford: Bookman and Librarian.* Littleton, Colo.: Libraries Unlimited, 1975.
3176. ———. "Ainsworth Spofford and the Copyright Law of 1870." *JLH* 6 (1971): 34–40.
3177. ———. "Ainsworth Spofford and the National Library." Doctoral dissertation, George Washington University, 1971.
3178. ———. "Ainsworth Rand Spofford: The Valiant and Persistent Librarian of Congress." *QJLC* 33 (1976): 93–115.
3179. ———. "A National Monument for a National Library: Ainsworth Rand Spofford and the New Library of Congress, 1871–1897." *RCHS* 48 (1973): 468–507.
3180. Grisso, K. M. "Ainsworth R. Spofford and the American Library Movement, 1861–1908." Master's thesis, Indiana University, 1966.
3181. Mearns, D. C. "Ainsworth the Unforgettable." *QJLC* 25 (1968): 1–5.
3182. Miller, C. H. "Ainsworth Rand Spofford, 1825–1908." Master's thesis, George Washington University, 1938.
3183. Putnam, H. "Ainsworth Rand Spofford: A Librarian Past." *TI* 65 (1908): 1149–55.
3184. Schubach, B. W. "Ainsworth Rand Spofford and the Library of the United States." Master's thesis, Northern Illinois University, 1965.
3185. Slade, W. A. "As It Was in the Beginning [Ainsworth Rand Spofford]." *PubL* 29 (1924): 293–96.

STEARNS, LUTIE EUGENIA

3186. Tannenbaum, E. "The Library Career of Lutie Eugenia Stearns (1867–1943)." *WMH* 39 (1956): 159–65.
3187. Stearns, L. E. "My Seventy-Five Years: Part I, 1866–1914." *WMH* 42 (1959): 211–18.
3188. ———. "My Seventy-Five Years: Part II, 1914–1942." *WMH* 42 (1959): 282–87.
3189. ———. "My Seventy-Five Years: Part III, Increasingly Personal." *WMH* 43 (1959–60): 97–105.

STEARNS, RAYMOND PHINEAS

3190. Brindenbaugh, C. "Raymond Phineas Stearns." *PMHS* 83 (1971): 157–60.

STEPHENSON, JOHN GOULD

3191. Carter, C. "John Gould Stephenson: Largely Known and Much Liked." *QJLC* 33 (1976): 77–91.
3192. Wood, R. G. "Librarian-in-Arms: The Career of John G. Stephenson." *LQ* 19 (1949): 263–69.

STILLWELL, MARGARET BINGHAM

3193. Stillwell, M. B. *Librarians Are Human: Memories In and Out of the Rare-Book World, 1907–1970.* Boston, 1973.

TAUBER, MAURICE FALCOLM

3194. Szigethy, M. C. *Maurice Falcolm Tauber: A Bio-Bibliography, 1934–1973.* Metuchen, N.J.: Published for Beta Phi Mu, Nu Chapter, Columbia University School of Library Service. Scarecrow Press, 1974.

THWAITES, REUBEN GOLD

3195. Turner, F. J. *Reuben Gold Thwaites: A Memorial Address.* Madison: State Historical Society of Wisconsin, 1914.

TIMOTHEE, LOUIS

3196. Blumenthal, W. H. "First Librarian of Colonial America [Louis Timothee]." *AN&Q* 1 (1963): 83–84.
3197. Friedman, W. "The First Librarian of America [Louis Timothee]." *LJ* 56 (1931): 902–03.

TITCOMB, MARY L.

3198. Wilkinson, M. S. "Mary L. Titcomb, 1857–1931." In *Pioneering Leaders in Librarianship*, First Series, edited by E. M. Danton, pp. 179–87. Chicago: American Library Association, 1953.

TORY, JESSE

3199. Teggart, J. F. "An Early Champion of Free Libraries [Jesse Tory]." *LJ* 23 (1898): 617–18.

TYLER, ALICE SARAH

3200. Richardson, C. E. "Alice Sarah Tyler: A Biographical Study." Master's thesis, Western Reserve University, 1951.
3201. Scott, C. R. "Alice Sarah Tyler, 1859–1944." In *Pioneering Leaders in Librarianship*, First Series, edited by E. M. Danton, pp. 188–96. Chicago: American Library Association, 1953.

VATTEMARE, ALEXANDRE

3202. Haraszti, Z. "Alexandre Vattemare." *MoreB* 2 (1927): 257–66.
3203. Richards, E. M. "Alexandre Vattemare and His System of International Exchanges." *MLAB* 32 (1944): 413–48.
3204. ———. "Alexandre Vattemare and His System of International Exchanges." Master's thesis, Columbia University, 1934.
3205. Quincy, J. P. "The Character and Services of Alexandre Vattemare." *PMHS* 21 (1884): 260–72.
3206. Winsor, J. "M. Vattemare and the Public Library System." *LW* 10 (1879): 185–86.
3207. ———. "The Results of Vattemare's Library Scheme." *LW* 10 (1879): 281–82.

VORMELKER, ROSE L.

3208. Magner, M. J. "The Businessman's Librarian–Rose L. Vormelker." Master's thesis, Western Reserve University, 1957.

WALTER, FRANK K.

3209. Bay, J. C. "Frank K. Walter in Retrospect." *CRL* 4 (1943): 309–11.

WARREN, ALTHEA

3210. *Althea Warren, Librarian.* Keepsake number 3. N.p.: California Library Association, 1962.
3211. Boaz, M. *Fervent and Full of Gifts: The Life of Althea Warren.* New York: Scarecrow Press, 1961.

WATTERSON, GEORGE

3212. Kennedy, J. A. *George Watterson, Novelist, "Metropolitan Author," and Critic.* Washington, D.C.: Catholic University of America, 1933.
3213. Matheson, W. "George Watterson: Advocate of the National Library." *QJLC* 32 (1975): 371–88.

WEST, ELIZABETH HOWARD

3214. Hester, G. A. "Elizabeth Howard West, Texas Librarian." Master's thesis, University of Texas, 1965.

WHEELER, JOSEPH L.

3215. Bell, M. V. "Joseph L. Wheeler: A Bibliography." *BB* 23 (1961): 127–32.
3216. Compton, C. H. "Joseph L. Wheeler." *BB* 21 (1955): 169–71.
3217. Edwards, M. A. "I Once Did See Joe Wheeler Plain." *JLH* 6 (1971): 291–302.

3218. Lydenburg, H. M. *Joseph Lewis Wheeler, Pathfinder and Pioneer* Baltimore: Enoch Pratt Free Library, 1945.
3219. "Three Tributes to Joseph Lewis Wheeler." *LJ* (1945): 283–85.
3220. "Tribute to Dr. Wheeler." *BL* 12 (1945): 7–8.
3221. Wheeler, J. L. "Happy Days." *ML* 27 (1961): 5–7.

WHITEHILL, WALTER MUIR

3222. *Walter Muir Whitehill: Director and Librarian, Boston Athenaeum, 1946–1973. A Bibliography and Verses by Friends Presented on His Retirement.* Boston: Boston Athenaeum, 1974.

WILLIAMS, EDWARD CHRISTOPHER

3223. Josey, E. J. "Edward Christopher Williams: A Librarian's Librarian." *JLH* 4 (1969): 106–22.

WILLIAMSON, CHARLES CLARENCE

3224. Reece, E. J. "C. C. Williamson: A Record of Service to American Librarianship." *CRL* 4 (1943): 306–08.
3225. Winckler, P. A. "Charles Clarence Williamson (1877–1965): His Professional Life and Work in Librarianship and Library Education in the United States." Doctoral dissertation, New York University, 1968.

WILSON, HALSEY WILLIAM

3226. "Halsey William Wilson, May 12, 1868–March 1, 1954." *WBL* 28 (1954): 665–68.

WILSON, LOUIS ROUND

3227. Barker, T. D. "Louis Round Wilson: A Tribute." *SEL* 1 (1951): 75–89.
3228. Johnson, W. H. "Louis R. Wilson, Teacher." *NCL* 18 (1959): 21–22.
3229. *Louis Round Wilson: Papers in Recognition of a Distinguished Career in Librarianship.* Chicago: University of Chicago Press, 1942.
3230. *Louis Round Wilson Bibliography: A Chronological List of Works and Editorial Activities Presented on the Occasion of His Centennial Celebration, December 2, 1976.* Chapel Hill: University of North Carolina Library, 1976.
3231. Mathis, G. R., ed. "Louis Round Wilson's Decision to Remain at the University of North Carolina." *JLH* 4 (1969): 256–64.
3232. Randall, W. M. "Louis R. Wilson and the Graduate Library School." *LQ* 12 (1942): 645–50.
3233. Rush, C. E. "Another Pioneer Is Honored in His Own Country [Louis R. Wilson]." *LQ* 12 (1942): 675–78.

3234. Tauber, M. F. "The Contributions of Louis Round Wilson to Librarianship [Since 1901]." *WLB* 31 (1956): 315–23.
3235. ———. *Louis R. Wilson: A Biographic Sketch*. Chapel Hill: Friends of the [University of North Carolina] Library, 1956.
3236. ———. *Louis Round Wilson: Librarian and Administrator*. New York: Columbia University Press, 1967.
3237. Thornton, M. I. "Bibliography of Louis Round Wilson." *LQ* 12 (1942): 339–42.
3238. Weaver, F. A. *Louis Round Wilson: The Years Since 1955*. [Chapel Hill: University of North Carolina Friends of the Library, 1976].

WINKLER, ERNEST WILLIAM

3239. Friend, L. "E. W. Winkler and the Texas State Library." *TL* 24 (May–June 1962): 89–114.

WINSHIP, GEORGE PARKER

3240. Whitehill, W. M. "George Parker Winship (1871–1952)." *PMHS* 71 (1953–57): 366–75.

WINSLOW, AMY

3241. Greenaway, E. "Amy Winslow." *BB* 20 (1952): 201–03.

WINSOR, JUSTIN

3242. Boromé, J. A. "The Life and Letters of Justin Winsor." Doctoral dissertation, Columbia University, 1950.
3243. Brundin, R. E. "Justin Winsor of Harvard and the Liberalizing of the College Library." *JLH* 10 (1975): 57–70.
3244. Cutter, C. A. "Justin Winsor." *Nation* 65 (1897): 335.
3245. Foster, W. E. "Justin Winsor, 1831–1897." *BB* 8 (1914): 2–3.
3246. Kilgour, F. G. "Justin Winsor." *CRL* 3 (1941): 64–66.
3247. Lane, W., and Tillinghast, W. "Justin Winsor, Librarian and Historian, 1831–1897." *LJ* 23 (1897): 7–13.
3248. Scudder, H. E. "Memoir of Justin Winsor." *PMHS* 12 (1899): 457–82.
3249. Sharma, R. N. "Winsor: The Quintessential Librarian." *WLB* 51 (1976): 48–52.
3250. Yust, W. F. *A Bibliography of Justin Winsor*. Cambridge, Mass.: Library of Harvard University, 1902.

WIRE, GEORGE EDWIN

3251. Beatty, W. K. "Medicine, Law, Librarianship: The Unique Contribution of George Edwin Wire." *LLJ* 68 (1975): 82–91.

WISTER, OWEN

3252. Mason, J. "Owen Wister, Boy Librarian." *QJLC* 26 (1969): 200–12.

WOOD, MARY ELIZABETH

3253. Huang, G. W. "Miss Mary Elizabeth Wood: Pioneer of the Library Movement in China." *JLIS* 1 (1975): 67–78.

WRIGHT, LOUIS B.

3254. Hard, F. "Louis B. Wright: A Biographical Sketch." In *Louis B. Wright: A Bibliography and an Appreciation*, pp. 1–75. Charlottesville: University Press of Virginia, 1968.

WROTH, LAWRENCE C.

3255. Adams, M. W., and Black, J. D. "List of the Published Writings of Lawrence C. Wroth to December 31, 1950." In *Essays Honoring Lawrence C. Wroth*, pp. 485–504. Portland, Me.: The Anthoensen Press, 1951.

WYER, JAMES INGERSOLL

3256. Cregan, F., and Strube, J. "James Ingersoll Wyer: Writings in Librarianship, and Education, 1899–1942." In *New York State Library School Register, 1887–1926*, pp. 45–51. New York: New York State Library School Association, 1959.

WYER, MALCOLM GLENN

3257. Gripton, J., and Bangoura, L. *Dr. Malcolm Wyer—A Bio-Bibliographical Study*. Denver: University of Denver, 1967.
3258. Parham, P. M. "Malcolm Glenn Wyer, Western Librarian: A Study in Leadership and Innovation." Doctoral dissertation, University of Denver, 1964.
3259. Wyer, M. G. *Books and People: Short Anecdotes from a Long Experience*. Denver: Old West, 1964.

YOUNG, JOHN RUSSELL

3260. Broderick, J. C. "John Russell Young: The Internationalist as Librarian." *QJLC* 33 (1976): 117–49.

Author Index

All references are to entries.

Abbot, G. M., 645
Abbott, J. C., 1807, 2940
Able, A. H., 1670
Abraham, M. L., 1966
Abrahams, A. J., 230
Abrahams, J. J., 339
Abrahamson, D., 2538
Adam, C., 1874
Adams, C. M., 1851
Adams, E. B., 231, 232, 233
Adams, E. M., 2813
Adams, F. B., 2132
Adams, H. B., 892
Adams, H. D., 234
Adams, K. B., 1676
Adams, L. G., 862
Adams, M. W., 3255
Adams, R. G., 1808, 2828, 3038
Adams, R. T., 1967
Adams, S., 2283, 2284, 2285, 2309, 2732
Adams, T. R., 1741, 1923
Adkins, B. M., 1128
Adkins, M. T., 2354
Adkinson, B. W., 2108
Adler, C., 2355
Adrian, J. M., 2457
Agard, W., 388
Agriesti, P. A., 1
Akers, N. M., 3104
Albrecht, T., 646
Albrecht, T. J., 2735
Aldrich, F. D., 1968
Aldrich, W. L. B., 1369
Alessios, A. B., 2286
Alexander, G. L., 1322
Alexander, W. A., 1705
Allan, J. M., 1828
Allanson, V. L., 94
Allen, A. W., 2287
Allen, D. L., 1511
Allen, J. M., 3112
Allen, M. E., 2539
Allen, W. C., 95
Almy, P., 1559

Altick, R. D., 96
Alvey, G. R., 1969
Ambler, B. H., 1467
American Library Association, 2540
Ames, S. M., 235
Amos, A., 1958
Anders, M. E., 893, 2541, 2542, 2543
Anderson, F., 894
Anderson, I. T., 2544
Anderson, K. E., 647, 1463
Anderson, M. T., 648, 649
Anderson, R., 1049
Andrews, C., 236
Andrews, F. E., 2, 1311
Andrews, T., 1560
Annan, G. L., 2545
Antrim, Mrs. S., 1389
Archer, H. R., 1687, 2227
Archer, N. W., 2546
Armour, A. W., 1561
Armstrong, C. M., 1323
Armstrong, E. V., 1897
Arnold, J. H., 2246, 2247
Arthur, A. W., 1390
Asheim, L. E., 2458
Ashley, F. W., 2356
Ashton, J. N., 649
Atkins, E., 896, 1932
Au, C., 2700
Axelrod, H. B., 2228
Axford, H. W., 1677
Ayer, C. W., 1250
Ayrault, M. S., 2547

Baatz, W. Y., 2357
Babb, J. T., 3048
Babcock, F. K., 3123
Babylon, E. R., 2043
Bach, H., 3
Back, H., 1562
Backus, J., 652
Bade, E. S., 2248
Bader, A. L., 389
Baer, E., 390
Bahnsen, J. C., 1852

220 Author Index

Bailey, A. H., 1143
Bailyn, B., 391, 392, 426
Baird, V. M., 2288
Baker, C. H. C., 2133
Baker, C. M., 237
Baker, F., 2549
Baker, H. S., 393, 394, 395, 653
Bald, F. C., 654
Baldwin, C. F., 1283, 2550
Baldwin, S., 396
Balkema, J. A., 2289
Ball, A. D., 2551
Ballance, P. S., comp., 1370
Ballard, H. H., 655
Ballard, J. F., 2552
Ballou, E. B., 397
Ballou, R. O., 2553
Bangoura, L., 3257
Banks, K., 3152
Barfield, I. R., 1115
Barker, E. C., 1935
Barker, G. E., 398
Barker, J. W., 1468
Barker, T. D., 97, 98, 99, 897, 3227
Barnes, G. S., 1512
Barnes, J. C., 400
Barnes, J. W., 1324
Barnes, R. W., 1324
Barnett, C. R., 2358
Barnett, L. F., 1391
Barnett, M. F., 1875
Baroco, J. V., 656
Baron, M. S., 1215
Barous, T. R., 1563
Barr, J. L. C., 1970
Barr, L. J., 2044
Barr, M. M., 401
Barrett, M., 1464
Barrett, M. A., 2045
Barrette, L. M., 2837
Bartlett, R. A., 4
Basler, R. P., 2359
Bassett, J. S., 1654
Batchelder, M. L., 898
Bates, N. P., 2736
Batten, S. S., 1371
Battle, M. E., 1853
Battles, F. M., 1392
Batty, D., 2737
Bauer, H. C., 1955
Bauersfeld, S. H., 1671
Baughman, N. C., 1876
Baughman, R. O., 1393
Baumann, C. H., 3079
Baumgartner, B., 1104
Bay, J. C., 2134, 2838, 3134, 3209

Baym, M. E., 239
Beagle, A. M., 100
Beamon, M., 1164
Beasley, K. E., 101
Beatty, W. K., 3251
Beck, E. R., 5
Beck, L. N., 240
Becker, J., 2109
Becker, M. B., 3133
Beddie, J. S., 102, 899
Beede, B. R., 113
Belanger, M. D., 1877
Belanger, S. E., 2360
Belfour, S., 2897
Bell, B. L., 900, 901
Bell, D., 1971
Bell, M. V., 3215
Bell, W. J., 2290
Benedetti, L. S., 1057
Benjamin, H. C., 2229
Bennett, H. E., 1325
Bennett, J. D., 2554
Bennett, J. P., 2556
Benson, S. H., 2972
Bentinck-Smith, 1742
Benton, J. H., 1216
Berelson, B., 902
Berg, V. A., 1144
Bergen, E., 1085
Bergquist, C. C., 6
Berkeley, D. S., 2841
Berkeley, E., 2841, 2842
Berkshire Athenaeum and Museum, 657
Bernier, B. R., 2291
Berninghausen, D. K., 103, 104
Berry, W. J. C., 2249
Berthel, J., 1829
Berthold, A. M., 2361
Bestor, A., 241
Beswick, J. W., 3063
Betancourt, J. A., 903
Bethke, R. D., 402
Bettie, Sister P. M., 2189
Biby, W. A., 1186
Bickford, C. P., 403
Bidlack, R. E., 658, 1809, 1810, 1811, 1812, 2738, 2909
Billings, J. S., 2292, 2362
Bird, M. F., 2046
Birkhoff, G., 1743
Bishop, C., 2190
Bishop, W. P., 404
Bishop, W. W., 1564, 1813, 2363, 2364, 2365, 2856, 2857, 2859, 2860, 2861, 2862, 2863, 2864, 3009

Bixby, Mrs. A. F., 1271
Bixler, P., 2701
Black, H., 405
Black, J. D., 3255
Blackshear, E. C., 105
Blair, J., 1394
Blair, M. G., 659
Blake, M., 242
Blanck, J., 406
Blanford, L., 1058
Blanks, E. W., 1181
Blazek, R., 7, 2459
Blegen, T. C., 407
Blinkhorn, M. E., 1198
Bliss, C. S., 2135
Bliss, R. P., 2047
Bloom, H., 904
Bloore, S., 2884
Blough, N. L., 106
Blumenthal, W. H., 3196
Boaz, M., 3211
Bobinski, G. S., 905, 1878, 2844, 2976
Bode, C., 408
Bogardus, J., 2230
Bogart, R. E., 1830
Bolden, E. E. M., 2892
Boll, J. J., 107, 1565
Bollenbacher, B., 1395, 1396
Bolton, C. K., 108, 660, 661, 662, 863, 1744
Bolton, S. K., 906
Bondurant, A. M., 243
Bone, L. E., 2702
Bonnell, A. H., 1831
Boone, H. H., 1397
Boorstin, D., 244
Boquer, H. F., 410
Borden, A. K., 109, 245, 907
Born, L. K., 110
Boromé, J. A., 2871, 3039, 3242
Borthwick, H. H., 908
Bostian, I., ed., 1145
Bostwick, A. E., 909, 2872, 2917
Bowden, C. N., 1398
Bowerman, G. F., 2557, 2876, 2877
Bowers, C. W., 1499
Bowes, F. P., 411
Bowker, R. R., 111, 412, 663, 2558
Bowman, J. N., 664
Boyce, G. K., 2136
Boyd, F., 1165
Boyd, J. P., 246
Boyd, W. D., 665
Boyer, P. S., 112
Boynton, H. W., 413
Bradley, N. B., 1399

Bradley, R., 247
Bradshaw, L. M., 1513
Bradsher, E. L., 666
Bradway, F., 2845
Brady, J. G., 1050
Brainerd, C., 864
Bramley, G., 2460
Brandt, B. S., 1532
Branscomb, L. C., 3148, 3149
Branyan, B. M., 1972
Brass, L. J., 1536
Bray, T., 616
Brayton, S. S., 248
Breedlove, J. P., 1854
Breen, M. H., 1327
Breisacher, R., 2366
Brennan, J. F., 1305
Bresie, M., 2979
Brewitt, T. R., 2986
Brewster, B., 2703
Brewster, E., 2559
Brichford, M., 8
Bridenbaugh, C., 414
Briggs, F. A., 865
Briggs, M. I., 1973
Briggs, R. T., 249
Briggs, W. B., 1745
Brigham, C. B., 2137
Brigham, H. O., 2560, 2561
Brindenbaugh, C., 3190
Brinkley, C., 2367
Brinton, E. H., 1296
Brisco, R., 1727
Brisley, M. A., 3124, 3125
Brock, C. A., 2250
Broderick, J. C., 3260
Broderick, J. H., 1746
Brodman, E., 2110, 2111, 2293, 2294
Bromiley, F., 2368
Bronson, B., 9
Brookover, B., 1400
Brooks, R. E., 2251
Brophy, E. D., 1086
Brough, K. J., 1566
Brown, A. W., 1728
Brown, C. C., 2048
Brown, C. H., 2831
Brown, E. F., 910
Brown, H. M., 1747
Brown, J. V., 2231
Brown, R. E., 2112
Browne, C. A., 250
Browning, W., 2562
Bruce, B., 11
Bruce, P. A., 251
Bruder, M., 1146

Brudvig, G. L., 1387, 1388
Brumbaugh, W. D., 1567
Brundin, R. E., 1645, 3243
Brunner, J. E., 1715
Brunton, D. W., 2563
Bryan, B. D., 1087
Bryant, D. W., 1568, 1748
Bryant, L. M., 1655
Buchanan, J. B., 1217
Buchanan, L. B., 1569
Buchanan, R. E., 1570
Buck, J. P., 1505
Buck, P., 1749
Budington, W. S., 2138
Bugbee, B. W., 415
Bull, J., 1716
Bullock, E. U., 1147
Bullock, J. Y., 1328
Bultmann, P. W., 617
Bultmann, W. A., 617
Burbank, M., 667
Burge, N. T., 1974
Burger, B., 2941
Burgess, R. S., 2461
Burgh, A. E., 113
Burich, N. J., 1272
Burke, B. L., 668, 1088
Burnett, P. M., 2049
Burnette, P. J., 2369
Burns, R. K., 114
Burrell, M. R., 1148
Burstyn, H. L., 2139
Burton, A. S., 1401
Bush-Brown, A., 1218
Butler, N. M., 1832
Butler, P., 10, 3010
Butrick, M. W., 1402
Buzzard, R. A., 1403
Byrd, R. E., 1944
Byrnes, H. W., 911, 2050

Cadbury, H. J., 252, 253, 254, 669, 1750, 1751, 1752, 1753
Cahill, A. M., 2051
Cain, S. M., 1962, 2462
Callaham, B. E., 2463, 2464
Cambell, K., 416
Cambridge, Mass., Public Library, 1219
Camp, D. N., 2140
Campbell, H. C., 912
Campbell, M. M., 2994
Campbell, R. W., 1975
Canavan, B., 1268
Canavan, M. J., 670, 1220
Canfield, J. H., 1833
Cannon, C. L., 255, 256

Cantrell, C. H., 417, 2466
Capozzi, M. R., 2052
Capps, J. L., 418
Cardwell, G. A., 809
Carlin, O. R., 1822
Carlson, W. H., 1895, 2564, 2739, 2895, 3053
Carlstadt, E., 1284
Carlton, W. N. C., 1571, 2896
Carnovsky, L., 2467, 2468, 2469
Carnovsky, R. F., 2967
Carpenter, C., 419
Carpenter, E. H., 2141
Carpenter, E. J., 1221
Carpenter, R., 11
Carr, L. D., 2887
Carrier, E. J., 913
Carroll, C. E., 2470, 2471
Carroll, F. C., 1976
Carter, C., 3191
Carter, M., 671
Caruth, E., 1117
Cary Memorial Library, Lexington, Mass., 1222
Casey, G. M., ed., 115
Casey, M., 3073
Castagna, E., 1199
Castagnetti, N. R., 672
Cazden, R. E., 420, 421
Cecil, H. L., 1977
Chadbourne, E. F., 673
Chadwick, J., 2295, 2296
Chalker, W. J., 2053
Chamberlain, L. C., 1672
Champman, M. L., 2565
Chancellor, J., 914
Chang, H. C., 116
Chapman, M., 2704
Champman, M. L., 2565
Charvat, W., 422, 423
Chase, V., 674
Chase, E., 1924
Chenery, F. L., 2191
Cheney, E. P., 1898
Chevalier, S. A., 2740
Childs, J. B., 3022
Chinard, G., ed., 424
Chinard, G., 2142
Christianson, E. B., 2113
Christie, C. C., 3143
Church, F. E., 1572
Churchwell, C. D., 2472
Cincinnati Public Library, 1404
Cincinnati Young Men's Mercantile Library Association, 675
Clancy, Sister M. M., 1688
Clapp, V. B., 2916

Clapp, V. W., 2370, 2971
Clark, A. J., 425
Clark, E. S., 1312
Clark, J. B., 1936
Clark, M. B., 3054
Clark, R. B., 1223
Clark, T. D., 676
Clarke, J. H., 1405
Clarke, M., 1089
Clarke, M. G. M., 1656
Clarke, O., 2252
Clayton, H., 1573
Clement, E. G., 2566
Clemons, H., 258, 1945
Clift, D. H., 2567, 2568
Clinefeller, R. W., 1879
Clive, J., 426
Clopine, J., 117
Clower, G. W., 259
Clymer, B. F., 2297
Coats, N. M., 2192
Cochran, M. A., 1937, 2054
Cody, N. B., 1514
Coffman, C., 2298
Cohen, H., ed., 427
Cohen, L. G., 2930
Cohen, M. L., 2253
Cohn, W. L., 2569
Coil, N., 118
Colbourn, H. T., 428, 429, 430
Colburn, E. B., 2570
Cole, G. L., 2371
Cole, G. W., 677, 1329
Cole, J. Y., 2372, 2373, 2374, 2375, 2376, 2377, 2378, 2379, 3175, 3176, 3177, 3178, 3179
Cole, T. J., 1978
Coleman, E. E., 1754
Coleman, G. P., 12, 13
Colkel, M. B., 2380
Colla, Sister M. B., 1657
Collett, J., 2705
Collier, F. G., 915
Collins, L. T., 1406
Colorado State Library, 1083
Colson, J. C., 14, 15, 1547, 1548
Columbia University School of Library Service, 2473
Comaromi, J. P., 2741, 2742
Cometti, E., ed., 1946
Commager, H. S., 260, 431
Commons, E., 2381
Compton, C. H., 1297, 1298, 1299, 2910, 3216
Conant, R. W., ed., 916, 917
Conduitte, G. G., 119

Coney, D., 1646
Conmy, P. T., 16, 678, 1059, 1060, 1061, 1062, 1063, 2055, 2572, 2573, 2574, 2575, 2904, 2989
Connecticut Library Association, 2576
Conner, M., 918
Connor, R. D. W., 2382
Consolata, Sister M., 2577
Constantine, J. R., 1167
Constantine, R., 679
Conyngham, M. H., 1224
Cook, R. U., 1755
Cook, V. R., 1106
Cooke, A. M., 1372
Cookston, J. S., 1979
Cooley, L. C., 1064
Coolidge, A. C., 1756
Coolidge, Mrs. O. H., 1528
Cooper, M. K., 2193
Coover, R. W., 2056, 2057
Copeland, E. F., 1407
Corcoran, S. R., 2743
Correll, L., 17, 2982
Corwin, M. A., 120
Couch, C. R., 2143
Coughlin, B., 1182
Council of National Library Associations, 2578
Countryman, G. A., 2579, 2834, 3135
Cowles, L. H., 2144
Coyte, D. E., 2254
Cramer, C. H., 1408
Cramner, J. C., 1409
Crandall, J. C., 432
Cranford, J. P., 1855
Crawford, H., 2886
Crawford, M. C., 680
Cregan, F., 3256
Crittenden, J. L. J., 1129
Crook, M. R., 681
Cropper, M. S., 2255
Cross, W. O., 433
Crouch, M. L., 1503
Crumpacker, G. F., 1187
Culver, E. M., 1192, 2058
Cummings, C. S., comp., 18
Cummings, M. M., 2846
Cunning, E. T., 2299
Cunningham, L. L., 2873
Curless, M., 1168
Currier, L. G., 2059, 2919
Currier, M., 2194, 2744
Currier, T. F., 2745
Curry, J. L., 1118
Cushing, J. D., 866
Custer, B. A., 2746

Cutler, S. B., 682
Cutliffe, M. R., 19
Cutter, C. A., 1330, 1757, 3244
Cutter, W. P., 2922
Cylke, F. K., 2383

Dain, P., 919, 1331
Dale, D. C., 2384, 3094
Dale, E. E., 434, 435
Dalphin, M., 683, 1332
Dana, J. C., 2114, 2580, 2931
Dane, C., 2581
Daniel, E. C., 1130
Daniel, H., 920
Danton, E. M., 3095
Danton, J. P., 121, 1575, 2474, 2706, 2707, 2708
Daughtrey, J. A., 1980
Davenport, F. B., 2475
David, C. W., 684, 1899
Davidge, I. B., 1981
Davidson, H. L., 2145
Davidson, J. S., 1900
Davis, C. C., 436
Davis, D. G., 20, 21, 2476, 2477, 2582, 2583, 2584
Davis, E. G., 685
Davis, E. R., 2747
Davis, F. C., 922
Davis, J. M., 1333
Davis, R. B., 261, 437, 438, 439
Davison, A. T., 1758
Dawe, G., 2942
Dawson, G. E., 2146
Dawson, J. M., 2748
Dax, E. R., 1410
Day, N. J., 686
Deale, H. V., 2585
DeAngelis, P., 1090
Dean-Throckmorton, J., 2300
Debaugh, J., 2586
Debons, A., 2478
Dedmond, F. B., 440
DeKaindry, W., 1107
Dekenis, A., 3024
Dengler, T. P., 1982
Dennis, A. W., 2195
Denton, G. B., 2301
Derby, J. C., 441
Devlin, E., 2749
Dexter, F. B., 262, 1091
Diamond, I. S., 2385
Diana, J. P., 1469
Diaz, A. J., 1856
DiCanio, F., 2587
Dick, E. J., 2588

Dickey, P. W., 1290
Dickinson, A. D., 3136
Dillon, R., 2147, 2148
DiPietro, L. N., 1470
Ditzion, S., 22, 687, 868, 923, 924, 925, 926, 927, 3057, 3058
Dix, W. S., 928
Dixon, E. I., 23, 24
Dixon, M., 2060
Doane, B., 2918
Doane, G. H., 2479
Dodge, A. C., 869
Doe, J., 2480
Doherty, F. X., 1576
Doms, K., 1471
Donaldson, L. L., 1983, 1984
Donley, V., 2302
Donnan, E., ed., 3074
Donovan, D. G., 2709
Donovan, M. J., 2589
Donze, S. L., 688
Dorf, A. T., 1689, 3011
Doud, M., 2874, 2875
Downing, M., 1515
Downs, R. B., 25, 442, 443, 1577, 1578, 1579, 2481, 3084
Doyle, Sister M. A., 1313
Draper, W., 2303
Drazan, J., 26
Drummond, D. R., 2997
Drury, J. W., 2061
Duane, F. P., 929
Dubois, P. Z., 2482
Ducsay, W. J., 122
Duffus, R. L., 930, 931
Dugger, H. H., 444
Dumbauld, E., 263
DuMont, R. R., 932
Dunaway, W. F., 1901
Duncan, A. M., 1673
Duncan, R. B., 1933
Duniway, D. C., 2196
Dunkin, P. S., 2750, 3126
Dunkley, G. C., 1985
Dunlap, C. R., 1580
Dunn, A., 2814
Dunn, E. C., 445
Dunning, A. E., 870
Durnell, J., 3119
Dutrow, K. E., ed., 1729
Dyer, J. R., 2590
Dyste, M. C., 2914

Earnshaw, J., 1902
Easterly, A., 2591
Eastlick, J. T., 1084

Eastman, L. A., 2881
Eaton, A. J., 446
Eaton, J. D., 1857
Eaton, T., ed., 123, 124
Eberhart, L., 933
Eckert, C. J., 1411
Eddy, G. G., 1065
Eddy, G. S., 264
Edelman, H., 1581
Edgar, N. L., 125
Edgar, W. B., 265, 266, 447
Edlund, P., 2751
Edmunds, A. J., 690
Edsall, M. H., 1947
Edson, H., 1169
Edward, J. P., 2115
Edwards, A., 691, 2149
Edwards, E., 934
Edwards, M. A., 3217
Egan, M. E., 2800
Egolf, J. L., 1472
Eisner, J., 1334
Ela, J., 1549
Elias, W. D., 1412
Elkins, K. C., ed., 1759, 1760, 1761
Elliot, C. A., 126, 2592
Elliot, E. M., 2593
Elliot, L., 2625
Elliot, L. M., 2256
Elliot, M. E., 1533
Ellis, H., 692
Ellis, M., 1529
Ellsworth, D. J., 27
Ellsworth, R. E., 2594
Elson, R. M., 448
Emberman, A., 1834
Emert, F. A., 2483, 2595
Engebretson, B. L., 693
England, J. M., 449
Engley, D. B., 1762
English, T. H., 1682
Enoch Pratt Free Library, 1201
Ensor, A., 450
Epstein, J. S., 935
Erickson, E. W., 1582
Esarey, L., 451
Esbin, M., 2062
Esterquest, R. T., 127, 936
Estes, D. E., 2596
Eury, W., 1373
Evans, A. P., 3109
Evans, C., 128
Evans, E. G., ed., 267
Evans, G. E., 2484
Evans, L. H., 1583, 2386, 2752
Evans, M. M., 2753

Evans, W. A., 268
Everhart, F. B., 1930
Evraiff, L. A. K., 2485
Exman, E., 452

Fain, E., 28
Falley, E. W., 1730
Fannin, G. M., 1335
Faries, E., 1413
Farlow, J. W., 2304
Farquhar, F. P. P., 3008
Farr, L. M., 2305
Farrow, M. H., 1858
Feaster, D. M., 1170
Fedder, M. B., 871
Feeney, R. B., 1986
Fell, Sister M. L., 453
Fenneman, N., 3146
Fenwick, S. I., 1987
Ferguson, E., 2597
Ferguson, M. J., 2878, 2943
Fess, M. R., 1336
Field, P. I., 3061
Fields, J. E., 269
Fiering, N. S., 454
First, E. W., 2971
Fisher, C. P., 2307
Fisher, D. C., 2893
Fisher, H. H., 2150
Fiske, M., 129
Fitch, A. W., 694
Fitz, L., 1306
Fitzgerald, W. A., 2598
Fitzpatrick, E. A., 3075
Flack, H. E., 2063
Flanagan, J. T., 270
Flanders, F. V., 695
Fleischer, M. B., 1414, 2486, 2599
Fleming, E. M., 130, 2879
Fleming, J. B., 1131
Flener, J. G., 696
Fletcher, C., 618
Fletcher, D. M., 872
Fletcher, M. P., 455
Fletcher, W. I., 131, 697, 698, 937, 938
Flick, H. M., 1337
Flournoy, M. W., 1374
Flower, E., 2165
Folmer, F., 2600
Fontaine, E. O., 3096
Fonville, E. R., 1045
Foos, D. D., 3045
Foote, H., 619
Ford, P. L., 456
Ford, W. C., 457, 2387
Foreman, C., 2601

Forney, D. J., 1415
Fortin, C. C., 1817
Foster, P. M., 1988
Foster, W. E., 1493, 2602, 2923, 3245
Fowler, S. P., 699
Francis, W. W., 2603, 2903
Franklin, H. R., 939
Franklin, W. D., 1338
Franklin Typographical Society, Boston, 2151
Frantz, R. W., 940
Frarey, C. J., 2754
Freeman, J., 700
Freund, C. E., 2308
Friedman, W., 3197
Friend, L., 3239
Frost, J., 2604
Frost, J. E., 2944
Frothingham, N. L., 3017
Fry, A., 2309
Fry, B. M., 2388
Fry, J. W., 132
Fulcino, S. A., 133
Fuller, H. M., 1658
Fulton, D., ed., 3072
Fulton, J. F., 2310, 2311
Fulton, S., 1516
Fund, C. K., 1225

Gabriel, R. H., 2389
Galbreath, C. B., 1416, 1417, 2064
Gallant, E. F., 1314
Galloway, M. L., 1989, 1990
Galvin, T. J., 2487
Gambee, B. L., 942, 1991, 1992, 2710, 2711, 2712, 2815
Gambee, R. R., 2815
Gapp, K. S., 1827
Gara, L., 146
Garceau, O., 943
Gardner, H. B., 1494
Garnder, O. M., 1375
Garfinkle, N., 458
Garnett, R., 1339
Garrison, B. S., 1376
Garrison, D., 134, 944, 945, 946, 947, 948
Garrison, F. H., 2847
Garrison, G., 2488
Gartland, H. J., 2390
Garwig, P. L., 2124
Gaskill, G. A., 701
Gaston, M., 1993
Gates, E. S., 1994
Gates, J. K., 1054
Gay, J., 702

Geary, S., 459
Gecas, J. G., 135
Geiger, M. J., 703
Gelfand, M. A., 1584
Geller, E., 136, 137, 1995, 3047
Gershevsky, R. H., 3171
Getchell, M. W., 2975
Gholdson, E., 2258
Giandonato, R. M. H., 2391
Gibson, F. E., 1285
Gibson, H. B. C., 1188
Gibson, T. J., 2065
Giddings, R. L., 1092
Gilchrist, D. B., 1585, 1835, 1836
Gill, S., 1119
Gillespie, D., 29
Gillespie, R. C., 1517
Gillies, M., 2606
Gillis, F. J., 1226
Gillis, M. R., 2067
Gilman, D. C., 949, 1659
Gilreath, J. W., 2197
Ginnell, F. W., 2259
Girvin, A. G., 1903
Girvin, C. M., 1473
Gittinger, N., 2060
Gittinger, N. M., 1192
Gladeck, A. A., 2152
Glasier, G. G., 2607
Glazier, K. M., 2713
Gloucester Lyceum and Sawyer Free Library, 1227
Godard, G. S., 2068, 2069
Godet, M., 138
Goff, F. R., 271, 272, 2392, 2393
Goggin, M. K., 2489
Goldberg, A., 1340
Goldhor, H., 30
Goldman, S., 2394
Goldschmidt, E., 3081, 3082
Goldstein, D., 1341
Goldstein, H., 2490
Golter, P., 2608
Gondos, V., 2395
Gooch, R. E., 1418
Goodale, G., 1419
Goodfellow, D. M., 704
Goodhue, A., 1763
Goodknight, J. L., 950
Goodrich, N. L., 2991
Goodrum, C. A., 2396
Goodspeed, T. W., 2915
Goodwillie, M. C., 1731
Goodwin, D., 705
Goodwin, J., 31
Gorchels, C. C., 1956

Gordon, D., 273, 274, 3070, 3071
Gordon, M. K., 3083
Gordon, N. S., 620
Gore, D. J., 1342, 2755
Gormley, D. M., 32
Gossage, W., 1586
Goudeau, J. M., 275, 276, 277, 460
Goudeau, L., 276, 277
Goulder, G., 706
Govan, J. F., 1506
Gower, C. W., 707
Grade, A. E., 461
Graham, C. A., 139
Graniss, R., 1925
Gray, A. K., 708
Gray, V. G., 709
Grayson, B. R., 1046
Graziano, E. E., 2756, 2757
Greathouse, C. H., 2397
Green, C. R., 1228
Green, C. S., 140, 951
Green, C. W., 1721
Green, E. D., 1291
Green, E. L., 1931
Green, S. A., 2198
Green, S. S., 952, 1229
Greenaway, E., 3241
Greenberg, H., 278
Greene, J. T., 1420
Greenman, E. D., 1996
Greenough, C. N., 462
Greer, J. J., 1732
Gregorie, A. K., 710
Grieder, E. M., 1764
Griffith, T. J., 2848
Grimm, D. F., 711, 712
Gripton, J., 3257
Grisso, K. M., 3180
Griswold, A. M., 1733
Griswold, S. B., 2260
Gropp, A. E., 2398
Gross, S. C., 713
Grotzinger, L. A., 2491, 2945, 3087, 3157
Grove, P. S., 2758
Guild, R. A., 1587, 3040
Gummere, R. M., 463
Gunjal, S. R., 2946
Gunn, M. H., 1292
Gunning, C., 2963
Gwynn, S. E., 1690

Hackett, A. P., 464
Haddonfield, N.J., Library Company, 714
Hadley, C., 2932

Haffner, G. O., ed., 279
Hagler, R., 33, 2759
Haines, H. E., 953, 3001
Hake, S. D., 1537
Hale, C., 2609
Hall, A. E., 1997
Hall, E., 1998
Hall, H. J., 280
Hallenbeck, C. T., ed., 715
Halmos, D., 2199
Halmos, D. M., 1859
Halsell, W. D., 34, 873
Hamill, R. F., 281
Hamlin, T. F., 1837
Hammitt, F. E., 1999
Hamner, P. N., 1273
Hand, M. E., 874
Handlin, O., 954
Hanson, E. R., 2760, 2761
Hanson, J. C. M., 2762, 2763
Handy, C. H., 2070
Handy, D. N., 2232
Hankins, F. D., 141
Hansbrough, I. C., 1507
Hansen, A. M., 1678
Hansen, R. W., 1647
Hanson, J. C. M., 3012
Haraszti, Z., 465, 1230, 1231, 3202
Hard, F., 3254
Harding, Sister M. F., 1495
Hardsin, T. S., 1588, 1589
Harding, W., comp., 282
Harlan, R. D., 466, 467, 3002
Harlow, N., 2947
Harlow, T. R., 3150
Harper, J. R., 1880
Harrell, L., 716
Harris, A. W., 2200
Harris, D. G., 717
Harris, G. W., 1838
Harris, H. J., 142
Harris, J. F., 2233
Harris, M. H., 20, 21, 29, 35, 36, 37, 38
  39, 40, 41, 42, 43, 44, 45, 46, 143, 144,
  283, 284, 285, 468, 469, 470, 471,
  472, 955, 956, 957, 1232, 2610, 3041,
  3042
Harris, S. M., 1132
Harris, V., 1959
Harris, W. S., 718
Harrison, J. L., 719, 958, 1233
Harshfield, L., 1421
Hart, J. D., 473
Hart, M. L., 47
Harwell, R., 959, 1590
Hasse, A. R., 2849

Hassenforder, J., 960, 961, 2948
Hatch, O. W., 720
Hauserman, D. D., 2933
Hausmann, A. F., 1093
Haverstick, D. C., 721
Havlik, R. J., 145
Havron, H. J., 1422
Hawthorne, N., 3018
Hayden, E. C., 1558
Hayes, C. D., 1839
Haygood, W. C., 2900
Haywood, W. C., 1343
Hazeltine, R. E., 1423
Healey, J. S., 2978
Heaney, H. J., 48
Heaps, W. A., 1977
Heard, J. M., 1234
Hecht, A., 1108
Heckel, J. W., 2611
Heckman, M. L., 1691, 2902
Hedrick, U. P., 474
Hegel, R., 1660
Heim, H. R., 1424
Heindel, S. W., 1860
Heisey, T. M., 2764
Heiss, R. M., 2765, 2766
Heisser, W. A., 1644
Heizmann, L. J., 1474
Held, R., 722, 723, 724, 875, 1066, 1067, 1068
Helms, C., 1274
Hemmer, P. B., 1196
Hemphill, W. Edwin, ed., 475
Hench, M., 2261
Henderson, J. D., 962
Henderson, K. L., 2767
Hendrickson, R. M., 2612
Henke, E. M., 1462
Henkle, H. H., 2312
Henne, F., 2000
Hensel, E. M., 2768
Hensley, H. C., 1069, 1070
Henry, W. E., 1171
Herdman, M. M., 963, 964
Herrick, C. A., 476
Herrick, M. D., 1723
Herring, B. G. U., 3020
Hershey, F. E., 3103
Heskin, M. K., 2201
Hesseltine, W. B., 146, 2965
Hester, G. A., 3214
Hewins, C. M., 1094
Hewitt, V. D., 2714
Heyl, L., 2984
Hibbs, J. E., 1425
Hicham, J. S., 2202

Hickey, D. J., 2769
Hickman, R. W., 1766
Hilker, E. W., 2153
Hill, D., 2399
Hill, L. D., 1235
Hillard, G. S., 1236
Hintz, C. W. E., 2071
Hirsch, C. B., 621
Hisz, E., 1344
Hitchcock, J. E., 2770
Hodges, E. J., 1237
Hoesch, M. J., 1275
Hoff, A., 1734
Hoffleit, D., 1767
Hoffman, C., 147
Hoffman, J., 2614
Hoffman, R. P., 1508
Hoffman, W. H., ed., 1300
Holden, O., 2001
Holder, E. J., 1861
Holingsworth, V., 2962
Holley, E. G., 49, 148, 1172, 1591, 2615, 2616, 2617, 2973
Holloway, D. P., 2262
Holt, A. C., 2313
Holzapfel, M. L., 1212
Homes, H. A., 2072, 2203
Honea, A. B., 2833
Hook, A., 2204
Hooker, M. W., 725
Hoole, M. D., 3030
Hoover, A. R., 1377
Hoover, F. R., 1534
Hopkins, L., 1426
Hopper, O. C., 1881
Horiuchi, I., 2924, 2949
Horrocks, N., 2715
Houk, J., 2559
Houlette, W. D., 286, 287, 477, 478, 622, 623
Howard, J. G., 1345
Howard, L., 479, 1133, 2073
Howard, P., 2400
Howe, D. W., 480
Howe, H. E., 2492, 3158
Howell, J. B., ed., 1294
Hoyer, M., 1823
Hoyle, N. E., 2002
Hoyne, T., 1152
Huang, G. W., 3253
Hubbard, C. L., 1963
Hubbell, J. B., 481
Hudon, E. G., 2263, 2264, 2265
Hudson, J. P., 1948
Hudson, Ohio, Library and Historical Society, 2205

Huggins, M. A., 2003
Hughes, D. E., 1268
Hughes, H. L., comp., 1315
Huleatt, R. S., 2234
Hull, T. V., 1173
Hume, E. E., 2314, 2315, 2316, 2317, 2318, 2319, 2320
Hunt, J. R., 2771
Hunter, C. P., 1378
Huntington, A. T., 2321
Hurd, H. M., 2850
Hurley, G., 482
Hurley, L. J., 1157, 1554
Hurst, J. F., 624
Hurwitz, J. D., 965
Husselbee, M. V., 1679
Hutchinson, V. L., 3021
Hutzler, H. C., 1134
Hyers, F. H., 1071, 3003
Hyland, L., 3120

Illinois, University of, Library School, 2493
Immroth, J. P., 2772, 2925
Ingalls, M. E., 1427
Ingraham, C. A., 483
Ingram, E. F., 726
Irrman, R. H., 288
Irshay, P. C., 1072
Irwin, F. T., 1307
Irwin, M., 1882
Irwin, R., 50

Jackl, W. E., 1202
Jackson, C. O., 2004
Jackson, R., 159
Jackson, S. L., 51, 149, 150, 151, 727, 966
Jackson, W., 1692
Jackson, W. A., 289, 3037
Jackson, W. V., 152
Jacobson, B., 1346
James, J. W., 1768
James, M., 2494, 2618
Jamieson, J. A., 2619
Jamison, A. H., 1135
Jamsen, E., 2074
Jantz, H. S., 484
Jarrell, P. H., 1500
Jast, L. S., 2950
Jeffress, I. P., 1518
Jeffrey, W., 2253
Jelin, V., 2116, 2235
Jenks, G. A., 1238
Jennings, J. M., 1949, 1950
Jerabek, E., 2206

Jevons, S. W., 967
Jewett, C. C., 153, 968
Joannes, E., 2236
Joeckel, C., 969
Johansen, D. O., 3034
Johns, A. W., 2117
Johns, H., 1538, 2620
Johns Hopkins University, 2322
Johnson, A. S., 970
Johnson, B., 2621
Johnson, C., 485
Johnson, C. L., 3065
Johnson, E. C., 1693
Johnson, E. D., 154, 155, 156
Johnson, E. R., 1592
Johnson, H., 2935
Johnson, K. R., 1047
Johnson, L. B., 1530
Johnson, M., 3069
Johnson, M. H., 2005
Johnson, M. L., 1669
Johnson, R. D., 290
Johnson, R. E., 2266
Johnson, Sister M. I., 971
Johnson, T. H., 486
Johnson, W. D., 1109
Johnson, W. H., 3228
Johnston, E., 2977
Johnston, G. A., 2267
Johnston, W. D., 728, 2401, 2402
Jonah, D. A., 1926
Jones, E. K., 3085
Jones, F. N., 1769
Jones, G. W., 291, 292, 293
Jones, H. D., 1840, 3137
Jones, H. E., 2495
Jones, H. G., 1593, 2403
Jones, H. M., 487
Jones, H. W., 2323
Jones, L. R., 729
Jones, P., 2894
Jones, R., 1841
Jones, S. B., 1904
Jordan, M., 2496, 3117
Josey, E. J., 3223
Joyaux, G. J., 488
Joyce, D. F., 294
Junior Service League, Independence, Mo., 2404

Kahn, E. M., 3005, 3006
Kahn, R. A., 1203
Kaiser, W. H., 973
Kalisch, P. A., 730, 1204, 1205
Kalp, M. E., 2494, 2618
Kanner, E. E., 157

Author Index

Kansas State Teachers College, 1713
Kansfield, N. J., 1594
Kaplan, L., 158, 295, 1595, 2816, 2817, 2818
Kaser, D., 159, 731, 489, 1596, 2865
Kato, Mother A., 1842
Kaula, N., 2405
Kebabian, B., 2773
Keen, W. W., 2324
Keep, A. B., 732, 876, 1843
Keifer, M., 490
Keim, A., 1475
Kell, B. F., 2622
Keller, J. D., 52
Kellogg, A. W., 733
Kelly, E. D., 734
Kelso, J. G., 735
Kendall, H. A., 1073
Kennedy, A. M., 736
Kennedy, J. A., 3212
Kennedy, I. W., 877
Kennedy, R. F., 2951
Kennett, Sister M. E., 1661
Kent, A. E., 3032
Keogh, A., 974, 1662, 2866
Kerr, R. A., 2983
Kerr, W. H., 3051
Kesselring, M. L., 491
Ketcham, J., 296
Ketchersid, A. L., 3114
Keys, T. E., 297, 298, 299, 300, 301, 302, 303, 2325, 3029, 3052
Khurshid, A., 2497
Kidder, N. T., 1239
Kieffer, E. C., 737
Kildal, A., 2716
Kilgour, F. G., 160, 2326, 3246
Kimball, C. F., 1153
Kimball, L. E., 492
King, C. S., 3086
King, D. M., 2207
King, M., 738
King, M. L., 1110
King, S., 2154
Kingsbury, M. E., 3035
Kipp, L. J., 2774
Kirby, M. B., 1735
Kirchem, C. E., 1465
Kirkpatrick, L. H., 739
Kirkwood, H. W., comp., 1074
Kitchell, J., 740
Kittelson, D., 53, 1686
Kittle, A. T., 975
Kittredge, G. L., 493
Klein, S. J., 1736
Klopenstein, M. J., 976

Klugiewicz, E., 1476
Knachel, P., 2165
Knachel, P. A., 2155
Knight, D. M., 977
Knighten, L., 1722
Knoer, Sister M. M. A., 1597
Koch, J. V., 1206
Koch, T. W., 978, 979
Koopman, H. L., 1496
Korey, M. E., 304
Kortendick, J. J., 2498
Korty, M. B., 305, 741
Koudelka, J. B., 2327
Kraft, Sister M. I., 1905
Kram, R. I., 1154
Kramp, R. S., 980
Kratz, E. A., 1155
Kraus, J. E., 878
Kraus, J. W., 161, 306, 1598, 1599, 1770, 2623, 2843
Krieg, C. J., 3138
Krueger, H. E., 1694, 1964
Krug, J., 162
Jrummel, D. W., 163, 3115
Kruzas, A. T., 2237
Kuhlman, A. F., 3023
Kulp, A. C., 1600
Kumar, P. S. G., 2952
Kunkle, H. J., 54, 2076, 2499
Kurts, B., 3153

LaBoone, E., 1683
Lacy, D. M., 164, 2406
Lacy, M. G., 2407
Ladd, J., 55
Ladenson, A., 1156
Lage, L. C., 2328
Lamberton, E. V., 307
LaMontagne, L. E., 2408, 2775, 2776
Lancaster, E. R., 494
Landau, R. A., 2880
Landram, C. O., 165
Landrum, G. W., 495
Lane, M., 2006
Lane, W. C., 1771, 1772, 1773, 1774, 3247
Langdell, M. E., 2624
Langner, M. C., 2118, 2238
Lanier, G. D., 2007
Lansberg, W. R., 2936
Larned, J. N., 742
Larsen, J. C., 2077, 2078
Lathrop, O. C., 2268
Laubach, H., 2239
Laudine, Sister M., 1648
Laugher, C. T., 625

Laurus, J., 496
Law, R. A., 2156
Lawson, R. W., 2870
Lawson, V., 2500
Lea, J., 2208
Leach, S., 1601
Learned, W. S., 981
Leary, W. M., 166, 497
Leasure, M. F., 2240
Lee, J. B., 1938
Lee, R. E., 982, 1519
Lehmann-Haupt, H., 498
Lehnus, D. J., 167, 2777
Leidecker, K. F., 2778, 3019
Leigh, R. D., 983
Lemke, A. B., 168, 1602
Lemley, D. E., 2008
Lenfest, G. E., 1304
Lenhart, J. M., 2209
Leonard, G., 743
Leonard, H. V., 1862
Leonard, I. A., 308
Leonard, L. E., 2779
Lester, C. B., 1551
Lester, E. L., 984, 985
Lester, R. M., 985, 986
Leverette, S., 2625
Levine, L. E., 2079
Lewis, D. F., 1174
Lewis, J. F., 744
Lewis, M. E., 1428
Lewis, W. P., 1308
Lewis, W. S., 860
Libby, D. C., 2210
Lichtenstein, J., 1075
Liebaers, H., 2717
Liebman, S. W., 499
Lillard, R. D., 500
Lincoln, Sister M. E., 1286
Lind, L. R., 1706
Linderman, W. B., 1844, 2502, 2953
Lingelbach, W. E., 2157, 2158
Lingfelter, M. R., 1477
List, B. T., 1863
Little, A. E., 2926
Little, E. N., 501
Littlefield, G. E., 502
Litto, F. M., 503
Livingood, J. W., 747
Lloyd, D. D., 2409
Lohrer, M. A., 2503
Long, H. G., 987, 2009
Longhway, M. W., 1287
Longworth, R. O., 1303
Lonie, C. A., 1276
Lonn, E., 748

Lopez, L. L., 3127
Lopez, M. D., 56, 2010, 2241
Lord, C. M., 1309
Lord, J. W., 988, 2011
Lord, M. E., 2410
Lorenz, J. G., 2411, 2718
Los Angeles County Free Library, 1076
Loughran, V., 3067
Lovett, R. W., 749, 1240, 1776, 1777, 1778, 1779, 1780
Low, J. F., 750
Lowell, M. H., 1603, 1707, 1708
Lowrey, S. G. R., 751, 1095
Loyola, Sister M., 2012
Luckett, G. R., 2412
Lum, L., 1316
Lundberg, D., 504
Lundean, J. W., 1695
Lunnon, B. S., 2013
Luther, K., 2504
Lydekker, J. W., 626
Lydenburg, H. M., 752, 1347, 1348, 2159, 2160, 2851, 2852, 2866, 3147, 3218
Lyle, G. R., 169
Lynch, D. N., 2014

McBride, M., 2819
MacCampbell, B. B., 1429
McCauley, E. B., 762, 763
McClaren, D. N., 2633
McClary, B. H., ed., 1934
McColl, M. C., 2331
McCord, D. T. W., 1242
McCord, J. L. V., 2634
McCorison, M. A., 311, 764
MacCormick, A. H., 2270
McCoy, D. R., 2416
McCrary, M. E., 1509
McCulley, K. M., 3078
McCulloch, S. C., 627, 628
McCullough, M. W., 1121
McCutcheon, R. P., 508, 765
McDaniel, W. B., 2635, 2636, 2835
McDermott, J. F., 312, 313, 314, 315, 316, 317, 509, 510, 511, 512, 513, 514, 515, 766
MacDonald, H., 1241
MacDonald, M., 1241
McDonald, M. F., 879
McDonough, J., 2417
McDonough, J., 3092
McElderry, S., 1605
McFadden, M., 1175
McFarland, M. M., 1906
McGowan, F. M., 2637

McGowan, O. T. P., 1243
McGregor, J. W., 2638
McGuire, L. P., 1183
McKay, G. L., 516
MacKay, M. B., 2080
McKelvey, B., ed., 1350, 1351
Mackenzie, A. D., 1077
McLean, P. T., 2166
MacLeish, A., 2413, 2414
MacLeod, D. I., 1552
MacLeod, R. D., 2954
McMullen, C. H., 1697, 1698
McMullen, H., 57, 58, 59, 60, 61, 172, 173, 174, 517, 518, 767, 768, 769, 990, 1717, 2120, 3013
McMurty, B. B., 1207
McNeil, G., 1055
McNiff, P. J., 1781
McSwain, M. B., 3033
McTaggart, J. B., 1907
McVee, M. F., 1352
Maddox, L. J., 2626
Madison, C. A., 505
Maestri, H. L., 753, 754
Maggetti, M. T., 2627
Magner, M. J., 3208
Magrath, Sister G., 2628
Mahoney, B. L., 1078
Mallison, D. W., 2888
Malone, E. G., 1553
Mamaronek, N.Y., Free Library, 1349
Manchester, N.H., City Library, 1310
Manley, M. C., 170
Manning, J. W., 506, 755
Maples, H. L., 1111
Marchman, W. P., 2161, 2162, 2163
Marco, G., 2164
Marion, G. E., 2629, 2630
Marke, J. J., 2271, 2631
Markuson, B. E., 2780
Markwell, D., 756
Marley, S. B., 2415
Marshall, A. P., 989
Marshall, J. D., comp., 171, 3160, 3164
Marshall, M., 2330
Marta, O. V., 757
Martel, C., 2781
Martens, A., 1604
Martin, D. V., 758
Martin Memorial Library, York, Pa., 1478
Martinez, A., 2119
Mason, A. P., 759
Mason, D. D., 112
Mason, D. E., 2165
Mason, G. C., 760

Mason, J., 3252
Mason, L. G., 1520
Mason, P. R., 1120
Massman, V. F., 2632
Massonneau, S., 2782
Matheson, W., 3213
Mathews, Brother S. G., 1883
Mathews, E. L., 1479
Mathis, G. R., ed., 3231
Matsushige, H., 1139
Matthews, A., 507
Mathews, J. P., 3056
Mauerer, M., 310
Mauseth, B. J., 1051
Maxfield, D. K., ed., 1696
Maxwell, M. N. F., 2905, 2906
May, H. F., 504
Mayer, V. J., 761
Maze, A. H., 3091
Mead, C. D., 62, 770
Meador, D. J., 318
Mearns, D. C., 2418, 2419, 2420, 3139, 3140, 3141, 3181
Mehl, W. R., 2639
Mellen, G. F., 3077
Melrose, L. H., 175
Melvin, Sister M. C., 2015, 2016
Memory, M. W., 1379
Menan, N. V., 63
Merritt, E. P., 629
Mershon, G. L., 771
Meshot, G. V., 1430
Metcalf, J. C., 319
Metcalf, K. D., 1606, 1782, 1783, 1784, 1785, 1786, 1787, 1788, 1789, 1790, 1798
Metcalfe, J., 176
Metz, C. A., 1431
Meyer, A. B., 177
Meyer, W. P., 1480
Meyerend, M. H., 1908
Meyers, J. K., 1884
Michel, J. G., 1646
Michelson, A. I., 2640
Michener, R., 959, 1724, 3066
Michigan, University of, 2830
Michigan, University of, Library, 1814
Michigan Board of Commissioners, 1277
Mickelson, P., 991
Middleton, E. H., comp., 1176
Miksa, F., 87, 178, 2927, 2928
Miles, E. A., 519
Miller, A. H., 1699
Miller, B. M., ed., 3025
Miller, C., 3099

Miller, C. E., 772
Miller, C. H., 3182
Miller, G. C., 1079
Miller, L. A., 1607
Miller, L. B., 2328
Miller, M. M., 1096
Miller, R. C., 2211
Miller, V. P., 1818
Miller, W. T., 1048
Mills, F. L., 1157, 1554
Mills, R. V., 520, 773
Miltimore, C., 2641
Minnich, H. C., 521
Minnick, N. F., 522
Mishoff, W. O., 64
Mitchell, A. C., 2643, 2644
Mitchell, M. W., 1097
Mitchell, S. B., 2505, 3100
Mitchell, S. W., 2854
Mohrhardt, F. E., 2421, 2867
Moloney, L. C., 1939
Moltenberry, F., 1208
Molz, J. B., 630
Molz, K., 179, 992
Monrad, A. M., 2783
Monro, I., 1117
Monroe, M. E., 993
Montgomery, T. L., 1481
Mood, F., 2422, 3007
Moore, B. L., 1380
Moore, E. T., 180
Moore, G. G., 1864
Moore, M. D., 2085
Moore, M. R., 2645
Moore, Mrs. J. T., 1510, 2212
Moore, M. V., 880
Moore, R. N., 3060
Moran, I. S., 1353
Morin, R. W., 1826
Morison, N. H., 1209
Morison, S. E., 320
Morris, D. A., 2332
Morris, W. J., 321
Morrisey, M., 2423
Morrison, H. A., 322
Morrison, T., 774
Morroni, J. R., 2646
Morse, C. R., 2929
Morse, D. B., 1293
Mosier, R. D., 523
Moss, J. R., 994
Moss, Mrs. F. C. B., 1432
Mott, F. L., 524, 525
Mount Union College, 1885
Moyers, J. C., 1535
Mugridge, D. H., 2424

Muller, R. H., 1608
Mullett, C. F., 526, 527
Mullins, L. S., 2121
Mumford, L. Q., 2425
Mumford, R. F., 775
Mumford, R. L., 775
Mumm, B., 2988
Munford, W. A., 2647
Munn, J. B., 1791
Munn, R., 181, 995, 1482, 1483, 1484
Munn, R. F., 1960
Munthe, W., 182
Murison, W. J., 996
Murphy, S. B., 1381
Murray, K., 1433
Murray, M. E., 1434
Mutschler, H. F., 1435
Myers, A., 2167
Myers, M., 183

Nagy, M. C., 1436
Napier, J., 528
Nash, R., 1244
Neal, P., 2648
Nehlig, M. E., 1909, 2507
Nelson, C. A., 2784
Nelson, J. K., 631
Nesbitt, E., 2508
Nestleroad, R., 1437
Neuman, R., 1122
New Haven Free Public Library, 1098
New York Public Library, 1354, 1355, 1356, 1357, 1358
New York State Library, 2086
Newark, N.J., 3046
Newark Public Library, 1317, 1318
Newell, M. M., 184
Newmyer, J., 185
Newson, H. E., 1539
Neyman, M., 776
Nichols, B. B., 1359
Nichols, C. H., 529
Nichols, I. C., 2998, 2999
Nichols, M. E., 1737, 1821
Nicholson, J. B., 777
Nicholson, J. M., 1865
Nields, J. P., 1105
Nietz, J., 530
Nitecki, J. Z., 186
Noble, A. D., 1113
Noel, M., 531
Nolan, C., 1438
Noonan, M. Z., 2017
Nonacs, M., 2333
North, N., 2426
Norton, C. B., comp., 1099

234 Author Index

Norton, F., 2506
Norton, W. T., 779
Nourse, E. S., ed., 977
Nourse, H. S., comp., 1245
Nourse, L. M., 1080
Nunis, D. B., 532
Nunmeker, F. G., 780
Nyhom, A. W., 2785
Nylander, E. P., 1289

Obenaus, K. M., 1123
Oboler, E. M., 187, 2649, 3113
O'Brien, Sister M. B., 1319
O'Connor, Sister M. V., 781
Oddon, Y., 1815
Odom, E. P., 1136
Oehlerts, D. E., 65, 997
O'Flynn, M. E., 3068
Okubo, S., 1140
Oldham, E. M., 782
Olech, J., 998
Oliphant, J. O., 323, 1910
Oliver, M., 11
Ollé, J., 66, 2898
O'Loughlin, Sister M. A. J., 2650
O'Malley, C. D., 2334
O'Neal, W. B., 1951, 324
Orians, G. H., 533, 534
Orlando, P., 1501
Orne, J., 1609
O'Rourke, Sister M. M., 881
Orr, A. P., 1866
Orr, M. F., 1540
Orr, R. S., 1610
Osborn, V. J., 2786
Osborne, G. E., 2544
Osborne, J. T., 1911
Osburn, H., 2509
Oswald, J. F., 2787
Ottley, A., 2988
Overton, J. M., 1360
Ownings, V. B., 1738

Packard, F. R., 784, 2335
Pafford, J. H., 189
Palmer, H. R., 785, 1497
Palmer, V. D., 2788
Palmer-Poroner, B. J., 786
Paltsits, V. H., 787, 2968
Pardee, H. L., 1439
Pargellis, S. M., 2890, 3116
Parham, P. M., 3258
Parker, J. A., 2719
Parker, W. E., 2912
Parker, W. W., 535, 536, 537, 788
Parks, E. W., 325, 538

Patane, J. S., 1124
Patrick, W. R., 326, 327, 539, 882
Patterson, M., comp., 1655
Paul, G. N., 1649
Paylore, P., 3118
Peabody, A. P., 3168
Peace, W. K., 2087
Pearl, E. E., 1246
Pearlove, S., 67
Pearsall, T. F., 1867
Pearson, E. L., 190, 3121, 3122
Pease, K. R., 1184
Pease, M. E., 2213
Peckham, H., 540
Peden, W. H., 328, 329, 541
Peebles, M., ed., 1294
Peer, S., 1361
Peirce, P., 191
Pendell, L., 1674
Pene du Pois, H., 330
Penland, P. R., 2510
Pennington, E. L., 632, 633, 634, 789
Perez, C. B., 3128
Perham, M., 2651
Perkins, F. B., 790
Perkins, T. E., 1868
Perres, M. J., 1125
Perrins, B. C., 2820
Perry, M. E., 1158
Peters, O. M., 1177
Peterson, C. E., 791
Peterson, K. G., 192, 1650
Peterson, L., 2272
Pette, J., 2789
Pettigrew, C. L., 2981
Petty, W. E., 2273
Phelps, D. J., 2088
Phelps, R. B., 2821
Philadelphia City Institute, 1485
Philadelphia Free Library, 1486
Philadelphia Library Company, 792
Philadelphia Mercantile Library Company, 793
Phillips, C. O., 2969
Phillips, J. W., 1912
Phillips, V., 1440
Pierpont Morgan Library, New York, 2168, 2169
Pilkington, J. P., 542
Pitcher, P. M., 1541
Pitkin, G. M., 2790
Plunkett, H., 3076
Poll, B., 999
Pomfret, J. E., 2170, 2171, 2172
Pond, P., 2652
Poole, W. F., 1000, 2653

Poor, A. M., 3105
Porritt, R. K., 1792
Poste, L. I., 2720
Potera, E. J., 1487
Potter, A. C., 331, 1793, 1794
Potter, H., 2654
Potter, J. C., 1957
Pound, R., 2274
Powell, B. E., 1611, 1612, 1613, 1869, 3110
Powell, J. H., 543
Powell, L. C., 193, 1651, 2913, 2992, 3101, 3131
Powell, N. L., 1210
Powell, R. A., 1961
Powell, S., 1001, 2018
Powell, W. S., 544
Power, F. M., 545
Power, L. S., 3106
Powers, Z. J., 1663
Prassel, M. A., 2655
Pratt, A. S., 1664, 1665, 1666
Pratt, C., 2019, 2020
Predeek, A., 194, 1002
Prentice, A. E., 1003
Prentis, G., 1004
Pressing, K. L., 2214
Preston, E. H., 2380
Price, O. M., 2275
Prichard, L. G., 1159
Prime, L. M., 2656
Proctor, M. M., 2276
Pugh, J. F., 795, 1870
Pulling, A. C., 2277
Pulling, H. A., 3064
Purcell, J. A., 546
Purdy, B. A., 1006
Putnam, H., 2427, 3183
Putnam, L. A., 2215

Quenzel, C. H., 547
Quincy, J., 796
Quincy, J. P., 1007, 3205
Quinn, D. B., 332, 548

Raddin, G. G., 883, 884
Radford, N. A., 1614, 1615
Radtke, L. S., 195
Rairigh, W. N., 196
Ramachandran, R., 1141
Rand, F. P., 1247
Randall, G. E., 2388
Randall, W. M., 3232
Ranganathan, S. R., 197
Ranz, J., 2791
Ratcliffe, T. E., 1700

Rathbone, J. A., 1008, 2021, 2657
Ray, F. K., 2336
Rayward, W. B., 198, 549, 2022, 2721, 2955
Read, K. T., 333
Rason, J., 1675
Redd, G. L., 1137
Reddie, J. N., 2792
Redding, B. N., 2023
Reece, E. J., 2511, 3224
Reed, M. M., 1441
Reed, S. R., 2512, 2513
Rees, G., 1009
Reese, G. H., 334
Regan, M. J., 797
Rehfus, R. O., 199
Reichman, F., 68
Reilly, P. G., 798
Reinke, E. C., 799
Reitzel, W., 550
RePass, E. W., 2337
Reynolds, H., 1616, 1617
Rhees, W. J., 200, 2428
Rhodehamel, J. D., 2911
Ribbens, D. N., 551
Rice, C., ed., 1248
Rice, D. M., 1211
Richards, E. M., 3202, 3204
Richards, E. S., 2089
Richardson, C. E., 3200
Richardson, E. R., 1913
Richardson, L. N., 552
Richie, J. F., 885
Rider, F., 1667, 2956
Ridgway, F. H., 1189
Ridpath, J. W., 800
Riggs, J. B., 2939
Ring, D. F., 1442
Ripley, E. F., 1249
Ristow, W. W., 2122
Roalfe, W. R., 2278, 3028
Robathan, D. M., 553
Robbins, C., 554, 1795
Roberts, A. S., 801
Roberts, E. D., 1796
Robinson, C. F., 335
Robinson, O., 802
Robinson, R., 335
Robinson, R. W., 803
Rochester, M., 2722
Rockwood, R. H., 2957
Roddy, Sister R., 1739
Roden, C. B., 2514
Rodgers, H., 336
Rodstein, F. M., 1443
Rogers, A. E., 337

Rogers, A. R., 201
Rogers, F., 1362, 2338
Rogers, F. B., 2855
Rogers, R. D., 3111
Rogers, T. W., 804
Rolfe, W. J., comp., 1250
Rollins, C. P., 3049
Rollins, O. H., 1363
Roloff, R. W., 1819
Romberg, A., 805
Root, M. E. S., 1010, 3026
Roper, D. F., 2658
Roper, F. W., 2515
Rose, E., 1011
Roseberry, C. R., 2090
Rosenbach, A. S. W., 338
Rosenberg, B., 3102, 3132
Ross, R. R., 806
Ross, Sister, M. C., 2659
Rossel, B. S., 1012
Roth, M., 555
Rothe, B. M., 2660
Rothstein, S., 1618, 1619, 2516, 2822, 2823, 2824
Rouse, R., 1620, 1940, 1941
Rowell, J. C., 807
Roxas, S. A., 2920
Ruderman, L. P., 3159
Ruffin, M. B., 2793
Rufsvold, M. I., 2024
Rugheimer, V. C., 808, 809
Rukus, A. T., 2025
Rush, C. E., 3233
Rush, N. O., 1723, 1725, 3161
Russy, E. N. de, 2279
Ryan, D. T., 2091
Ryberg, H. T., 1444

Sabine, J., 2937
Sabine, J. E., 810, 811, 1320
Sahlin, N. G., 2173
Salamanca, L., 2429
Salfas, S. G., 1251
Salinas, A., 2993
Salton, G., 2123
Samuels, C., 2661
Sanborn, F. B., 812
Saniel, I., 2662
Saracevic, T., 2794
Sargent, M. E. F., 1252
Sasse, M., 2026
Satterfield, H. C., 1138
Satterfield, V., 1684, 1685
Saucerman, K., 1555
Saviers, S. H., 1886
Savin, M. B., 339

Schabas, A. H., 2795
Schad, R. O., 2174, 2175
Schenk, R. K., 2517
Schick, F. L., 202, 203, 556, 1013
Schiller, A. R., 204
Schink, R. J., 1887
Schlachter, G. A., 69
Schlesinger, A. M., 557
Schley, R., 2796
Schmeckebier, L. F., 2430
Schmidt, V. L., 205
Schmutz, C. A., 2242
Schorr, A. E., 1621
Schoyer, G., 1888
Schryver, N. E., 1445
Schubach, B. W., 3184
Schullian, D. M., 340
Schullman, D. M., 2337
Schultz, C. K., 2124, 2663
Schultz, F. A., 1193
Schunk, R. J., 2664
Schwartz, A. E., 2431, 2723
Schwartz, B., 2665
Schwarz, P. J., 70
Schwerin, K., 2278
Scoggin, R. B., 1382
Scott, C. D., 2432
Scott, C. R., 3201
Scott, E., 1718, 2797, 3014, 3015
Scott, K. J., 1197
Scriven, M., 2216
Scudder, H. E., 1014, 2027, 3248
Seabrook, M., 2666
Sealts, M. M., 558
Searcy, H. L., 635
Sears, D. A., 559, 813
Seeber, E. D., 341
Seigel, J. P., 560
Selmer, M. L., 2798
Sensabaugh, G. F., 561
Serebnick, J., 206
Serrill, K. W., 814
Servies, J. A., 1952, 2799
Sessa, F., 71
Seth, O. C., 2028
Settlemire, C. L., 2092
Setton, K. M., 3031
Severance, H. O., 1824, 1845
Severns, H., 2832
Sevy, B., 2339
Seybolt, R. F., 1797
Sexton, M. M., 1701
Shaffer, E., 342, 562, 887, 1488
Shali, M. S., 636
Shamp, B. K., 1446
Sharma, R. N., 3249

Sharp, H. A., 207
Sharp, K., 208, 1160, 1702
Shaw, B., 1680
Shaw, D. R., 3088
Shaw, R. K., 2995
Shaw, R. R., 563
Shaw, S. S., 815
Sheehan, D., 564
Sheffield, H. G., 1447
Sheldon, H. D., 1896
Shellem, J. J., 1914
Shelton, W., 2667
Shepherd, G. F., 1846
Shepley, H., 1798
Shera, J. H., 72, 73, 74, 209, 816, 888, 1015, 1016, 2125, 2518, 2668, 2800
Sherman, C. E., 2980
Sherman, S. C., 817, 1498
Shewmaker, J. D., 1448
Shiflett, O. L., 1622
Shinn, M. E., 1915
Shipley, J. B., 343, 565
Shipton, C. K., 2176, 3169
Shirley, N., 1365
Shirley, W., 3162
Shoemaker, E. C., 566
Shoemaker, R. H., 2801
Shores, L., 75, 76, 77, 78, 210, 1623, 3163, 3165
Short, O. C., 2825
Shove, R. H., 567, 2669
Sibley, A. M., 568
Siebens, C. R., 1253
Siggins, J. A., 2724
Sills, R. M., 79
Silva, Sister M. F. C., 1889
Silver, R. A., 1449
Silver, R. G., 569
Simmons, B. S., 2093
Simmons, C. M., 2340, 2341
Simon, H. W., 570
Simpson, W. S., 344
Sims, E. E., 2217
Singer, A. R., 2029
Singleton, M. E., 2519
Sioussat, St. George L., 345
Sitter, C. L., 1942
Sittig, W. J., 2974
Sive, M. R., 3004
Skaar, M. O., 2030
Skallerup, H. R., 346, 818
Skearns, E. I., 199
Skeel, E. E. F., ed., 571
Skeen, J. R., 2243
Skelley, G. T., 572, 1624
Skidmore, W. L., 2218

Skipper, J. E., 1890
Slade, W. A., 1017, 3185
Slavens, T. P., 1712, 1847, 1848, 1849, 2985, 3151, 3172
Sloan, R. M., 1018
Smail, H. A., 2219
Smart, G. K., 347
Smith, C., 2095, 2096
Smith, C. A., 1681
Smith, C. E., 2094
Smith, C. W., 819, 2670
Smith, D., 1652
Smith, D. J., 1916, 1917
Smith, E., 3154
Smith, G., 637
Smith, G. W., 211
Smith, J. C., 1625
Smith, J. M., 80, 212
Smith, L. E. 2433
Smith, M., 2031
Smith, M. B., 1799
Smith, M. H., 1489
Smith, M. H. K., 1521
Smith, M. J., 2126
Smith, P. C., 213
Smith, R. C., 1194, 2434
Snapp, E., 2435
Snyder, F. B., 3055
Solberg, T., 2436
Somerville, S. A., 1450
Songer, F. H., 2032
Sowerby, M., comp., 348, 349
Spain, F. L., 820, 821, 822
Sparks, C. G., 2671, 2868
Sparks, E. C., 1295
Spaulding, V. A., 1451
Spector, B., 2836
Speir, C. H., 1019
Spell, L. M., 2177
Spencer, G. S., 1161
Spiegler, G., 1232
Spivak, C. D., 2342
Spofford, A. R., 1020, 2437, 2438
Springer, N. P., 1710
Spruill, J. C., 350
Spurlin, P. M., 573, 574, 575
Stafford, M., 576
Stallmann, E. L., 2520
Stanbery, G. W., 2521
Standlee, M. W., 3156
Stanford, E. B., 214, 1626
Stanley, E. L., 1711
Starke, A., 577
Starr, H. K., 3016
Stearns, L. E., ed., 1556, 3187, 3188, 3189

Steele, H. M., 2439
Steig, L. F., 1081, 2725
Stein, J. H., 1891
Steinbarger, H., 2672
Steiner, B. C., 638, 639
Stephens, H. H., 1714
Stephenson, H. S., 2097
Stern, M. B., 351, 578
Stetson, W., 1100
Steuernagel, B., 1162
Stevens, E. L., 2127
Stevens, H., 3062
Stevens, M. H., 2440
Stevens, N. D., 27, 81, 1630
Stevens, W. F., 2673
Stevenson, G., 2802
Stevenson, V. F., 2996
Steves, N. E., 1254
Stewart, J., 1052
Stewart, N., 82, 1631
Stewart, W. L., 1383
Stibitz, M. T., 1021
Stiffler, S. A., 823
Stillman, M. E., 2441
Stillwell, M. B., 3193
Stinson, D., 2178
Stiverson, G. A., 579
Stobridge, W., 580
Stock, L. F., ed., 3074
Stolt, C. A., 2033
Stone, E. W., 215
Stoneman, R. E., 2179
Storie, C. P., 1627, 1628
Storm, C., 2829
Story, J., 2442
Story, R., 824
Stovall, F., 581
Strable, E. G., 2244
Straka, M., 2803
Strang, M., 3107
Stratton, G. W., 1452
Strauss, L. H., 1629
Street, T. W., 352
Stringfellow, K., 1502
Strother, J. V., 1542, 2098
Stroup, E. W., 2726
Strube, J., 3256
Stuart-Stubbs, B., 216
Sturdevant, E., 2443
Suen, M. T., 2964
Suhler, S. A., 1522
Sullivan, P., 2674, 2727, 3097
Sumner, J. S., 217
Sussman, J., 2728
Sutton, W., 582
Suzuki, Y., 2729

Swan, M. M., 825
Swan, M. W. S., 1800
Swarthout, A. W., 218
Swartz, R. G., 1301
Sweeney, J. L., 1801
Swogetinsky, B. A., 1523
Synder, E. B., 1185
Szigethy, M. C., 3194
Szkudlarek, M. E., 1453

Tachiata, C., 1142
Tai, Tse-Chien, 2522
Takeuchi, S., 2958
Talbert, N. J., 353
Talcott, M. T., 1255
Tannenbaum, E., 3186
Tanselle, T. G., 583, 584
Tapley, H. S., 585
Tarlton, S. M., 1871
Tate, E. L., 2804
Tatum, G. M., 1581
Tauber, M., 1918
Tauber, M. F., 2805, 3234, 3235, 3236
Taylor, J., 1384
Taylor, K. L., 2839
Taylor, M. V., 1178, 2099
Taylor, R. M., 2444
Taylor, R. N., 3155
Teague, A. H., 1524
Tebbel, J., 586
Teeter, L. W., 826
Teggart, J. F., 3199
Terrell, D., 1802
Thackston, F. V., 2806
Theriot, B. C., 3166
Thomas, A., 2774
Thomas, E. F., 827, 2180
Thomas, E. H., 2343
Thomas, M. A., 2100, 2445
Thomas, M. E., 1454
Thomassen, C., ed., 2034
Thomison, D., 69, 2675, 2676, 2677, 2678
Thompson, C. S., 828, 1022, 1919
Thompson, D. E., 83
Thompson, H. P., 640
Thompson, K. S., 2344
Thompson, L. B., 1023
Thompson, L. S., 1632, 1633
Thompson, L. W., 1719
Thompson, M. C., 2826
Thompson, S. O., 2730
Thornton, E. M., 2101
Thornton, M. I., 3237
Thorpe, J., 1850
Thurber, E., 1634, 1635

Author Index 239

Thurner, A. W., 1278
Thwaites, R. G., 2220, 2966
Ticknor, A. E., 2908
Tietjen, L. M., 1256
Tilghman, G., 2245
Tillinghast, C. B., 1257
Tillinghast, W., 3247
Tillman, R. H., 1056
Tinklepaugh, D. K., 2035
Titcomb, M. L., 1212
Titley, J., 2345
Tolles, F. B., 355
Tolzmann, D. H., 829
Tope, M., 587
Topley, H. S., 830
Tourtellot, A. B., 588
Tower, E. B., 2679
Towne, J. E., 1816, 1965, 2221, 2827
Towner, L., 2181, 2182
Translyvania University, 1720
Trask, W. B., 3043
Trautman, R., 2959
Trautman, R. L., 2523
Travous, R. L., 831
Trent, R. M., 3167
Troxel, W., 2680
Troxell, G. M., 1668
Truman, L. S., 2280
Trumbull, J., 1101
Tryon, W. S., 589
Tuck, R. S., 1490
Tucker, J. S., 1892
Turner, F. J., 3195
Truner, H. M., 2681
Turrell, G. H., 832
Tuttle, H. W., 1636
Tuttle, J. H., 356, 357, 358, 359
Tuttle, M. L., 2682
Tyler, L. G., 1953
Tyler, M. C., 1024

Uhler, P. R., 1213
Ulrich, C., 1025
Ulveling, R., 1026
Ulveling, R. A., 1279
Unger, C. P., 1027
Upshur, A. F., 360
U.S. Bureau of Education, 219
U.S. Library of Congress, 2281
U.S. Library of Congress, Map Division, 2446, 2447
U.S. National Agricultural Library Associates, 2448
U.S. Works Progress Administration, Florida, 1126
Utica, N.Y., Public Library, 1366

Utley, G. B., 2683, 2684, 2685, 2686, 3170

Valentine, Sister M., 1920
Van, S. K., 2524, 2525, 2526
Van Allen, S. J., 2036
Van Beynum, W. J., 833, 834
Van Hoesen, H. B., 1927
Van Horne, B., 3036
Van Ingen, P., 2346
Van Male, J. E., 2102
Van Oesen, E., 1385
Van Orman, R. A., 590
Vance, J. T., 2449
Vandemark, P., 1456
Vann, S. K., 2524, 2525, 2526, 2547
Vannorsdall, M. M., 2103
Varner, Sister C., 2128
Vaughan, B., 1195
Vaughan, J. E., 2037
Veaner, A. B., 220
Veit, F., 1637
Vermilya, N. C., 1893
Vermont Free Public Library Commission, 1531
Vitz, C., 2882
Vleeschauwer, H. J., 84
Vloebergh, H. E., 2104
Vonnegut, T. F., 591
Vosper, R., 2731
Vought, S. W., 2450
Vrooman, F., 2451

Wachtel, L., 1029
Wade, B. A., 1545
Wade, R. C., 592
Wadlin, H. G., 1258
Wadsworth, R. W., 1638
Waggoner, L. B., 1102
Wagner, L. F., 1921
Wainwright, N. B., 2222
Waldeck, F., 2183
Waldron, R. K., 2223
Wales, B., 1525
Walker, C. S., 3044
Walker, D. D., 593
Walker, M. H., 2224
Walker, M. J. D., 2687
Wall, J. F., 2899
Wallace, A., 221, 1030, 1031
Wallace, D. H., 835
Wallace, J. O., 1639
Wallace, W. S., 1543
Walter, A. L., 2807
Walter, F. K., 889
Walter, F. L., 1820

Walther, L. A., 1179
Walton, G. M., 1280
Wang, S. Y., 1803
Wannarka, M. B., 2347, 2348
Waples, D., 594, 1032
Ward, B. A., 1544
Ward, T., 836
Warfel, H. R., 595, 837
Warheit, I. A., 2388
Waring, J. I., 2349
Warner, H. J., 2350
Warren, A., 596, 2990, 3061
Waserman, M. J., 2452
Washburn, D., 2328
Washburn, W. E., 2453
Wasserman, P., 222
Waterman, J. S., 361
Waters, E. N., 3142
Watson, H. R., 362
Wead, E., 3089
Wead, K. H., 1103
Weakley, M. E., 2351
Weaver, F. A., 3238
Webb, D. A., 2527
Webber, M. L., 838
Weber, D. C., 1640, 2808
Webster, J. P. 2352
Wecter, D., 839
Weeks, S. B., 363, 840
Weis, F. L., 1259
Weis, L. A., 1457
Welborn, E. C., 841, 842
Welch, E. W., 2225
Wellard, J. H., 1033, 1034, 1035, 1036
Weller, J. M., 1458
Wellisch, J. B., 1037
Wellman, H. C., 3173
Wells, S. B., 223
Welsh, W. J., 2916
Wenger, E. M., 2038
Werdel, J. A., 2732
Werkley, C. E., 1038
Werner, J. M., 597
Wesson, J. J., 2039
West, E. K., 2129
Wetzel, N. P., 3090
Weyant, R. G., 598
Whalum, C. G., 2688
Wheatland, H., 2184
Whedbee, M. M., 1386
Wheeler, J. L., 1082, 1214, 2528, 3108, 3144, 3221
Wheeler, J. T., 364, 599, 600, 601, 641, 642, 890
White, A. W., 1546
White, C. M., 2529

White, J. L., 224
White, L. W., 2689
White, R. A., 1943
Whitehill, W. M., 643, 843, 844, 1260, 1261, 1262, 3240
Whitelaw, R. T., 360
Whitenack, C. I., 2040
Whitman, J. B., 2690
Whitney, E. M., 1491
Whitney, J. L., 1263
Wicklzer, A. F., 2530
Wiesner, J., 2531
Wiggin, C. B., 845, 846, 847
Wigglesworth, E., 848
Wight, E. A., 1039
Wight, W. E., 225
Wikander, L. E., 1264
Wilcox, B. H., 2691
Wilcox, H. M., 891
Wilcox, L. E., 1703
Wiley, A. N., 3145
Wilgus, A. C., 2692
Wilkins, B., 85
Wilkins, J., 1190
Wilkins, M. J., 2809
Wilkinson, M. S., 3198
Willet, M. M., 2693, 2810
William L. Clements Library, 2185
Williams, D. A., 849
Williams, E. E., 1748, 1804, 3093
Williams, J. R., cont., 365
Williams, M. D., 1114
Williams, R. V., 86, 1740
Williams, S. R., 850
Williams, Sister M. L., 226, 2694
Williamson, C. C., 1040, 2960
Williamson, I. R., 2733
Williamson, R., 2282
Williamson, W. L., 3130
Willis, D. E., 2454
Willoughby, E. E., 602
Wilson, B., 2695
Wilson, E. H., 1653
Wilson, F. A., 1265
Wilson, J. E., 366
Wilson, J. S., 603
Wilson, L. R., 227, 851, 1641, 1872, 1873, 2105, 2532, 2533, 2696, 2891, 3050, 3098
Wilson, W. J., 2353
Wilt, M. R., 2697
Winans, R. B., 604
Winckler, P. A., 3225
Wine, E., 1459
Winfrey, D. H., 2106
Wing, D. G., 1669

Wing, M. J., 2534
Winger, A. K., 1492
Winger, H., 87, 228
Winne, J., 367
Winser, B., 1321, 2935
Winser, M. c., 2698
Winship, G. P., 1928
Winship, S. G., 2921
Winslow, A., 969
Winslow, E., 852
Winsor, J., 1041, 1042, 1266, 1267, 1642, 3206, 3207
Winterich, J. T., 605
Winthrop, R. C., 1805
Winston, C., 606
Wisconsin, University of, Library School, 2536
Wisconsin Free Library Commission, 1557
Wisconsin Library School Association, 2535
Wofford, A., 2041, 2042
Wolcott, M. D., 853
Wolf, E., 368, 369, 370, 371, 372, 373, 374, 375, 376, 377, 378, 379, 380, 854, 855, 856, 857, 858, 1922, 2253
Wolf, N. E., 2226
Wong, R., 1367
Wood, M. E., 1043
Wood, R. F., 2911
Wood, R. G., 3192
Woodberry, G. E., 859
Woodford, F., 88
Woodford, F. B., 1282
Woodman, J., 1526
Woods, B. M., 89
Woodward, D. M., 1268
Woodwell, R. H., 1269
Woolf, H., 607
Worcester, Mass., Free Public Library, 1270
Work, R. L., 1806
Works Progress Administration, 1191
Worley, M. M., 1127
Wormann, C. D., 2734
Worthington, C., 743
Wright, A. E., 2970
Wright, C. C., 608
Wright, L. B., 381, 382, 383, 384, 609, 610, 611, 612, 2186, 2187, 2188
Wright, L. M., 2107, 2885
Wright, L. T., 2869
Wright, N., 613
Wright, P. B., 1302
Wright, T. G., 385
Wright, W. E., 2811, 2812

Wroth, L. C., 614, 644, 860, 1929
Wyatt, E. A., 861
Wyche, B., 1527
Wyer, J. I., 2537
Wyer, M. G., 3259

Yanchisin, D. A., 2130
Yates, B., 90
Yenawine, W. S., 1704
Yockey, R., 1460
Yost, G., 386
Young, A. P., 2699
Young, B., 3059
Young, B. A., 1368
Young, M. J., 1461
Yueh, N. N., 1643
Yust, W. F., 3250

Zabel, J. M., 2455
Zachert, M. J. K., 91, 92, 93, 387, 2131
Zafren, H. C., 1894
Zimmerman, C. R., 1044
Zimmerman, M., 1180

Subject Index

All references are to entries.

Abington Library Society (Jenkintown, Pa.), 800
academic libraries, 3, 64, 82, 1559–1965, 2706, 2713, 2818, 2822–2824, 2826
accreditation of library schools, 2468, 2484, 2486, 2487, 3510. *See also* education for librarianship
Adams, Charles Kendall, 1965
Adams, John, 239, 290, 465, 553
Adams, John Q., 321
Adams, Randolph G., 2828–2830
Addison, Joseph: his *Cato* in America, 503
adult services, 904, 914, 933, 982, 993, 1021, 1352. *See also* immigrants, library service to
advertising libraries, 2244
Agassiz, Louis, 1806
Akron (Ohio) Law Library, 2262
Akron (Ohio) Public Library, 1391, 1394, 1439, 1457, 1461
Akron (Ohio) University Library, 1879
Alabama public libraries, 1045–1048
Alabama Library Association, 2614
Alaska: bibliography of library history of, 26; private libraries in, 236, 322; public libraries in, 1049–1052
Alaska Department of Library Service, 2088
Alexandria (Va.) Public Library, 1352
Alger, Horatio: and libraries, 944
Allegan County (Mich.) Public Library, 1274
Allegheny College (Pa.) Library, 1916, 1917, 1922
Allen Memorial Art Museum Library (Oberlin, Ohio), 2217
Allentown (Pa.) Public Library, 1473
American Antiquarian Society (Worcester, Mass.), 2137, 2149
American Association of Colleges of Pharmacy, Committee on Libraries, 2544
American Association of Law Libraries, 2607, 2611, 2625, 2631, 2638
American Association of School Librarians, 2652
American Book Center for War Devastated Libraries, 2578
American Documentation Institute, 2124
American Hauser Libraries (Germany), 2726
American Library Association, 87, 143, 944–948, 2558, 2566, 2573, 2574, 2578, 2581, 2592, 2593, 2599, 2601, 2602, 2610, 2615–2617, 2619, 2626, 2628, 2632, 2647–2650, 2658, 2661, 2665, 2668, 2671, 2675–2678, 2685, 2686, 2688, 2699, 2710–2712, 2738, 2758–2760, 2784, 2856, 2907, 2941–2960, 3094–3098
American Library Institute, 2683
American Library in Paris, 2702, 2730
American Merchant Marine Library Association, 2640
American Philosophical Society (Philadelphia) Library, 345, 2157, 2158
American Society for Information Science, 2663
American Sunday School Union, 879. *See also* Sunday school libraries
American Theological Library Association, 2639, 2682
Ames, William, 359
Amesbury (Mass.) Public Library, 1269
Amherst (Mass.) College Library, 1762
Andrews, Clement Walker, 2831
Anglican Church, 615–644
Anglo-American Code, 2789, 2811
Annhurst College Library (South Woodstock, Conn.), 1661
Anthony, Susan B., 240
Antioch (Ohio) College Library, 1884
architecture, 32, 65, 83, 95, 107, 179,

201, 908, 984, 997, 1214, 1225, 1262, 1345, 1355, 1357, 1466, 1524, 1560, 1565, 1569, 1608–1610, 1617, 1700, 1786, 1787, 2221, 2309, 2378, 2379, 2827, 3079, 3123
Arizona: academic libraries in, 1644; public libraries in, 1053
Arkansas public libraries, 1054–1056
Ashtabula (Ohio) Social Library, 694
Ashton, Ralph, 377
Askew, Sarah B., 2832
Asplund, Julia Brown, 2833
Association of American Library Schools, 2476, 2477, 2494, 2582, 2584, 2618, 2657, 2669
Association of College and Research Libraries, 2609
Association of Hospital and Institution Librarians, 2695
Association of Research Libraries, 2569, 2637
associations, 2538–2699. *See also individual associations*
Astor Library (New York), 2160, 2167
athenaeums. *See social libraries*
Athol (Mass.) Public Library, 1255
Atlanta Public Library, 1128, 1135
Augusta (Ga.) Public Library, 1131
Augustana College Library (Rock Island, Ill.), 1693
Austin (Tex) Public Library, 1522
Australian libraries, 2715
automation and libraries, 160, 176, 2123, 2780, 2782, 2795, 2801, 2846

Babcock, Sidney, 403
Baldwin, Clara F., 2834
Baldwin-Wallace College Library (Berea, Ohio), 1875
Ballard, James F., 2835, 2836
Baltimore and Ohio Railroad Library, 2240
Baltimore Archdiocesan Library Council, 226, 2279
Baltimore Bar Library, 2279
Baltimore Library Company, 746, 817
Barrette, L. M., 2837
battleship libraries, 2126
Bay, J. Christian, 2838, 2839
Baylor University Library (Waco, Tex.), 1940, 1941
Beals, Ralph A., 2840
Beaumont (Tex.) Public Library, 1520
Beckley, John, 2841, 2842
Bedford (N.H.) Social Library, 686
Beer, William, 2843

Belleville (Ill.) Public Library, 1162
Benezet, Anthony, 252, 254
Bentley, William, 296
Berkeley, Bishop George, 1658, 1659, 1662, 1750
Berkeley, Norborne, 386
Berkshire (Mass.) Athenaeum, 655, 657
Bernhisel, John M., 2075
Bertram, James, 2844
Bessemer (Ala.) Public Library, 1045
Bethany Biblical Seminary Library (Chicago), 1691
Bethesda (Md.) Public Library, 1198
Bethlehem (Pa.) Public Library, 1472
Bibliographic Center for Research, 2129
Billings, John Shaw, 2847–2855
Birmingham (Ala.) Public Library, 1048
Bishop, William Warner, 2856–2868
Black, William, 318
Blacks: library service to, 633, 896, 900, 901, 989, 1045–1047, 1118, 1125, 1128, 1129, 1137, 1190, 1290, 1342, 1369, 1380, 1501, 1507–1509, 1512, 2869
Blackstone's *Commentaries*, 361
blind: library service to, 140, 184, 877, 951, 1341, 1346, 1447, 1460, 2286, 2996
Blue, Thomas Fountain, 1190, 2868
Board on Cataloging Policy and Research, 2805
Bonham (Tex.) public libraries, 1521
book catalogs, 2736, 2743, 2791, 2793, 2801
book collecting. *See private libraries*
bookmobiles, 910, 922, 1327, 1385, 1386, 1403, 1433, 1477, 1557
Books Across the Sea Library, 2720
book trade, 390, 393, 394, 409, 413, 414, 420–423, 444, 452, 457, 459, 460, 464, 466–473, 483, 487, 489, 492, 496, 498, 502, 505, 508–516, 518, 520, 524, 532, 535–537, 546, 550, 562, 564, 566, 567, 569, 571, 572, 576–578, 580, 582–587, 589, 591, 592, 595, 599, 600, 603, 604, 606, 607
Booth, Mary Josephine, 2870
Boston Athenaeum, 433, 650, 661, 663, 680, 691, 698, 733, 796, 797, 824, 825, 843, 844, 848, 852, 3222
Boston Library Society, 815
Boston Medical Library, 2295, 2304
Boston Mercantile Library Association, 701

Boston parochial libraries, 619, 629, 643
Boston Public Library, 462, 816, 1216, 1217, 1220, 1221, 1225, 1226, 1230–1232, 1236, 1242, 1244, 1258, 1260–1263, 1266, 1267, 2740, 3242–3250
Bostwick, Arthur Elmore, 2871–2875
Bowdoin College Library (Brunswick, Maine), 1723, 1724
Bowerman, George F., 2876, 2877
Bowker, Richard Rogers, 2878–2880
Bradford, John, 685
branch libraries, 1434. See also individual libraries
Bray, Thomas, 615–644
Brett, William Howard, 2881–2883
Bridgeport (Conn.) Public Library, 1085
Brientnall, Joseph, 2884
Brigham, Johnson, 2885
British Museum, 2733
Bronson Library (Waterbury, Conn.), 1097
Brookfield (Vt.) Public Library, 1529
Brooklyn College Library, 1840
Brooklyn Public Library, 879, 1353
Brown, Charles Harvey, 2886
Brown, John Carter, Library, 1923, 1925–1929
Brown Library (Rugby, Tenn.), 731
Brute Library (Vincennes, Ind.), 341
Bucknell University Library (Lewisburg, Pa.), 1910
Buffalo (N.Y.) Public Library, 742, 1330, 1336, 1340
Buffington, Willie Lee, 2887
Bulen, Henry Lewis, 2888
Buncombe County (N.C.) Medical Library, 2305
business: library service to, 998, 1122, 1317, 1318, 1445, 2227–2245, 3208
Business Information Bureau, Cleveland Public Library, 1445
Butler, Pierce, 2889–2891
Butler, Susan Dart, 2892
Byrd, William, II, 256, 257, 345, 369

Cabel, Joseph Carrington, 429
California: academic libraries in, 1645–1652; bibliography of library history in, 54; book trade in, 532, 580; private libraries in, 247, 351, 393–395, 482; public libraries in, 1057–1082; school libraries in, 875, 1997; social libraries in, 652, 653, 665, 678, 703, 722–724, 807; special libraries in, 2135, 2141, 2150, 2166, 2170–2172, 2174, 2175, 2177, 2183
California, University of (Berkeley), Library, 1646, 1650, 1652
California, University of (Los Angeles), Library, 2992
California Academy of Sciences and Early History of Science in the West, 2211
California Library Association, 16, 2563, 2572, 2573, 2621, 2904
California State Library, 2055, 2067, 2076, 2499
Calument (Mich.) public libraries, 1278
Cambridge (Mass.) Public Library, 1219, 1250
Canton (Ohio) Public Library, 3090
Carey, Mirian E., 2894
Carey and Lea (Philadelphia), 489
Caritat, Hocquet, 492, 883, 884
Carlson, William H., 2895
Carlton, William, 2896
Carnegie, Andrew, 894, 895, 905, 906, 929, 950, 976, 978, 985, 986, 991, 995, 1038, 1040, 1116, 1141, 1377, 1519, 1524, 1547, 1548, 1552, 2844, 2897. See also Carnegie Corporation
Carnegie Corporation, 894, 905, 906, 978, 985, 986, 995, 1141, 1519, 1524, 1563, 1564, 1615, 2715, 2722
Carnegie Library School (Atlanta), 2463, 2464, 2521
Carnovsky, Leon, 2900, 2901
Carroll College Library (Waukesha, Wis.), 1964
Carter, Robert, 333, 365
Caruthers, William, 436
Cassel, Abraham Harley, 2902
cataloging and classification, 1342, 2326, 2504, 2735–2812, 2916, 2922–2929, 2941–2960, 3009–3016, 3126
Cataloging and Classification Division, American Library Association, 2540
Cathedral Free Circulating Library (New York), 881
Catholic Library Association, 2577, 2598, 2659, 2697
Catholic University of American Library School (Washington, D.C.), 2498
censorship. See intellectual freedom
Central City (Colo.) libraries, 522
centralized processing, 2739, 2748, 2771, 2779, 2780, 2786. See also cataloging and classification

Subject Index   245

certification of librarians, 1980, 2008
Champaign (Ill.) Public Library, 1155
Charleston (S.C.) Library Society, 615, 710, 783, 789, 799, 808, 809
Charlotte (N.C.) College Library, 1871
Charlotte (N.C.) Public Librry, 1374, 1377
Charlton, Margaret, 2603, 2903
Chatham (N.J.) Public Library, 1316
Chatham Square Branch of the New York Public Library, 1367
Chattanooga (Tenn.) Public Library, 1506
Chelan County (Wash.) Public Library, 1541
Chemung County (N.Y.) Public Library, 1333
Chester County (Pa.) public libraries, 1489, 1490, 1500
Chestnut Hill College Library (Philadelphia), 1905
Chicago, University of, Library, 1687, 1689, 1690, 1697–1699, 3009–3016
Chicago Art Institute Library, 2179
Chicago Association of Law Libraries, 2587
Chicago Historical Society Library, 2210
Chicago Lutheran Theological Seminary Library, 1695
Chicago Public Library, 1146, 1149, 1150, 1152, 1154, 1156, 1159, 1161, 1163
children's librarians, 988, 2508
children's literature, 403, 405, 406, 419, 432, 448, 449, 453, 456, 458, 485, 490, 502, 505, 521, 523, 530, 562, 587, 595, 887, 1995, 2004, 2022. See also children's services in public libraries; school libraries
children's services in public libraries, 942, 972, 987, 988, 1001, 1006, 1027, 1164, 1170, 1335, 1360, 1399, 1453, 1457, 1467, 1536, 1987, 1991, 2009, 2010, 2021, 2700, 2930, 3024–3026, 3104–3106, 3133. See also school libraries
Christ Church Parochial Library (Boston), 629
Church Historical Society Library, 2191
church libraries. See theological libraries
Cincinnati Law Library, 1404, 1458
Cincinnati Young Men's Mercantile Library Association, 671, 675
circulating libraries, 492, 599, 863, 866, 876, 877, 880–886, 888, 890
circulation services, 1607
Citizen's Library Movement (N.C.), 1373, 1375
Civil War: and libraries, 211, 225, 547
Clackamas County (Ore.) libraries, 1465
Claremont (Cal.) College Library, 1648
Clark, George Thomas, 2904
Clark, William Andrews, Library, 1651
Clark (N.J.) Public Library, 1319
classification. See cataloging and classification
Clements, William L., 1808, 2905, 2906
Clements Library (Ann Arbor, Mich.), 2185, 2828–2830
Cleveland Public Library, 1395, 1396, 1399–1402, 1405–1408, 1420, 1427, 1434, 1436, 1440, 1442, 1443, 1445–1447, 1449, 1456, 1460, 2881–2883, 3208
Clift, David, 2907
Cogswell, Joseph Green, 2908
Coke, Sir William, 527
Cole, Agnes M., 2785
Colelazer, Henry, 2909
collection development, 1575, 1576, 1581, 1592, 1595, 1598–1603, 1611, 1624, 1625, 1636, 1638, 1643, 1687, 1785, 1800, 1852
college libraries. See academic libraries
Colorado: academic libraries in, 1653; private libraries in, 522; public libraries in, 1083, 1084; special libraries in, 2112
Colorado Historical Society Library, 2223
Colorado Library Association, 2559
Colorado State Library, 2102
Columbia Union College (Tacoma Park, Md.), 1733
Columbia University libraries, 1566, 1829, 1831–1833, 1837, 1841, 1843–1845, 1850, 2796, 2803
Columbia University Library School, 2473, 2502, 2523
Columbus (Ga.) Public Library, 1129
comparative librarianship, 960, 974, 1575, 2700–2734
Compton, Charles, 2910
computers and libraries. See automa-

tion and libraries
Concord (N.C.) Public Library, 1376
Congregational Library Association, 2571
Congress, Library of. *See* U.S. Library of Congress
Connecticut: academic libraries in, 1654–1669; bibliography of library history of, 47, 79; public libraries in, 751, 1085–1103; school libraries in, 1103, 1967, 1971, 1994, 2025, 2029; social libraries in, 668, 672, 702, 751, 833, 834; special libraries in, 2140, 2144
Connecticut Agricultural Experiment Station Library, 2391
Connecticut Library Association, 2576
Connecticut School Library Association, 2539
Connecticut State Library, 2068–2070
consortia, 1602, 1603
Conway (Mass.) Public Library, 1248
Coolbrith, Ina, 1061, 2911
Coonskin Library (Ames Township, Ohio), 761, 776, 777
cooperation, 139, 158, 161, 210, 216, 1640. *See also* centralized processing; consortia; storage libraries
copyright, 389, 400, 403, 404, 412, 415, 425, 446, 496, 549, 563, 1752, 2374
Cornell University Library (Ithaca, N.Y.), 949, 1838, 1846
Coulter, Edith M., 2912, 2913
Council of National Library Associations, 2597
Council of Books in Wartime, 2553
Countee Cullen (N.Y.) Regional Branch Library, 1368
county libraries, 962, 1065, 1074, 1076, 1078, 1080, 1104, 1123, 1132, 1133, 1138, 1140, 1164–1166, 1168–1170, 1172–1175, 1207, 1210, 1212, 1223, 1274, 1291, 1295, 1302, 1332, 1333, 1368, 1371, 1374, 1381, 1382, 1389, 1401, 1409, 1419, 1438, 1454, 1465, 1489, 1490, 1492, 1499, 1500, 1502, 1505, 1514, 1518, 1533, 1537, 1539, 1541, 1544, 1558
Countryman, Gratia A., 2914
Crawford County (Ohio) Public Library, 1422
Creole libraries, 275–277, 317, 326, 327
Crerar, John, 2915
Crerar Library (Chicago), 2134
Cronin, John, 2916
Crunden, Frederick M., 2917, 2918

Culver, Essae M., 2059, 2919
curriculum of library schools, 2511, 2512
Currier, Thomas F., 2920
Curry, Arthur R., 2921
Cutter, Charles Ammi, 2922–2929
Cuyahoga County (Ohio) Public Library, 1401
Cuyahoga Falls (Ohio) Library Association, 750

Dallas (Pa.) Public Library, 1487
Dallas (Tex.) Public Library, 1513
Dana, John Cotton, 2698, 2930–2937
Danton, J. Periam, 2938
Darby (Pa.) society libraries, 803, 814, 828
Dartmouth College Library, 1825, 1826
Davenport (Iowa) Public Library, 1182
David, Charles Wendell, 2939
Davis, Raymond Casallis, 1807, 2940
Dayton, University of, Library, 1883
Dayton (Ohio) Public Library, 1403, 1459
Decatur (Ill.) Public Library, 1158
Defoe, Daniel, 462
DeGolyer Foundation Library, 2143
Delaware: academic libraries in, 1670, 1671; public libraries in, 1104, 1105; social libraries in, 775
Delaware, University of, Library, 1670, 1671
Delaware Historical Society Library, 2214
Delaware Library Association, 2554
Delaware State Archives, 2100, 2445
Delaware State Library Commission, 2089
dental libraries, 2298, 2301, 2328, 2330, 2331
Denver, University of, Library School, 2489
Denver Medical Society Library, 2337
Denver Public Library, 1084, 2347
departmental libraries: in academic libraries, 1632
DePauw University Library (Greencastle, Ind.), 1709
deposit libraries. *See* storage libraries
Depository Library Act of 1962, 135
Depression, the, 594, 931, 963, 964, 980, 1032
Des Moines (Iowa) Public Library, 1181, 1185
Detroit Public Library, 658, 1279, 1282
Dewey, Melvil, 2778, 2941–2960

Dewey Decimal Classification, 2737, 2738, 2741, 2742, 2746, 2778
Dickinson, Emily, 418
Dickinson College Library (Carlisle, Pa.), 1912
disadvantaged, library service to. *See* Blacks; blind; Puerto Ricans
dissertations on library history: bibliography of, 38, 69
District of Columbia: academic libraries in, 1672–1675; law libraries in, 2252, 2261, 2263–2265, 2281, 2282; medical libraries in, 2283, 2284, 2314–2320, 2323, 2325, 2343, 2353, 2354; public libraries in, 1106–1114; special libraries in, 2146, 2154, 2155, 2165, 2186–2188
District of Columbia Library Association, 2551, 2555, 2557, 2634, 2666, 2672
District of Columbia Public Library, 1106, 1107, 1109, 1110, 1112, 1113, 2876, 2877
district school libraries. *See* school district libraries
Doe, Janet, 2961
Doren, Electra Collins, 2962
Downs, Robert B., 2963, 2964
Drake University Library (Des Moines, Iowa), 1712
Draper, Lyman Copeland, 2965, 2966
Drexel Institute Library (Philadelphia), 1909
Drexel University Library School, 2488, 2507
Duke University Library (Durham, N.C.), 1854, 1869, 2806
Duluth (Minn.) Public Library, 1289
Drummer, Jeremiah, 1655, 1664
Dunkin, Paul S., 2967
Durham (Conn.) Book Company, 833, 834

Eames, Wilberforce, 2968
Earlham College Library (Richmond, Ind.), 1711
Early, Peter, 387
Eastern Baptist Theological Seminary Library (Philadelphia), 1907
Eastman, Linda A., 2969, 2970
East Palestine (Ohio) Public Library, 1415
East Texas State University Library, Science Department (Commerce), 2457
Edmunds, John, 2971

Educational Film Library Association, 2588
education for librarianship, 2456–2537, 2955
Eleanor Squire Memorial Library (Cleveland), 2219
Elkins, William McIntire, 342
Elliot, Charles, 1761
Elliot, Leslie Robinson, 2972
"Elmwood" (Va.) Library, 258
Elon (N.C.) College Library, 1868
Emerson, Ralph Waldo, 282, 433, 440, 499, 517
Emory University Library (Atlanta), 1682
Emory University Library School, 2500
endowments for libraries, 152. *See also* Carnegie, Andrew; philanthropy and libraries
enlightenment in America, 391, 392, 426, 428, 431, 504, 515, 573–575
Enoch Pratt Public Library (Philadelphia), 1199–1202, 1204–1206, 1214
Erie (Pa.) Public Library, 1476
Eureka (Calif.) Public Library, 1073
Evans, Charles, 2973
Everett, Edward, 1232
extension services, 1385, 1418, 2124, 2125. *See also* bookmobiles; state libraries

faculty status for librarians, 1578–1580
Fairfax County (Va.) public libraries, 1533
Fairfield (Conn.) Public Library, 1087
Fairmont (W.Va.) State College Library, 1961
Fall River (Mass.) Public Library, 1243
Farmington (Conn.) Village Library Company, 702
federal aid to libraries, 115, 126, 132, 135, 140, 145, 178, 179, 184, 213, 214, 1022, 1037, 1178, 1194, 1435, 1442, 1515, 1625, 1626, 2108
Fellows Dorkas, 2975
fiction, 459, 604, 913, 944
Fields, James T., 589
films in libraries, 1567, 2190. *See also* microforms in libraries
Fisk University Library (Nashville, Tenn.), 1932
Fitchburg (Mass.) Athenaeum, 759
Fletcher, William Isaac, 2976
Flexner, Jennie M., 2977
Florida: academic libraries in, 1676–1681; bibliography of library history

248 Subject Index

in, 6; public libraries in, 1115–1127; school libraries in, 2013; social libraries in, 656, 827
Florida, University of, Library (Gainesville), 1676, 1680
Florida Atlantic University Library (Boca Raton), 1677
Florida Library Association, 2565, 2641, 2684
Florida State Library, 2053
Florida State University Library School (Tallahassee), 2490
Fogarty, John E., 2978
Foik, Paul J., 2979
Folger Shakespeare Library (Washington, D.C.), 2146, 2154, 2155, 2165, 2186–2188
Forbes Library (Northampton, Mass.), 1224, 1233
Force, Peter, 295
Fort Vancouver (Wash.) Regional Library, 1539
Fort Worth (Tex.) Public Library, 1515, 1527
Foster, William E., 2980
Franklin, Benjamin, 242, 264, 305, 343, 345, 368, 370, 373, 379, 565, 588, 708, 711, 712, 727, 741, 767, 784, 791, 792, 854–858
Franklin, Louise, 2981
Franklin Institute Library (Philadelphia), 2152, 2153
Franklin Typographical Society (Boston), 2151
Freedley, George R., 2982
Freemont (Ohio) Public Library, 1418, 1423
Friends' Meeting Library (Philadelphia), 669, 709
friends of libraries, 1518, 1863
Frost, Robert, 461

Galesburg (Ill.) Ladies Library Association, 1148
Gallaudet College Library (Washington, D.C.), 1674
Galveston (Tex.) Public Library, 1512, 1525
Gary (Ind.) Public Library, 1177
Gay, Frank Butler, 2983
genealogy in libraries, 1426
general stores and books, 468–470, 472
Geneva (Ill.) Public Library, 1147
Georgetown Public Library (Washington, D.C.), 1111, 1114
Georgetown University Library (Washington, D.C.), 1672
Georgia: academic libraries in, 1682–1685; public libraries in, 1128–1138; school libraries in, 2032
Georgia, University of, Library (Athens), 1683
Georgia Library Association, 2546, 2596
German public libraries, 2704
German singing society libraries (Texas), 646
German university libraries, 2706
gerontological concepts and librarianship, 157
Gerould, James Thayer, 2984
Gillet, Charles Ripley, 2985
Gillis, James L., 2986–2988
Gillis, Mabel Ray, 2789, 2790
Gilmer, Francis Walker, 437
Glennville (W.Va.) State College Library, 1958
Gloucester (Mass.) Lyceum and Sawyer Free Library, 1227
Goodrich, N. L., 2991
Goodwin, John E., 2992, 2993
Goshen (Ind.) College Library, 1710
Goucher College Library (Towson, Md.), 1730, 1735
government documents, 543
government libraries, 86, 2283–2285, 2291, 2314–2320, 2323, 2325, 2343, 2353, 2354, 2455
Green, Samuel Swett, 2995
Greenough, Horatio, 613
Greenwich (Conn.) Public Library, 1096
Gregg County (Tex.) public libraries, 1514
Griffin, Etta Josselyn, 2996
Grosse Pointe (Mich.) Public Library, 1275
Grosvenor Library (Buffalo, N.Y.), 1336
Grothaus, Julia, 2997
Guest, John, 376
Guilford (Conn.) College Library, 1858
Guilford (Conn.) Public Library, 1088
Gunter, Lillian, 2998
Gustavus Adolphus College Library (St. Peter, Minn.), 1818

Haddonfield (N.J.) Library Company, 714
Hadley, Chalmers, 3000
Haines, Helen E., 3001–3004
Hall, David, 466
Hallidie, Andrew S., 3005–3007

Hamilton College Library (Clinton, N.Y.), 1828
Hamilton (Ohio) Public Library, 1398
Hamilton County (Ohio) Public Library, 1433
Hammond, George, 3008
Hampton Falls (Mass.) social libraries, 812
Hanson, J. C. M., 3009–3016
Harper and Brothers, 452
Harris, Thaddeus Mason, 666, 3017–3019
Harris, William Torrey, 2778
Harrison, Alice S., 3020
Hart, Gilbert, 3021
Harvard, John, 253, 331, 493, 1752
Harvard University libraries (Cambridge, Mass.), 613, 1566, 1742–1746, 1748–1761, 1763–1774, 1776–1780, 1782–1791, 1793–1795, 1797, 1798, 1800–1806, 2246, 2247, 2274, 2277, 2313, 2744, 2745, 2774, 2793, 3093, 3168, 3169, 3242–3250
Haskell, Rachel, 500
Hasse, Adelaide R., 3022
Hatboro (Pa.) Union Library, 715
Hawaii: academic libraries in, 1686; bibliography of library history in, 54; public libraries in, 1139–1142; social libraries in, 667; special libraries in, 2127
Hawaii, University of, Library, 1686
Hawaii Library Association, 2586
Hawthorne, Nathaniel, 491, 551, 596
Hay, John, 316
Hayes Memorial Library (Freemont, Ohio), 2161–2163
Hebrew Union College Library (New York), 1894
Hegel and American cataloging, 2756, 2757
Henry, Edward Atwood, 3023
Hepburn Libraries (New York), 1363
Hewins, Caroline M., 3024–3026
Hewitt, Charles N., 300
Hicks, Frederick G., 3027, 3028
Highland County (Ga.) Public Library, 1138
High Point (N.C.) Public Library, 1383
Hiram (Ohio) College Library, 1886, 1891
historical society libraries, 2189–2226
Hollis, Thomas, 1795
Holmes, Oliver Wendell, 501
Holmes, Thomas J., 3029
Holy Family College Library (Philadelphia), 1920
Honolulu Library Association, 667
Hoole, William Stanley, 3030
Hoover Institute on War, Revolution, and Peace Library (Stanford, Calif.), 1649, 2150, 2166
hospital libraries, 1329
hotel libraries, 2241
Houghton Mifflin, 397
Howard University Library (Washington, D.C.), 1673, 1675
Howland, Arthur C., 303
Hudson (N.Y.) Public Library, 1365
Hudson (Ohio) Library and Historical Society, 2205
Hudson (Ohio) Public Library, 1409
Hume, David, 597
Huntington County (Pa.) Public Library, 1492
Huntington Library (San Mareno, Calif.), 2170–2172, 2174, 2175
Hutchins, Frank, 3032

Ideson, Julia B., 3033
Illinois: academic libraries in, 1687–1704; book trade in, 469; private libraries in, 237, 238, 270, 285; public libraries in, 1143–1163; school libraries in, 1999, 2017, 2034; social libraries in, 768, 779, 831; special libraries in, 2134, 2164, 2179, 2181, 2182, 2210, 2213, 2227
Illinois, University of, Library (Champaign-Urbana), 1700, 1701, 1703, 1704, 2213, 2768, 2826, 2963, 2964
Illinois, University of, Library School, 2491, 2493, 2504
Illinois Historical Society Library, 2213
Illinois Library Association, 2689
Illinois State Library, 2046, 2093
image of librarians, 125
immigrants, library services to, 932, 990, 1402, 1436, 1440, 1443, 1501
Indiana: academic libraries in, 1705–1711; private libraries in, 283, 284, 341, 468; public libraries in, 1164–1180, 2099; school libraries in, 1164, 1976, 1999; social libraries in, 679, 692, 740, 768, 849; special libraries in, 2145
Indianapolis and Marion County (Ind.) Public Library, 1164, 1166, 1169, 1170, 1172–1175
Indiana Public Library Commission, 1178
Indiana State Library, 2044, 2083

Indiana University Library (Bloomington), 1705, 1707, 1708
information retrieval, 176. See also automation and libraries
Insurance Library Association Library (Boston), 2232
intellectual freedom, 103, 104, 112, 129, 133, 136, 137, 162, 166, 180, 187, 196, 206, 241, 260, 497, 533, 944, 946, 994, 1019, 1523, 1995
international relations, 2700–2734, 2859, 2867
Iowa: academic libraries in, 1712; public libraries in, 1181–1185
Iowa State Library, 2062, 2107
Iowa State Medical Library, 2300
Irving, Washington, 2167
Isom, Mary Frances, 3035, 3036
Ithaca (N.Y.) Public Library, 1361

Jackson, William A., 3037
Jackson County (Ohio) Public Library, 1454
Jackson (Miss.) Public Library, 1290, 1292
Jacksonville (Fla.) Public Library, 1118
Jamaica (N.Y.) Public Library, 1325
Japanese libraries, 2724, 2729
Jefferson, Thomas, 230, 234, 241, 260, 261, 263, 271, 324, 325, 328, 329, 339, 346, 348, 349, 361, 384, 424, 429, 430, 437–439, 538, 598, 603, 1945, 1946, 1951, 2371, 2408, 2420, 2424, 2799, 3038
Jefferson Medical College Library (Louisville, Ky.), 2299
Jewell College Library (Liberty, Mo.), 1822
Jewett, Charles C., 3039–3043
Johns Hopkins University Library (Baltimore), 1726, 1731, 2322, 2327
Johnson, Alvin S., 2844
Johnson, C. Smith University Library (Charlotte, N.C.), 1853
Johnston County (N.C.) Public Library, 1371
Johnstown (Pa.) Public Library, 1475
Jones, Samuel, M., 3044
Josephson, Aksel G. S., 3045
Journal of Education for Librarianship, 167
junior college libraries, 1639, 1645

Kaiser, John B., 3046
Kansas: academic libraries in, 1713, 1714; public libraries in, 1186–1188;
social libraries in, 707
Kansas City (Mo.) Public Library, 1300, 1302
Kansas State Library, 2061
Kansas State Teacher's College Library (Emporia), 1713, 1714
Kelso, Tessa, 3047
Kensington (Conn.) Public Library, 1090
Kent (Ohio) Public Library, 1429
Kent (Ohio) State University Library, 1875
Kent State University Library School, 2482
Kentucky: academic libraries in, 1715–1720; law libraries in, 2254; public libraries in, 1189–1191; school libraries in, 1989, 1990; social libraries in, 685, 769; special libraries in, 2120
Keogh, Andrew, 3048, 3049
Kern County (Calif.) Public Library, 1058
Ketchikan (Alaska) Public Library, 1051
Kidder, Ida Angeline, 3053
King's Chapel Library (Boston), 619, 643
Kingsbury, Mary A., 3054
Kingston (N.J.) Public Library, 771
Kittitas County (Wash.) Public Library, 1537
Knox, Henry, 457
Knoxville (Tenn.) Public Library, 1507
Koch, Theodore W., 3055
Kuhlman, A. F., 3056

Ladies Library Associations (Mich.), 1271, 1273, 1275
Lafayette College Library (Easton, Pa.), 1921
Lagrange County (Ind.) public libraries, 1168
Lakeside Press (Chicago), 2227
Lakewood (Ohio) Public Library, 1441
Lancaster (Mass). Public Library, 1259
Lancaster (Pa.) libraries, 737
land-grant college libraries, 1625, 1634, 1635
Land (Ohio) Public Library, 1410
Lanier, Sidney, 551
Lansing (Mich.) Public Library, 1272
Larned, Josephus N., 3057–3059
La Salle College Library (Chicago), 1913
La Retema (Tex). Public Library, 1517
law libraries, 376, 377, 601, 2246–2282

Subject Index   251

2444, 2449, 2455, 2587, 2590, 2607, 2611, 2625, 2638, 2753, 3251
laymen's libraries. *See* Bray, Thomas
Lee, Molly H., 3060
Lee County (Miss.) Public Library, 1291
legislation for libraries, 1179, 1187, 1299, 1334, 1384, 1968
legislative reference libraries, 2063
Legler, Henry E., 3061
Lenin, V. I., 2719
Lennox, James, 3062
Lenox (Mass.) Public Library, 1241
Leonard Case Library (Cleveland), 1400
Leominster (Mass.) Public Library, 1196
Lexington (Ky.) libraries, 592, 685
Lexington (Mass.) Public Library, 1222
Leypoldt, Frederick, 3063
Library Association (Great Britain), 2711, 2712
Library Journal, 141, 2648
library literature, 1596, 1980, 2255, 2635, 2648, 2814
Library Quarterly, 199
Library Services Act, 132
Lilly Library (Bloomington, Ind.), 2145
Lima (Ohio) Public Library, 1393
Lisbon (Ohio) Public Library, 1424
literary society libraries, 1588, 1589, 1620, 1627, 1628, 1706, 1723, 1724, 1777, 1778, 1797, 1877, 1886, 1891, 1900
Lloyd, Edward, 374
Lloyd Library (Cincinnati), 2340, 2341
Logan, James 370–372, 375, 380
Logassa, Hannah, 3064
Longfellow, Henry, 1800, 3065, 3066
Longview (Wash.) Public Library, 1538
Los Angeles Public Library, 1064, 1071, 1076
Louisiana: academic libraries in, 1721, 1722; circulating libraries in, 882; private libraries in, 275–277, 326, 327, 539; public libraries in, 1192–1195; school libraries in, 1979; social libraries in, 753, 754, 765.
Louisiana State Library, 258–260, 2097, 2919
Louisiana State University Library (Baton Rouge), 1721
Louisville (Ky.), University of, Library, 1715, 2254
Louisville (Ky.) Law Library, 2281
Louisville (Ky.) Medical Institute Library, 2345
Louisville (Ky.) Public Library, 1190, 1191

Lowe, John A., 3068
Ludington, Flora B., 3069
Lummis, Charles F., 3070, 3071
lyceums, 475, 707, 716, 735, 770, 1227
Lydenburg, Harry Miller, 3072
Lynch, Thomas, Jr., 269

McCarthy, Charles, 3073–3076
McClung, Calvin M., 3077
McCoy, Isaac, 312
McDiarmid, Errett W., 3078
Macdonald, Angus S., 3079
McGuffey, William Holmes, 521, 523, 587
McKay, Donald, 311
McKinley, Archibald, 323
MacLeish, Archibald, 2665, 2677, 3080–3082
Macon (Ga.) Public Library, 1137
Madison, James, 2433
Madison (Conn.) Public Library, 1095
Madison (Wisc.) Public Library, 1549, 1553
Madison (Wisc.) school libraries, 1982
Magruder, Patrick, 3083
Maine: academic libraries in, 1723–1725; circulating libraries in, 886; public libraries in, 1196, 1197; social libraries in, 673
Mamoroneck (N.Y.) Public Library, 1349
Manchester (N.H.) Public Library, 1310
Manhattanville College Library (Purchase, N.Y.), 1842
Mann, Horace, 3084–3086
Mann, Margaret, 3087–3089
maps in libraries, 1322, 2121, 2122, 2446, 2736, 2798
Marine Biological Laboratory Library (Woods Hole, Maine), 2360
Martin, Mary P., 3090
Martin, Wilton D., 1478
Maryland: academic libraries in, 1726–1740; book trade in, 890; circulating libraries in, 599, 890; parochial libraries in, 620, 622–626, 630, 632, 633, 636–642; private libraries in, 364, 366; public libraries in, 1198–1214; social libraries in, 817
Maryland, University of, Library (College Park), 1727
Maryland State Library, 2052, 2056, 2057
Massachusetts: academic libraries in, 1741–1806; circulating libraries in, 863; private libraries in, 239, 249,

250, 253, 262, 278, 282, 290, 331, 335, 354, 356–359, 385; public libraries in, 749, 1215–1270; social libraries in, 655–657, 661, 663, 664, 670, 680, 691, 698, 701, 773, 796, 797, 812, 815, 816, 824, 825, 830, 843–848, 852, 859; special libraries in, 2137, 2139, 2149, 2151, 2184, 2194, 2195, 2198
Massachusetts Historical Society Library, 2195, 2198
Massachusetts State Library, 2051, 2082
Mather, Increase, 356, 358
Mayo, William W., 301
mechanics and mercantile libraries. *See* social libraries
Medford (Mass.) Public Library, 1252
medical libraries, 279, 293, 298–301, 303, 340, 366, 601, 2283–2353, 2443, 2452, 2787, 2809, 3251
Medical Library Association, 2545, 2552, 2562, 2589, 2603, 2627, 2635, 2636, 2656, 2679, 2680, 2903
medical library education, 2480, 2496, 2515
MEDLARS, 2284, 2885
Meehan, John Silva, 3092
Melville, Herman, 558
Memphis (Tenn.) Public Library, 1508
Menlo Park (Calif.) Public Library, 1057
Mennonite Historical Library (Goshen, Ind.), 1710
Mentor (Ohio) Public Library, 1450, 1451
Metcalf, Keyes D., 3093
Methodist Publishing House, 542
Miami (Fla.), University of, Library, 1679
Miami (Fla.) Public Library, 1115, 1119, 1122
Michigan: academic libraries in, 1807–1816; book trade in, 409; law libraries in, 2268; public libraries in, 1271–1282; social libraries in, 654, 658
Michigan, University of, Library (Ann Arbor), 1808–1815, 2185, 2827–2830, 2909
Michigan State Library, 2074, 2077, 2078, 2084
Michigan State University Library (East Lansing), 1816
microforms in libraries, 110, 220
Middle States Association of Colleges and Secondary Schools, 1584
Mid-West Interlibrary Center (Chicago), 1595
Milam, Carl H., 3094–3098
military libraries, 2723. *See also* U.S. Air Force libraries; U.S. Army Medical Library; U.S. Army Post Library Service; U.S. Army Walter Reed Medical Center Library; U.S. Naval Academy Library; U.S. Veterans Administration Library
Miller, Charles, 3099
mill-town libraries, 762, 763
Milton, John, 479, 507, 561
Milton (Mass.) Public Library, 1239
Minneapolis Athenaeum, 693
Minneapolis Public Library, 1285, 1286, 1288, 3135, 3141
Minnesota: academic libraries in, 1817–1820; bibliography of library history of, 53; public libraries in, 1283–1289; school libraries in, 1973; social libraries in, 693; special libraries in, 2128, 2706, 2707
Minnesota Historical Society, 2206, 2207
Minnesota Library Association, 2550
mission libraries, 247
Mississippi: academic libraries in, 1294, 1821; bibliography of library history of, 34; public libraries in, 1290–1295; school libraries in, 1294, 1993, 2039; special libraries in, 1294
Mississippi, University of, Library (University), 1821
Mississippi Library Association, 2642
Missouri: academic libraries in, 1822–1824; book trade in, 444, 509–515; private libraries in, 390; public libraries in, 1296–1302; social libraries in, 766, 772, 828
Missouri, University of, Library (Columbia), 1823, 1824
Mitchell, John, 291, 309
Mitchell, Sidney B., 3100–3102
Monessen (Pa.) Public Library, 1468
Monroe, James, 292
Montana: public libraries in, 1304
Monterey (Calif.) Library Society, 807
Montgomery (Ala.) Public Library, 1046
Monti, Minnie Sweet, 3103
Moore, Anne C., 3104–3106
Morgan State College Library (Baltimore), 1738
Morgantown (W.Va.) Public Library, 1545

Subject Index   253

Morrill, Justin S., 2417
Morristown (Pa.) Public Library, 1491
Morsch, Lucile, 3108
Mount Holyoke College (South Hadley, Mass.), 1775
Mount Union College Library (Alliance, Ohio), 1880, 1885
Mount Vernon (Ohio) Public Library, 1428
Muhlenberg College Library (Allentown, Pa.), 1900
Mumford, L. Quincy, 3110, 3111
Muncie (Ind.) Public Library, 1176
Murphy (N.C.) Public Library, 1372
museum libraries, 2189–2226
Museum of Modern Art Film Library (New York), 2190
music in libraries, 1106, 1185, 1324, 1446, 1638, 2164
Music Library Association, 2556, 2646

Nahant (Mass.) Public Library, 1265
Nantucket (Mass.) Public Library, 1253
Napoleon (Ohio) Public Library, 1437
Nashville (Tenn.) Public Library, 1509
nationalism and libraries, 936, 940
Nebraska: public libraries in, 1304; social libraries in, 730
New Britain (Conn.) Institute, 2140, 2144
New Castle County (Del.) Public Library, 1104, 1105
New Castle (Del.) Library Company, 775
New England Deposit Library, 1576
New Hampshire: academic libraries in, 1825, 1826; public libraries in, 1305–1310; social libraries in, 686, 762, 763
New Hampshire State Library, 2048
New Harmony (Ind.) Working Man's Institute Library, 849
New Haven (Conn.) Public Library, 1091, 1098, 1100
New Jersey: academic libraries in, 1643, 1827; public libraries in, 1311–1321; school libraries in, 2006; social libraries in, 714, 771, 810, 811, 1320
New Mexico Library Association, 2667
New Mexico State Library, 2045, 2049
New Orleans Public Library, 754, 1193, 2843
New Philadelphia–Tuscarawas County (Ohio) Public Library, 1141
New York (state): academic libraries in, 1828–1850; bibliography of library history of, 56, 63; book trade in, 876, 883, 884; circulating libraries in, 492, 876, 881, 883, 884; private libraries in, 272, 330, 367, 398, 436, 474; public libraries in, 1322–1368; school libraries in, 869, 2035, 2036, 2038; social libraries in, 2132, 2136, 2159, 2160, 2168, 2169
New York Association of the Bar Library, 2249
New York Herald Tribune Library, 2233
New York Public Library, 879, 1322, 1326–1328, 1331, 1335, 1339, 1341–1347, 1354–1358, 1367, 1368, 2755, 2845–2855
New York Society Library, 732, 738
New York State Library, 2086, 2090, 2104
New York State Library School, 2537. See also Columbia University Library School
New York State Medical Library, 2336, 2350
New York Times Library, 2228
New York University Library, 2271, 2289
New Zealand libraries, 2722
Newark (N.J.) Public Library, 810, 811, 1317, 1318, 1320, 1321
Newberry County (S.C.) Public Library, 1499
Newberry Library (Chicago), 2164, 2181, 2182, 3115, 3116
newspaper libraries, 2228, 2233
Newtown (Pa.) social libraries, 803
nonprint media in libraries, 2758, 2759
Norris, Isaac, 304
North Carolina: academic libraries in, 1851–1873; bibliography of library history of, 11; book trade in, 546; private libraries in, 353, 362, 363; public libraries in, 1369–1386; school libraries in, 1974, 2003, 2023; social libraries in, 700, 778, 795, 840, 851; state library in, 2105
North Carolina, University of, Library (Chapel Hill), 1851, 1852, 1855–1857, 1859–1864, 1866, 1870, 1872, 1873, 2297, 3231
North Carolina, University of, Library School, 2534
North Carolina Agricultural and Technical College Library (Raleigh), 1867
North Carolina Library Association, 2696

North Carolina Library Commission, 2105
North Carolina Supreme Court Library, 2444
North Dakota: public libraries in, 1387, 1388
Northeast Regional Library (Miss.), 1295
Northwestern University Library (Evanstown, Ill.), 2278
Norton's Literary Gazette, 163
Notre Dame (Md.) College Library, 1737
Norwegian libraries, 2708
Norwich (Conn.) Public Library, 1101

Oakland (Calif.) Library Association, 678
Oakland (Calif.) Public Library, 1060–1062
Oberlin (Ohio) College Library, 1892
Oberly, Eunice R., 3112
Oboler, Eli M., 3113
Ocala (Fla.) Public Library, 116
Odd Fellows' Library Associations (Calif.), 723
Ohio: academic libraries in, 1873–1894; bibliography of library history of, 1, 55; book trade in, 420; private libraries in, 288; public libraries in, 1389–1461; school libraries in, 1968; social libraries in, 651, 671, 675, 694, 706, 750, 757, 758, 761, 768, 776, 777, 780, 826, 850, 853; special libraries in, 2161–2163, 2193, 2197, 2204, 2205, 2217–2219, 2224
Ohio Agricultural Experiment Station Library, 2426
Ohio Historical and Philosophical Society Library (Columbus), 2204
Ohio Penitentiary libraries, 2273
Ohio State Library, 2094–2096, 2103
Ohio State University Library (Columbus), 1881, 1888, 1890
Ohio Wesleyan University Library (Delaware), 1882
Oklahoma: public libraries in, 1462
Old Saybrook (Mass.) libraries, 1256
Omaha (Neb.) Library Association, 730
Orange County (Calif.) Public Library, 1074
Orange (N.J.) Public Library, 1312
Oregon: academic libraries in, 1895, 1896; private libraries in, 323, 520; public libraries in, 1463–1466; social libraries in, 659, 681, 745, 755, 773

Oregon, University of, Library (Eugene), 1896
Oregon State Library, 2066, 2071
Osler, Sir William, 2325
Otterbein College Library (Westerville, Ohio), 1876, 1893
Ouachita (La.) Parish Library, 695
Owen, Thomas M., 3114
Ozark Regional Library (Mo.), 1301

Pacific Northwest Library Association, 2670
Paddy's Run (Ohio) social libraries, 850
Palm, Swante, 337
Palm Beach (Fla.) Society of the Four Arts Library, 827
Palo Alto (Calif.) Public Library, 1079
paperbound books, 556
Pargellis, Stanley, 3115, 3116
parochial libraries. *See* Bray, Thomas
Peabody College Library (Nashville, Tenn.), 1933
Peabody Institute Library (Baltimore), 1203, 1208 1209, 1213
Peabody Museum Library (Baltimore), 2194
Pearson, Edmund L., 3119–3122
Peninsula (Ohio) Library and Historical Society, 2218
Pennsylvania: academic libraries in, 1897–1922; bibliography of library history of, 41; book trade in, 414; circulating libraries in, 866, 877; private libraries in, 242, 252, 254, 264, 305, 307, 342, 343, 345, 355, 368, 370–373, 375–380, 402; public libraries in, 1467–1492; school libraries in, 1966, 2015, 2016; social libraries in, 669, 689, 690, 704, 708, 709, 711, 712, 715, 727, 737, 741, 744, 747, 767, 784, 786, 791, 792, 798, 800, 803, 806, 835, 836, 854–858; special libraries in, 2157, 2158, 2201
Pennsylvania, University of, Library (Philadelphia), 1897–1899, 1902, 1904, 1908, 1915, 1919, 2331, 2749, 2796
Pennsylvania Genealogical Society Library, 2226
Pennsylvania Historical Society Library, 2222
Pennsylvania Hospital Library (Philadelphia), 2290, 2335, 2344
Pennsylvania State College Library (University Park), 1901
Pennsylvania State Library, 2047, 2081

Pensacola (Fla.) Library Association, 656
Pensacola (Fla.) Public Library, 1125
Peoria (Ill.) Public Library, 1143
personnel policies in libraries, 159, 205
Persons, Frederick T., 3123
Peterborough (N.H.) Public Library, 1305, 1307
Petersburg (Va.) social libraries, 861
philanthrophy and libraries, 894, 895, 903–906, 929, 950, 976, 978, 985, 986, 991, 995, 1038, 1040, 1116, 1141, 1199–1201, 1203, 1204, 1206, 1208, 1363, 1478, 1518, 1519, 1524, 1547, 1548, 1552, 1610, 1615
Philadelphia Apprentices' Library, 744
Philadelphia City Institute Library, 1485
Philadelphia College of Physicians Library, 2308, 2324
Philadelphia Commercial Museum Library, 2201
Philadelphia Free Library, 798, 1467, 1470, 1471, 1485, 1486, 1488
Philadelphia Library Company, 645, 689, 690, 708, 711, 712, 727, 741, 767, 784, 791, 792, 798, 854–858, 2884, 3196, 3197
Philadelphia Mercantile Library Company, 793, 798
Phoenix (Ariz.) College Library, 1644
physically handicapped: and libraries, 1346, 1460. *See also* blind
Pierce, Cornelia M., 3124, 3125
Piercy, Esther J., 3126
Pierpont Morgan Library (New York), 2132, 2136, 2159, 2168, 2169
Pittsburgh (Pa.) Public Library, 1482–1484
Poe, Edgar Allen, 416
Polk, Mary, 3127, 3128
Poole, William Frederick, 3129, 3130
Portland (Maine) Public Library, 1197
Portland (Ore.) Library Association, 647, 745
Portland (Ore.) Public Library, 1463
Powell, Lawrence Clark, 3131, 3132
Power, Effie Louise, 3133
Princeton (N.J.) University Library, 1827, 2796, 2861
prison libraries, 2266, 2269, 2270, 2273, 2455
private libraries, 230–387, 390, 393, 395, 398, 407, 416, 417, 429, 438, 444, 447, 454, 468, 477, 482, 494, 506, 508, 588, 611, 614, 696, 820–822, 841, 842, 1336, 1342, 1347, 1651, 1656, 1716, 1751, 1752, 1793, 1806, 1810, 1829, 1847, 1912, 1923–1929, 2132–2188, 2287, 2288, 2424, 2435, 2864, 2905, 2906, 2915, 3062
Progressive Librarian's Council, 2623
proprietary libraries. *See* social libraries
Providence (R.I.) Athenaeum, 719, 743
Providence (R.I.) Public Library, 1493–1495, 1498
provincial libraries. *See* Bray, Thomas
public libraries, 71, 762, 763, 892–1558, 1987, 1991, 2004, 2009, 2021, 2347, 2348, 2821–2825
Public Library Inquiry, 902, 943, 983
public services in libraries, 1605. *See also* circulation services; reference work in libraries
Publishers Weekly, 130
Puerto Ricans: library service to, 903
Puritans, 560
Putnam, Herbert, 3134–3142
Putnam County (Tenn.) public libraries, 1505

Queens Borough (N.Y.) Public Library, 1328
Quillin, Rev. William, 259
Quincy (Mass.) Public Library, 1235

Racine (Ill.) Public Library Lectures, 1157
Racine (Wisc.) Public Library, 1554
Radcliffe College Library (Cambridge, Mass.), 1792
railroad libraries, 885, 2240, 2245
Raines, Caldwell W., 3143
Ranck, Samuel H., 3144
Randolph (Vt.) Public Library, 1530
Ratchford, Fannie, 1942, 3145
Rathbone, Josephine A., 3146
Ravenna (Ohio) Public Library, 1412
Reading (Pa.) Public Library, 1474, 1480
Redwood Library (Newport, R.I.), 760, 764, 781, 801, 860
reference work in libraries, 2813–2826
rental libraries. *See* circulating libraries
Resources and Technical Services Division, American Library Association, 2547, 2570
Rhode Island: academic libraries in, 1923–1929; private libraries in, 248, 336; public libraries in, 1493–1498; social libraries in, 705, 719, 743, 760, 764, 781, 785, 801, 860
Rhode Island School of Design Library

(Providence), 1924
Rice, Paul North, 3147
Richardson, Ernest Cushing, 3148, 3149
Roanoke College Library (Salem, Va.), 1948
Robbins, Thomas, 3150
Rochester (N.Y.), University of, Library, 1835, 1836, 1839
Rochester (N.Y.) Public Library, 3124, 1350, 1351, 1364
Rockingham County (N.C.) Public Library, 1381
Rockingham (Va.) Public Library, 1534, 1535
Rockwell, William W., 3151
Rocky Bottom (S.C.) Transient Camp Library, 1501
Rocky River (Ohio) Public Library, 1414
Rogan, Octavia R., 3152
Rollins College Library (Winter Park, Fla.), 1678
Roman, Anton, 351
Rome (Ga.) Public Library, 1134
Roosevelt, Theodore, 272
Roosevelt Library (Hyde Park, N.Y.), 2368, 2382, 2416
Rosary College Library (Chicago, Ill.), 1688
Rousseay, Jean, 575
Rowell, Joseph C., 3153
Russell Library Company (Middletown, Conn.), 672
Rutland (Vt.) Public Library, 1528

St. Charles Borromeo Seminary Library (Overlook, Pa.), 1914
St. Johns College Library (Annapolis, Md.), 1728, 1736
St. Johns University Library (Collegeville, Minn.), 1819
St. Joseph College Library (West Hartford, Conn.), 1657, 1739
St. Louis (Mo.) Free Congregation Library, 829
St. Louis (Mo.) Mercantile Library, 772
St. Louis (Mo.) Public Library, 1297, 1298
St. Petersburg (Fla.) Public Library, 1124
St. Thomas College Library (St. Paul, Minn.), 1817
Salem (Mass.) Athenaeum, 649, 845–847, 859
Salem (Mass.) Philosophical Library, 2139, 2184
Salem (Ohio) Public Library, 1397
Salisbury (N.C.) Public Library, 1369
San Diego (Calif.) Public Library, 1082
San Francisco (Calif.) earthquake: and libraries, 1063
San Francisco (Calif.) Mercantile Library Association, 652
San Francisco (Calif.) Public Library, 1069, 1070, 1075
Sanders, Minerva, 3154
Sandusky County (Ohio) Public Library, 1418, 1423, 1432
Sandusky (Ohio) Library Association, 853
Sandwich (Mass.) Public Library, 1254
Saunders, Frederick, 389
Scheuber, Jennie S., 3155
Schomburg, Arthur A., 294
Schomburg Collection (New York Public Library), 1342, 2755
school district libraries, 868, 869, 875, 891. See also school libraries
school librarians, 2026, 2485, 2503
school libraries, 64, 78, 898, 942, 1103, 1164, 1966–2042, 3020, 3166. See also school district libraries
Scott, Sir Walter, 410
Scoville Memorial Library (Salisbury, Conn.), 1099
Seaboard Air Line Railway Free Traveling Library System, 2245
seamen's libraries, 818
Seattle (Wash.) Public Library, 1536
selection of books. See collection development
Seguin–Guadalupe County (Tex.) Public Library, 1518
serials, 2747, 2790
Shakespeare, William, 445, 570, 590, 602
Sharp, Katharine, 3157, 3158
Shaw, Henry, 315
Shera, Jesse, 3159
Shirley Wayne, 3160–3163
Shoe String Press, 195
Shortess, Lois F., 3166
Shreve Memorial Library (Shreveport, La.), 1195
Sibley, John Langdon, 3168, 3169
Silver Springs (Md.) Public Library, 1211
Sitka (Alaska) Public Library, 1050
Skinner, Mark, 3170
Smith, Charles, 3171
Smith, Henry Preserved, 3172

Smithsonian Institution Library (Washington, D.C.), 2355, 2362, 2402, 2428, 2438, 2453
Smyth, Thomas, 352
social libraries, 645–861, 971, 1240, 1320, 2139, 3099
Society for the Propagation of Christian Knowledge. See Bray, Thomas
Society for the Propagation of the Gospel. See Bray, Thomas
Society of Printers (Boston), 1244
Sohier, Elizabeth P., 3173
Somersworth (N.H.) Manufacturers' and Village Library, 762, 763
South Bend (Ind.) Public Library, 1180
South Carolina: academic libraries in, 1930, 1931; bibliography of library history of, 85; book trade in, 606; private libraries in, 265, 266, 447; public libraries in, 1499–1502; school libraries in, 2041; social libraries in, 710, 783, 789, 799, 808, 809, 820–822, 841, 842
South Carolina, University of, Library (Columbia), 1931, 2349
South Carolina College Library (Orangeburg), 1930
South Dakota: public libraries in, 1503, 1504
South Dakota State Library, 2080
Southeastern Library Association, 2541
Southwestern Library Association, 2687
Southwestern Louisiana Institute Library (Lafayette), 1722
special librarians: education for, 2465, 2480, 2483, 2495, 2496, 2515
special libraries, 2108–2455, 2818, 2820
Special Library Association, 2483, 2560, 2561, 2580, 2595, 2605, 2612, 2629, 2630, 2643, 2644, 2654, 2698
Spofford, Ainsworth Rand, 2372–2379, 3174–3185
Springfield (Mass.) Public Library, 1215, 1251
Springfield (Ohio) Public Library, 1390
Standard and Poor's Library (New York), 2242
standards for school libraries, 1992, 2008
Stanford (Calif.) University Library, 1566, 1647, 1649
state libraries, 2043–2107
Statesboro (Ga.) Regional Library, 1133
statistics: history of use of, in libraries, 155, 172–174, 202, 203
Stearns, Lutie Eugenia, 3186–3189
Stearns, Raymond Phineas, 3190
Stephenson, John G., 3191, 3192
Sterne, Lawrence, 555
Stetson University Library (De Land, Fla.), 1681
Stevens, Henry, 289, 535–537
Stillwell, M. B., 3193
Stockbridge Library (Pittsfield, Mass.), 664
Stoddard, Solomon, 454
storage libraries, 1576, 1600. See also cooperation
Story, Joseph, 2442
storytelling: for children, 1170, 1335, 1969
Stoughton (Mass.) Public Library, 1268
Strahan, William, 467
Sturgis Library (Barnstable, Mass.), 1218
subject divisional plans in college libraries, 1592
subscription books, 576
subscription libraries. See social libraries
Sunday opening of public libraries, 925
Sunday school libraries, 862, 867, 870, 871, 873, 874, 879, 887, 889
Sunday-School Union, 562
surveys: use of, in libraries, 169, 1582, 1614, 1630
Sutro Library (San Francisco, Calif.), 2147, 2148, 2177, 2183

Takoma Park (Washington, D.C.) Public Library, 1108
Talbot County (Mass.) Free Library, 1223
Tallahassee (Fla.) Public Library, 1121
Tampa (Fla.) Public Library, 1127
Tardireau, Barthelemi, 313
Tauber, Maurice F., 3194
Taylor Memorial (Cuyohoga Falls, Ohio), 750
Teackle, Thomas, 360
Teaneck (N.J.) Public Library, 1314
technical library assistance to foreign countries, 2703
technical service. See cataloging and classification
Teenage Library Association of Texas, 2633
Temple University Library (Philadelphia), 1918, 2339
Tenafly (N.J.) Public Library, 1311

258 Subject Index

Tennessee: academic libraries in, 696, 1932–1934; public libraries in, 1505–1510; social libraries in, 696, 731
Tennessee Historical Society Library, 2208, 2212
Tennessee State Library, 2085, 2092
Tennessee Valley Authority, 213, 914
Tennessee Valley Library Council, 2543
Terre Haute and Vigo County (Ind.) Public Library, 1165
Teton County (Wyo.) Public Libraries, 1558
Texas: academic libraries in, 1935–1942; private libraries in, 337, public libraries in, 1511–1527; school libraries in, 1983, 1984, 1986, 2001, 2019, 2020, 2028; social libraries in, 646, 805; special libraries in, 2156, 2200
Texas, University of, Library (Austin), 1937, 1939, 1942
Texas College of Arts and Industries Library (Kingsville), 1938
Texas History Center (Austin), 2200
Texas Library Association, 2622, 2655
Texas Southern University (Houston), 2276
Texas State Library, 2054, 2065, 2087, 2106
theater libraries, 17, 1344, 2982
theological libraries, 205, 217, 218, 224, 296, 341, 352, 601, 1427, 1594, 1597, 1604, 1827, 1847–1850, 1862, 1907, 1911, 1914, 1947, 1959, 2191, 2209, 2571, 2577, 2682, 2972, 3123, 3150, 3151
Thomas, Isaiah, 1825
Thwaites, Rueben G., 3195
Ticknor, George, 354, 1232
Timothee, Louis, 3196, 3197
Titcomb, Mary L., 3198
Toledo (Ohio) Public Library, 1425, 1426, 1453, 1455
Topeka (Kans.) Public Library, 1186
Tory, Jesse, 3199
Transylvania College Library (Lexington, Ky.), 1718, 1720
traveling libraries, 1327, 1557, 2061, 2094. *See also* bookmobiles
Trenton (N.J.) Public Library, 1313
Truman Library (Independence, Mo.), 2404, 2409
Trumbull Manuscript Collection on Connecticut library history, 79
trustees, 1003, 1013

Twain, Mark, 450
Tyler, Alice Sarah, 3200, 3201
Typewriters in libraries, 100

union catalogs, 2735, 2810
Union Library Company (Hatboro, Pa.), 803, 806
unions in libraries, 117, 1285
Union Theological Seminary Library (New York), 1847–1849
United Nations Library (New York), 2384, 3094
U.S. Air Force libraries, 2441
U.S. Army Medical Library, 2283, 2284, 2314–2320, 2323
U.S. Army Post Library Service, 2367, 2369
U.S. Army Walter Reed Medical Center Library, 2443
U.S. Atomic Energy Commission Library, 2388
U.S. Bureau of Education and libraries, 126, 145, 2592
U.S. Bureau of Standards Library, 2366
U.S. Department of Agriculture Library, 2407, 2421
U.S. Department of Health, Education, and Welfare Library, 2381
U.S. Department of Labor Library, 2439
U.S. Department of State Library, 2361
U.S. Department of Interior Library, 2400
U.S. Federal Library Committee, 2423
U.S. Geological Survey Library, 2454
U.S. Information Agency Library, 2705
U.S. Information Service libraries, 2728
U.S. Library of Congress, 67, 2354, 2356, 2359, 2363–2365, 2370–2380, 2387, 2389, 2392, 2393, 2396, 2398, 2401, 2405, 2406, 2408, 2410, 2411, 2413–2415, 2417–2420, 2422, 2424, 2425, 2427–2429, 2433–2438, 2442, 2446, 2447, 2449, 2451, 2718, 2751, 2753, 2754, 2763, 2772, 2775, 2799, 2807, 2819, 2841, 2842, 2974, 3080–3083, 3110, 3111, 3134–3142, 3174–3185, 3212, 3260
U.S. National Archives, 2395, 2403
U.S. National Institutes of Health Library, 2343
U.S. National Library of Medicine, 2291, 2294, 2325, 2338, 2353, 2845–2855
U.S. Naval Academy Library, 2412
U.S. Office of Education Library, 2450
U.S. Supreme Court Library, 2252, 2261, 2263–2265, 2282

Subject Index 259

U.S. Tariff Commission Library, 2432
U.S. Treasury Department Library, 2385
U.S. Veterans Administration Library, 2357, 2390
U.S. Weather Bureau Library, 2394
university libraries. *See* academic libraries
Urbana (Ill.) Free Library, 1144
Ursinus College Library (Collegeville, Pa.), 1911
Ursuline College Library (Cleveland), 1889
Utah: social libraries in, 739
Utah State Library, 2075
Utica (N.Y.) Public Library, 1366

Van Wert County (Ohio) Public Library, 1389, 1431
Vassar College Library (Poughkeepsie, N.Y.), 1834
Vattemare, Alexander, 618, 2078, 3202–3207
Vermont: academic libraries in, 1943; book trade in, 535–537; public libraries in, 1528–1531
Vincennes (Ind.) social library, 679, 740
Virginia: academic libraries in, 1943–1954; bibliography of library history of, 29; book trade in, 528; private libraries in, 230, 234, 235, 241, 251, 256–261, 263, 267, 271, 273, 274, 286, 287, 289, 291–293, 309, 310, 319, 324, 325, 328, 329, 332, 334, 339, 344–350, 360, 361, 365, 369, 370, 381–384, 386, 428–431, 437–439, 477, 478, 494, 495, 544, 548, 579, 609; public libraries in, 1532–1535; school libraries in, 1985, 2002; social libraries in, 861
Virginia, University of, Library (Charlottesville), 324, 1944–1946, 1951, 1954, 2351
Vormelker, Rose, 3208

Wabash College Library (Crawfordsville, Ind.), 1706
Wabasha (Minn.) Public Library, 1287
Wake Forest College Library (Winston-Salem, N.C.), 1865
Walla Walla (Wash.) Public Library, 1540
Walter, Frank K., 3209
Warren, Althea, 3210, 3211
Warren (Ohio) Public Library, 1444
Washington (state): academic libraries in, 1955–1957; public libraries in, 1536–1544; school libraries in, 1988; social libraries in, 819
Washington, University of, Library (Seattle), 1955–1957
Washington County (Md.) Public Library, 1210, 1212
Washington Library Association, 2564, 2620
Washington (D.C.) Library Company, 728
Watterson, George, 3212, 3213
Watts, Isaac, 1665
Webster, Noah, 566, 595
Weems, Mason Locke, 483, 571
Wellesley (Mass.) College Library, 1747, 1796
West, Elizabeth Howard, 3124
West Boxford (Mass.) Public Library, 1246
West Hartford (Conn.) Public Library, 1092
West Virginia: academic libraries in, 1958–1961; public libraries in, 1545, 1546
West Virginia, University of, Library (Morgantown), 1960
Westbury (N.Y.) Public Library, 1360
Westchester County (N.Y.) public libraries, 1332
Westchester (N.Y.) Public Library, 1359
Western Library Association (Ames Township, Ohio), 651
Western Maryland College Library (Westminster), 1733
Western North Carolina Library Association, 2690
Western Reserve Historical Society Library (Cleveland), 2197, 2224
Western Reserve University Library (Cleveland), 1878
Western Reserve University Library School, 2475, 2518
Weston (Mass.) Public Library, 1249
Wheeler, Joseph L., 90, 3215–3221
Whitcomb, Samuel, Jr., 541
Whitehill, Walter Muir, 3222
White House National Advisory Commission on Libraries, 114
Whitman County (Wash.) Public Library, 1544
Wichita (Kan.) Public Library, 1188
Wilkinson Library (Hartford, Conn.), 1089
William and Mary College Library (Williamsburg, Va.), 1949, 1950, 1952, 1953

Williams, Edward C., 3223
Williamson, Charles C., 3224, 3225
Willoughby (Ohio) Public Library, 1448
Wilmington (Del.) Public Library, 1105
Wilson, Halsey William, 3226
Wilson, Louis R., 1641, 3227, 3228
Wilson Library Bulletin, 94
Windsor (Conn.) Public Library, 1086
Winkler, E. W., 3239
Winship, George P., 3240
Winslow, Amy, 3241
Winsor, Justin, 1772, 3242–3250
Winston-Salem (N.C.) Public Library, 1370, 1380
Winteringham, Rev. John, 285
Winter Park (Fla.) Public Library, 1117
Winthrop, Rev. John, 250, 278
Wire, George E., 3251
Wisconsin: academic libraries in, 1962–1965; bibliography of library history of, 70; public libraries in, 1547–1557; school libraries in, 1982, 1998, 1999
Wisconsin Historical Society Library, 2220, 2221
Wisconsin Library Association, 2613, 2624, 2651, 2691
Wisconsin Library Bulletin, 105
Wisconsin, University of, Library School (Madison), 2479, 2501, 2517, 2535, 2536
Wisconsin State College (Oshkosh), 1963
Wisconsin State University Library (Whitewater), 1962, 1965, 2030
Wisconsin State University Library Science Department, 2462
Wister, Owen, 3252
Withers Public Library (Bloomington, Ill.), 1153
women and libraries, 18, 111, 113, 120, 134, 168, 183, 185, 204, 223, 229, 350, 500, 947, 948, 1148, 1271, 1273, 1275, 1972
Wood, Mary Elizabeth, 3253
Woodstock (Md.) College, 1732
Woodstock (N.Y.) Public Library, 1362
Woolman, John, 355
Worcester (Mass.) Public Library, 1270
world's fairs and libraries, 166, 1583
World War I and libraries, 127, 936, 979, 1025
World War II and libraries, 166, 1583
Wright, Louis B., 3254
Wroth, Lawrence C., 3255
Wyer, James I., 3256

Wyer, Malcolm, 3257–3259
Wyoming: public libraries in, 1558
Wyoming Library Association, 2606

Yakima (Wash.) Public Library, 1543
Yale, Elihu, 1669
Yale University Library (New Haven, Conn.), 1566, 1655, 1658–1660, 1662–1666, 1668, 1669, 2251, 2310, 2311, 2329, 2770, 2783, 2793
Young, John R., 3260
Young Men's Christian Association (YMCA) Libraries, 872, 878
Youngstown (Ohio) Library Association, 826
Youngstown (Ohio) University Library, 1887
York (Pa.) Public Library, 1478

Abbreviations of Journal Titles

AAJ	American Art Journal
AALSNL	AALS Newsletter
AAr	American Archivist
AB	Antiquarian Bookman
ABAJ	American Bar Association Journal
ABC	American Book Collector
ABooks	About Books
AcaB	Academic Bookman
ACHS	American Catholic Historical Society
ACJ	Autograph Collectors' Journal
A&E	Architecture & English
AG	American Genealogy
AGQ	Amherst Graduates Quarterly
AH	American Heritage
AHB	Atlanta Historical Bulletin
AHILQ	AHIL Quarterly
AHM	American Historical Magazine
AHQ	Arkansas Historical Quarterly
AHR	American Historical Review
AJ	Antiques Journal
AJE	American Journal of Education
AJLH	American Journal of Legal History
AL	American Literature
AlaHQ	Alabama Historical Quarterly
AlaL	Alabama Librarian
ALib	American Libraries
AMAn	Albany Medical Annals
AmCAB	American Congregational Association Bulletin
AmD	American Documentation
AMH	Annals of Medical History
AmO	American Oxonian
AN	American Neptune
AnI	Annals of Iowa
AN&Q	American Notes and Queries
AQ	American Quarterly
AQR	American Quarterly Register
ARHHS	Annual Report of the Hawaiian Historical Society

ArizL	Arizona Librarian
ArizQ	Arizona Quarterly
ArizW	Arizona and the West
ArkL	Arkansas Libraries
AS	Adult Services
ASch	American Scholar
ASIB	American Swedish Institute Bulletin
ASLHM	American Society Legion of Honor Magazine
AtlM	Atlantic Monthly
BA	Berkshire Athenaeum
BALA	Bulletin of the American Library Association
BB	Bulletin of Bibliography
BBPL	Bulletin of the Boston Public Library
BC	Book Collector
BCCQNL	Book Club of California Quarterly News Letter
BCHSP	Bucks County Historical Society Papers
BCSLA	Bulletin of the California School Library Association
BFHA	Bulletin of Friends' Historical Association
BHM	Bulletin of the History of Medicine
BHPSO	Bulletin of the Historical & Philosophical Society of Ohio
BHSSC	Berkshire Historical and Scientific Society. Collections
BL	Between Librarians
BMSJ	Boston Medical & Surgical Journal
BNYPL	Bulletin of the New York Public Library
BookB	Book Buyer
BPAU	Bulletin of the Pan-American Union
BPLA	Bulletin of the Philippine Library Association
BPLQ	Boston Public Library Quarterly
BSCHS	Bulletin of the Shawnee County Historical Society
BSL	Bay State Librarian
CalL	California Librarian
CarnM	Carnegie Magazine
CBJ	Connecticut Bar Journal
CCH	Catalogers and Classifiers Handbook
CCY	Catalogers and Classifiers Yearbook
ChiSJ	Chicago Schools Journal
CHSP	Cambridge Historical Society Publications
CHSQ	California Historical Society Quarterly
CJ	Classical Journal
CLB	California Library Bulletin
CLC	Columbia Library Columns
CLitW	Catholic Literary World
CLJ	Canadian Library Journal
CLW	Catholic Library World
CMHS	Collections of the Massachusetts Historical Society
CO	Chronicles of Oklahoma

ConnHSB	Connecticut Historical Society Bulletin
ConnM	Connecticut Magazine
Cosmo	Cosmopolitan
CQ	Congregational Quarterly
CR	Contemporary Review
CRL	College and Research Libraries
CSJ	Catholic School Journal
CSL	California School Libraries
CULB	Cornell University Library Bulletin
CUQ	Columbia University Quarterly
DAM	Dartmouth Alumni Magazine
DanHSC	Danvers Historical Society Collections
DCL	D.C. Libraries
DCLB	Dartmouth College Library Bulletin
DE	Downeast
DH	Delaware History
DLQ	Drexel Library Quarterly
DN	Delaware Notes
EAL	Early American Literature
EB	Education Bulletin
EeB	Education et Bibliothèque
ELB	Education Libraries Bulletin
ELIS	Encyclopedia of Library & Information Science
FAR	French-American Review
FBJ	Federal Bar Journal
FCHQ	Filson Club History Quarterly
FEd	Florida Education
FitchHSP	Fitchburg Historical Society Proceedings
FL	Franklin Lectures
F&L	Field and Laboratory
FLB	Florida Library Bulletin
FP	Firelands Pioneer
FSUS	Florida State University Studies
GAQ	Goucher Alumnae Quarterly
GaR	Georgia Review
GGC	Gazettte of the Grolier Club
GHQ	Georgia Historical Quarterly
GP	Guide Post
GranM	Granite Monthly
HAHR	Hispanic American Historical Review
HarAB	Harvard Alumni Bulletin
HB	Horn Book
HCEI	Historical Collections of the Essex Institute
HEQ	History of Education Quarterly
HGM	Harvard Graduate Magazine
HLAJ	Hawaiian Library Association Journal

HLB	Harvard Library Bulletin
HLN	Harvard Library Notes
HLQ	Huntington Library Quarterly
HLS	Herald of Library Science
HMPEC	Historical Magazine of the Protestant Episcopal Church
HNH	Historic New Hampshire
HRBC	Historical Review of Berks County
HSSCQ	Historical Society of Southern California Quarterly
HuntLB	Huntington Library Bulletin
IARB	Inter-American Review of Bibliography
ICSJ	International College of Surgeons Journal
IJHP	Iowa Journal of History and Politics
IL	Idaho Librarian
IllL	Illinois Libraries
IMH	Indiana Magazine of History
IMich	Inside Michigan
IMPLB	Ingalls Memorial Public Library Bulletin
IndL	Indian Librarian
IntLR	International Library Review
IntR	International Review
IQB	Indiana Quarterly for Bookmen
ISMSJ	Iowa State Medical Society Journal
JAH	Journal of American History
JAmS	Journal of American Studies
JCC	Journal of Catalogers & Classifiers
JCE	Journal of Chemical Education
JEGP	Journal of English & German Philology
JEL	Journal of Education for Librarianship
JELH	Journal of English Literary History
JEMSS	Journal of the Elisha Mitchell Scientific Society
JFrI	Journal of the Franklin Institute
JHAM	Johns Hopkins Alumni Magazine
JHBS	Journal of History of Behavioral Science
JHI	Journal of the History of Ideas
JHMAS	Journal of the History of Medicine & Allied Sciences
JISHS	Journal of the Illinois State Historical Society
JLA	Journal of Library Automation
JLE	Journal of Legal Education
JLH	Journal of Library History
JLIS	Journal of Library and Information Science
JMH	Journal of Mississippi History
JNHCHS	Journal of the New Haven Colony Historical Society
JPH	Journal of Presbyterian History
JPL	Journal of Philippine Librarianship
JrH	Junior History
JSF	Journal of Social Forces

JSH	Journal of Southern History
JSocH	Journal of Social History
JSS	Journal of Social Science
KHQ	Kansas Historical Quarterly
KLAB	Kentucky Library Association Bulletin
KMJ	Kentucky Medical Journal
LACUNYJ	LACUNY Journal
LAR	Library Association Record
LC	Library Chronicle
LHQ	Louisiana Historical Quarterly
LHR	Library Historical Review
LibR	Library Review
LibT	Library Trends
LIF	Long Island Forum
LIS	Library & Information Science (Mita Society)
LivA	Living Age
LJ	Library Journal
LLAB	Louisiana Library Association Bulletin
LLJ	Law Library Journal
LM	Library Mirror
LNDUL	Library Notes of Duke University Library
LO	Library Occurrent
LQ	Library Quarterly
LRTS	Library Resources & Technical Services
LW	Library World
MA	Mid-America
MadQ	Madison Quarterly
MAH	Magazine of American History
MaineHSNL	Maine Historical Society Newsletter
MAQR	Michigan Alumnus Quarterly Review
MassLAB	Massachusetts Library Association Bulletin
MBGB	Missouri Botanical Gardens Bulletin
MBJ	Missouri Bar Journal
MedH	Medical History
MedHR	Medford Historical Register
MenQR	Mennonite Quarterly Review
MH	Magazine of History
MHM	Maryland Historical Magazine
MHR	Missouri Historical Review
MHSB	Missouri Historical Society Bulletin
MHSP	Missouri Historical Society Publications
MichHM	Michigan History Magazine
MichL	Michigan Librarian
MinnH	Minnesota History
MinnL	Minnesota Libraries
MinnUB	Minnesota University Bulletin

ML	Maryland Libraries
MLAB	Medical Library Association Bulletin
MLAN	Music Library Association Notes
MLAQ	Missouri Library Association Quarterly
MLB	Maine Library Bulletin
MLCB	Massachusetts Library Club Bulletin
MLHJ	Medical Library Historical Journal
MLNews	Mississippi Library News
MLQ	Massachusetts Law Quarterly
MLR	Massachusetts Law Review
MM	Massachusetts Magazine
MoreB	More Books
MP	Modern Philology
MS	Military Surgeon
MVHR	Mississippi Valley Historical Review
NAR	North American Review
NatH	National History
NatM	National Magazine
NC	Nineteenth Century
NCHR	North Carolina Historical Review
NCL	North Carolina Libraries
NCLife	North Country Life
NCMJ	North Carolina Medical Journal
NDHQ	North Dakota Historical Quarterly
NDLNN	North Dakota Library Notes and News
NEHGR	New England Historical and Genealogical Register
NEJM	New England Journal of Medicine
NEM	New England Magazine
NEQ	New England Quarterly
NH	Nebraska History
NLB	Newberry Library Bulletin
NMHR	New Mexico Historical Review
NMLB	New Mexico Library Bulletin
NNCL	News Notes of California Libraries
N&Q	Notes and Queries
NWOQ	Northwest Ohio Quarterly
NYH	New York History
NYLAB	New York Library Association Bulletin
NYSJM	New York State Journal of Medicine
OAHQ	Ohio Archaeological and Historical Quarterly
OakL	Oak Letter (Oakland, Calif.)
OEM	Ohio Education Monthly
OFB	Outlook for the Blind
OH	Ohio History
OHQ	Oregon Historical Quarterly
OLAB	Ohio Library Association Bulletin

Abbreviations of Journal Titles xvii

ON	Occasional Notes
ONGQ	Old Northwest Genealogical Quarterly
OTNE	Old-Time New England
PAAS	Proceedings of the American Antiquarian Society
PACHS	Papers of Albemarle County Historical Society
PacS	Pacific Spectator
PAPS	Proceedings of the American Philosophical Society
PASCH	Papers of the American Society of Church History
PBHS	Publications of the Buffalo Historical Society
PBSA	Papers of the Bibliographical Society of America
PCSM	Publications of the Colonial Society of Massachusetts
PDK	Phi Delta Kappan
PennH	Pennsylvania History
PETHS	Publications of East Tennessee Historical Society
PF	Pennsylvania Folklife
PIAS	Proceedings of the Indiana Academy of Science
PJE	Peabody Journal of Education
PL	Public Libraries
PLAB	Pennsylvania Library Association Bulletin
PLHS	Proceedings of the Lancaster Historical Society
PLMN	Pennsylvania Library and Museum Notes
PLN	Pennsylvania Library Notes
PMHB	Pennsylvania Magazine of History and Biography
PMHS	Proceedings of the Massachusetts Historical Society
PMJ	Philadelphia Medical Journal
PMLA	Publications of the Modern Language Association of America
PNHCHS	Papers of the New Haven Colony Historical Society
PNJHS	Proceedings of the New Jersey Historical Society
PNLAQ	Pacific Northwest Library Association Quarterly
PNQ	Pacific Northwest Quarterly
POSAHS	Publications of Ohio State Archives & Historical Society
PSCHA	Proceedings of the South Carolina Historical Association
PubL	Public Libraries
PULC	Princeton University Library Chronicle
PW	Publishers Weekly
QJLC	Quarterly Journal of the Library of Congress
QN	Quarterly Newsletter
RASHPS	Report of the American Scenic & Historical Preservation Society
RB	Reprint Bulletin
RCHS	Records of the Columbia Historical Society
RDB	Revue des Bibliothèques
RDLC	Revue de Littérature Comparée
RH	Rochester History
RHSP	Rochester Historical Society Publications

RKSHS	Register of the Kentucky State Historical Society
RMMJ	Rocky Mountain Medical Journal
SAB	South Atlantic Bulletin
SanDHSQ	San Diego Historical Society Quarterly
SAQ	South Atlantic Quarterly
SB	Studies in Bibliography
SchL	School Libraries
SchLJ	School Library Journal
SCHM	South Carolina Historical Magazine
SCL	South Carolina Librarian
SCQ	Southern California Quarterly
SDLB	South Dakota Library Bulletin
SE	Studies in Education
SEL	Southeastern Librarian
SHBN	Stechert-Hafner Book News
SHQ	Southwestern Historical Quarterly
SJR	Social Justice Review
SL	Special Libraries
SLAGMDB	Special Libraries Association Geography Map Division Bulletin
SM	Scribner's Monthly
SMB	Stanford Medical Bulletin
SMQ	School Media Quarterly
SR	Sewanee Review
SS	Senior Scholastic
S&S	School and Society
SunM	Sunset Magazine
TA	Trinity Archive
TAPS	Transactions of the American Philosophical Society
TCLG	Trinity College Library Gazette
TCPP	Transcript of the College of Physicians of Philadelphia
THM	Tennessee Historical Magazine
THQ	Tennessee Historical Quarterly
TI	The Independent
TL	Texas Libraries
TLJ	Texas Library Journal
TMCHS	Transactions of the McLean County Historical Society
TQHGM	Tyler's Quarterly Historical and Genealogical Magazine
TR	Texas Review
TULB	Temple University Library Bulletin
TUN	Temple University News
UBL	UNESCO Bulletin for Libraries
UFLR	University of Florida Law Review
UHQ	Utah Historical Quarterly
UMSMB	University of Maryland School of Medicine Bulletin
UNCM	University of North Carolina Magazine

UnivS	University Studies
URLB	University of Rochester Library Bulletin
USCB	University of South Carolina Bulletin
UTSE	University of Texas Studies in English
VC	Virginia Cavalcade
VH	Vermont History
VL	Virginia Librarian
VLB	Vermont Library Bulletin
VMHB	Virginia Magazine of History and Biography
VMM	Virginia Medical Monthly
VQ	Vermont Quarterly
VQR	Virginia Quarterly Review
WCHSB	Westchester County Historical Society Bulletin
WestHQ	Western Historical Quarterly
WHQ	Washington Historical Quarterly
WintP	Winterthur Portfolio
WisLB	Wisconsin Library Bulletin
WLB	Wilson Library Bulletin
WLR	Wyoming Library Roundup
WMH	Wisconsin Magazine of History
WMQ	William and Mary Quarterly
WPHM	Western Pennsylvania Historical Magazine
WQR	Wesleyan Quarterly Review
WSHSC	Wisconsin State Historical Society Collections
WW	World's Work
WWO	Wonderful World of Ohio
YR	Yale Review
YULG	Yale University Library Gazette